Advance Praise for *The Arab Spring: Pathways of Repression and Reform*

"By far the most ambitious and convincing analysis of the recent Arab uprisings in comparison to failed and successful democratic transitions in the rest of the world."
Alfred Stepan, Wallace Sayre Professor of Government, Columbia University. Co-author with Juan J. Linz of *Problems of Democratic Transition and Consolidation*

"***The Arab Spring: Pathways of Repression and Reform*** is one of the most comprehensive accounts of the politics underlying the Arab Spring. This authoritative and well-researched book is both theoretically rigorous and empirically rich. The authors have put together a magnificent account of the Arab Uprisings. Anyone interested in acquiring a sophisticated understanding of these events must read this book."
Amaney Jamal, Edwards S. Sanford Professor of Politics, Princeton University. Author of *Of Empires and Citizens: Pro American Democracy or No Democracy at All?*

"This is the book with which everyone interested in the Arab upheavals of 2011 must now grapple. It puts forward parsimonious and counter-intuitive explanations for the different results we see across the Arab world from those momentous events, and grounds those explanations in sophisticated and informed empirical analysis. It engages with larger theoretical debates but never loses its focus on the Arab Spring itself. It is a perfect teaching book, because it makes big arguments in a clear way. It will define the social science debate on the Arab Spring."
F. Gregory Gause, III, John H. Lindsey '44 Chair, Professor of International Affairs, Bush School of Government, Texas A&M University. Author of *The International Relations of the Persian Gulf*

"***The Arab Spring: Pathways of Repression and Reform*** explains why the optimism that developed in 2010 and 2011 proved to be unjustified. In its analysis of the delayed democratic transition in most of the Middle East, it is incisive, parsimonious, compelling, and—perhaps above all—sobering."
Donald L. Horowitz, James B. Duke Professor of Law and Political Science Emeritus, Duke University. Author of *Ethnic Groups in Conflict*

"***The Arab Spring*** represents an important step forward in the systematic, theoretical analysis of the political turbulence which rocked the region beginning in late 2010. Placing the region firmly in comparative perspective and rigorously assessing the limited outcomes of the protest wave, The Arab Spring offers a parsimonious explanation of these events which establishes a new standard for political scientists."
Marc Lynch, Director, Institute for Middle East Studies and Professor of Political Science, The George Washington University. *Author of The Arab Uprising: The Unfinished Revolutions of the New Middle East*

"The uprisings collectively described as the Arab Spring are the most dramatic political events, to date, in our young century. The story is distressingly familiar — initial euphoria as dictators fell, the sobering challenge of building democracy on the ruins of autocracy, then the grim setback in Egypt and the paroxysms of Libya, Syria, and Yemen. If we hope to understand this critical region, our current political era, and the prospects for democracy to take root in unfamiliar soil, we need to make sense of the Arab Spring. Brownlee, Masoud, and Reynolds are uniquely equipped for this task, bringing expertise on the history, culture, economy, geopolitics, and institutions that drove the uprisings and the politics that followed. The book reveals patterns amid complexity and separates solid evidence from speculation. We will be debating the Arab Spring for generations and updating how we understand it. But Brownlee, Masoud, and Reynolds provide the foundation. All the scholarship to come will build on this book."
John M. Carey, John Wentworth Professor in the Social Sciences Government Department, Dartmouth College. Author of *Presidents and Assemblies: Constitutional Design and Electoral Dynamics*

The Arab Spring

Pathways of Repression and Reform

Jason Brownlee, Tarek Masoud, and Andrew Reynolds

OXFORD
UNIVERSITY PRESS

OXFORD
UNIVERSITY PRESS

Great Clarendon Street, Oxford, OX2 6DP,
United Kingdom

Oxford University Press is a department of the University of Oxford.
It furthers the University's objective of excellence in research, scholarship,
and education by publishing worldwide. Oxford is a registered trade mark of
Oxford University Press in the UK and in certain other countries

First Edition published in 2015

Impression: 6

Published in the United States of America by Oxford University Press
198 Madison Avenue, New York, NY 10016, United States of America

British Library Cataloguing in Publication Data
Data available

Library of Congress Control Number: 2014954011

ISBN 978–0–19–966006–3 (hbk.)
ISBN 978–0–19–966007–0 (pbk.)

Printed and bound by
CPI Group (UK) Ltd, Croydon, CR0 4YY

For my son, Mac
JB

For my father, El-Miselhy Abdel Hamid Masoud
(1940–2001)
TM

For my wife, Layna
AR

Acknowledgments

The manuscript for *The Arab Spring* was long in the making. We were guided in our journey by the comments, critiques, corrections and suggestions of an esteemed group of scholars of Middle Eastern and comparative politics. Participants at manuscript workshops at the University of North Carolina in November 2011 and the University of Texas in August 2012 included: Zoltan Barany, Matt Buehler, John Carey, David Edwards, Ali Reza Eshraghi, Jack Goldstone, Kimberly Guiler, Peter Harris, Don Horowitz, Charlie Kurzman, Peter Mohanty, Curtis Ryan, Dan Slater, Al Stepan, Jillian Schwedler, Zeynep Tufekci, Nicolas van de Walle, Kurt Weyland, and Carrie Wickham.

We benefited from the research assistance of Ryan Triche, Bryce Loidolt and Paula Mukherjee at UNC Chapel Hill, Steven Brooke at UT-Austin, and Andrew Ma, Nada Zohdy, Duncan Pickard, and Safia Trabelsi at Harvard. Our theory was made stronger by the invaluable insights of Michael Baldassaro, Robert Becker, Melani Cammett, Abhishek Chatterjee, Phil Costopoulos, Vincent Dacruz, Larry Diamond, F. Gregory Gause III, Eugene Gholz, Mohamed Hamed, Mostafa Heddaya, Clement Henry, Catherine Herrold, Simon Hix, Julie Hughes, Lila Jaafar, Alex Keyssar, Pete Moore, Jawad Nabulsi, Roger Owen, Marc Plattner, Mansour Sadeghi, Lotfi Saibi, Joshua Stacher, Niklaus Steiner, Denis Sullivan, Hermann Thiel, Robert Vitalis, Sean Yom, Malika Zeghal, and Daniel Ziblatt.

At Oxford University Press we are indebted to the editorial team of Olivia Wells, Rosie Chambers, Ellen Carey, Elizabeth Suffling, and Sarah Parker for shepherding the manuscript through the production process. We particularly appreciate the support and patience shown by Dominic Byatt, our terrific editor at OUP.

Brownlee is grateful to Steven Brooke, who improved the manuscript tremendously by carefully critiquing and editing it. Brownlee also thanks Gary Freeman for enabling the book workshop at UT-Austin.

Masoud is particularly indebted to Andrew Ma and Nada Zohdy, who went far beyond the call of duty in reading and commenting on every aspect of this volume, to the Carnegie Corporation of New York and the Middle East Initiative of the Harvard Kennedy School for supporting this research, and to Mary Anne Baumgartner.

Reynolds owes a particular debt of gratitude to his long-time friend and collaborator John Carey.

Contents

List of Figures xi
List of Tables xiii

Introduction: The Third Arab Spring 1

1. Theorizing the Arab Spring 18
2. Lineages of Repression 40
3. Breakdowns and Crackdowns 64
4. Post-Breakdown Trajectories 98
5. Why Breakdowns Did Not Always Produce Transitions 169
6. Limits and Legacies of the Arab Spring 211

Notes 229
Bibliography 291
Index 315

List of Figures

2.1	Causal Pathways of the Arab Spring	61
4.1	Results of First Round of 2012 Presidential Election	118
5.1	Transition Outcomes in Four Cases of Regime Breakdown	174
5.2	State Effectiveness in Four Cases of Regime Breakdown	176
5.3	Per Capita Income in Four Cases of Regime Breakdown	185
5.4	Historical Rates of Urbanization in Egypt and Tunisia	207
5.5	Egyptians' and Tunisians' Views on Sharia and Personal Status Laws	209
6.1	Per Capita GDPs of Eastern European (1990) and Arab Countries (2010) Compared	218

List of Tables

1.1 Institutional Profile of Selected Arab Regimes Prior to the Uprisings 33

1.2 Percentages of World Values Survey Respondents in Selected Arab Countries (2010–2014) Who Report Obtaining Information From the Internet Daily, Weekly, Monthly, Less Than Monthly, or Never 37

2.1 Per Capita Value of Oil and Gas Production in Selected Arab States (2009) 54

2.2 Succession Patterns in Select Arab States (2010) 59

2.3 The Structure of Arab Regime Change, 2010–2012 60

4.1 Egyptian Election Results, November 28, 2011 to January 11, 2012 114

4.2 Results of Tunisian Constituent Assembly Election, October 23, 2011 138

4.3 Results of Election for Libya's General National Congress, July 7, 2012 161

4.4 Features of the Transition Process in Four Cases of Regime Breakdown 166

5.1 Indicators of Military Centrality in Egypt and Tunisia 191

5.2 Pluralism in Founding Elections, Tunisia and Egypt 197

5.3 Self-Reported Rates of (Present or Past) Organizational Membership in Tunisia and Egypt Compared (2013) 205

6.1 Freedom House Scores for the Countries of the Arab Spring, 2010–2014 213

6.2 Freedom House Scores for Warsaw Pact Countries, 1989–1992 216

Introduction: The Third Arab Spring

For those yearning for an exit from the Arab world's long record of autocracy and political dysfunction, the late 1980s seemed like a period of hope and possibility. An almost decade-long war between Iraq and Iran, which had seen hundreds of thousands of lives lost on both sides, finally came to an end. The countries of North and South Yemen, long divided politically, began to take concrete steps toward unification. Protests in Tunisia, capped by a bloodless coup by a self-styled modernizer, pushed aside a dictator who had ruled for three decades. Nearby, in Egypt, opposition parties and civil society organizations brought the country a degree of political dynamism not seen since the "liberal" 1920s. Their counterparts in Jordan appeared to be following suit, as the country conducted its first legislative elections in decades. Mass protests in the North African state of Algeria prompted that country's president to make genuine promises of reform, including constitutional amendments and free elections. Change even seemed possible in the grim standoff between Israelis and Palestinians, as an uprising in the West Bank and Gaza Strip appeared to refocus the attentions of both Israeli and Palestinian leaders on the business of peace.

The end of the Cold War seemed likely to accelerate these trends toward a new, more democratic status quo. The Soviet Union's collapse robbed some autocrats of a patron, and seemed to render moot the United States' reason for supporting others. However, the early 1990s delivered destruction rather than emancipation. Iraq invaded

Kuwait in August 1990 and was expelled in the US-led Operation Desert Storm seven months later. When Kurds and Shia Arabs tried to topple Saddam Hussein, his military proved more than capable of brutally enforcing domestic control. The country of Yemen, which had unified into a republic in 1990, soon descended into civil war. Egyptian president, Hosni Mubarak, slammed the door on electoral competition, staging legislative "elections" (in 1990 and 1995) that set new standards for repression and fraud. Tunisian president, Zine El Abidine Ben Ali, proved just as adept at running a security state as the man he had ousted. The brief Jordanian political opening was slammed shut once it appeared that conservative Islamists were its greatest beneficiaries. The much-heralded Oslo Accords between Israelis and Palestinians did not give birth to a new Palestinian democracy, but rather to an entity, the Palestinian Authority, that mimicked the internal repressive practices of sovereign Arab autocracies.

The biggest calamity occurred in Algeria. Islamist movements, led by the Front Islamique du Salut (Islamic Salvation Front, or FIS), handily won local elections in 1990. The religious current offered a historic departure from the hybrid of single-party and army rule that had gripped Algeria since its independence from France in 1962. The FIS also outperformed its competitors in the first round of parliamentary elections in December 1991. The following month, the Algerian military put a stop to the Islamic juggernaut. Voting was suspended and martial law imposed. Supporters of the coup argue that it was necessary to prevent the inauguration of a new theocracy; opponents contend that it smothered in the cradle the most promising democratic experiment in Arab history. What cannot be debated is that the action led to one of the region's bloodiest civil wars.

It would be fifteen more years before the Arab world would again see a political opening comparable to the aborted one of the late 1980s. In January 2005, newly elected to a second term, George W. Bush and his foreign policy principals contended that "freedom was on the march" in Arab countries. The invasion of Iraq, originally justified with reference to weapons of mass destruction that later proved illusory, was now described as the opening salvo in a noble effort to bring democracy to the Arabs.[1] The year 2005 marked the zenith of Bush's "Freedom Agenda." Lebanese protesters expelled Syrian military forces from their country, Iraqis freely elected a new constitutional assembly, Egyptians chose, for the first time, between multiple presidential candidates (albeit in a process far less competitive than Iraq's), and Palestinians went to the polls to choose a legislative council in an election widely certified as free and fair.[2] But unlike the first "Arab Spring" of the late 1980s, this second spring was isolated to a few countries where Washington had keen interests and close ties. Like its more momentous precursor, however, the second Arab Spring foundered. Only a year after it had begun, the ostensible moment of liberalization was gone, swallowed by the dark fog of Iraq's civil war, a new crackdown in Egypt, internecine strife between Palestine's newly elected Hamas government and the incumbents it had come to replace, and a war between Israel and Hezbollah that took the lives of more than five hundred Lebanese civilians.[3] Another Arab Spring had passed, replaced by what Bush's chief diplomat called "the birth pangs of a new Middle East."[4]

There are echoes of these earlier seasons of discontent in the series of uprisings that began in Tunisia in December 2010 and quickly spread to Egypt, Yemen, Libya, Bahrain, and Syria in 2011 and 2012. The mass mobilization constituting this third "Arab Spring" has delivered a mix of outcomes simultaneously more emancipatory, more violent, and more confounding than either of its forerunners. While events took their most dramatic course in the six mentioned countries, protesters elsewhere—such as in Morocco, Algeria, and Jordan—also took to the streets to call their rulers to account. Such demonstrations marked a historic escalation in the region's contentious politics, even as they paled in comparison to the surge of activism in the other cases. But it was the popular revolts in Tunisia, Egypt, and Yemen that were to prove truly unprecedented, delivering twin blows that were absent from the previous Arab Springs: *leadership change* (i.e., the removal of the incumbent in response to mass demands) and *institutional change* (i.e., a process of renegotiating the rules of the game, in which the public played a historic role).

In Bahrain and Syria, peaceful uprisings fell quickly to state repression, replaced in Bahrain by low-key civil activism and in Syria by high-intensity civil war. Unelected leaders survived, and the grammar of politics in these states—oligarchic and coercive as they were—remained essentially unchanged. These violent outcomes recall the crackdowns begun in Iraq and Algeria in the early 1990s—a tragic parallel between the first and third Arab Springs. Though Libya, too, experienced regime change, it shares much with the more doleful cases of Bahrain and Syria. In that beleaguered country, the removal of the autocrat came not because protesters forced the defection of the coercive apparatus, as in Egypt and Tunisia, but because international military intervention effectively overwhelmed a coercive apparatus willing to go to great lengths to secure the tenure of the ruler. Absent the "no-fly zone" imposed by NATO—which tipped the balance not only in the air but also on the ground—Qaddafi would likely still be in power.

Countless observers of and participants in the new Arab uprisings yearned for political transformations that would be both revolutionary and democratic. In most instances, the immediate outcomes were neither. Disappointment came not only from the cases where protests never crystallized into revolts (Jordan, Morocco, Algeria) or from the countries where states suppressed peaceful demonstrators in an all-too-familiar pattern (Bahrain, Syria), but also in some of the places that held the most promise. The sites of some of the Arab world's most historic popular revolts have delivered, at least so far, less-than-monumental reforms.

In Egypt, free and fair elections gave rise to a long-feared Islamist dominion. As partisans of the Muslim Brotherhood set about trying to capture the institutions of the state, their opponents turned for salvation to the military, which moved with alacrity to abrogate a democratic experiment with which it had never been comfortable. In Yemen, multi-party elections have yet to even take place, as a top-down process of limited reform is commanded by the selfsame political elite that dominated under the deposed autocrat (who himself continues to play an outsized role in the country's politics). The situation in Libya after Qaddafi has borne an unnerving resemblance to post-Saddam Iraq: initial elections producing governments that enjoy only the authority local militias allow them. Only Tunisians have managed to overturn the old security state and generate meaningful opportunity for civilians to acquire and exercise political power through democratic and constitutional processes. Thus, as of this writing, more than three years after the fall of Tunisia's dictator, it is possible to conclude that the season of protest known as the Arab Spring has yielded a depressingly modest harvest.

Springs Through History

The meager yield of the latest uprisings invites the question: If these moments of popular mobilization mostly result in civil war, state failure, and authoritarian renewal, what is spring-like about the present period and its antecedents? Ironically, the volatility of 2010–2014, when commentators have swung from elation to despondency, is precisely what links the latest Arab Spring to its Western precursors, "the springtime of the peoples" in Europe in 1848 and the "Prague Spring" of Czechoslovakia in 1968.[5] Those moments of promise also ended with devastated protesters and emboldened autocrats, imbuing the political usage of "spring" with the dual connotation of tremendous potential and inevitable setback. In fact, upon examination one finds instructive similarities between the patterns of revolt and repression in the European springs and their Arab analogues.

The revolutions of 1848 erupted after crowds in Paris ousted King Louis-Philippe and ushered in a new republic. Soon demonstrators were conquering the streets and challenging monarchs across Prussia, the Austrian Empire, Italy, and northern Europe. The common denominator was a demand to curb absolutist rule. Some monarchs, as in Sweden, Denmark, and the Netherlands, made brisk political concessions, allowing more liberal constitutions or forming more representative governments. The revolts climaxed, however, before they could shatter the power of hereditary rule, and they were followed by a bitter conclusion. Amidst a popular surge that threatened to spread republicanism across mid-nineteenth-century Europe, local opposition forces had proven fractious, unable to translate their tactical victories at the barricades into structural changes in the capitals. As monarchs outmaneuvered dissidents, incipient democracy gave way to dictatorship. Even the French Second Republic—touchstone of the revolutionary wave—collapsed. Louis-Napoleon Bonaparte, elected president in December 1848, pioneered the modern *autogolpe* (self-coup) by dissolving the Constituent Assembly in December 1851 and declaring himself "emperor of the French" (Napoleon III) a year later. Elsewhere, counterrevolution came from the near abroad. In Central Europe, the Russian troops of Nicholas I intervened as a backstop to local absolutism. Bolstered by the tsar, incumbents in the German states broke powersharing agreements and "annulled the Basic Rights of the German People," a democratic charter in the mold of the US Declaration of Independence (Merriman 2010: 613–643).

Unlike the springtime of the peoples, which changed a ruler in France and temporarily shifted the rules of the game in a number of other countries, the Prague Spring of 1968 was more modest, resulting in a brief relaxation of restrictions on speech and political activity. In January of that year, the Communist Party of Czechoslovakia tapped the reform-minded Alexander Dubček as first secretary and, by extension, head of state. For a period of months Dubček presided over a veritable social and political renaissance amid the repressive regimes of the Eastern Bloc. This experiment ended abruptly in August 1968, when Soviet premier Leonid Brezhnev sent half a million troops, and an imposing set of tanks, into the Czechoslovakian capital. The crackdown quelled not only local proponents of democratic change, it also served notice to Dubček's admirers in other states of the Warsaw Pact that they followed his example at their peril. In autumn, Brezhnev announced his eponymous doctrine, arrogating to the USSR the right to intervene directly in communist countries to shore up their single-party rule domestically and their alignment with Moscow in foreign affairs (Merriman, 2010). It would take over twenty years for that policy to collapse and non-communists to rise to power in Czechoslovakia and the five other Eastern Bloc countries (Poland, East Germany, Hungary, Bulgaria, Romania).[6]

The lessons for the Arab world of these earlier episodes, from a very different region and under distinct historical circumstances, are abstract yet informative. Students of politics should not be surprised that popular mobilization is more often met by reactionary violence than by visionary reforms. Incumbents, whatever the century in which they rule, enjoy advantages of resources and political coordination that turn grassroots campaigns into uphill battles. This is especially the case when they command fierce repressive organizations. As Samuel Huntington, quoting Thomas Hobbes, once noted: "Clubs are trumps" (1968: 196). Furthermore, autocrats who find their domestic coercive capacities under strain are often able to call on foreign patrons for backup. Accordingly, the latest Arab Spring conforms to a great extent with its regional and international forerunners, both in the breadth of contentious challenges and the overwhelming backlash. In this volume we explore the causes of rebellion—and quiescence—in this period, and the limits of change in those few countries that actually experienced uprisings.

Research Agenda

The historical nature of the latest Arab Spring certainly merits attention. But does it warrant another book? Since 2011 over a dozen monographs and edited volumes, as well as countless articles, have addressed the subject.[7] Although this literature has expanded rapidly, however, much of the writing has not connected contemporary events to prior theories of comparative politics. It would be a gross mischaracterization to call the corpus of work on the Arab Spring "atheoretical." At the same time, the nature of the theoretical contributions remains fragmentary. Part of the problem may be timing. Dissertation supervisors caution their students not to study "moving targets," preferring to direct them to objects of study in which the outcome is safely in the rear-view, not subject to change just as the student goes to defend their dissertation or their scholarship goes out to readers. In 2011 and 2012 the fluidity of politics in the leading cases of the Arab Spring was exactly what authors hoped to capture. There was an inherent trade-off to chasing events, however. For one thing, it was hard to determine, over a relatively short period of time, just how lasting the gains of the opposition would be. In addition, observers lacked the distance to venture broader claims. Arguments naturally gravitated toward proximate variables, particularly the attitudes of the actors involved.

Whatever the reason for this trend, it is one that we aspire to break. Until now readers have encountered important explanatory variables—from the uses of social media to the calculations of repressive agencies to the power of diffusion—but seldom found an overarching explanatory *framework*. The literature to date has not delivered a conceptual apparatus that can help us understand the latest uprisings and also hold the potential to "travel" outside the Arab world. Our aim in writing this book is to fill that gap with a testable—and disprovable—theory of major political outcomes during 2010–2014. Subsequent chapters develop the theory in detail and place it in dialogue with earlier explanations.

Before proceeding to an overview of our argument, let us tackle one other elephant in the room: Should Arab countries be grouped together and, if so, does this denote that they are exceptional or outside the bounds of conventional social science? Our answers to these questions are yes and no respectively.

The region of the Arab majority countries (or "Arab world") is analytically useful because the states in question do share certain characteristics that are germane for questions of regime change.The most obvious of these are language and religion. Though we do not subscribe to theories that locate the sources of Arab authoritarianism in these factors, we also recognize that the sharing of these characteristics potentially facilitates the diffusion both of repressive techniques and revolutionary tactics across borders. Second, Arab countries exhibit several shared patterns of economic development (itself an important variable in any study of regime type), from oil-rich rentier states such as Algeria, Libya, and the monarchies of the Arabian Guf, to the lower-middle income countries of the Levant and North Africa (although, as we shall see, there is considerable diversity within these subtypes).

The third, and perhaps most important reason for considering the regimes of the Arab world together is that they are all embedded in, and shaped by, a single international security environment. Ever since the Iranian Revolution of 1978–1979, the Arab Middle East has been a bulwark of the United States' vision of regional security. Centered on the defense of Israel, the containment of Iran, and the protection of Gulf energy resources, US policy has driven extraordinary spending by Arab autocracies on weapons of war and domestic repression. These security states flourished after the end of the Cold War, while regimes elsewhere felt pushed to adopt democratic or quasi-democratic institutions (Levitsky and Way 2002). In sum, the Arab despots threatened in 2010–2012 were inordinately repressive and resilient, yet their exceptionalism derived from politics and history (not immutable cultural factors). Specifically, the Middle East became populated by what might be called "externally unconstrained security states" thanks to a confluence of existing domestic authoritarianism and systematic US support from the 1970s onward. Though we conceptualize the Arab uprisings as primarily domestic processes, those uprisings occured in the context of (and despite) decades of great power patronage of Arab autocrats.

An Overview of the Arab Spring

The basic narrative of the Arab Spring begun in 2010–2011 requires little recapitulation. Since narratives are laden with theoretical premises, however, it is worth presenting our perspective on the empirics before specifying the variables we think are best suited to explain those empirics.

Most accounts of the Arab Spring begin with the recounting of a single dramatic action: On December 17, 2010, twenty-six-year-old Tarek al-Tayeb Mohamed Bouazizi set himself on fire in front of a local municipal office after being harassed by police officers in the central Tunisian town of Sidi Bouzid. His actions were followed by demonstrations and riots in his hometown, where protesters railed against poor economic opportunities and rampant unemployment. Bouazizi's shocking death may have been the trigger for a wave of uprisings, but the spark his sacrifice ignited might have fizzled like many before, if the dictatorships of North Africa had not already piled high a flammable powder keg of societies repressed, angered, and humiliated by their leaders. Even then, the diffusion of protest and revolution in the Arab world that began in 2011 was not inevitable: it was a mixture of serendipity and momentum, as ordinary people looked across borders and were emboldened by the possibility of change on a grand scale.

The uprisings that began in Tunisia spread rapidly across the region, not just to Bahrain, Egypt, Jordan, Libya, Syria, and Yemen but beyond—protests of varying intensity arose in Algeria, Iraq, Mauritania, Morocco, Sudan, and the Gulf states. In the first thirty months after December 2010, approximately 90,000 people in sixteen countries died in Arab Spring related violence, but autocrats only fell in four.

If the simmering hatred unleashed against dictators with dramatic force in 2011 was unforeseen, regime durability and survival in the face of popular challenge was somewhat more explicable. Across the region, the initial fates of dictators turned on the choices of domestic militaries and foreign powers. In Tunisia the army threw its lot in with the ruled rather than the ruler, and it only took dissidents four weeks to force President Zine El Abidine Ben Ali into exile. In Egypt, the army equivocated briefly before determining that Mubarak was a liability, cutting him adrift after just eighteen days of protest. In Bahrain and Libya, armies stayed loyal to the autocrat, and it was left to foreigners to tip the scales—in favor of the regime in Bahrain, and of the rebels in Libya. In Yemen, the army fractured but did not split. The besieged president, Ali

Abdullah Saleh, narrowly escaped assassination in June 2011 and then convalesced for months in Saudi Arabia while violence escalated. In November 2011, he signed a Gulf Cooperation Council plan that gave him and his family immunity from prosecution in exchange for him relinquishing his office. Finally, in Syria, the protests that began in February 2011 have, as of this writing, metamorphosed into a civil war and humanitarian catastrophe, as that country's military proved willing to back its leader, Bashar al-Assad, to the hilt.

Thus, while the uprisings constituted the most serious challenge to authoritarian regimes in the Middle East and North Africa since the Cold War, when the dust settled, the results were relatively limited: mass protests rocked less than half the region's dictatorships, and revolts replaced incumbents in only four countries: Tunisia, Egypt, Libya, and Yemen. This variation is puzzling. After all, there was much about the protests that was similar across borders: Arab dissidents took advantage of the same new information technologies, and benefited from a shared repertoire of contentious collective action. Moreover, the opponents they faced—what we have called "externally unconstrained security states"—were also broadly similar. Yet movements in different countries experienced very different degrees of success. Explaining this variation is the book's first task.

If the Arab Spring's balance sheet is modest with respect to protest, it is even more so with respect to democratization in those places where protests actually succeeded. In Tunisia, the post-Ben Ali period has been characterized by active, often contentious, but always peaceful negotiation among the country's diverse political forces. Conversely, in Egypt the military took the reins of power after withdrawing from Mubarak, while Islamists and their non-Islamist rivals failed to construct a durable coalition that would finally enshrine the principle of civilian sovereignty in a country long bereft of it. In Libya and Yemen the regime's military machine fragmented as generals defected from autocrat to opposition and took their soldiers with them. However, regional and clan allegiances have remained strong, serving as the building blocks of the new states. Increasingly, it appears as if a seat at the table in

Libya or Yemen is bought with packs of armed fighters rather than with votes. The result has been political institutions that reflect sub-national power conflicts rather than overarching conceptions of the national interest. Explaining these seemingly disparate outcomes is the book's second task.

A Structural Approach

In *The Arab Spring,* we place the above events in a theoretical and comparative framework that, we believe, offers a distinct contribution beyond the initial, proximate accounts in most prior works. We address two outcomes of major interest: leadership change and institutional change. Further, we apply scope conditions that resolve the "moving target" problem by setting the outcomes clearly in the past. For example, we explain leadership change, and its contrast space of leadership continuity, during the period December 18, 2010 (the beginning of major protests in Tunisia) until February 27, 2012 (when Yemeni President Ali Abdullah Saleh left office). Hence, analysis of the uprisings and their effects on leadership are confined to 2010–2012. We utilize similar parameters for the institutional changes that delivered new electoral and constitutional rules. For those outcomes our focus is 2011–2013. We recognize that *additional* leadership and institutional changes were ongoing as this manuscript went to press. Further, many more shifts in policy and personnel are likely in the months to come. Nonetheless, our focus on 2010–2013 provides us meaningful analytic distance from the objects of explanation while allowing us to join contemporary debates on Middle Eastern and comparative politics.

Our scope conditions are geographic as well as temporal. As noted, we restrict our study to Arab countries. This means we set aside the Islamic Republic of Iran, an authoritarian regime in a non-Arab country. Iran experienced an uprising in 2009 and may be amenable to analysis through the framework we propose. At the same time, Iran merits close consideration in its own right and we leave it to specialists of that country to determine whether the present theory illumines events there. Similarly, we exclude Turkey and Israel. Though both countries have experienced bouts of popular mobilization, they are excluded from our analysis because their governments experience regular, peaceful rotation of power among competing parties, the defining feature of electoral democracy.

Even within the Arab world, we have restricted the scope of our analysis. Most notably, Iraq and Lebanon are not examined. Citizens in Lebanon experience a form of proto-democracy that differs qualitatively from the political conditions in the other Arab states of interest. As for Iraq, we believe that its experience of a recent foreign intervention and a subsequent effort at nation-building make it difficult to compare that country's recent experience with those of its counterparts elsewhere in the Arab world.

These parameters—Arab countries that were autocratic at the outset of the Arab Spring and not under foreign occupation—produce a set of fourteen majority Arab States: Algeria, Bahrain, Egypt, Jordan, Kuwait, Libya, Morocco, Oman, Qatar, Saudi Arabia, Syria, Tunisia, United Arab Emirates, Yemen). Rulers and masses in all of these countries were exposed to the "shock" of the Arab Spring, which delivered different processes of contentious politics and varying degrees of political change. Six countries witnessed uprisings, politically oriented mass protests stretching for multiple days in multiple sites. In three of these states (Tunisia, Egypt, Yemen) domestic demonstrations culminated in "authoritarian breakdown" and leadership change (Geddes 1999). In two others (Bahrain, Syria) rulers survived uprisings through violent crackdowns. Finally, in the case of Libya, Qaddafi repressed his opponents violently but foreign military intervention ensured authoritarian breakdown and the ouster of the autocrat.

We first are interested in explaining this variation in outcome, the dramatic difference between leadership change and leadership continuity. Our approach to explanation is inductive—geared toward theory building, rather than theory testing. Deep investigation of the cases in question has shown that two variables provide significant explanatory leverage. The first variable is the extent of non-tax hydrocarbon (mainly oil) rents. Such rents are causally significant because they shore up support within the armed forces and police, helping to reinforce the regime's coercive capacity during moments of unrest. The second variable is the nature of the ruling elite and whether the ruler himself came to power through a process of hereditary succession. Like rents, hereditary succession helps to bind the agents of state violence to the incumbent. Rulers who assumed power through domestic hereditary succession processes appear to enjoy greater loyalty among state security agencies and, correspondingly, a greater capacity to quell uprisings. The rent and succession variables stretch the explanation further back historically and causally than more proximate claims relating to the professionalism of the security forces or the tech savvy and grievances of activist cadres.

Our second aim is to explain variation in outcomes of the four cases that experienced regime breakdown. Linz and Stepan (1996: 3) famously laid out a simple test by which one can determine whether a country has completed a transition to democracy—that is, if free elections have brought to power a government that has *de facto* authority to make policy and does not have to share *de jure* power with generals or autocrats. By that standard, Yemen's transition is incomplete, as the country has yet to conduct multiparty elections. Egypt's transition was thwarted as its elected legislature and presidency were abrogated by agents of the state—the judiciary in the former case, the military in the latter. Libya is a more difficult case—elections in 2012 brought democratically elected government with de jure authority, but endemic state weakness has limited the extent to which that government can be considered to have anything more than notional authority. According to Stepan (2012: 90) only in Tunisia, which since October 2011 has been governed by representatives of the people, can democracy be said to have taken root. What explains this?

Scholars have offered two sets of accounts. The first are largely structural and deterministic, locating the durability of authoritarianism (even as individual authoritarian regimes have proven fragile) in such factors as Arab culture, Islam, or in the region's low levels of economic development and literacy. The second are largely voluntaristic, locating countries' democratic prospects in the actions of political parties, civil societies, and militaries during the transition period. *The Arab Spring*, following Karl (1990), argues for a combination of these perspectives. We argue that the decisions of political actors mattered, but that these were shaped by distal structural factors. To put it simply, we suggest that successful transitions to democracy required the presence of two factors: strong states and a sufficient degree of pluralism within the pro-democratic forces. The former channels political competition into formal democratic institutions rather than toward the battlefield. The latter prevents losers in one election from concluding that their chances of acquiring power are better under dictatorship. Where either of these things did not exist, democracy failed to take root or foundered shortly thereafter.

Layout of the Book

The six chapters of this book develop this explanation of the major leadership and institutional outcomes of the Arab Spring. Chapter 1, "Theorizing the Arab Spring," situates the popular uprisings and ousters of autocrats in the literature on comparative authoritarianism. It evaluates the relative weight of major agential and structural approaches, and it provides the basis for our focus on the outcomes of authoritarian breakdown, rather than democratization and revolution. Our causal explanation for the variations in coercion that drove these phenomena forms the subject of Chapter 2, "Lineages of Repression." There is a general consensus that the posture and cohesion of repressive forces were pivotal in determining whether regimes cracked down or broke down. Because such claims can verge on tautology, we move further back in the causal process, turning "repressive capacity" into an intermediate variable—despotic power—that merits explanation. We then draw from prior literature on the comparative politics of the Middle East to build a parsimonious theory in which material rents and hereditary succession help explain the difference between leadership change and continuity across the fourteen Arab states under consideration. Chapter 3, "Breakdowns and Crackdowns," traces the empirical processes of breakdowns and crackdowns in the six core cases that experienced uprisings.

Chapters 4 and 5, "Post-Breakdown Trajectories" and "Why Breakdowns Did Not Always Produce Transitions," move from the uprisings that changed leaders (Tunisia, Egypt, Libya, Yemen) to the transitions that followed. Chapter 4 offers detailed accounts of the unfolding processes of negotiation and contention among political actors that have resulted in democracy in Tunisia, a military coup in Egypt, a near-civil war in Libya, and authoritarian continuity in Yemen. In doing so, it focuses our attention on key features of each country's transition process—specifically, the role played by oppositionists and incumbents in post-breakdown governance; the extent of voice accorded to civil society and political parties in determining the rules to govern political competition; the outcomes of free and fair elections; and the ability of new governments to actually govern their territories.

Chapter 5 turns to explain the variation carefully laid out in Chapter 4. It argues that the success or failure of transitional processes was less due to contingent factors—such as particular institutional choices or the foresight or political acumen of particular politicians—than to structurally defined power imbalances among relevant political actors. Specifically, we argue that well developed and articulated civil societies were more likely to give rise to democratic actors who could prevent militaries and state elites from dominating transitions, and which were likely to be able to conclude and enforce deals *among themselves* instead of appealing to the men with guns for help. Thus, in Egypt, a weak civil society dominated by Islamic institutions gave rise to a post-breakdown political landscape dominated by Islamist parties, leaving non-Islamists little choice but to appeal to the military and to elites within the state apparatus (such as judges) to protect their basic interests. In Tunisia, in contrast, a strong civil society, anchored in a dynamic and cohesive national labor union, meant that non-Islamist actors never felt the need to withdraw from the democratic game. Yemen and Libya offer yet another contrast—both are tribal societies in which state authority is limited. As a result, in Yemen, democratic actors have proven supine before a dominant security apparatus that has dictated the terms of the transition from above (ostensibly in order to avoid civil war—which it may yet fail to do). In Libya, the absence of such a security apparatus has led to armed conflict among tribal militias. Neither offers propitious terrain for democracy.

The conclusion to this volume reviews our principal findings, considers rejoinders to our argument, and offers thoughts for a research agenda on the third Arab Spring and its unfolding aftermath. It ends by reflecting on the potential for consolidation of Tunisia's fledgling democracy, for further change in Egypt, Yemen, and Libya, as well as the prospects of democratic progress in countries such as Jordan and Morocco which have eschewed the revolutionary path.

1

Theorizing the Arab Spring

The Arab Spring surprised students of Middle Eastern politics, who had been researching robust authoritarianism for over a decade (Posusney and Angrist 2005; Gause 2011). Scholars seeking to explain the dynamics of this period were immediately thrust between literatures on democratic transitions and durable authoritarianism. Initial outcomes were more diverse than the political transformations of Southern Europe and Latin America begun in the mid-1970s (O'Donnell, Schmitter, and Whitehead 1986). They were also distinct from the more recent "fourth wave" of democratization in post-communist states and subsequent "electoral revolutions." Post-communist democracies and hybrid regimes emerged from the balance of power between old elites and new activists, often in the context of an uneven electoral playing field (Bunce and Wolchik 2011; McFaul 2002).

Contrary to the picture painted by some in the media, and indeed academia, most Arab countries did not witness extraordinary social upheaval. In Morocco, Algeria, and nearly all Gulf monarchies protests were limited in number and scope, and they did not concentrate political disaffection on incumbent rulers—as occurred in Tunisia, Egypt, Libya, Yemen, Syria, and Bahrain. Arguably the most fitting regional analogue for the Arab Spring is sub-Saharan Africa. Between 1988 and 1992, twenty-eight of forty-two sub-Saharan African states saw massive popular protests. Although by 1994, eleven of the region's countries had held new democratic elections nearly 75% remained authoritarian. Today the area continues to host some of the world's most persistent and repressive regimes, for example, Equatorial Guinea, Ethiopia, and Gabon (Bratton and van de Walle 1997: 117, 286–287).

Thus while the political whirlwind of early 2011 seemed to sweep away prior claims about "durable authoritarianism," the range of outcomes shows that many of the variables used to explain autocratic resilience remained valid—if not for explaining the persistence of individual leaders, then for explaining the durability of authoritarianism as the region's modal regime type. Recalling the heterogeneity of Africa's "democratic experiments" twenty years ago, this chapter situates the Arab Spring in scholarship on democratization *and* authoritarianism. Given the breadth of these literatures, our treatment is necessarily selective. Our primary goal is to assess what the leading explanatory frameworks of democratization and authoritarianism can say about Tunisia, Egypt, and other Arab states rocked by demonstrations in 2010–2011. We begin by delineating the scope of our dependent variables for the first part of the book and specifying the universe of cases.

After summarizing the type of cases we aim to explain, we address prior political-science theories that shed light on the uprisings. Theories rooted in the phenomenon of protests from below and the distribution of power between opposition forces prove to be more compelling than voluntarist theories emphasizing elite pacts or innovative activism. Yet the importance of power asymmetries begs the question: what determines the relative influence of incumbents and oppositionists? On this score, classic regime *type* classifications prove less instructive than the material and coercive resources of those regimes. After covering the pre-2011 literature, we turn to recent works on the Arab Spring, including arguments based on technology, diffusion, and demography. In general, the narrow temporal focus of these accounts limits their ability to explain observed variation or to bring the cases of the Arab Spring into a dialogue with our existing knowledge about protest and revolution. Recent work on monarchism and oil wealth provides the grist for our theory explaining variations in the repressive response of regimes, contained in Chapter 2, "Lineages of Repression."

Sorting Outcomes: Uprisings and Authoritarian Breakdown

Although the spectacle of millions of demonstrators from Tunis to Sanaa captured headlines, the importance of the Arab uprisings for political life and political science will be measured in their lasting effect on a region dominated by authoritarianism: to what extent did they appreciably alter who rules and how? To be clear about our narrow focus, we are primarily concerned in this half of the book with uprisings and authoritarian breakdown. In the second half of the book, we will attend to the question of whether and under what conditions regime collapse ushered in democratization.

From December 2010 through mid-2013, six countries of the Arab Spring—Tunisia, Egypt, Bahrain, Yemen, Libya, and Syria—displayed basic commonalities in process and wide variance in outcomes. The common trend was the presence of "uprisings," which we consider a major type of contentious collective action (McAdam, Tarrow, and Tilly 2001). Three features characterize an uprising:

1. the eruption of non-violent mass protests over multiple days,
2. the spread of protest to multiple geographic sites, and
3. the seizure and control by protesters of public spaces—for example, Bourguiba Avenue in Tunis, Tahrir Square in Cairo, the Pearl Roundabout (Dawwār al-Lu'lu'ah) of Manama, and Bahrain.

Uprisings exceed conventional demonstrations in their size, national resonance, and persistence. They differ from armed insurgencies in the methods used by their organizers. Although in Syria, Libya, and, to a lesser extent, Yemen, peaceful protest morphed into violent rebellion, the two phenomena are distinct. Militias do not require uprisings to emerge and uprisings do not necessarily produce militias.

The *effects* of uprisings vary widely. The quintessential Arab uprising before 2011 might have been the Palestinian *intifada* of 1987–1993, yet its participants did not effect the political change they sought: an end to the Israeli occupation of the West Bank and Gaza Strip. The record of later uprisings in the Arab world is a mix of failure and success. On the one hand, Tunisian protesters unified across lines of class and geography to force their president to resign. On the other hand, Bahrainis protested in higher per capita terms than their peers in other Arab states, yet a brutal crackdown ended their mobilization.[1]

The success of uprisings during 2010–2012 was most visible in the replacement of autocratic leaders in Tunisia, Egypt, and Yemen. We term these events a form of authoritarian breakdown, based on widescale popular pressure rather than, for example, a military putsch. Authoritarian breakdown entails the involuntary "replacement of incumbent rulers by an alternative set of elites" (Brownlee 2009: 519; Geddes 1999: 19). It excludes an assassination of the executive that leaves in place the top echelon. For example, while Egyptian president Anwar Sadat's killing in 1981 did not constitute breakdown, Hosni Mubarak's removal in 2011 did. Breakdown marks the endpoint of one period of authoritarianism. It may be followed by more authoritarianism or by a more democratic system.

We compare instances of authoritarian breakdown with periods of regime continuity during *domestically driven* political challenges. These take place when a mass movement, as in an uprising, impels a change of leader. Although military figures may remove the leader, the element of social pressure is sufficient that the breakdown is not a simple coup. Three regimes—Tunisia (2010–2011), Egypt (2011), and Yemen (2011–2012)—met these criteria and qualified as domestically driven breakdown. Tunisians pushed Ben Ali into exile on January 14, 2011; Egyptians forced Mubarak to relinquish the presidency on February 11, 2011; Yemenis forced Saleh to resign on February 27, 2012. Although in these cases the armed forces were instrumental in ushering dictators from power, they were responding directly to a groundswell of nonviolent street activism and they operated without active military assistance from foreign states.

Authoritarian breakdown almost always involves a change of leader. It may also entail a change of regime. Regarding the Arab Spring, however, we largely avoid applying the term "regime change." The term "regime" can carry a broad meaning, encompassing the set of established and customary rules that govern politics. Robert Fishman defined it as "the formal and informal organization of the center of political power, and of its relations with the broader society" (1990: 428). For the most part, the organization of political power and regime–society relations did *not* change radically in the core cases, even when the ruler was toppled in Egypt and Yemen—hence our preference to explain breakdown rather than regime change.

There is one exception: foreign imposed changes or FIRCs. FIRCs involve outside powers and may bear little resemblance to a purely internal overthrow (Werner 1996; Downes and Monten 2013). A FIRC occurs when foreign armies play a determining role in the removal of the incumbent ruler, including through significant and direct repressive assistance. The US-led Operation Iraqi Freedom in 2003, which overthrew Saddam Hussein, and the NATO-directed Operation Unified Protector of 2011, which enabled rebels to topple Qaddafi's regime in Libya, are the most recent FIRCs in the MENA region. In both instances there is a clear counterfactual case to be made that had the foreign military *not* attacked, the regime would have persisted during the immediate period in question. For this study Libya presents an instance of authoritarian breakdown through a FIRC.

In the remaining cases, the classification of no breakdown signifies an uninterrupted line of rulers, or a single ruler, during the period in question. Ten regimes belong in this category during 2010–2012: Algeria, Bahrain, Jordan, Kuwait, Morocco, Oman, Qatar, Saudi Arabia, Syria, and the United Arab Emirates. Lack of breakdown does not mean that these countries were politically stagnant or devoid of consequential shifts in institutions and personnel. This category contains a spectrum—from places with cosmetic but unsubstantive change (i.e., Qatar) to failed mobilizations (e.g., Bahrain) to regime endurance in the face of civil war (e.g., Syria). Beyond those cases, some Arab rulers have flirted with reforms and allowed limited elections. Yet such initiatives, while noteworthy and *potentially* momentous, do not in themselves remove incumbents. To the contrary, they often bolster incumbents and fragment the opposition (Heydemann 2007; Dobson 2012; Stacher 2012).

Recognizing our focus on uprisings and breakdowns, what do we have to say about revolutions and democratization? Immediately after Mubarak lost power, much ink was spent arguing about whether or not Egyptians had accomplished a revolution. There is little utility in reviving that debate. Popularly, the semantic conflict has been settled: Egyptians overwhelmingly embrace the term "revolution" for their eighteen-day struggle against Mubarak. But analytically, we part ways. Because we are speaking to a scholarly literature we must choose our terms precisely. Comparativists steeped in Skocpol's analysis of the French, Russian, and Chinese revolutions and accustomed to her definition of revolutions as a rapid, structural transformation of the state (and, for social revolutions, of society), will acknowledge that neither Egypt nor the other Arab Spring cases clear the bar (Skocpol 1979).

It is also difficult to discuss uprisings without addressing the question of democratization. Like revolution, democratization is a major dependent variable spawning a rich and vast literature. Like "revolution," however, talk of "democratization" in the Middle East has sometimes gotten ahead of developments on the ground. At the time of this writing, the Arab uprisings have yielded no stable democracy among the Arab countries we cover: only Tunisia currently meets the minimal standards of electoral democracy. Democratization's absence, however, does not mean authoritarianism has not been shaken—a consequential, and rare, outcome even during the Arab Spring. Because we are interested in explaining variation in the occurrence of such ruptures, we focus here on authoritarian breakdown rather than democratization.

Because we home in on the outcome of breakdown, our theory here speaks more to questions of comparative authoritarianism than to issues of comparative democratization. Nonetheless, the contrast we find among the Arab Spring cases is highly instructive for understanding variations in repressive capacity. Regime persistence and the absence of popular opposition reveal one dimension of authoritarian control: the ability to inculcate quiescence, if not consent (Lukes 1974; Gaventa 1980). Lack of breakdown *in the face of* popular opposition shows a more basic feature of authoritarianism: the ability to defeat dissent through force. Two uprisings failed to spur regime change: in 2011 Bahrain, and since 2011 in Syria. The conjunction of popular revolt and regime *continuity* gives our analysis cautionary examples of "successful" repression: crackdowns. By showing regimes under strain, such crackdowns provide valuable contrast examples of authoritarian breakdown (Brownlee 2002).

A word is warranted about our coding of Bahrain and Syria. Some observers may question whether the Bahraini royal family's survival in 2011 is really evidence of the regime's durability. After all, Saudi Arabia led a Gulf Cooperation Council (GCC) military force into Bahrain a month into the uprising. The Saudi intervention suggests that regime continuity may have depended on foreign support. It is, of course, impossible to test the counterfactual of how the Bahrain regime would have fared without the GCC military units. However, by all accounts, GCC forces did not take the vanguard in the regime's offensive. Rather, they served mainly to secure key installations around the country. In this respect, the GCC army was a reserve or backup source for the Bahraini Defense Force: a fail-safe, rather than a mainstay of the regime's response (ICG 2011: 6–7). More importantly, the crackdown itself showed Bahrain's repressive apparatus cohered. There were no fissures in the armed forces.

A similar pattern manifested in Syria. There the uprising descended into a full-blown civil war. The state's crackdown is ongoing and unyielding, with tanks, helicopter gunships, and bombers devastating major cities. Although the outcome of this *military* conflict remains to be determined, we think it is not premature to code the peaceful mass revolt as having been unsuccessful. By 2013 it appeared that only a FIRC would remove Bashar al-Asad from power. That prospect, however, was taken off the table after US and Russian diplomats reached a deal for removing Syria's chemical weapons stockpiles.

How well do existing theories—created before the uprisings or in response to them—account for these outcomes? The remainder of the chapter addresses this question, beginning with explanations based on relations between and relative power of key actors.

Actor-Based Approaches

In the transitions paradigm, outcomes hinge on the decisions and strategies of the actors involved, particularly the so-called soft-liners of the regime and their moderate interlocutors in the opposition (O'Donnell, Schmitter, and Whitehead 1986). Such approaches are best suited for situations of political parity and open-endedness. The paucity of regime change in the Arab Spring suggests it was characterized by less uncertainty and indeterminism than O'Donnell, Schmitter, and their collaborators found in the transitions from authoritarianism in Latin America and Southern Europe. Initial outcomes across the region underscore the importance of the domestic balance of power in disrupting or sustaining extant power arrangements.

O'Donnell and Schmitter's "tentative conclusion," that transitions begin with an intra-regime rift between soft-liners and hard-liners, subsequently acquired a semi-canonical quality (1986: 19). This approach has been incredibly influential in the study of Middle Eastern politics, where scholars have sought to explain variations in elite conflict and the conditions under which insiders could partner with oppositionists in negotiated "pacts" (Brownlee 2007; Wickham 2004).

The transitions framework was not a theory of democratization, however. For example, the conditions dividing elites were not specified, and the approach suffered from a dearth of testable "if, then" propositions (Bunce 1995: 123). Moreover, as Valerie Bunce observed, the seminal examples of transitions differed substantially from subsequent cases of democratization, such as the transformation of post-communist states:

> In southern Europe and Latin America, the issue *was* democratization; that is, a change in political regime. Indeed, the circumscribed character of political change in southern Europe and Latin America is one reason why students of comparative democratization could reduce democratic transitions to a process involving interactions among a handful of political elites. By contrast, what is at stake in Eastern Europe is nothing less than the creation of the very building blocks of the social order. (1995: 120–121, emphasis in original)

Ending authoritarianism in many countries outside of Latin America and Southern Europe put far more issues on the table than the transfer of rule from a military junta to a civilian government. Consequently, when comparativists explaining democratization grappled with processes other than "transitions" they found non-elite actors playing a much more significant role than originally postulated (e.g., Bratton and van de Walle 1997; Yashar 1997). Here we can follow Bunce and consider an instructive non-Arab regional analogue: the post-communist transitions begun in 1989 and 1991.

The *Transitions from Authoritarian Rule* volumes speculated that democratization was most likely when incumbents and opposition forces were equally matched. Such parity would enable regime soft-liners and moderate oppositionists to negotiate among themselves and institutionalize the rotation of power (O'Donnell and Schmitter 1986; see also Rustow 1970; cf. Bermeo 1997). Subsequent work in comparative democratization has found a contrary pattern, namely that a clean break from authoritarianism is most likely when the power of challengers exceeds that of incumbents. Analyzing twenty-eight post-communist regimes, Michael McFaul reported that uncertainty among the main participants in the negotiation of a new regime produced conflict rather than a pro-democratic compromise. The stage was then set for internal violence, in Tajikistan, or competitive authoritarianism, which took hold in Ukraine and Russia. "Conversely," he wrote, "the two other transition pathways had more certain distributions of power and therefore much less confrontation" (2002: 224). A pro-challenger balance of power yielded stable democracy (Poland, Hungary); an asymmetry favoring old regime elites produced durable authoritarianism (Kazakhstan, Turkmenistan) (McFaul 2002: 227).

Power asymmetries between regimes and oppositions are a dominant feature of the Arab Spring. Regimes have not collapsed in domino-like fashion as in the Eastern Bloc in 1989 (Kuran 1991). The most successful protests took weeks, rulers dithered before resigning, and security forces only broke with incumbent autocrats after demonstrators held their ground in public spaces. In Tunisia the domestic balance of power favored challengers during the transition. The immediate result was a civil society-driven process of institutional reforms, clean elections, and constitutional deliberation. By contrast, the balance of power has favored the regime in all cases without uprisings (Morocco, Algeria, Jordan, Saudi Arabia, etc.). Only in Egypt, Libya, Bahrain, Syria, and Yemen can the balance of power be described (at best) as "even or uncertain," in Michael McFaul's framework.

The salience of political elites in *later* stages of the challenge to authoritarianism during the Arab Spring also differs significantly from the situation in Latin America and Southern Europe, where political change reportedly *began* from the top of the regime. The uniformed military in Tunisia and Egypt carried out leadership changes, but they hardly initiated them. To the contrary, the uprisings coalesced "from below," through marches, rallies, sit-ins, and public demonstrations demanding reform or regime change. In this respect, the core dynamics of the Arab Spring resembled challenges to authoritarian rule in Eastern Europe and Africa during the late 1980s and early 1990s (Bratton and van de Walle 1997; Bunce 1999; Linz and Stepan 1996). Protests came from different sectors and reflected different grievances. Working-class demonstrators in Tunisia rose up far from the capital to contest economic deprivations. In Egypt, middle- and upper-class Internet activists organized the initial "Police Day" protests in Cairo. Although they included an improved national minimum wage in their initial demands, the thrust of their critique was against the president and his minister of interior, whose resignation they sought. Once contentious collective action broke out, countries followed different paths, toward constitutional changes in Tunisia and Egypt and toward armed conflict in Libya and Syria.

In their study of sub-Saharan African transitions, Michael Bratton and Nicolas van de Walle reported that twenty-eight of forty-two countries experienced political protests during 1988 and 1992, and that all twenty-eight enacted liberalizing reforms by the end of 1992. However, only eleven of these states (39%) had held democratic elections by December 1994, the endpoint of the authors' analysis (1997: 117). A major contrast between Africa's democratic experiments and the Arab uprisings is that the early political trajectory in Arab states has trended toward conflict rather than political liberalization. We reason this difference comes in large part from a power distribution in Arab countries that continues to favor incumbents, even in the face of emboldened opposition.

Institutional Differences

Anti-regime forces in the Arab world may face a steeper climb than their counterparts in other regions because of the form of authoritarianism they confront. Therefore it is worth considering whether the power asymmetries and rarity of pacts derive from institutional variations that have characterized the states in question.

Responding to what they saw as an excessive voluntarism in the transitions literature, comparativists have worked to situate the agency of incumbent and opposition actors in political contexts that predate pacts about changing the regime. "Structured contingency" became a way of integrating the effect of slow-changing structures with the fluidity of negotiations and maneuvers during periods of transformation (Karl 1990). Such an approach "allows that people can make their own history, even if not under conditions of their own choosing" (Bratton and van de Walle 1996: 45). Within the literature on authoritarianism, one of the institutions that, belatedly, received significant attention is *the regime* (see Snyder and Mahoney 1999). To quote Bratton and van de Walle once more: "the outcome of political struggles depends critically on the way that power was exercised by the rulers of previous regimes" (1997: 89). Sharing this intuition, comparativists have investigated extensively the nature of the elite—the political and material bases of its authority—and the extent to which the regime permits public contestation and participation—typically through constrained elections (Chehabi and Linz 1998; Diamond 2002; Gandhi and Przeworski 2007; Geddes 1999; Levitsky and Way 2002; Schedler 2002).

For claims that antecedent institutions can account for variance in regime change the Arab world initially presents a conundrum. The prevalence of highly repressive forms of authoritarianism across the region seemingly reduces the explanatory power of regime types. In the Arab Spring, a spectrum of new movements bursts from an apparently monochromatic tableau, characterized by hegemonic executives and feeble opposition forces. In 2010, Freedom House and Polity scores (the two most widely employed datasets in statistical comparisons of democratization) gave little indication that a year later Tunisians would enjoy epochal levels of political pluralism while neighboring Algerians remained under the heel of a military junta. All six countries that witnessed major uprisings had been recently classified as "Not Free" by Freedom House (with the country average of Political Freedom and Civil Liberties scores ranging between 5.5 and the worst possible rating of 7). Five of them had highly autocratic (negative) Polity scores (Bahrain was not coded). The dynamism of activists from Tunis to Manama was not foreseen or captured ahead of time by the major cross-national indices of political freedom. This is not a retrospective indictment of the Freedom House or Polity data. Rather, it invites additional *prospective* consideration of institutional factors that correlate with subsequent variance.

Comparative studies of democratization and authoritarian durability provide additional measures of institutional variation across nondemocracies. Robert Dahl's classic study of political systems, *Polyarchy*, arranged regimes by their level of participation and contestation, with polyarchies rating high on both variables (1971). Subsequent authors adopted the same indices to separate inclusionary and exclusionary autocracies. The first set exhibited high levels of participation but low levels of contestation, while the second group scored low in both areas (Remmer 1985–1986: 71).

Bratton and van de Walle mapped the regimes of sub-Saharan African onto Dahl's grid, using the presence of elections and the winning party's seat share to operationalize participation and contestation (1996: 140–143). Nearly all of their cases fit in three subtypes: military oligarchy (low in both areas), plebiscitary one-party system (with medium levels of participation but low levels of contestation), and competitive one-party systems (with medium scores on both axes) (1996: 78). They found a mix of relationships between these regime types and differences in a) levels of protests, b) the enactment of political liberalization, and c) the execution of democratic transitions. Among the authoritarian cases, protests, liberalization, *and* democratization were most likely in regimes that previously allowed elections (even though a single party dominated them), and least likely in the exclusionary military regimes (1996: 144, 188, 220–221). As it happens, initial trends among the Arab cases reflect a similar pattern. The Middle East's "plebiscitary" and "competitive" dominant-party autocracies (Egypt, Syria, Tunisia, Yemen) delivered the bulk of major uprisings and, in Egypt and Tunisia, some measurable liberalization. Conversely, the region's most exclusionary regimes (whether military or monarchical) seldom witnessed comparable levels of contestation (e.g., Algeria, Saudi Arabia). Revolts in Libya and Bahrain depart from this trend, but do not undermine the general impression that opposition forces have done best in the Arab pseudo-republics.

Upon closer examination, however, differences across the Arab Spring may have less to do with the elections autocrats allowed than with the organizations on which they depended. A 2002 special issue of the *Journal of Democracy* triggered investigation of so-called hybrid regimes that combine inclusionary institutions with repression, corruption, and dirty tricks to prevent the opposition from winning power (Diamond 2002; Levitsky and Way 2002; Schedler 2002). But distinctions among "competitive" and "hegemonic" electoral authoritarianism provide limited traction on the developments unfolding in Tunisia, Egypt, and other Arab states. Whereas prior statistical work has established a significant positive relationship between vigorous electoral contestation under the *ancien régime* and subsequent democratization, none of the Arab states previously qualified as competitive authoritarian systems (Brownlee 2009; Levitsky and Way 2010). In this sense, whatever democratizing promise Tunisia, and to a lesser extent Egypt, showed in 2011, it emerged—as far as the leading hybrid regime types are concerned—de novo, out of police states in which the opposition never controlled even a third of parliament.

Turning to the variable of personalism, there are two sets of categories to consider. The first comprises monarchies and non-monarchies. The second includes extremely personalistic (or so-called sultanistic) regimes and their more conventional counterparts.

Michael Herb has accounted for the historic success of Arab monarchs at foiling coup plotters and would-be revolutionaries (1999). This pattern appears to hold during 2010–2012. Arab kingdoms and emirates exhibited greater resistance to protest and change than other regimes. We return to the phenomenon of apparent monarchical resilience in Chapter 2.

Regarding broader theories of personalism and sultanism, we again face a generally uniform political profile on one hand and a variety of outcomes on the other. In their authoritative study of democratization and democratic consolidation, Juan Linz and Alfred Stepan elaborated the long-term negative effects of sultanism on democratic development (1996: 51–56; see also Chehabi and Linz 1998). The Cold War era was rife with sultanistic regimes from the Caribbean to the Eastern Pacific, including "Haiti under the Duvaliers, the Dominican Republic under Trujillo, the Central African Republic under Bokassa, the Philippines under Marcos, Iran under the Shah, Romania under Ceausescu, and North Korea under Kim Il Sung" (Linz and Stepan 1996: 51). Although this category allows for significant variation (one could, for example, identify numerous contrasts between the Philippines under Marcos and communist North Korea), sultanistic regimes differ substantially from classic authoritarian regimes (such as Franco's Spain). Specifically, they lack a mobilizing ideology, but possess a "pseudo-ideology not believed by staff, subjects, or [the] outside world." They also exhibit low levels of formal institutionalization and strong tendencies toward dynasticism (Linz and Stepan 1996: 44–45).

Based on these criteria, it could be argued that at the time of the Arab Spring, the Middle East contained numerous sultanistic regimes: Syria under the Assads, Tunisia under Ben Ali, Egypt under Mubarak, Yemen under Saleh, and Libya under Qaddafi. In light of Linz and Stepan's work, prospects for democratization in these cases are exceedingly limited. Sultanistic regimes suffer from a dearth of soft-liners and moderate oppositionists, virtually precluding the classic transition path of *reforma pactada-ruptura pactada* (Linz and Stepan 1996: 61). Events of the Arab Spring strongly validate this notion, particularly in cases like Libya where, following Linz and Stepan, "democratic consolidation would entail the task of simultaneously crafting not only political and economic society, but also every single arena of a democracy [a constitution, citizenship, legislature, etc.] as well" (54). The Tunisian example, though, signals democratic opportunities may emerge from a state where the ruler's personality cult infiltrated both public and private life. In this respect, Tunisia's relative success betrays social and political undercurrents that survived excessive personalism at the regime's peak and which, in turn, direct attention to alternative approaches. We formulate an alternative approach to personalism and monarchism, but note there that the metrics of prior literature would logically place all six cases of Arab uprisings in the sultanistic regime family.

Table 1.1 presents the institutional variances in the six Arab cases of major uprisings and two contrast cases, Algeria and Saudi Arabia.

Table 1.1. Institutional Profile of Selected Arab Regimes Prior to the Uprisings

	Freedom House (2010)	Polity (2010)	Bratton and van de Walle (1996)*	Diamond (2002)***	Geddes (1999)	Linz and Stepan (1996)*	Outcome
Tunisia	6	–4	Plebiscitary one-party	Hegemonic electoral authoritarian	Single-party	Sultanistic	Regime change
Egypt	5.5	–3	Competitive one-party	Hegemonic electoral authoritarian	Personal/ military/ single-party	Sultanistic	Regime change
Libya	7	–7	Military oligarchy	Non-electoral authoritarian	Personal	Sultanistic	Foreign imposed regime change
Yemen	5.5	–2	Competitive one-party	Hegemonic electoral authoritarian	Personal	Sultanistic	Regime change
Syria	6.5	–8	Plebiscitary one-party	Hegemonic electoral authoritarian	Personal/ military/ single-party	Sultanistic	Civil war and regime continuity
Bahrain	5.5	N.A.	Monarchy**	Non-electoral authoritarian	Monarchy**	Sultanistic	Regime continuity
Algeria	5.5	2	Military oligarchy	Hegemonic electoral authoritarian	Single-party/military	Authoritarian	Regime continuity
Saudi Arabia	6.5	–10	Monarchy**	Non-electoral authoritarian	Monarchy**	Sultanistic	Regime continuity

* Codings of Arab cases are the authors' judgment based on the classification criteria of the prior works.

** Monarchies omitted in original studies.

*** Codings are from 2004 data, using the most recent executive election (Brownlee 2009).

Initial Literature on the Arab Spring

Existing analytic frameworks draw attention to the variation between the Arab states and other regions, thus providing limited leverage on the question of where uprisings emerged among the Arab states, and where those uprisings changed regimes. Scholars of the Middle East thus sought new theoretical tools and frameworks, often based on factors that were prominent in the events themselves, such as the profile of protesters or the tools they adopted. To conclude our overview of prior literature, we address three of the most prominent variables regarding the uprisings: demography, technology, and repressive capacity. In Chapter 2 we turn to two additional variables, oil rents and hereditary succession, which we utilize to craft a new structural theory of regime change during 2010–2012.

Before homing in on specific variables it is worth noting that the initial studies of the Arab Spring have largely shared in common a proximate focus, that is, their principal explanatory variables have been relatively close to the events they aim to explain. Such accounts, which are often highly voluntarist, have struggled to explain the many outcomes that have characterized the Arab Spring. Authors focus their attention on the proverbial dogs that barked (Tunisia, Egypt, etc.), rather than considering the MENA region as a whole (Hilsum 2012). Moreover, instead of taking the past seriously, many early accounts offered reductionist versions of history (see Fischer 1970: 172–175): the Tunisian revolution supposedly began with a fruitseller's self-immolation on December 17, 2010, while the Egyptian uprising sprung from a YouTube video in which a female activist exhorted her countrymen to join her in Tahrir on January 25, 2011 (Saddy 2011; Ismail 2011). While these events "mattered," they may also have been segments in a longer causal chain that remains mostly unspecified.

The first line of argument cites the profile of protesters themselves to explain why and where the uprisings took place. Scholars have pointed to the "youth bulge" of the Arab countries as one driver of protest, claiming that when a disproportionate share of the total population is relatively young (under twenty-five years of age), the country is vulnerable to revolt. Hence Mark Haas and David Lesch write that in the MENA region "roughly one out of every three people is between the ages of twenty and twenty-four. Youth bulges are particularly pronounced in those countries that experienced the most widespread and powerful protests during the Arab Spring" (2013: 3). A look at the data across the cases that had major uprisings and those that did not, however, reveals there is not a statistically significant difference in median age between the two groups (average of 24 years and 4 months for countries with uprisings, 26 years for countries without uprisings).

Perhaps it is not the presence of youth but their grievances against the government that provokes mass unrest. To address such a contention, youth unemployment (specifically *male* youth unemployment) is a stronger indicator than median age. Here too, a look at the data shows no significant difference across uprising and non-uprising cases. The portion of unemployed young males was 21.2% in the countries that experienced uprisings: only marginally higher than the 20.4% rate in their less turbulent neighbors.

Apart from domestic economic complaints, both young and older persons might be frustrated by their government's foreign policies. In his close examination of Arab attitudes, Shibley Telhami reasons that the "revolts were about restoring dignity" (2013:18). That goal entailed challenging both internal repression and the behaviors of key external powers:

> In their own minds, Arabs have never fully divorced the authoritarianism of their rulers from the Western-dominated international order that they see as having cultivated and entrenched these rulers in power from the very inception of the modern political system in the Arab world at the end of World War I. (19)

Here again the variable in question—opposition to Western foreign policy behaviors—appears more compelling as a correlate of regional attitudes than a causal explanation of intra-regional variance. Indeed, the rulers whom protesters challenged exhibited very different profiles vis-à-vis the West, from close clients like Mubarak and Saleh to veritable rogues like Assad and Qaddafi.

A second line of argument turns from the profile of protesters to their organizational tools, specifically the use of the Internet and social media (Ghonim 2012; Lynch 2011; Noueihed and Warren 2012; Tufekci and Wilson 2012). But the narrative of youthful pluck and technological savvy only went so far. Activists from Rabat to Riyadh had access to Twitter, Facebook, and YouTube, and yet the story of most democratic activists in the Arab world remains one of disappointment and defeat. The limits of information technology as causes of the uprisings are illustrated in Table 1.2, which displays the self-reported rates of Internet usage for ten Arab countries surveyed as part of the sixth wave of the World Values Survey in 2010 to 2014.[2] None of the Arab autocracies with the highest rates of Internet usage—Kuwait (55.1% of respondents reporting that they obtain information from the Internet every day), and Qatar (57.5%), and Algeria (39%)—were sites of significant mass protest. In contrast, Egypt (where only 12.8% say they receive information from the Internet on a daily basis, and almost 78% say they never do) and Yemen (where only 6.6% say they get information from the Internet every day, as opposed to the 73.4% who say they never do) both featured uprisings and regime change. At the very least, these patterns suggest that the role of Internet connectivity in generating the latest wave of Arab uprisings is outweighed by other factors.

Unsurprisingly, the most systematic examination to date of the effects of Internet and texting reached modest conclusions. In their book, *Democracy's Fourth Wave?: Digital Media and the Arab Spring*, Philip Howard and Muzammil Hussain vet an enormous amount of cross-national data on their subject. They find, however, that new technologies were not causes of uprisings or regime change, so much as intermediate linkages. "Digital media . . . provided the fundamental infrastructure for social movements and collective action . . . 'connective action' . . . In every single case, the inciting incidents of the Arab Spring were digitally mediated in some way" (2012: 118, 123).

Table 1.2. Percentages of World Values Survey Respondents in Selected Arab Countries (2010–2014) Who Report Obtaining Information from the Internet Daily, Weekly, Monthly, Less than Monthly, or Never

	Algeria	Iraq	Jordan	Kuwait	Lebanon
Daily	39.0	21.8	24.8	55.1	41.2
Weekly	10.5	7.9	11.6	16.3	13.2
Monthly	5.2	4.3	4.4	6.4	11.3
Less than monthly	11.1	7.9	4.0	9.1	10.0
Never	31.3	56.8	55.2	7.6	22.5
No answer	2.9			4.8	
Don't know		1.2		0.6	1.8
N	1,200	1,200	1,200	1,303	1,200
	Qatar	Libya	Tunisia	Egypt	Yemen
Daily	57.5	39.3	32.0	12.8	6.6
Weekly	11.6	10.4	8.3	5.1	5.1
Monthly	3.4	4.6	2.1	2.5	1.0
Less than monthly	8.2	4.0	6.6	1.7	2.9
Never	19.4	38.6	49.5	77.9	73.4
No answer		0.6			
Don't know		2.6	1.6		11.0
N	1,060	2,131	1,205	1,523	1,000

Source: World Values Survey, 6th Wave.

Of course, "digital mediation" is not digital causation. The relatively limited role of the Internet and SMSing—compared to deeper factors—becomes more apparent in the events themselves. "Perhaps the best evidence that digital media were an important causal factor in the Arab Spring is that dictators treated them as such," the authors write. "The months during which the Arab Spring took place had the most national blackouts, network shutdowns, and tool blockages to date" (2012: 69). Targets of repression are not necessarily causes of regime change. We would not infer, for examples, that marches were a causal factor just because dictators tried to suppress them with truncheons and tear gas.

Finally, whereas the objects of regime repression were intermediate factors, so too was that repression itself a segment in a longer causal process. Perhaps the strongest point of consensus in recent studies is that Arab militaries played the role of switchman in the uprisings. Eva Bellin noted that protesters succeeded in toppling autocrats where the military was institutionalized, rather than personalized (2012: 132–133). Zoltan Barany and F. Gregory Gause observed that the military supported demonstrators in countries that were ethnically homogenous (Tunisia, Egypt), while it fragmented or fired upon the opposition when tribal or sectarian interests superseded the armed forces' corporate identity (Barany 2011: 30; Gause 2011). Similarly, Jack Goldstone argued that professional soldiers in Tunisia and Egypt were offended by their presidents' cronyism, whereas in Yemen and Libya factions of the military remained bound to the regime through extended familial connections (2011: 12–13). These studies move the field forward by pointing to systematic variations in the capacity of Middle East regimes to repress.

At the same time, following how the coercive apparatus responded to challenges from below begs the question of why, under certain circumstances, uniformed officers realigned in favor of the opposition and why, under other conditions, they defended incumbents. It is easy to argue in hindsight that the Egyptian military was more professionalized—and less loyal to the president—than Syria's, it is much harder to identify variables that in 2010 or earlier could have forecast the defections of militaries in Tunisia and Egypt and the military's loyalty in Syria. In fact, a priori few would have predicted that Egypt's military would follow the Tunisian army's lead and break from the incumbent. After all, though Tunisia has boasted a long tradition of civilian control over the military that might explain the army's reluctance to back Ben Ali, the scholarly wisdom on Egypt had long held that the army and the regime were one (Abdel-Malek 1968). Thus, most post-Arab Spring accounts of military behavior have been exercises in curve-fitting—reading the generals' attitudes from their actions. While coercion should be considered an intervening variable, the drivers of that capacity must be treated in light of more distal causes.

Finally, authoritarian breakdown in the Middle East and North Africa can be viewed through the prism of "structured contingency," meaning actors challenge authoritarianism under historically shaped circumstances (Karl 1995: 10–11; Bratton and van de Walle 1997: 45–48; see also Yashar 1997: 3). Though dissidents could take advantage of the diffusion of new "toolkits" that gave them an unprecedented ability to disseminate their message and coordinate mass protests, their success in bringing about change was ultimately determined by *longue durée* factors (Bunce and Wolchik 2010). More specifically, society's ability to challenge authoritarian regimes, and the regime's capacity to repel those challenges, are demarcated by historical legacies of resource wealth and hereditary rule.

Conclusion: Toward a Structual Explanation

Social scientists studying the Arab Spring have made significant contributions on the dynamics of protest, the breakdown of autocracy, and the establishment of democracy.[3] Yet like their predecessors covering transitions from authoritarianism in Southern Europe and Latin America, scholars of the Arab uprisings have homed in on proximate causes, emphasizing the agency of activists and officers. In Chapter 2, "Lineages of Repression," we build on arguments about petroleum resources and dynastic leadership to formulate a structural explanation of regime change and continuity in the Arab Spring.

2

Lineages of Repression

Despite the popular narrative of a wave of mass mobilization that swept the Middle East, toppled dictators, and established democracy, very few Arab countries experienced anything of the sort. The Arab Spring's modest harvest—a record far less inspiring than the Eastern European revolutions of 1989 or the political transitions of sub-Saharan Africa in the early 1990s—cries out for explanation. Why did fewer than half of the Arab-majority states experience popular uprisings? Further, why did authoritarian breakdown—the unseating of longstanding dictators—take place in only four of those states?

This chapter develops a political explanation of uprising outcomes from the Arab Spring of 2010–2012. Our framework owes an intellectual debt to prior studies discussed in Chapter 1, "Theorizing the Arab Spring." At the same time, our approach differs from its precursors in empirical breadth and causal depth. First, we seek to account for variance: from the dramatic overthrow of Ben Ali in Tunisia to the political endurance of Assad in Syria. Second, we step back from proximate variables, such as the diffusion of social networking tools and the posture of the army, to examine economic and historical regime characteristics that determined the relative balance of power between incumbents and oppositionists (McFaul 2002). By rooting our explanation in structural variables that could have been observed and measured prior to the Arab Spring, we avoid the risk of generating a post-hoc narrative that imputes causes from outcomes.

State violence was the political fulcrum of the Arab Spring: Regimes faltered only when armies turned against autocrats. Variations in levels of repression and restraint, however, do not constitute an explanation: they must be explained. This chapter does so. The key dependent variable in our analysis is what Michael Mann (1984) called "despotic power"—that is, the capacity of the state to coerce. Like other traits of the modern state, despotic power emerged over time through historical and international process. We discuss these lineages of repression and how they distinguished the Middle East from other developing regions. The security designs of outside powers during the twentieth century played an oversized role in sustaining atypically high levels of despotic power. Hence, over the *longue durée*, international flows of ideas and material played a constitutive role in the course of the Arab uprisings, even as the immediate outcomes depended largely on domestic actors. Shifting from cross-regional variations to intra-regional contrasts, we trace levels of despotic power back to two variables: oil rents and hereditary rule. Polities with these resources, economic and personal, exhibit a resilient merger between the state's political leadership and its coercive agencies. Amid a situation of revolt, this fusion of executive decision-making with the means of concerted violence brought devastating amounts of despotic power upon the regime's opponents.

In summary, the chapter uses a combination of long-term historical variables found internationally and domestically to answer two major concerns raised by the Arab Spring: Why do regimes in the Middle East continue to exhibit extraordinary durability relative to their counterparts in other regions? What explains the recent contrast between authoritarian breakdown and authoritarian continuity among Arab regimes?

Regarding the first question, the cases of the Arab Spring displayed a very different post-Cold War legacy than otherwise similar autocracies in the developing world. The end of Washington's superpower rivalry with Moscow appeared to encourage liberalization and even democratization in Latin America, Eastern Europe, and parts of Africa and East Asia (Levitsky and Way 2010). By contrast, the United States and local Arab regimes turned their attention from the Soviet Union to the new bête noire of radical Islam. The American pursuit of regional security over democracy dated back to longstanding interests in a US-led security framework, and cordial ties with Arab energy exporters. The political impact was to reinforce Arab *mukhabarat* (security) states. Thus in 2010–2012 protesters faced well-equipped coercive agencies, often supported from abroad and committed to preserving authoritarianism in a putatively liberal age.

After explaining cross-regional and intra-regional variations in despotic power, we apply our framework to the fourteen Arab autocracies of 2010. We find no structural preconditions for the *emergence* of uprisings: the stochastic dynamics of protest diffusion meant that a wide variety of regimes faced popular challenges. However, the *success* of a domestic campaign to oust the ruler was structurally preconditioned by two variables: oil wealth (which endows the ruler with material resources needed to mute challenges before they arise, or to cement the security apparatus' loyalty in case they do), and the precedent of hereditary succession (which is accompanied by the heightened fealty of coercive agents to the executive). Regimes lacking *both* major oil revenue *and* a prior hereditary succession succumbed relatively quickly and non-violently to domestic uprisings. By contrast, where dictators had inherited rule (whether through traditional monarchism or corrupted republicanism) or commanded vast oil rents, their repressive forces remained sufficiently loyal and capable of conducting brutal crackdowns, often resulting in outright warfare.

By explaining the sources and variance in repressive capacity (despotic power), the present approach advances a fuller explanation of the course of the Arab Spring to date. We also hope that it brings us closer to a general theory of protest success, one that can potentially account for similar waves of regime change and continuity in other places and at other times.

Revisiting Despotic Power

Comparativists have given incredible attention to variations in state capacity. There is a rich field of works explaining why some states are efficacious while others appear unable to channel politics in nationally useful directions (Evans 1995; Haggard 1990; Kohli 2004; Migdal 1988). Hence scholars have sought to explain the salutary actions of state officials, such as reducing poverty, combatting illiteracy, and achieving high levels of economic growth. These outcomes are all tokens of state strength. Specifically, they denote the presence of what Michael Mann called "infrastructural power," defined as "the capacity of the state actually to penetrate civil society, and to implement logistically political decisions throughout the realm" (1984: 185).

Infrastructural power is the commonly understood separator between strong and weak states (Migdal 1988). Developing countries exhibit infrastructural power to varying degrees, while the United States and leading Western democracies enjoy it in an unprecedented fashion. Writes Mann:

> The state can assess and tax our income and wealth at source, without our consent or that of our neighbors or kin (which states before about 1850 were never able to do); it stores and can recall immediately a massive amount of information about all of us; it can enforce its will within the day almost anywhere in its domains; its influence on the overall economy is enormous; it even directly provides the subsistence of most of us (in state employment, in pensions, in family allowances, etc.). The state penetrates everyday life more than did any historical state. (1984: 114)

The ability to reach into society means the state not only deters and prevents behaviors, it shapes them. Infrastructurally strong states can mobilize their citizenry in novel and innovative ways. Their dexterity and creativity make Hobbes's Leviathan look like a clumsy oaf by comparison.

Yet brute force still involves a kind of power. Coercion alone may not make the trains run on time. It seldom produces valuable exports. But if we consider the problem of political survival, as opposed to economic development, the ability to mete out violence is of significant value. Even as he delineated his idea of infrastructural power, Mann nevertheless recognizes that this is built upon more traditional means of domination, which he called "despotic power." Whereas infrastructural power entails negotiations between state leaders and social constituencies, despotic power refers to the actions that can be taken outside of such relationships. Such actions are necessarily limited in range. They mainly include the use or threat of force on those subjects the state can physically reach. "Great despotic power," Mann describes, "can be 'measured' most vividly in the ability of [absolutist monarchs] to shout 'off with his head' and have their whim gratified without further ado—provided the person is at hand" (1984: 113). Writing in a similar vein, Nazih Ayubi (1995) distinguished "strong" states (i.e., those that command the ability to conceive and execute national policies) from those that were merely "fierce" (i.e., able to rain brutality upon opponents). The former possess Mann's infrastructural power; the latter only the despotic variant.

To some degree, this ability to inflict punishment may seem analytically uninteresting. A coercive apparatus is the sine qua non of states. To the extent that despotic power is ubiquitous, one might argue that this element of state power does not demand explanation. However, modern Arab states exhibit varying degrees of such power—as the disparate outcomes of the Arab uprisings attest. Thus, the amount of despotic power a ruler enjoys may determine whether he falls to a popular revolt or crushes it. In this respect, despotic power remains a variable that, in some contexts, must still be explained and theorized (even while in other contexts, such as the advanced industrialized democracies, the ability to mete out violence is less important than the ability to muster up votes).

We argue, with Ayubi (1995) that a surfeit of despotic power separated the Arab regimes from their counterparts elsewhere. Middle Eastern autocracies ran the gamut in terms of infrastructural power. Tunisia evinced significant economic development, while its neighbor Libya soaked up oil rents without developing national infrastructure. Other countries could be placed along a spectrum of state strength, with Egypt and Syria near the middle and Yemen close to Libya. In terms of despotic power, however, the Arab regimes clustered at the high end. Nearly a decade before the Arab uprisings, Brownlee (2002: 57) compared breakdown and continuity in regimes where despotic power was prevalent. He found rulers in Tunisia, Libya, Syria, and Iraq all survived potent challenges, crises that toppled similar regimes in other regions, through repression. Thus it is the command and use of despotic power that distinguishes the regimes that Arab protesters confronted during the uprisings of 2010–2012. We turn to this large and important cross-regional variation before scrutinizing the subtler differences in despotism among the Arab cases.

Explaining Cross-Regional Variation: Unconstrained Security States

The Middle East and North Africa have intrigued social scientists because almost all of the region's regimes survived the third wave of democratization and those few that fell were followed by new autocracies (Huntington 1991). In the 2000s, comparativists revisited the question of Middle Eastern exceptionalism (Berman 2002; Fish 2002; Stepan and Robertson 2003). Was there something about the region's history, culture, or dominant religion (Islam) that exacerbated authoritarianism? Scholars of the region responded that while the MENA autocracies were more durable than their counterparts elsewhere, the causes of robust authoritarianism were fundamentally political (Posusney 2004; Posusney and Angrist 2005). Consequently, the MENA regimes were not exceptions to the relationships social scientists had observed between institutions or economics, on one side, and political outcomes, on the other. Rather, these enduring autocracies exhibited new levels of variance for those explanatory and dependent variables. In particular, regimes from Morocco to the Persian Gulf relied on high levels of domestic repression and a general lack of international pressure (constituting what we call "unconstrained security states"), especially in comparison to regimes that fell during the third wave (Bellin 2004; Brownlee 2002; Snyder 1991; Skocpol 1979). This common condition presents a contrast to the nature of authoritarianism in other regions.

In most of Latin America, Southern Europe, and Eastern Europe, as well as in the Philippines, post-World War II autocracy interrupted a democratic heritage but did not erase it. Despite the repression of juntas and kleptocrats, opposition groups enjoyed old networks and broad constituencies. These mass movements eventually overthrew dictators or convinced army leaders to return to the barracks. Although Cold War geostrategy long mitigated foreign pressure for democracy, by the 1980s, the United States and other Western powers had begun to accept, if not embrace, the need for democratic leadership in these regions. In Latin America, for example, international pressure combined with a powerful domestic impetus to squeeze autocrats and hasten their exit from power (Carothers 1991). In the much less propitious setting of sub-Saharan Africa, democracy seldom emerged during the post-colonial period. Nonetheless, foreign powers incentivized political and economic change through a combination of sticks and carrots. During the early 1990s, they bolstered a domestic push toward liberalization, sometimes leading to democratization (Bratton and van de Walle 1997: 182–183).

Political scientists observed that the end of the Cold War brought a period of unrivaled US influence and an unprecedented opportunity to spread democracy and capitalism abroad (Fukuyama 1989; Levitsky and Way 2002). Until 2011 they also puzzled over the stark absence of democratization or even serious liberalization in the Arab world. The sources of the post-1989 political divergence between the Arab world and neighboring regions merit attention here. Given that the Arab Spring unfolded in this seemingly extraordinary context, understanding what made the Arab regimes different will help clarify why unprecedented uprisings often delivered modest outcomes.

There is little question that US–Soviet rapprochement and the Soviet Union's collapse during 1989–1991 posed a "critical juncture" for democratization and authoritarianism (Collier and Collier 1991). When opposition movements tore down the Iron Curtain they opened political vistas. Within and without the post-communist world, societies that had lived under harsh autocracy for decades leapt toward democracy in a matter of years or, in some cases, months. Between 1989 and 1994 the global number of electoral democracies increased by 50%, from 69 to 113. In this moment of seemingly unbounded contingency and possibility, however, enduring interests and relationships worked to shape the course of democratic development.

Where the United States and the European Union could easily expand their influence and gain partners in the former Eastern Bloc, democracy flourished. Elsewhere in Africa and Asia the end of superpower rivalry gave authoritarian regimes a second wind. Yet Western governments did not oppose authoritarianism and encourage democratization uniformly. There remained "pockets of permissiveness" where geostrategy eclipsed local democracy (Levitsky and Way 2002: 7–8).

The Arab world remained a large crevasse in the world's democratic terrain for reasons international and domestic. Michael Hudson reported that Arabs from Morocco to the Gulf lived under a "*mukhabarat* state, an authoritarian-bureaucratic Leviathan whose stability derives more from fear than legitimacy" (1991: 408). Washington's pursuit of regional security over democracy dated back to traditional interests in a US-led security framework and cordial ties with oil-rich Arab states. Administrations from both major parties had long backed pro-US Arab tyrants to preserve oil flows and defend Israel. These behaviors stemmed from historic changes in the 1970s, including Great Britain's departure from the Persian Gulf in 1971, the 1973 War and oil shock, and, in 1979, the Iranian Revolution and Soviet invasion of Afghanistan.

In 1971 the sun set on the British Empire and the United Kingdom completed its withdrawal from positions "east of Suez," including its bases in the Persian Gulf. As the former imperial power retreated, the United States advanced. Washington established a toehold in the Gulf in the new island state of Bahrain, which began hosting a modest US naval presence in 1971.[1] Over subsequent years the United States fortified its strategic position in the Gulf as it responded to war and revolution in the Middle East.

On October 6, 1973, months before the third wave's seminal transition in Portugal, Egypt and Syria launched a surprise attack into the Israeli-occupied Sinai Peninsula and Golan Heights. The foray ended in military calamity for the Syrians and a diplomatic stalemate for the Egyptians, but it brought an economic windfall to Saudi Arabia and Arab member states of the Organization of Petroleum Exporting Countries (OPEC). In response to a US resupply of Israel during the war, Saudi King Faisal bin Abdul Aziz spearheaded a reduction in oil production and cut Arab oil exports to the United States and, eventually, a small set of developed countries, including Japan. The actual drop in global supplies was limited because other producers compensated for the so-called Arab embargo. Nonetheless, domestic policies in the United States and elsewhere stoked panicking and hoarding. During the "oil price shock" the nominal value of a barrel of oil quadrupled, vastly enriching Saudi Arabia and its fellow monarchies in the Persian Gulf (Katzenstein 1978; Yergin 2009).

The 1973 War and accompanying oil crisis intensified concerns over political instability in the Arab world. Hence, just as a democratic wave was about to break over much of the world, Arab regimes were anchored by Western powers, led by the United States. US worries about regime change were realized on February 11, 1979, when the Iranian revolution replaced the Shah, a long-time ally and faithful US weapons patron, with the defiant Ayatollah Ruhollah Khomeini. On December 24, the Soviet Union invaded Afghanistan. The combination of a hostile religious regime and a putative Soviet advance toward the Indian Ocean prompted Carter to issue his eponymous doctrine, vowing to defend the free flow of Middle East oil, with force if necessary. This pledge presupposed extensive logistical support from Arab allies. Without a network of regional partners, the United States would lack the capacity to project force to areas Carter's defense secretary called "far from but vital to us" (Brown 1980). Although the seminal mission under the Carter Doctrine—an attempt to liberate hostages held at the US Embassy in Tehran—ended in tragedy and scotched the president's reelection bid, Carter had established a strategic framework successive presidents would expand. His Rapid Deployment Force grew under Ronald Reagan into Central Command (CENTCOM), with an operational area stretching from Egypt to Pakistan. In addition, the Egyptian–Israeli peace treaty Carter had brokered shortly after the Shah fell enabled unprecedented military and intelligence cooperation between Washington and Cairo.

The United States' historic interest in the Middle East and neo-suzerainty over the Persian Gulf influenced the course of the Arab regimes after the watershed of 1989–1991. No sooner had the USSR dissolved than US officials identified a new rival on the global stage: political Islam and the movements that propagated it. On December 26, 1991, the day the Soviet Union ceased to exist, Algerians voted in their country's first multi-party legislative elections. First round results pointed to a landslide victory for the religiously conservative Islamic Salvation Front (known as the "FIS," based on its French acronym). The Algerian military never allowed the runoff to take place and instead seized power for themselves, a move endorsed by France and the United States. Ranking officials of the George H. W. Bush administration later admitted they had backed the coup because stopping the FIS was more important than supporting Algerian democracy, wherever it might lead (Gerges 1999). This stance presaged two decades of bipartisan backing for Mubarak and other autocrats who pledged to hold Islamists at bay and preserve US influence across the region.

Just as ostensibly anticommunist tactics carried much broader spillover effects during the Cold War, the Arab security states swept aside radical Islamists before repressing peaceful activists. Thanks to a lack of democratizing pressure and the rise of sprawling security apparatuses, by the first decade of the twenty-first century Arab autocracies shared little in common with the competitive authoritarian regimes elsewhere that were embroiled in change. Whereas opposition movements in Central Europe and Sub-Saharan Africa had incrementally broken elites' monopoly on power, challenger parties in the Arab states were almost completely shut out. Opposition parties were mostly legal in Egypt, Tunisia, and Yemen, but they operated under such severe constraints that *de jure* multipartyism belied *de facto* single-party rule. In the presidential autocracies (Egypt, Tunisia, Syria, Yemen), incumbents invariably took over three-quarters of the vote, a sure sign of exclusionary authoritarianism (Brownlee 2011). When members of the opposition managed to eke out seats in the legislature, they often behaved more like adjuncts than dissidents. The most vociferous critics of authoritarianism decried formal institutions altogether and took to the streets, but they seldom achieved a mass following.

With few exceptions, US assistance did not create the Arab world's authoritarian regimes and their despotic capacities. Algeria and Egypt, for example, had emerged from colonialism with preponderant militaries and weak civilian parties. Over time, however, US relations with Arab autocracies contributed to their growing repressive abilities during a period of world history in which dozens of other countries were moving in the opposite direction. If war built the European state, internal wars built up the security state, justifying indefinite States of Emergency, presidencies-for-life, and massive policing of the local population (Tilly 1985).

Explaining Intra-Regional Variation: Rents and Dynasties

The Arab states share a familial resemblance as unconstrained security states, but they displayed varying levels of despotic power during 2010–2012. Those variations in turn made the difference between breakdowns that ousted rulers and crackdowns that crushed the opposition.

Therefore, we seek to explain why three leaders fell to domestic uprisings while the remainder survived or, in the case of Libya, fell to a combination of internal and foreign military forces. We are also interested in identifying whether the uprisings themselves can be explained through major antecedent variables or whether they were contingent or agential. Our principal finding is that a combination of structural variables can account for the *success* of domestic uprisings, but that massive protest emerged due to local ingenuity and courage rather than larger variables. Through two variables—oil rents and traditions of dynasticism—we capture the posture of the repressive apparatus and the corresponding capacity of Arab rulers to maintain control through despotic power.

By considering antecedent sources of despotic power we move from tautology—regimes with sufficient repressive capacity survive—to causality. Specifically, we trace the contrasts in coercion to the historical accumulation of oil rents begun after October 1973 and the inception of dynastic rule through hereditary succession (Yergin 2009). Whereas the effects of oil on development and democracy are highly debatable, their influence on regime stability is well substantiated. The link we draw between dynasticism and political cohesion is more surprising. The transfer of executive power from father to son is rare in the post-World War II era (Brownlee 2007). We argue that such events, whether they occur through convention in monarchies or innovation in autocratic republics, signal that the state's repressive agents have rallied around the executive to an extraordinary degree. We elaborate on both variables presently.

Oil Rents

Though most autocrats have some measure of affluence, oil wealth endows dictators with extraordinary means to stave off mass challenges. Scholars of the Middle East have long maintained that the oil-rich regimes of the region experience a distinctive form of politics, based largely on their command of spectacular resources earned without the need for taxation, that is, "rents" (Karl 1997; Smith 2007; Anderson 1987; Mahdavy 1970). Michael Ross's statistical study of rentierism offers one of the most comprehensive tests of the theory in its various forms (2001). He considered not only oil wealth, but also rents from non-oil minerals (such as diamonds). Further, Ross probed the intervening mechanisms that generated significant cross-national correlations. One of his tests examined whether oil and non-oil mineral wealth was linked to higher levels of government spending on the military. Earlier scholars deemed this "repression effect" an important factor in the rise of security states across the Persian Gulf (Gause 1995). The data validated that hypothesis, showing that major oil exporters spent significantly more on their militaries than states without great oil rents (Ross 2001: 350). Subsequently, Benjamin Smith cast doubt on the link between oil and repression, suggesting that while oil stabilized authoritarian regimes, it operated through other mechanisms (2004: 238–239). In the same article, though, Smith found a significant negative relationship between oil wealth and social protest (2004: 241).

A recent wave of research on the rentier state and accompanying resource curse has complicated the relationship between oil wealth and democratization while affirming the connection between oil rents and regime continuity or lack of breakdown (see Smith 2013). Comparativists have cautioned against simplistic determinism, such as equating the presence of oil with rigid regime types (Brynen et al. 2012: 193–212). For example, whether oil is owned by private companies or by the state makes an incredible difference in its political effects (Jones Luong and Weinthal 2001). Even in authoritarian settings, oil interacted with local politics to produce different relationships between rulers and ruled. Sean Yom traced the historical paths through which regimes accumulated and utilized oil rents. Paying off the population often proved an effective alternative to coercion. Hence, some Arab monarchs practiced "popular rentierism" cultivating support from below and, over time, enjoying genuine mass support, as opposed to persisting through "despotic rentierism" (217–218). In addition to these important qualifications, Stephen Haber and Victor Menaldo delivered the strongest refutation to Ross's original article and the general notion that oil rents support authoritarianism. Using a new variable that measured the extent of "reliance" on hydrocarbon exports, they conclude: "oil and mineral reliance does not promote dictatorship over the long run. If anything, the opposite is true" (2011: 25).

Interestingly, however, even this broadside to the reigning consensus suggests that when it comes to the Arab Spring, oil resources may have indeed been a curse for the opposition. Haber and Menaldo's very broad and comprehensive dataset places recent country–years, from the period of modern Arab security states, alongside much earlier periods. There is thus reason to question whether their treatment may have diluted the causal importance of oil rents on *recent* regime endurance. In fact, Andersen and Ross reviewed Haber and Menaldo's same data and argued that the oil curse applies strongly after 1973, as the governments of oil-exporting countries took greater control over oil production and price setting (2014). Further, even Haber and Menaldo acknowledge that particular regimes may enjoy stabilizing benefits from oil rents, even if a "sweeping, lawlike" correlation is absent (2011: 25). Therefore, the bulk of evidence supports an expectation that major oil exports will enjoy higher levels of despotic power. As Benjamin Smith soberly concludes in his tour d'horizon of scholarship on rents and regimes: "Unfortunately, the evidence suggests that [resource wealth] may stabilize precisely the kinds of status quo we normatively want to become less prevalent" (2013: 20).

On balance, the evidence suggests oil-rich states will exhibit higher levels of despotic power than their peers that lack high levels of non-tax revenue. To operationalize this variable we divide the fourteen Arab countries under consideration into two groups based on whether they are major oil exporters. We code as oil-rich the Arab OPEC members (Algeria, Kuwait, Libya, Qatar, Saudi Arabia, UAE), as well as Oman and Bahrain. As shown in Table 2.1 these countries produced between $1,930 and $24,940 in oil and gas in 2009. By contrast, the remaining six countries (Egypt, Jordan, Morocco, Syria, Tunisia, Yemen) had negligible oil resources, ranging from zero dollars to $450 in per capita value.

Chapter 3, "Breakdowns and Crackdowns," traces the process by which the six core regimes applied despotic power to varying effect against domestic uprisings. Here it is worth making a broader

Table 2.1. Per Capita Value of Oil and Gas Production in Selected Arab States (2009)

Oil-Rich Countries	Oil-Poor Countries
Qatar $24,900	Syria $450
Kuwait $19,500	Yemen $270
United Arab Emirates $14,100	Egypt $260
Oman $7,950	Tunisia $250
Saudi Arabia $7,800	Jordan —
Libya $6,420	Morocco —
Bahrain $3,720	
Algeria $1,930	

Source: Michael L. Ross, *The Oil Curse: How Petroleum Wealth Shapes the Development of Nations* (Princeton, NJ: Princeton University Press, 2012), 20.

observation in passing that oil-exporting states overtly used their wealth to stem popular discontent in 2010–2012. For example, on January 18, 2011—days after the flight of Ben Ali and a week before the onset of Egypt's revolution—the Kuwaiti government announced a grant of 1,000 Kuwaiti dinars ($3,500) to every man, woman, and child, as well as a year's worth of free staples such as sugar, oil, rice, and milk.[2] The government of Saudi Arabia followed suit one month later, announcing a $10.7 billion dollar package of wage hikes for public-sector employees, payments for the unemployed, and higher stipends for university students. The Saudi state also dedicated a further $70 billion for low-income housing.[3] In September 2011, the government of Qatar—not usually included among the autocracies thought to be at risk of popular uprising—declared that it would spend more than $8 billion to raise public-sector salaries and pensions by 60%.[4]

However, while rentier states excel at dispensing "carrots," we are most interested in their use of "sticks." Ross found that "oil-poor Tunisia . . . spent $53 per capita on its armed forces in 2008 [while] its oil-rich neighbor, Algeria, spent $141 per capita and had far fewer protests" (2011). Saudi Arabia, Bahrain, and Algeria led the region in the size of their international arms purchasing agreements during 2006–2009 at $29.5 billion, $14.2 billion, and $6.8 billion respectively (Grimmett 2010). Saudi Arabia ranks among the top ten arms procurers worldwide, neck-in-neck with such great powers as India and Germany.[5] Naturally, heavy weapons purchases do not ensure domestic stability (as the Shah of Iran discovered in 1978–1979). For the Arab regimes of 2010–2012, however, the gratuitous consumption of cutting-edge defense hardware was emblematic of a tight relationship between rulers and armies. It was this political bond—rather than the arms themselves—that enabled vast despotic power when an oil-rich regime, as in Libya and Bahrain, confronted mass revolt.

Dynastic Personalism

Comparativists have drawn attention to the personalized nature of politics in Middle Eastern regimes (Ayubi 1995; Brownlee 2002). To a great extent, these regimes share traits of extreme neopatrimonialism with their sub-Saharan African peers (Bratton and van de Walle 1997: 61–63). When politics boils down to the whims of one "boss," then personal connections to that figure will logically play a dominant role in the conduct and capacity of the repressive apparatus.

Operationalizing the loyalty of the regime's coercive agents is a difficult task. As noted earlier, other studies have by necessity inferred the value of this variable from the military's actual behavior during an uprising—a post hoc patch that is not conducive to theory-building. We argue, however, that a more reliable indicator of such loyalty—and one that can be observed a priori—is the successful transfer of power from one family member to another. In such regimes, the coercive apparatus has pledged its fealty to a particular family, and is thus likely to go some distance to protect it.

Why is hereditary succession such a powerful indicator of regime cohesion? Moments of succession in authoritarian regimes are inherently perilous. Former allies plot against one another, and palace intrigues often mean that succession processes end up concluding in ways the departed autocrat did not anticipate or want.

Given all of this, it is nothing short of remarkable when a moment of regime transition results in the orderly passing of power from father to son (or other family member).

We recognize that this assumption goes against much of the literature on authoritarian regimes. Since Weber, social scientists have debated whether rulers who concentrate power in their family are more resilient than those who adhere to a more rational–legal tradition (Linz 1975). In comparative politics, extremely personalistic—or so-called sultanistic—regimes have generally been considered less resilient than their peers (Chehabi and Linz 1998; Geddes 1999; Snyder 1992; Brownlee 2002). As Jack Goldstone (2011) put it in a recent article on the Arab uprisings: "Although such [sultanistic] regimes often appear unshakable, they are actually highly vulnerable, because the very strategies they use to stay in power make them brittle, not resilient. It is no coincidence that although popular protests have shaken much of the Middle East, the only revolutions to succeed so far—those in Tunisia and Egypt—have been against modern sultans."

Though we agree that both Ben Ali and Mubarak bore some similarities to the sultanistic regimes of prior literature, the corruption and nepotism they exhibited does not seem to have exceeded levels observed in most "garden variety" authoritarian regimes. We argue that a higher threshold needs to be set for separating "sultans" from conventional autocrats, and that hereditary succession provides the appropriate threshold. Moreover, we argue that once this analytical move is made, we observe—contra Goldstone—a *positive* relationship between the genuinely intense personalism that characterizes true dynastic regimes, and the durability of those regimes.

To illustrate the difference between a genuinely sultanistic regime and a merely authoritarian one, let us consider Mubarak's Egypt and the Assads' Syria. A visitor to the two countries before the Arab Spring would have been struck by how differently the executive's family and his regime interacted. Surveying the names of ranking army officers in Syria would have turned up dozens of relatives of al-Assad (including his younger brother, Maher, who commands the Republican Guard and the army's Fourth Armored Division), while the same exercise in Egypt would have discovered none of Mubarak's kin among the senior officer corps.

Perhaps most importantly, these contrasts in regime profiles were not of recent vintage: they could be traced back to the 1990s, when Hafez al-Assad was establishing familial rule with the consent of the Syrian military. That regime made no attempt to hide plans for dynastic succession. According to Lisa Wedeen (1999: 60), Basil al-Assad, the president's eldest son and first choice as successor, was presented as "a potential incorrupt leader," and the president publicly took the honorific "Abu Basil" (the father of Basil), explicitly establishing a link between Hafez and his designated successor. When Basil died, dynastic expectations fell on Bashar, who suddenly began to appear alongside his father and dead brother in the state's official iconography. From that point, a host of notables from the security state converged around the father-son duo to support Bashar's succession in 2000. Therefore, after the elder Assad died, "what transpired was not the work of elites unconsciously following a dead president's command. The evidence indicates that elites from the central regime branches united behind Bashar's candidacy," writes Joshua Stacher. "The elites came to a decision about [Hafez] al-Assad's successor and then returned to their home institutions to ensure that the consensus was executed without disruption or dissent" (2011: 205).

In contrast, hereditary succession was a much more contentious issue in Egypt, and the regime was much more coy about it. Reflecting the touchiness of the succession issue, the son was forced to publicly rebuff the notion that he would ascend to the presidency, declaring in 2005 that "I am absolutely clear in my mind and the president's mind that this story of father and son has nothing to do with reality."[6] By 2009, according to a US State Department document, the elder Mubarak was deemed to have assumed a "hands off approach to the succession question," leaving it in the hands of the security apparatus, which was widely rumored to be inhospitable to the notion of Gamal inheriting his father's post.[7] This is not to say that succession plans were off the table in Egypt. But the Egyptian regime's difficulty in implementing those plans, contrasted with the ease and inevitability of succession in Syria indicate the Assads enjoyed qualitatively stronger bonds between their executive and repressive apparatus than the Mubaraks did.

It follows that the prior execution of hereditary succession demarcates a line that sets Syria apart from the other Arab republics that experienced uprisings. Therefore, with respect to Arab and non-Arab regimes, we favor replacing the general notion of sultanism with the more precise and replicable indicator of dynasticism, measured simply as the inheritance of executive authority.[8] Where dynasties exist, we argue, despotic power follows. Far from being brittle, highly personalized regimes are actually stronger than their depersonalized counterparts, able to close ranks in the face of social protest while others fracture.

The hereditary succession variable helps account for the survival of Arab monarchies through a political process that is also present in other regimes. Sean Yom and Gregory Gause attributed the "new monarchical exceptionalism" to a conjunction of societal support and access to resource rents or foreign aid. "The prospects for popular revolution in the Arab kingdoms will remain slim," they conclude, "so long as their leaders continue to maintain broad-based coalitions, secure access to hydrocarbon rents, and enjoy bountiful support from foreign patrons" (2012: 76). Although Western funding may play a role in stability, the greatest Arab beneficiary of such aid, Mubarak, was neither a monarch nor a political survivor of the Arab Spring. Oil rents, meanwhile, have bolstered non-monarchs, such as the Algerian president, as well as royal autocrats. Finally, the "cross-cutting coalitions" that preserve authoritarianism are "historical alliances linking different social constituencies to the ruling family." According to Gause and Yom, participants in these alliances yoke their fortunes to the regime, making "the payoff of authoritarian continuity . . . significantly higher than the 'payoff' of revolutionary turnover" (2012: 81). On this point we argue that it is not societal groups but the repressive apparatus that must be bound to the regime for it to survive. Hence, in 2011 Syria's hereditary republic and the Bahraini kingdom both trumped historic

Table 2.2. Succession Patterns in Select Arab States (2010)

Hereditary Regimes	Non-Hereditary Regimes
Bahrain	Algeria
Jordan	Egypt
Kuwait	Libya
Morocco	Tunisia
Oman	Yemen
Qatar	
Saudi Arabia	
Syria	
United Arab Emirates	

opposition from constituencies that preferred revolution to continued authoritarianism.

We code the fourteen Arab countries dichotomously, based on whether or not they had undergone hereditary succession in the post-colonial period. Our periodization of this variable is important. If one were surveying the states of the Arab world in the 1950s, one might have come to the opposite conclusion from ours, as dynastic regimes collapsed in Egypt (1954), Iraq (1958), Libya (1969), Tunisia (1957), and Yemen (1968). However, we contend that those regimes are qualitatively different from present-day dynasties in one important respect—all were sustained, not by purely domestic pacts between a family and the state apparatus, but by foreign powers as well. In this sense, our reasoning about succession—like Ross's latest findings on oil—apply most strongly to the post-1973 period. We identified as hereditary regimes the six states of the GCC plus Morocco, Jordan, and Syria. All of these regimes, save for Syria, are monarchies (see Table 2.2).

Explaining Outcomes

Having described the causal logic behind each of the explanatory variables we are now ready to combine them in a parsimonious framework. Based on rents and succession precedents, we sort the regimes of the Arab world into four families (see Table 2.3). We also identify the countries that experienced uprisings and authoritarian breakdown, the principal outcomes of which we seek to explain. Bold-faced type indicates the presence of an "uprising." Countries in all caps experienced breakdown. An asterisk (*) indicates "foreign-imposed regime change." In Chapter 3, we follow the course of the uprisings as they produced momentous breakdowns or, when despotic power prevailed through rents or personalism, repressive crackdowns.

As shown in Table 2.3, uprisings occurred across all four of the cells, that is, in all four of the configurations of hereditary/non-hereditary and oil-rich/non-oil-rich regimes. Tunisia's uprising began, on December 17, 2010. Ferment then spread rapidly to Egypt (January 25, 2011), Yemen (February 3, 2011), Bahrain (February 14, 2011), Libya (February 15, 2011), and Syria (March 15, 2011). We address the spread of protests across structurally dissimilar contexts below. The relationship between the main explanatory variables and the outbreak of uprisings was indeterminate. Stronger correlations emerge, however, when we shift our focus to explaining regime change. Though activists emerged everywhere, their aspirations were not self-fulfilling. Many who took to the streets in countries other than Egypt, Tunisia, and Yemen seemingly overestimated their chances and misjudged the staying power of local regimes (Weyland 2012; McAdam 1982).

Table 2.3. The Structure of Arab Regime Change, 2010–2012

	Oil-Rich Regimes	Oil-Poor Regimes
Non-hereditary regimes	Algeria **Libya***	**Egypt** **Tunisia** **Yemen**
Hereditary regimes	Bahrain Kuwait Oman Qatar Saudi Arabia United Arab Emirates	Jordan Morocco Syria

Source: A prior version of this table appeared in our essay "Tracking the 'Arab Spring': Why the Modest Harvest?" *Journal of Democracy* 24 (October 2013): 29–44.

* Foreign-imposed regime change (FIRC).

How does our explanatory framework account for this variation in outcomes? Oil exporters were able to withstand the shocks of domestic protest. The one instance of regime change among this family of countries, Libya, came via NATO's sustained campaign of aerial bombardment. There is considerably more variation, though, among oil-poor regimes. An alliance of civilian dissidents and disgruntled generals replaced dictators in Egypt, Tunisia, and Yemen. The hereditary regimes of Jordan, Morocco, and Syria, on the other hand, remain in place (although the latter at a significant cost of life). The pattern of regime stability during 2010–2012 revealed that oil wealth and hereditary rule were each individually sufficient for authoritarian continuity—unless external powers intervened on behalf of the opposition. Figure 2.1 illustrates the causal pathways followed by the two major groupings of cases.[9] Recall that the emphasis here is on explaining intra-regional variations. Hence, the idea that the cases of breakdown had *limited* despotic power is necessarily relative. (Compared to average regimes outside the Middle East coercive capacity was high across the board.)

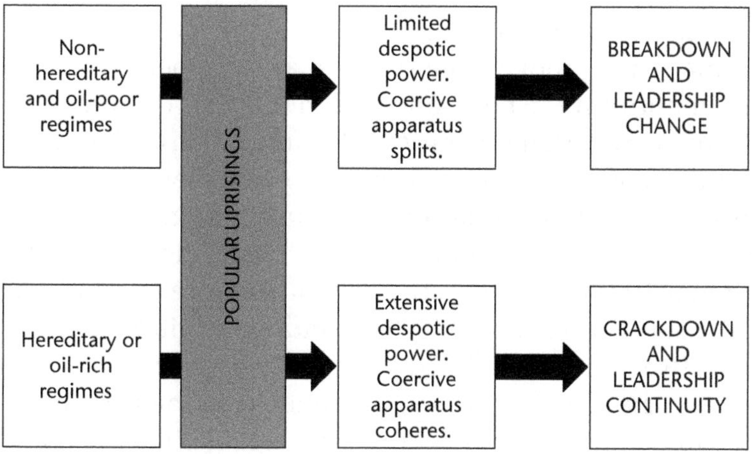

Figure 2.1. Causal Pathways of the Arab Spring.

Uprisings Independent of Opportunity

Uprisings occurred across all quadrants of our regime typology. This diversity of conditions affirms the voluntarist stream of the literature on the uprisings we discussed in Chapter 1, "Theorizing the Arab Spring." New technologies and activist repertoires have permeated the region and enabled unprecedented challenges to authoritarian rule. Uprisings are generated and driven by ingenuity and courage, irrespective of the macro-historical context in which their organizers find themselves. Inverting Skocpol's dictum about social revolutions, the Arab uprisings did not come: they were made. Because the role of human agency and chance looms large, seeking a parsimonious theory of where uprisings will occur may be a fool's errand.

Though there was no structural prerequisite for uprisings, we do find that the most propitious conjunction of variables for the emergence of protest was a non-hereditary regime that did not enjoy significant oil export rents. Indeed, in terms of the Arab authoritarian regimes considered here, that combination appears to have been sufficient to observe an uprising. Yet the uprisings in Libya, Bahrain, and Syria caution us against over-interpreting this pattern. Looking at the scope of cases, the biggest lesson is that agents, not structures, drove the uprisings.

Yet many who took to the streets may have perceived a structural opportunity where one did not exist (Weyland 2014; McAdam 1982). Demonstrations "diffused" partly because of a misperception that regimes were vulnerable. Moreover, unlike what Charles Kurzman has observed in the Iranian Revolution, protesters' visions of opportunities were not self-fulfilling (Kurzman 1996). It follows that the dissonance in expectations held by social scientists reflected a more complicated empirical clash between newly mobilized protesters and (still) heavily fortified autocrats. In short, Arab regimes remained durable, but their opponents, in some countries, were willing to take new risks to challenge them.

Conclusion: The Continuing Power of Coercion

In the Arab Spring, dissidents made the first noises, but soldiers had the last word. The despotic power that had become the hallmark of Arab regimes was on full display during 2010–2012. Whether officers held back or opened fire, they carried veto power in two directions—obstructing rulers, as in Tunisia, or decimating their opponents, as in Syria. All the regimes that faced major insurrections commanded notoriously fierce coercive agencies. Explaining the posture of those agencies—the intra-regional variations in despotic power—is therefore integral to understanding why the some political-security coalitions split apart while others cohered. In Chapter 3, "Breakdowns and Crackdowns," we trace this process, linking the structural variables of oil rents and dynasticism to processes of authoritarian breakdown and continuity.

their variables can explain probability of uprisings and success of uprisings

3

Breakdowns and Crackdowns

The initial results of the Arab Spring vindicated those who believed in the capability of mass movements to coalesce spontaneously and press for change. Yet the limited scope of political transformation across the Arab states also underscored the continuing durability of autocratic institutions, particularly the fabled "coercive apparatus" that has kept the opposition in check for decades. This chapter moves from our core explanatory variables to the causal links connecting them to major outcomes: regime breakdown and regime continuity, through repressive crackdowns.

Most Arab countries—from Morocco and Algeria in North Africa to five of the Gulf monarchies (all of the Gulf Cooperation Council except Bahrain)—did not witness extraordinary social upheaval. Protests were limited in scope and they did not concentrate political disaffection on the removal of incumbents. These negative cases of political continuity, in which uprisings did not occur and regimes did not break down, displayed one or both of the structural variables, dynasticism and oil wealth. Our focus here is on the much more intense political contestation of the remaining six authoritarian regimes of the Arab Middle East. To explain variance in these cases, we trace the processes of mass challenge and regime response, showing that these outcomes corresponded to antecedent structural traits rather than more proximate correlates (George and Bennett 2004).

Two paths link structural variables in the nature of the regime to the ultimate outcomes of protests. In the first trajectory, the armed forces realigned, partly or completely, to back demonstrators. This process played out in Tunisia, Egypt, and Yemen. At the moment of the uprisings, protesters impelled the coercive apparatus to break with the regime and help force the incumbent to relinquish power. Activists were integral to this process, but they were not the *cause* of regime breakdown. In addition, the outcomes were not merely functions of the professionalism or self-restraint of the military during the upheavals. Rather, the causes of uprising success and incumbent downfall originate in the structural traits, discussed above, that predated the revolts. The lack of both significant oil revenues and a cadre of uniformed officers who were not enmeshed in the ruling clique through prior dynastic succession generated the possibility of expelling long-ruling despots. Under these conditions, incumbents enjoyed neither the resources nor the personal connections to mount a unified coercive response. Under strain from historic popular protests, the existing bond between the ruler and the armed forces proved brittle. Bereft of the means to crack down, regimes instead broke down.

The second course was concerted military repression, which stemmed from either a long legacy of oil-based rentierism, an inherited tradition of dynasticism, or both. Three countries—Bahrain, Syria, and Libya—translated hydrocarbon wealth and/or hereditary rule into regime cohesion in the face of mass uprisings. Processes in these countries embodied the crushing power of brute force to defeat nonviolent demonstrators. As in the cases of regime breakdown, however, their roots stretched back for years. In manpower and force of arms, the Bahraini, Syrian, and Libyan militaries did not stand apart from their peers in Egypt, Tunisia, and Yemen before 2011. Rather, what separated these two otherwise similar groups was the structure of regime–military relations, specifically whether the incumbent enjoyed the loyalty of the officers to such an extent that they preferred to turn on the people instead of against the ruler. Unless foreign states entered the fray and shifted the balance of military power in favor of the opposition, as occurred in Libya between February and October 2011, unconstrained despotic power prevented regime breakdown and delivered political continuity.

From here the chapter deals with the core uprisings in two groups: the cases of breakdown and the cases of continuity. With respect to Bahrain and Libya, we devote particular attention to integrating the varying extent of foreign intervention into our domestically centered explanatory framework. Syria also receives special consideration, because of the nature of its ongoing civil war and the role of foreign support for the opposition.

Opposition Success in the Non-Hereditary, Oil-Poor Regimes

Prior to December 2010, few comparativists would have judged the Tunisian, Egyptian, or Yemeni regimes susceptible to revolt. At the heart of these security states, however, stood coalitions that could endure normal times but were vulnerable to fragmentation under stress. Such weaknesses do not mean that authoritarianism was frail, only that it was more prone to breakdown under mass pressure *relative* to even more resilient peers in the region. In these three countries opposition groups benefited from a political structure in which the coercive apparatus had not previously united behind the ruler in a hereditary succession. In addition, Ben Ali, Mubarak, and Saleh lacked lucrative rents to purchase military loyalty or social quiescence. This combination of variables produced a structural opportunity for ousting long-ruling incumbents that activists managed to exploit to historic effect.

Tunisia

In Tunisia, Ben Ali used as much despotic power as he could muster, but in the toughest showdown of his career, the backstop of the coercive apparatus, the uniformed military, soon abandoned him. The army broke away because it could. The coercive apparatus enjoyed autonomy from the political leadership through modern Tunisian statehood. Uniformed officers had never been fused to the regime through rents or dynasticism. Thus, the underlying sources of an effective challenge to the regime had been laid long before Bouazizi's dramatic self-immolation in December 2010.

Structural opportunities for regime breakdown mean little if the opposition remains quiet. In Tunisia, the successful uprising began from preexisting networks of dissent that centered on prior challenges to Ben Ali, particularly from the country's organized workers (Chomiak 2011: 72–73). The uprising occurred as a sub-national cascade of protests, which began in the hinterlands of the south and moved toward the capital and affluent coastal area. In this process the General Union of Tunisian Workers (UGTT) played a prominent role. Unlike labor federations under some Arab regimes, such as Egypt, the UGTT had a tradition of defying Tunisian rulers (cf. Posusney 1997). In 1978, a series of escalating strikes by the Union incurred President Habib Bourguiba's wrath. The Tunisian president ordered the UGTT headquarters be stormed, a decision that left hundreds dead or injured (Bellin 1995: 129–130). Still, the organization continued to function as the principal representative of the country's workers. Prior to the 2010–2011 revolt, the UGTT included "24 regional unions, 19 labor federations, and 21 general unions" (Schraeder and Redissi 2011: 13). These networks enabled large but unsuccessful workers' rights protests in the mining region of Gafsa during 2008 and early 2010. When riots broke out in Sidi Bouzid, the UGTT resumed its challenge against the state and ensured that the wave of dissension Bouazizi had triggered spread beyond its origin site (Alexander 2011).

Educational unions within the UGTT organized unemployed college graduates and channeled their dissatisfaction with the regime into genuine activism. Legal rights advocates, including the Tunisian Bar Association, and opposition party members bolstered the movement. "In this way, a broad coalition of civil society organizations has connected bread-and-butter employment grievances with fundamental human rights and rule-of-law concerns," reported Christopher Alexander in the midst of the uprising. "They also pull together constituencies that transcend class and regional distinctions—unemployed young people in Sidi

Bouzid, Menzel Bouzaiene, and Regueb, and lawyers and journalists in Monastir, Sfax, and Tunis" (Alexander 2011). Online videos and social media enabled groups to share experiences instantaneously and circumvent the regime's strictures on public discourse. In this respect, the seminal "broadcast" was the video bringing the small demonstration for Bouazizi in Sidi Bouzid to millions of viewers online (Beinin and Vairel 2011: 238–239). One should not overstate the impact of Facebook and other social networking sites. After all, they had been operating for years before 2011 without triggering revolt. Tunisians, though, were simultaneously one of the most politically repressed *and* most electronically connected populations of the developing world (at that point, a third of Tunisians used the Internet and about a fifth of the population had a Facebook profile). Facebook was the primary source of information for students following the protests in December and January (Schraeder and Redissi 2011: 11).

A week into the uprising, the Ministry of Interior began firing live ammunition. Two demonstrators were shot dead on December 24 and over two hundred would die in the weeks to follow (Schraeder and Redissi 2011). On January 9, regime forces killed demonstrators in the city of Kasserine, the first instance of police shooting at a crowd in over twenty-five years (Beinin and Vairel 2011). Three days later, Ben Ali ordered the army to attack civilians in Kasserine. Paradoxically this command—a drastic overreach in a state with an autonomous military—tipped the uprising in the opposition's favor.

For two decades Ben Ali had built a vast personality cult and profiteering network around himself and his family (Angrist 2013: 547). The military, though, remained relatively uncorrupted and, in the midst of the uprising, eschewed the role of authoritarian enforcers. Armed Forces Chief of Staff General Rachid Ammar disobeyed the order to attack the Kasserine protestors, signaling to the dictator and his apparatchiks the military would not abet their lethal campaign. This is not to say that the army remained neutral: the men in uniform soon joined the fray, just not on Ben Ali's side. Rather than repelling the crowds, Ammar sheltered them, deploying soldiers into the streets of Tunis and other cities to protect against further assaults by the Ministry of Interior. With no other option, Ben Ali fled the country on January 14. "[Ammar] subsequently ordered troops to secure the major cities and crossroads," write Peter Schraeder and Hamadi Redissi, "but made it clear that neither he nor the military had any intention of playing any political role beyond protecting the demonstrators and the Tunisian public more generally and ensuring the formation of a civilian-led democracy" (2011: 13–14). The consequences of this detachment from national politics would play out over subsequent years, as civilians, not soldiers, led a fractious, but by regional standards, promising, transition.

Of the core cases, Tunisia presents the starkest example of a split in the coercive apparatus, with the police obeying the ruler and the army defying him. This cleavage stemmed from decades-old differences in the two institutions. Whereas the Tunisian police represented a conventional arm of the regime, a vicious and politically loyal security force that shared the practices of peer Arab security states, the military remained separate from politics and domestic repression. This tradition, of defending the nation instead of ruling it, dated back to independence in 1956 and the establishment of the Tunisian republic the following year. It was reflected in the profile of the republic's first leader: Habib Bourguiba, Tunisia's founding father and its longest ruling autocrat. Bourguiba stood apart from Arab rulers of his era, for he hailed neither from a military background nor from a ruling family. His status as a civilian prompted the Tunisian president to keep his country's military small and distant from politics (Kamrava 2000: 78n39). Meanwhile, the police that were responsible for monitoring and punishing Tunisians' behavior grew prodigiously. Bourguiba and, after 1987, Ben Ali expanded the domestic security forces to 130,000 (commensurate with the police: population ratio in Mubarak's Egypt), nearly four times the size of Tunisia's formal military (Schraeder and Redissi 2011: 6). More important than the size of the military was their distance from the regime's excesses, such that when a crisis erupted, they refused to crack down and instead sided with the citizenry.

The pivotal influence of the military also showcased how the process of authoritarian breakdown was largely a domestic phenomenon.[1] The alignment of coercive power within the country—which pulled the floor out from Ben Ali—occurred far more briskly than the foreign policy shifts of governments abroad. Rather than leading events, for example, the Obama administration followed them. The White House's first major statement, on January 14, blandly called on "all parties to maintain calm and avoid violence," and "on the Tunisian government to respect human rights, and to hold free and fair elections in the near future that reflect the true will and aspirations of the Tunisian people."[2] Even more embarrassing than America's tardy and ginger repudiation of Ben Ali, though, were offers by the French Foreign Minister two days prior to send in French police to help the Tunisian police restore calm.[3]

Tunisia watchers did credit the Obama Administration with communicating to Ben Ali that he would not be allowed to take refuge in the United States (Schraeder and Redissi 2011: 14). But by the time Obama hailed the Tunisians' victory, Ben Ali had already been in Saudi Arabia over ten days. The US president declared during his State of the Union address on January 25, 2011, "the will of the people proved more powerful than the writ of a dictator. And tonight, let us be clear: The United States of America stands with the people of Tunisia, and supports the democratic aspirations of all people."[4] That stirring rhetoric aside, for the most part the United States would prove content to repeat its tepid early response to Tunisia's uprising when confronted with other protests across the region. When uprisings threatened pro-US autocracies, the White House preferred a "wait and see" approach, reserving strong support until *after* the opposition had bested the despot. This position helped ensure that local militaries—and not foreign patrons—remained the switchmen of the Arab uprisings.

Egypt

While Tunisians were revolting against Ben Ali, copycat self-immolations had begun in Egypt. Members of preexisting activist groups, however, hoped to replicate Tunisians' mass actions, rather than Bouazizi's self-sacrifice. Whereas labor formed the nexus of dissent in Tunisia, anti-Mubarak networks generated the initial movement of the Egyptian uprising. Organizers from the "April 6" and "We Are All Khaled Said" groups, both of which denounced Mubarak's police state and his thinly disguised plans for hereditary succession, channeled widespread frustration into collective action (Masoud 2011a: 23–24; International Crisis Group 2011: 2). There was already a resonance between Tunisians' hardships under Ben Ali and Egyptians' tribulations under Mubarak. The case of Khaled Said, a young entrepreneur whom Egyptian police had bludgeoned to death the previous summer, bore basic parallels to Bouazizi's death; both men graphically lost their lives in situations of police abuse (Ismail 2012: 435). But Said's death, while a cause célèbre, had not triggered a national rebellion. Organizers thus attempted to rekindle, through social media and traditional publicity (flyers, word of mouth), what had spontaneously erupted in Tunisia. Tunisians, led by workers, rose up from the countryside and then converged on the capital. Egyptians would follow urban-based youth activists, in Cairo and other cities.

Notwithstanding these differences in the oppositionists' geographic and vocational profile, the fulcrum for regime change in both states remained the military. Ammar's counterpart in Egypt, Defense Minister Field Marshal Hussein Tantawi, also eventually acceded to popular pressure and compelled Mubarak to step down. There are reports that Mubarak's family alienated the army by attempting to position the dictator's son, Gamal, as heir apparent (Bakry 2012). As opposed to cases in which the military had lined up behind a dynastic succession (Syria) and would back the regime to the hilt in later years, in Egypt the top figures in the coercive apparatus balked at the prospect of such a hereditary power transfer.

Through new and old media, Egyptian activists called for a "Day of Wrath" on January 25, 2011. On that day tens of thousands responded to the call of April 6 member Asmaa Mahfouz, who had made the case on YouTube: "We want our rights. We don't want anything else. This whole government is corrupt. The president is corrupt. State Security is corrupt."[5] Despite Mahfouz's broadside, the initial demands coming from the streets of Cairo were circumscribed. Banners invoked the triple goal of "Bread, Freedom, Social Justice, and Human Dignity" (Fahmy 2012: 350). Protesters called for the interior minister's resignation, a decent monthly minimum wage, repeal of the Emergency Law, dissolution of the current parliament, and term limits on the presidency (International Crisis Group 2011; Beinin and Vairel 2011).

While the mass of protestors converged on Tahrir Square, similar marches snaked through other Egyptian cities. The regime responded promptly. Conscripts in the Central Security Forces (CSF), the main riot police, choked Tahrir Square with tear gas and forced protesters to regroup during the night (El-Ghobashy 2011). Organizers then worked on reviving their campaign in a "Friday of Anger." Escalating their campaign, they planned on demanding that Mubarak resign.

Many Egyptians who participated in the Friday of Anger recall it as the real moment of revolution, when the coercive apparatus fell to people power. Such narratives reflect the significant triumph of mass protests on that day as well as the *subsequent* decision of the army, over the next two weeks, not to regain the control of public space the police had lost.

On the morning of January 28 the regime disabled the Internet in a futile bid to stop citizens from congregating. In the afternoon, after Friday prayers ended, tens of thousands made their way toward Tahrir Square, and cried, "The people want to topple the regime!" The sheer number of marchers overwhelmed the ministry of interior. In dramatic scenes, the police retreated from bridges and intersections. As El-Ghobashy describes:

> At 5 pm on the afternoon of January 28, when reports started rolling in of police stations burning down, one after another, al-Adly capitulated and ordered the removal of his forces from the streets. It was a sight unseen in modern Egyptian police rule—the one and only time that Egypt's [disparate] protest subcultures were able to jointly defeat the coercive apparatus that had existed to keep them apart. (2011)

That evening Mubarak spoke on national television. Though he tried to pay lipservice to calls for democracy and poverty reduction, he did not resign. Inured to the magnitude of the crisis, he instead announced a cabinet shuffle.[6] The next day he appointed intelligence chief Omar Suleiman as vice president.

As soon as the police retreated, the Egyptian army moved into the streets. Defense Minister Field Marshal Tantawi had long opposed Mubarak's plans to pass power to his son, and the uprising provided the military an opportunity to scotch Mubarak's incipient dynasty while retaining its own privileged status. On the Monday Mubarak installed a "security cabinet" of military men headed by Lieutenant General Ahmed Shafiq as prime minister.[7] This cabinet shuffle ushered out the civilian technocrats who surrounded Gamal Mubarak and further expanded the military's role in crisis management. The army soon announced it would not fire upon peaceful demonstrators, thereby emboldening more Egyptians to join the throngs against Mubarak while positioning Tantawi as the people's champion.[8]

Like the Tunisian uprising, domestic processes outpaced international responses. For decades, Washington had contributed to the resilience of the Egyptian police state through political and material assistance (Brownlee 2012). When popular revolt, occurred, top decision makers tried in vain to find an exit strategy that would safeguard US interests whether Mubarak prevailed or fell. After days of bemusement, the While House settled on a strategy of "orderly transition" during the first weekend of the uprising. Initially, on January 25, US Secretary of State Hillary Clinton had called for restraint by all sides and assessed "that the Egyptian government is stable and is looking for ways to respond to the legitimate needs and interests of the Egyptian people."[9] The following Sunday, she was on the US Sunday morning talk shows supporting an "orderly transition" from Mubarak to Suleiman.[10] In this manner, the Obama administration sought to ensure the stability of a geostrategic ally while appearing to advocate steady democratization.[11]

In week two of the uprising there was no orderly transition on the horizon. Instead of cutting a deal with Mubarak and Suleiman, and then going home, protesters across Egypt called for the regime to fall. On February 1, Mubarak made another television appearance. He forswore seeking another term or passing power to his son, but he still refused to step down. The next day, thugs riding horses and camels stormed into Tahrir and attacked demonstrators. After this "Battle of the Camel," regime agents are alleged to have sniped at demonstrators from rooftops and lobbed Molotov cocktails into the square.[12] In turn, squatters in Tahrir jerry-rigged barricades and shields (Shokr 2011: 16–18). In two days of violence, over a thousand were wounded and Tahrir became a veritable battle zone.[13] The "Friday of Departure" on February 4 attracted an estimated one hundred thousand people.

In a bid to regain control, Mubarak and his top lieutenants shifted from repression to inclusion. Vice President Suleiman invited the Muslim Brotherhood and the loyal opposition into a national dialogue, which they quickly accepted. But the crowds in Tahrir rejected Suleiman's entreaties, refusing to let him direct public discontent into private pacts. As a result, Suleiman's "dialogue" collapsed on February 6. On February 8, the Real Estate Tax Collectors' Union and three other labor organizations added their voices to the call for Mubarak to step down. Tens of thousands of workers across various industries (cement, hospitals, the Suez Canal, petroleum, telecommunications) went on strike or participated in protests (Beinin and Vairel 2011: 247).

The tide was turning against Mubarak, but Mohammed Tantawi was no Rachid Ammar. Having blocked the hereditary succession project that had troubled them for years, Egyptian officers wanted the crowds to subside (El-Menawy 2012). When it became clear the uprising would not abate until Mubarak resigned, Tantawi acted. On Thursday, February 10, The Supreme Council of the Armed Forces (SCAF), met independently of Mubarak. Led by Tantawi, the SCAF was composed of the twenty highest-ranking Egyptian officers. The council announced it would remain in session indefinitely and work to guarantee the accomplishments of the Egyptian people. Members took this step only because Mubarak had failed to stop the protests (Albrecht and Bishara 2011: 15–16).

"If [the regime] were able to succeed [in quelling the uprising through police action]," they later admitted to the *Washington Post*, "nothing would have happened. We would have pulled our people back to the barracks."[14] The following afternoon, the SCAF stated in Communiqué No. 2 that its members would oversee a transition toward a new constitution, free elections, and, when circumstances permitted, the end of the country's hated State of Emergency. Vice president Suleiman announced Mubarak had stepped down. Instead of cracking down, the Egyptian army had brought the breakdown of Mubarak's order. Although the months that followed were fraught with tension, the public had induced a leadership transition.

Tantawi and the generals promptly took charge. They enjoyed the support of White House and Pentagon officials who had become frustrated that Suleiman had not enacted substantive measures—such as ending the State of Emergency—to placate protesters earlier. The resulting Mubarak–Tantawi transition would not be quite as orderly as the Obama administration wanted, for the SCAF would have to suspend the Egyptian constitution and rule directly. The process would, however, maintain Egypt's critical position in US strategy. Facing either continued unrest with Mubarak in power or a leadership change that sustained the regime overall, US officials accepted the second course.

Yemen

Of the three successful uprisings, Yemen represented the newest state but had the longest-serving ruler. Formed in 1990 through the unification of the Yemen Arab Republic ("North Yemen") and the People's Democratic Republic of Yemen ("South Yemen"), the country had been ruled since that point by Ali Abdallah Saleh and his party, the General People's Congress. Saleh had also led North Yemen for twelve years before the unification (Durac 2012: 163). Regime breakdown in Yemen took longer than in Tunisia and Egypt, and it more heavily involved external powers negotiating the incumbent's exit. All the same, the major structural components of leadership change—lack of massive oil wealth and the absence of a dynastic tradition—provided an opportunity for critics of President Ali Abdullah Saleh that was analogous to the opening exploited by dissidents in the other two countries.

Demonstrations began in Sanaa on January 15, the day after Tunisians ousted Ben Ali. Protests continued into February, prompting Saleh to pledge he would not seek reelection in 2013.[15] This initial concession (much like Mubarak's speeches) did not deter activists, who insisted on Saleh's immediate departure. They mobilized twenty thousand for a "Day of Rage" on February 3.[16] The night of February 11, hours after Mubarak stepped down, chanters echoed the mantra of their Egyptian peers: "*al-sha'b yurīd isqāṭ al-niẓām* (the people want to topple the regime)." Tens of thousands took part in demonstrations in at least eight cities on Friday, February 18.[17] On February 21 a tent city in Taghir (Change) Square began forming. (Regime forces had preemptively seized the capital's Tahrir Square (Durac 2012: 164).) Although the cries from Taghir Square all centered on deposing Saleh, demonstrators' ideas varied widely. One group comprised newly emboldened youth activists campaigning for national political reform. They were aligning, however, with regional rebels. In the north, an armed group of Shias was pushing for independence. Named for a fallen commander, Hussein Badreddin al-Houthi, the Houthis had long been a thorn in Saleh's side.[18] At the other corner of Yemen, a group known as the Southern Movement or simply "The Movement" (Hirak) had chafed at northern domination since 1994, when the country's post-unification civil war ended (Gelvin 2012: 91). In the uprising, Houthis and the Hirak advanced sub-national goals while students made national political demands. Nonetheless, their numbers grew. On March 18 in Sanaa and May 29 in Taiz snipers killed dozens of protesters. Like the "Battle of the Camel" in Cairo, these attacks by regime supporters hardened the opposition and intensified the uprising (Thiel 2012).

With the onset of bloodshed it was the regime's agents of coercion who would tip the scales, gradually, against Saleh. On this point, the Yemeni case offers subtle and instructive contrasts with

Tunisia and Egypt. Saleh had gone much further toward establishing familial rule than had Ben Ali or even Mubarak. The president's tribe, the Sanhan Hashid, "dominate[d] the commissioned ranks of the Yemeni armed forces." Saleh's nephew Yahya commanded the Central Security Service, and his son Ahmed was chief of the Republican Guard (Jones 2011). However, Saleh had been unable to establish a coalition of the security forces in support of Ahmed. In fact, powerful elements of the Yemeni elite had signaled their opposition to the dynastic project.[19] Whereas an accomplished hereditary succession brings cohesion between the political leadership and the coercive apparatus, Saleh's scheming had the opposite effect:

"For years," Alley reports:

[Saleh] had ruled Yemen through a complex web of tribal and regional patronage. Broad inclusion had been the key to overall stability. Saleh threw all that away, however, and alienated his own partners . . . by resolving to settle the succession upon his son at the expense of longtime allies (2013: 77).

In short, top Yemeni officers, like their Egyptian counterparts, bristled at the idea of a hereditary succession. When given the opportunity they were quick to disrupt the president's dynastic plans (Thiel 2012). Thus while Saleh could muster significant despotic power over a prolonged period, he could not command the level of loyalty available in the monarchies and the hereditary republic of Syria.

For a month the Yemeni president retained the support of the 138,000-person strong armed forces. But after the March 18 shooting of protesters in Sanaa, General Ali Mohsen al-Ahmar followed his Tunisian and Egyptian counterparts. On live television he vowed the First Armored Division would shield civilian demonstrators. "Within minutes," Gregory Johnsen describes, "several other top army commanders had joined the nascent rebellion. By the end of the day Yemen's military had split" (Johnsen 2013: 270–271).

In Yemen, as in Egypt, the general maneuvered not out of noblesse oblige, but to advance his own agenda. Long an opponent of hereditary succession, al-Ahmar had long-standing motives for throwing his lot in with Saleh's opponents (Barany 2011).

Whereas the president had tapped al-Ahram to fight critical battles in the south in 1994 and in the country's north since 2004, Saleh had deliberately promoted Ahmed Saleh at the expense of Al-Ahmar (Johnsen 2013: 270). The break between the president and his right-hand military man carried major implications for the uprising. al-Ahmar's realignment drove a political fissure through the regime's core. Writes Marc Lynch, "[al-Ahmar's] move was followed by a cascade of resignations and defections" that included uniformed and civilian elites (Lynch 2012: 156).

In the flurry of opposition activity, a fairly conservative delegation emerged. Traditional parties, from Islamists to socialists and regime defectors, grouped in the Joint Meeting Parties (JMP) and became Saleh's chief interlocutor (Carapico 2011). With the JMP the embattled president was able to engage in a protracted negotiation over the outcome of the revolt, precisely what US officials had hoped Mubarak and Suleiman would achieve in the second week of the Egyptian uprising. It followed that Yemen appeared headed toward a much more orderly transition than in Egypt. In April the JMP embraced a Gulf Cooperation Council (GCC) proposal that would allow Saleh to resign and escape prosecution. Negotiations between Saleh and JMP notables, including army defectors, constituted an elite-centered "reshuffling of the political deck" in the JMP's favor (ICG 2012: i). In this respect, a groundswell of mass mobilization had given way to the building of a new elite consensus.

The domestic push for leadership change gained steam when influential external forces advocated Saleh step aside. Seeing the writing on the wall, Saudi Arabia and the United States concurred that Saleh would need to depart from power. Rather than waiting for events to play out on their own, Riyadh led diplomatic efforts to quell the uprising politically. The Saudi leaders' motive was simple: preempt potential contagion of neighboring states (including their own). In this respect, the Saudis' *diplomatic* intervention in Yemen followed the same self-preservation calculus as their *security* involvement in Bahrain, addressed below.

Having weathered an uprising for months, Saleh was in no hurry to concede. His strategy was to satisfice, and relinquish as little political power as possible. The risks of this approach were punctuated in early June by a rocket attack on the presidential compound that nearly took Saleh's life and left him badly injured. More broadly, battles between loyalists and army defectors had brought Yemen to the "brink of civil war" (Alley 2013: 78). At this moment of polarization, the assassination attempt brought an opportunity for all sides to reconsider their positions: Saleh was rushed to Saudi Arabia for emergency medical attention. There the White House advised him to step down and accept the GCC plan.[20] Instead the embattled autocrat convalesced for months while violence inside Yemen escalated. Three months later, he returned to Sanaa and resumed his bid to retain power.[21] By this point, however, the Libyan regime had fallen and Muammar Qaddafi was on the run. Regional efforts to resolve the Yemeni uprising escalated to the United Nations.

On October 21, 2011, the United Nations Security Council adopted Resolution 2014, pushing for Saleh to honor his own pledges to step down. The Resolution:

> *calls on* all parties in Yemen to commit themselves to implementation of a political settlement based upon this initiative, *notes* the commitment by the President of Yemen to immediately sign the Gulf Cooperation Council initiative and encourages him, or those authorized to act on his behalf, to do so, and to implement a political settlement based upon it, and *calls* for this commitment to be translated into action, in order to achieve a peaceful political transition of power, as stated in the Gulf Cooperation Council initiative and the Presidential decree of 12 September, without further delay.[22]

With a divided regime at home, the incumbent of thirty-three years capitulated to an internationally designed resolution. A month later, on November 23, Saleh signed the GCC plan, receiving immunity from prosecution for himself and his family in exchange for his resignation.

Saleh's exit was ratified on February 21 2012, when his vice president (and ex-minister of defense), ʿAbd Rabbuh Manṣūr al-Hādī, became president through a single-candidate referendum. Hardly a radical figure, Hadi was a "consensus-candidate" of the regime and regime's mainstream interlocutor.[23] Though this transition constituted the breakdown of Saleh's regime category, it remains to be seen whether Hadi will play midwife to democracy, consolidate power in his own hands, or allow for a member of Saleh's clan to take power at a later date (Thiel 2012: 46). Indeed, for months youth activists had scorned the JMP for pursuing the kind of limited political reshuffling that the Saleh–Hadi handover appeared to deliver (Durac 2012; Alley 2013).

Repression in the Oil-Rich and Hereditary Regimes

During the Arab Spring, political change was the exception and political continuity the norm. Countries in which uprisings occurred but did not culminate in domestically driven leadership changes shed light on the mechanisms of authoritarian reproduction. Whereas the defection of military elites prevented incumbents from mounting an overwhelming coercive response in Tunisia, Egypt, and Yemen, the fealty of such figures enabled massive crackdowns in the contrast cases of Libya, Bahrain, and Syria. This capacity in itself merits explanation, for it is the key intervening variable that connects the shock of mass revolt to the divergent outcomes of authoritarian breakdown and authoritarian continuity. Despotic power obviously cannot be taken for granted. It was lacking in the cases discussed above, and its presence in the next set of countries must be explained.

As discussed in Chapter 2, "Lineages of Repression," we do not account for the cohesion of the regime's coercive forces in terms of the immediate characteristics of the opposition (bold, tech savvy, hungry for dignity) or in terms of the profile of the uniformed military (professional or corrupt). Instead, we posit that prior material and institutional patterns either fused the coercive apparatus with the political leadership, or allowed the two to remain distinct. The following section traces the uprisings and crackdowns of regimes that benefited from oil largesse (Libya), loyal ruling coalitions (Syria), or both (Bahrain). These traits enabled them to hold the repressive apparatus together and violently suppress the opposition. To date, such repression only failed to keep rulers in power in the breach, when, as in Libya, foreign militaries deployed even greater violence in favor of the insurrection.

Libya

Muammar Qaddafi overthrew the monarchy of King Idris in 1969. Hence, by 2011 his tenure had stretched for over four decades. During this extraordinary time he survived coup attempts, US military strikes, and international isolation. Dirk Vandewalle attributed the regime's resilience to a combination of oil wealth and Qaddafi's unique brand of pseudo-populism, which together atomized social life while erecting a pervasive security apparatus (1998: 137). The Libyan "Brother Leader" (he eschewed republican titles like "president") used hydrocarbon rents to incorporate his people into politics superficially, through popular committees, while preventing them from acting collectively. In early 2011, this formula appeared to fail, as opponents of Qaddafi began massing as never before.

Like Yemenis, Libyans took inspiration from Mubarak's ouster. After the Egyptian president stepped down, Libyans in Switzerland and the United Kingdom began online calls against Qaddafi. Anticipating large-scale rallies inside the country, regime officials clamped down in Tripoli and the east. Despite this preparation, the regime was stunned by the demonstrations that gripped the eastern city of Benghazi on February 15, 2011 (ICG 2011: 3). The first "Day of Rage" was Thursday, February 17. Qaddafi responded with an unrepentant speech on February 20. When his son Seif echoed the message two days later, the opposition abandoned any hopes that this allegedly reform-minded younger Qaddafi would pursue a political solution (Hilsum 2012: 37). The regime buttressed its threat of coercive sticks with the kinds of carrots only petro-states can afford: "a $24 billion fund for housing and development" (Brynen et al. 2012: 28). When this bribe did little to stem the uprising, the regime stopped opening its purse and instead deployed its tanks.

By early March, the country was in the throes of a violent revolt (ICG 2011a: 3). Libyans were slowly wresting territory from the regime, village by village. The opposition National Transition Council (NTC) issued its first statement on March 5 from Benghazi, which included the following:

> The Council derives its legitimacy from the city councils who run the liberated cities, and who had been formed by the revolution of the 17th February to fulfill the revolutionary gains in order to achieve their goals . . . The Council declares that it is the sole representative of all Libya with its different social and political strata and all its geographical sections.[24]

Such statements were more aspirational than operational. Libyans coped with the same kinds of regional, tribal, and class cleavages that hampered Yemenis. The NTC was working to bridge those divides. But there were additional political challenges. Libyans hoping to build horizontal linkages also confronted the legacy of Qaddafi's deliberate cultivation of anarchy. The lack of public life precluded Libyans from coming together in a fashion similar to the JMP in Yemen. "The idiosyncratic and dictatorial nature of the Qaddafi regime," note Rex Brynen and his coauthors, "and the weaknesses of long-repressed Libyan civil society . . . meant that the rebels inherited few organizational resources upon which to build alternative state structures" (2012: 29). For these reasons, a cohesive national political movement did not emerge. Instead, local fighters—many of them civilians who were taking up arms for the first time—liberated their own towns or neighborhoods. Their connection to the NTC was mainly a vague sense of anti-Qaddafiism (ICG 2011).

The escalating struggle brought out cracks in Qaddafi's military, which numbered some 76,000. The armed forces began splintering along regional lines as soon as the first demonstrations broke out in Benghazi. "[T]he army and air force units based in and near Benghazi and Tobruk in eastern Libya defected more or less in their entirety," writes Zoltan Barany, "while large segments of units stationed in Kufra, Misrata, the Western Mountains, and Zawiya deserted as well" (2011: 34). In February, two bomber pilots flew to Malta rather than assault their fellow citizens (Hilsum 2012: 42). Meanwhile, those portions of the coercive apparatus with regional and tribal affiliations to Qaddafi remained loyal. These desertions, however, did not generate the kind of momentum for the uprising that Ammar, Tantawi, and Al-Ahmar had brought. Rather, loyal elements of the Libyan military proved eminently capable of defeating the protesters, armed or unarmed. Ironically, it was the potency of Qaddafi's coercive instruments that eventually provoked foreign intervention.

The uprising was barely a month old when Qaddafi's forces prepared to assault Benghazi in mid-March. The impending attack came in the context of a broad offensive to regain control of the east. Expecting a bloodbath, France began a push for intervention. Leaders in Washington soon joined with their counterparts in Paris and other European capitals to support the imposition of a United Nations-backed no-fly zone (Gazzini 2011). At that point there was every expectation that Qaddafi and his regime would survive, and many oppositionists, would die, if international forces did not shift the military asymmetry between a rent-fueled, unrestrained army and a rag-tag group of disparate fighters.[25] To be sure, the Libyan regime was facing armed resistance in portions of the country—hence the regime's plan to attack—but scattered rebellions looked incapable of overthrowing the dictator. Foreign intervention came like a deus ex machina to beleaguered Libyan dissidents.

On March 17, the United Nations Security Council voted 10-0-5 to authorize international military action against the Libyan regime. (The move also enjoyed an Arab League imprimatur, thanks largely to intense lobbying by Qatar (Gazzini 2011).) Specifically, UNSCR 1973 authorized member states to take action to enforce a no-fly zone *and* "to protect civilians and civilian populated areas under threat of attack in the Libyan Arab Jamahiriya, including Benghazi."[26] (It was left to the North Atlantic Treaty Organization to actually execute this mission.) The no-fly zone promised to upend Qaddafi's military advantage and, according to its proponents, was instrumental in saving the uprising from defeat. "[I]f we waited one more day," President Obama contended, "Benghazi, a city nearly the size of Charlotte, could suffer a massacre that would have reverberated across the region and stained the conscience of the world"[27] In addition to the humanitarian argument, there were pragmatic considerations about the use of military force, factors which would cut the other way when it came to Syria. The geography of Libya and the fighting reduced the likelihood of a regional contagion. Further, US strategists envisioned the air campaign would minimize American losses and not involve a major ground assault. There were trade-offs to this approach. While avoiding an Iraq-style imbroglio for US troops, this strategy prolonged the struggle for Libyan rebels, who took months to capture Tripoli and Qaddafi's hometown of Sirte.

Acting from the air, NATO forces immediately changed the dynamic on the ground. On March 19, the United States, the United Kingdom, and France began striking at Qaddafi's forces that were headed to Benghazi while also destroying "radar, communications, fuel storage and air defenses around Tripoli and Misrata" (Hilsum 2012: 207–212). Thus NATO's enforcement of the "no-fly zone" went far beyond patrolling Libya's skies.[28] In a short time, foreign governments were directly aiding Libyan rebels. Qatar provided some twenty thousand tons of weapons, France and Great Britain sent Special Forces to train the insurgents, and Tunisia offered a sanctuary and staging ground to Libya's west (Hilsum 2012: 215, 220). Still, Western and Arab support did not amount to a blitzkrieg against the Libyan armed forces. Rather, foreign military assistance enabled incremental gains against Qaddafi's regime, such as breaking a long siege of Misrata (Hilsum 2012: 213). From there local rebels advanced westward, capturing Tripoli in August and, finally, in October, Sirte.

Foreign air strikes also proved critical in bringing about Qaddafi's demise and the inauguration of a post-Qaddafi order. On October 20, 2011 a US Predator drone fired a missile into a large stream of vehicles fleeing Sirte. The convoy scattered, only to be struck by "two 500-pound bombs" from a French jet

(Gazzini 2011). These initial attacks killed loyalists of Qaddafi but not the leader himself, who was among the group leaving Sirte in search of refuge elsewhere. With no prospect of making further progress by ground, Qaddafi hid in a drainpipe. Rebels soon discovered and killed him.[29] Three days after the brutal incident of victor's justice, the NTC declared Libya fully liberated (ICG 2011b: 6). The next month an interim cabinet was formed (Brynen et al. 2012: 30).

The process of the Libyan uprising entailed both crackdown and breakdown. This unique combination among the core cases speaks, first and foremost, to the sources of despotic power, which in Qaddafi's case derived primarily from massive oil rents. Secondarily, the Libyan example spotlights the ways in which foreign intervention can deliver an opposition victory amid unfavorable conditions. Here we agree wholeheartedly with the counterfactual reasoning of Claudia Gazzini:

> Without the intervention, Qaddafi would certainly have clung to power and the revolt would likely have been crushed within a few weeks. Without NATO air strikes, without the Qatari forces advising the rebels on the ground, without the . . . equipment airlifted to rebel strongholds in the mountains south of Tripoli, the opposition would hardly have been able to break the stalemate of the late spring, let alone liberate Tripoli and topple the regime (2011).

Such speculation is strongly supported by the evidence of our remaining cases. Under similar structural conditions as in Libya, when such interventions did not occur, the opposition forces fared poorly.

Bahrain

Bahrain is the least populous of the core cases. However, it experienced the largest uprising on a per capita basis. "At their peak," writes Frederic Wehrey, "the demonstrations would involve about a fifth of Bahrain's half a million people" (Gazzini 2013: 116). Despite its proportional breadth, the revolt was the third shortest of the Arab Spring (thirty-three days, compared with eighteen days in Egypt and twenty-seven days in Tunisia). It was also the only traditional monarchy of the six countries that witnessed revolts. The al-Khalifas run the island kingdom (until 2002 an "emirate") as a fully dynastic monarchy, with princes controlling the top government posts (Herb 1999). In addition to its familial control, the Bahraini monarchy benefits from significant oil wealth ($3,720 per capita in 2009 dollars), which helps ensure the loyalty of domestic political elites, as well as local and foreign security agents (Ross 2013: 20). Brynen and colleagues point out that Bahrain's leadership also "receives significant, though unaccounted for, financial support from Saudi Arabia." All of these rents reinforced Emir (and later King) Shaikh Hamad ibn Isa al-Khalifa, when he succeeded to the throne in 1999: "Ruling-family members reportedly saw their monthly stipends increase, while other local elites enjoyed generous housing grants in new developments near the capital, Manama" (2012: 81).

Bahrain was the first Arab autocracy to survive 2011 through a repressive crackdown. Because the violence coincided with foreign intervention, a word is warranted about our explanation of the causal process. When Bahraini security forces rolled into the Pearl Roundabout in the middle of March 2011, they had backup from soldiers from Saudi Arabia and the Gulf Cooperation Council. It was the Bahraini coercive apparatus, however, that struck demonstrators and cleared the streets. Therefore, the inclination by some students of the Arab Spring to see continuity in Bahrain as the mirror image of change in Libya is empirically unsound.[30] Less than a handful of days separated regime restabilization in Bahrain (beginning March 14, 2011) and foreign imposed regime change in Libya (starting with the March 17 UNSC vote), yet the latter was not the inverse of the former. The Bahraini regime was not rescued from breakdown by external forces. Rather it exhibited precisely the kinds of cohesive despotic power that regularly spell defeat for opposition movements in authoritarian settings. The GCC forces were, in essence, overkill, a reservoir for repression that, in the event, was never tapped. For these reasons, the case narrative gives primary causal weight to the domestic variables of hereditary rule and petrodollars, rather than to the actions of external powers.

Bahraini organizers consciously emulated their Egyptian peers, calling for a "Day of Rage" on February 14, 2011. Also as in Egypt, the core of the demonstrations comprised newly mobilized activists who operated apart from existing opposition groups. (Parties per se are not permitted in Bahrain, although so-called societies provided a functional equivalent. Of these, al-Wifaq has been the leading political representative of Bahraini Shias in the country's parliamentary life (see Wehrey 2013).) Tens of thousands of Bahrainis participated in the first day of protests. The majority of participants came from Bahrain's Shia majority, long the subject of discrimination by the Sunni al-Khalifas. The protestors did not call for the fall of the regime, but rather for its reform, including the replacement of hard-line prime minster and member of the royal family Khalifa bin Salman al-Khalifa. Activists also "demanded constitutional reform, free elections [for parliament], release of prisoners of conscience, and an end to torture" (Gelvin 2012: 136). This moderate programme did not stop the government from responding violently. Security forces killed seven protesters during the first four days of the uprising. As the movement pressed on, Shiʿa parliamentarians and members of the judiciary joined the cause. Demonstrators eventually seized the Pearl Roundabout in Manama and turned it into a tent city—Bahrain's own Tahrir.

The regime, stood firm, keeping Prime Minister al-Khalifa in place and balking at calls for reform (ICG 2011: 6).[31] The longer the protests continued, the more participants escalated their demands from reforming the system to toppling it (Gelvin 2012: 136). In terms of sheer numbers as well, the regime's initial repression brought a second, and much larger wave of protesters into the streets, much like as had occurred in Egypt on January 28 (Lynch 2012: 136).

Like the rebellions in Libya, contentious collective action in Bahrain drew international attention. The examples of Ben Ali and Mubarak suggested there was a meaningful possibility that the demands of protesters could escalate from political reform to political transformation and, if they applied enough pressure, could perhaps topple the monarchy and establish some form of government more accountable to disfranchized Bahraini Shias. Western and regional powers took notice and considered their options. Foreign forces would eventually enter the small oil state, although the process of the uprising was primarily autochthonous, a relentless crackdown by a rentier, hereditary regime.

The al-Khalifas had come to power in 1783. During the nineteenth century the country became a British protectorate. It gained independent statehood in 1971, the year the United Kingdom withdrew from its military bases "east of Suez."[32] At that point, Bahrain acquired new patrons: the United States and Saudi Arabia. Taking up Britain's role in the Persian Gulf, the Pentagon established the Administrative Support Unit in Bahrain in 1971, a precursor to the facilities that would later host the US Navy's Fifth Fleet. In addition, Bahrain and Saudi Arabia became physically linked. The al-Khalifa's monarchy lay just sixteen miles from the much larger, much wealthier kingdom of the al Saud family, a distance literally bridged by the King Fahd Causeway since 1986.

These connections reflected the interests of two of the region's most powerful actors. When the uprising persisted longer than the Tunisian and Egyptian revolts, decision makers in Washington and Riyadh fretted about the fate of the small but critical nation. Bahrain's geographic proximity to Iran and to the half-Shia eastern province of Saudi Arabia meant revolution could overturn US and Saudi influence in one swoop, putting a natural ally of Iran on Saudi Arabia's doorstep. From a strategic perspective, this was an unconscionable prospect (Sanger 2012: 298–299).

The US response to Bahrain's uprising combined rhetorical pressure for reform with steady political support for the regime. Nearly four weeks into the uprising US defense secretary Robert Gates visited the country and deferred to King Hamad bin Isa al-Khalifa and the Crown Prince to calm the situation: "Obviously, leading reform and being responsive is the way we'd like to see this move forward." As in Egypt, though, the opposition was not interested in a "dialogue" that did not remedy their economic and political deprivation.[33] Meanwhile, the Saudi royal family took an even more hard line, conservative stance, signaling to their Bahraini counterparts that no concessions should be made at all (Lynch 2012: 137).

Elements inside the Bahraini royal family ultimately adopted the Saudi position, to devastating effect. A month after the Day of Rage, the Bahraini Defense Forces began clearing the Pearl Roundabout violently (ICG 2011: 6). On March 14, two days after Gates spoke, Saudi Arabia sent a thousand troops across the causeway into Bahrain. Five hundred UAE soldiers and a small Qatari contingent subsequently joined them. Kuwait provided naval support. This GCC force did not repress the demonstrators in the Pearl Roundabout but rather protected key installations around the country. Bahraini security forces began cracking down on March 15. By March 18 the roundabout had been cleared of people, the area's pearl-topped statue razed, and the country placed under martial law (Bahrain Independent Commission of Inquiry: 134–147; Wehrey 2013: 116; Lynch 2012: 137). Afterward, domestic repression intensified as the regime stalked protesters, sent oppositionists to military trials, and collectively punished Bahrain Shias (Faramarzi 2011: 41; Lynch 2012: 138). Bold dissidents continued criticizing the monarchy—and its foreign backers—but the uprising had ended in less than five weeks.

Scholars may debate the counterfactual question: Was the GCC intervention necessary for the Bahraini regime to survive? We reason the answer is no, because GCC forces were not involved in repressing demonstrators. They did provide a deterrent to further popular mobilization and offered some leeway for the Bahraini government. (Gelvin goes so far as to say the GCC "free[d] up Bahraini's own military and security forces to partake in a binge of repression" (2012: 138).) Still, the auxiliary role performed by foreign troops does not indicate the Bahraini regime itself lacked the coercive capacity to defeat the uprising. In fact, on the issue of despotic power, there is little room for debate. Bahrain's military did not split at all. Unlike Tunisia, Egypt, and Yemen, there were no defectors. In the absence of a Bahraini Ammar or Tantawi, one can expect that the security forces would have persisted in using concerted violence against demonstrators even if GCC troops were not standing in reserve locally. In short, the most logical answer to the counterfactual is that the crackdown might have taken longer without GCC support, but it still would have succeeded.[34]

Once again guns were trumps and the effectiveness of the coercive apparatus demands explanation. The regime in Bahrain had inculcated political loyalty in the coercive apparatus by staffing the military, police, and intelligence forces with members of the dominant Sunni minority and Sunni foreigners. In recent years the monarchy had even gone so far as to offer citizenship to non-native Sunni Arabs serving in the military (ICG 2011: 7). This amalgam of rentierism and personalism yielded political dividends. During the uprising there were no major breaks between the conventional armed forces and the other wings of the state. After protesters occupied the Pearl Roundabout, the Bahraini Defense Force took the lead in expelling demonstrators and regaining control over public space.

Next to Libya, Bahrain displayed the most active foreign involvement in a major case of the Arab Spring. Notably, the United States did not pressure the regime. After tying itself to the anti-Mubarak opposition on February 11, the Obama administration was at pains to rationalize its complicity in the Bahraini regime's repression. Responding in November 2011 to skepticism about US intentions, Secretary of State Clinton acknowledged that America's stakes in the region's autocracies influenced the US response to popular calls for democracy:

> Sometimes, as in Libya, we can bring dozens of countries together to protect civilians and help people liberate their country without a single American life lost. In other cases, to achieve that same goal, we would have to act alone, at a much greater cost, with far greater risks, and perhaps even with troops on the ground. But that's just part of the answer. Our choices also reflect other interests in the region with a real impact on Americans' lives—including our fight against al-Qaida, defense of our allies, and a secure supply of energy . . . As a country with many complex

interests, we'll always have to walk and chew gum at the same time. That is our challenge in a country like Bahrain, which has been America's close friend and partner for decades.[35]

While stressing America wants to be "on the right side of history," Clinton acknowledged that US strategic interests (in oil, anti-terrorism, etc.) would continue to be taken as given, not reformulated to match the priorities of populations in the region. In short, Washington would keep backing repressive dictators until their people removed them. Those domestic outcomes continued to hinge on the balance of power between demonstrators and soldiers.

Syria

The last major Arab uprising occurred in Syria. Although battles still rage at the time of this writing, the impact of state violence was apparent in 2011, when repression quelled peaceful demonstrations and ushered in a civil war. The Assad's regime recovery from the initial wave of protests was surprising in light of events in Tunisia and Egypt, but not unusual in the context of Syrian history. In recent memory, Syria had provided a classic case of regime restabilization, through repression, when Hafez al-Assad crushed the Hamah rebellion in 1982 and killed an estimated ten thousand to twenty thousand people (Brownlee 2002: 42–43). Since the 1973 War with Israel, Syria had maintained one of the most active and politically loyal militaries in the Middle East. By 2010, a decade into Bashar al-Assad's rule, Syria hosted the largest per capita military of the six Arab countries that experienced uprisings: over four hundred thousand troops for a population of twenty million. The officer corps was staffed extensively, although not completely, with Alawis, the co-confessionalists of the Assad family that comprise 12% of the country's population.[36] Syria's minoritarian, Alawi-dominated system is a product of colonial French divide-and-rule tactics that retains implications for regime cohesion during crises (Landis 2012). Alawi elites and their non-Alawi coalition partners had supported

Bashar's succession from his father and bolstered him during the most serious challenge to date of his presidency.

Syrians took inspiration from Tunisia and Egypt, and then from Libya. Activists first gathered in relatively small protests in smaller cities during February (ICG 2011b: 1). After weeks of these scattered events, major demonstrations began on March 15, 2011, the country's first organized "Day of Rage." The uptick in collective action came from a conjunction of local and international events. One crucial domestic episode occurred in the southwestern town of Dara'a, near the border with Jordan. On March 6, security forces had arrested fifteen schoolchildren, all of them minors, for spray painting the Arab Spring mantra: "The People Want the Regime to Fall" (Abouzied 2011).[37] When the children were incarcerated in some of Syria's most notorious installations crowds began demanding their release (Leenders 2012: 421). Rebuffed by politicians, they took to the streets where regime agents attacked them (ICG 2011b: 4). Assad's forces killed five and surrounded Dara'a, but the episode inspired kindred protests elsewhere.[38] On the international stage, Western and Arab signals to join the battle against Qaddafi appeared to give Syrian dissidents hope that they would share the success of their Libyan counterparts (Lynch 2012: 180). For a multitude of reasons, this aspiration soon appeared misplaced and the uprising remained a domestic affair in which the regime held the upper hand.

Antagonism against Assad grew in localities where security forces killed or brutalized crowds demanding reform and accountability. A cycle of repression and counterattacks spread across the country, imbuing the uprising with a heavy degree of reciprocal violence from its first months (ICG 2011b: 6). Local coordinating committees soon sprouted up across the countryside, offering an underground network as protesters retreated before tanks and house-to-house raids. After laying siege to Daraʿa in April, tanks moved against towns outside of Damascus and around the country in subsequent months. While opposition movements within and without Syria sought to push reforms or usher Assad from power, the Syrian president continued using live ammunition and heavy artillery to quell protests. Not all Syrian troops obeyed the orders to shoot. "Tens of thousands of rank-and-file conscripts," as well as over four-dozen high-ranking (non-Alawi) officers, joined the opposition (Heydemann 2013: 66). Crucially, though, Bashar's aides-de-camp continued supporting him. There were no defectors to the uprising from the regime's core (Black 2011).

At a mass level, the spirit of revolt failed to spread, never triggering the kind of popular groundswell that occurred in Bahrain. Despite grassroots defiance in Dara'a, Homs, and other quarters, the bulk of Syrians did not gravitate to the resistance. Many observers reject the shibboleth that sectarian conflict between the country's Alawi minority (a sliver of which holds top security posts in the regime), Christians and Sunni Muslims would plague a post-Assad Syria. That scenario, however, had been a mainstay of official ideology and, in 2011 it probably deterred much of the population, including Damascus and the commercial hub of Aleppo, from joining the uprising. Those who were pushing for Assad's ouster were also divided among themselves. Within the country, the opposition's "National Coordination Committee" was willing to negotiate with Assad on the condition that the Syrian army and security forces pull back from the towns they were occupying, stop attacking protesters, and release all political prisoners. Meanwhile, the broader Syrian National Council (based in Europe and Turkey) rejected any discussions with Assad not premised on his exit.

Some members of the National Council pushed for an internationally imposed no-fly zone (Slim 2011). However, a number of factors combined to obstruct the prospect of foreign military intervention. First, Moscow maintained a naval base in Syria, emblematic of security ties with the Assad regime, which meant that Russia would block any international attempts to threaten its ally. In addition, even the United States did not appear eager to pursue a Libya-style solution for Syria, sitting as it was in the heart of the Middle East instead of in the North African desert. Further, the possibility of having a second cauldron, after Iraq, for sectarian violence generated a different calculus than in Libya. Unlike in Bahrain, Yemen, and Egypt, Washington was not put in the embarrassing position of supporting a repressive regime. US ambassador to Syria Robert Stephen Ford lent moral support to Syrian demonstrators in Hama and may have forestalled a regime attack by visiting the city in July 2011 (Lynch 2012: 190). Still, the Obama administration did not materially alter the strategic asymmetry between tanks and civilians, apparently calculating that the risks of substantive intervention outweighed the benefits.

Although the State Department deplored the violence, there appeared to be no external check on Assad's repression. Saudi Arabia funneled money and arms to the Syrian opposition, but the support only prevented outright defeat; it did not deliver victory. Meanwhile, Russia and China were content to use their veto in the UN Security Council anytime council members proposed condemning Asad or taking other measures aimed at "ending the bloodshed in Syria" (Gladstone 2012).[39] Unchallenged by the military power of another state (or coalition of states), the Assad regime could act with impunity. Hence, by summer 2012 observers commented that Syria was descending into civil war. That was true in terms of the costs in lives lost. Yet Syria's war was a lopsided conflict, as helicopter gunships and tanks from the Assad regime devastated villages and cities where guerrillas and civilians mixed. Heightened militarization of the opposition provided little sign of progress. As Joshua Landis commented, "The Free Syrian Army (FSA) being assembled in Turkey . . . is no match for the Syrian Army" (2012). This dominance showed in the control of territory a year later. In fall 2013, Steven Heydemann wrote that Assad had: "reclaim[ed] authority over most of the country's urban 'spine' from Homs in the north to Damascus in the south . . . The regime now dominates the strategically important Mediterranean coast and every major city except Aleppo" (2013: 64).[40]

Even though the war continues as this book goes to press, there is an outcome to be explained: the turn in 2011 from uprising to crackdown. Here Syria resembles Bahrain's more than any other of the core cases: massive repression that kept the incumbent in power. Thus the reasons why Bashar outlasted Mubarak, Ben Ali, and Saleh can already be identified, for the pivotal difference came early on: Syrian repressive institutions shielded the ruler instead of abandoning him.

Aside from a few isolated defections from the armed forces, the coercive apparatus did not split and the military, in all its manifestations, remained a staunch regime backer. Additionally, the core of the repressive apparatus in the Republican Guards and intelligence services stood in lockstep behind Bashar. Syria specialist Bassam Haddad provides a detailed description of the regime's despotic capabilities:

> More than a dozen security services in Syria continue to be both the most "loyal" and the most cohesive part of the regime's coercive apparatus. Their loyalty is matched only by the elite Republican Guard units directly under the control of Mahir al-Asad, the president's brother. The combination of the above formations, with the latter having an edge of sorts, represents by far the most powerful and well-trained lines of defense and offense the regime possesses. (Haddad 2013)

As a result, the domestic strategic balance did not tip in favor of the opposition, neither over a period of weeks nor over a stretch of several years.

Whether or not Assad and his entourage survive the current war is as much a question of military science as political science (Stinchcombe 1965). Nonetheless, the comparative evidence underscores the resilience, not the fragility, of the regime. The armed Syrian opposition has failed to hold major swaths of territory. Meanwhile the regime has kept its military cohesive and active. This outcome of durability through repression derives to a significant degree from the regime's dynastic characteristics.

Conclusion: Theorizing Repression

For social scientists seeking to build general knowledge, the Arab uprisings present a potentially confounding array of explanatory factors. There are six core cases, two main outcomes (breakdowns and crackdowns), but numerous viable theories. This chapter has distilled the complexity of the Arab Spring by setting some variables ahead of others in the causal change. Specifically, we showed how two variables—rents and dynasticism—provide considerable leverage in understanding the complex processes of popular challenges and regime responses that stunned the world in 2010–2012. This parsimonious approach places other rival variables—such as internet savvy and military professionalism—later in the causal chain, as descriptive aspects of the uprisings themselves, rather than up-front as explanatory variables, that could be observed in 2010 or years ealier.

The notion of despotic power (repression) is central to our framework for understanding when regimes broke down and when they instead cracked down. Many scholars concur that Arab armies played a pivotal role in determining whether autocratic rulers would weather mass protest. We have *theorized* the coherence of the repressive apparatus. Antecedent variables related to the loyalty of coercive agents (measured through prior dynastic transfers of power) and a surfeit of state revenues (measured by oil rents) help explain the orientation of Arab security forces and the regime outcomes they drove. "Clubs were trumps," as Huntington (following Hobbes) put it—and prior regime structures determined where the clubs would fall and whom they would topple.

When it comes to repression, regional commonalities (as externally unconstrained security states discussed in Chapter 2, "Lineages of Repression") and intra-regional differences (the subject of this chapter) help explain why the Arab autocracies have been more resilient than their counterparts in other regions but locally vulnerable to popular opposition in 2010–2012. The uniformed military, police, and security forces have been far more prominent in the Arab world than in comparable regions dominated by authoritarianism during the late twentieth and early twenty-first century. In general, these forces have benefited from sympathetic patrons, including the world's oldest democracy. This context contributed to outcomes that were violent even when regimes collapsed quickly. Even in Tunisia, for example, the police killed hundreds before the military broke with Ben Ali.

While MENA regimes share the characteristic of being externally unconstrained security states, they also provide intriguing intra-regional variance in despotic capacity and coherence and their susceptibility to change. During the uprisings of 2010–2012 there were two types of repressive response. In Egypt, Tunisia, and Yemen the military accepted popularly imposed regime change. In Syria, Bahrain, and Libya (before Western intervention) the security apparatus executed a massive campaign of violence that pushed the uprising into armed conflict or quelled it. This variation is significant, and it derives from the material wealth of these regimes and whether or not rulers had secured the commitment of the armed forces through a prior hereditary succession or material payoffs.

After the point of regime breakdown, opposition members, militaries, and the satraps of the ousted incumbents, began jockeying for power in the post-breakdown order. We turn in Chapter 4, to those processes and their initial outcomes.

4

Post-Breakdown Trajectories

In each of our four cases of regime breakdown—Tunisia, Egypt, Libya, and Yemen—celebrants soon realized that the strongman's exit was not a moment of victory, but the opening scene in a much more difficult and protracted struggle to shape the post-authoritarian order. In each country, actors who had previously joined together to bring down dictators now found themselves in competition as their attention shifted from toppling regimes toward building new, ostensibly more democratic, ones. Revolutionaries were forced to confront basic disagreements over fundamental issues (most notably, the proper role of Islam in political life) while simultaneously contending with remnants of the old power structures—from ruling party apparatchiks and loyalist bureaucrats distributed throughout the state apparatus, to the very militaries whose defections had proven so vital to revolutionary success. As of this writing, more than three years after the resignation of Zine El Abidine Ben Ali of Tunisia, the trajectories of our four cases of authoritarian collapse have made plain the difficulties of crafting democracy out of the ruins of autocracy.

In Egypt, a period of military tutelage after Mubarak's overthrow gave way to a brief democratic interregnum that was marked by strife between Islamists and their non-religious rivals, particularly after the former swept both parliamentary and presidential elections. Disputes over the Muslim Brotherhood's monopoly over government and Islamist dominance of the constitution-making process, all taking place against a backdrop of economic decline, sparked mass protests throughout the country, culminating in the so-called Tamarrod (Rebel) movement that brought millions to the streets of Cairo and other Egyptian cities in late June 2013. On July 3, 2013, Minister of Defense ʿAbd al-Fattāḥ al-Sīsī, ostensibly responding to this popular demonstration of discontent, announced the removal of President Muhammad Morsi and the abrogation of the country's popularly ratified constitution. In May 2014, al-Sīsī was elected to the presidency, with a reported 96% of the vote, in what appeared to many to be a restoration of the pre-revolutionary status quo.[1]

The story in Yemen is similarly uninspiring to readers hoping that autocratic collapse would bring democratic victory. Though the country appears to have avoided the descent into civil war feared by many after Ali Abdullah Saleh's resignation in November 2011, the institutions that undergirded the old authoritarian regime appear to have remained intact.[2] As of this writing, the country is governed by Saleh's vice president, ʿAbd Rabbuh Manṣūr al-Hādī, who was elevated to the presidency in a February 2012 election in which he ran unopposed. A Gulf Cooperation Council-sponsored "National Dialogue" of Yemen's leading political forces concluded in early 2014, but the country has yet to draft a constitution and is the only one of our "success" cases not to have held a multi-party election since the fall of the autocrat. Struggles among the country's various tribes, an active al-Qaeda presence, an insurgency in the north of the country among Shīʿī al-Ḥūthīs, and a potential secessionist movement in the south, threaten the country's territorial integrity and the durability of any political settlement.

If Egypt represents a democratic reversal and Yemen a fragile authoritarian stasis, the story in Libya is more complicated. That country's political leaders—from former technocrats of the Qaddhafi regime to tribal leaders to Islamist activists—have managed to establish and maintain the institutions of electoral democracy, but they have been less successful at establishing the institutions of a functioning state in a country long bereft of one.[3] As a recent report put it, "Libya's parliament agrees on little, its interim government has no army to enforce security let alone impose its will, and a new constitution meant to forge a sense of nation remains undrafted."[4] In February 2014, a Libyan general named Khalīfa Ḥiftar mounted an aborted military coup, and has since been engaged in armed conflict with both the state and with Islamist militias in the east of the country.[5] By the time this book appears, a parliamentary election will have been concluded. Whether these contests will mark the completion of Libya's transition to democracy remains to be seen, but if a functioning state is a prerequisite to any kind of political democracy (Linz and Stepan 1996), the prognosis cannot help but be a grim one.[6]

Only in Tunisia—the country that touched off the protests of the Arab Spring—can those searching for signs of hope amid the upheavals of the last three years find some modicum of comfort. After the military's abandonment of Ben Ali in January 2011, civil society actors long excluded from government managed to seize for themselves a role in determining the course of the transition. Though the conflict between Islamists and non-Islamists that wracked Egypt was also reproduced in Tunisia—where October 2011 elections gave Islamists a plurality in the constituent assembly and control of the government—Tunisia's fledgling democratic institutions have so far remained intact. In February 2014, Tunisians adopted a constitution that has been hailed as "a positive example of successful constitution-making and conflict resolution, not just for the Arab region, but for much of the rest of the world as well."[7]

Explaining these variations—the democratic success in Tunisia and the doleful outcomes everywhere else—is the aim of the second half of this book. This chapter lays the groundwork for our inquiry.

Charting Transitions

Our investigation in this half of the book continues to confront the main analytic challenge we have confronted throughout: that the outcomes we seek to explain are not yet settled. Samuel Huntington (1991: 267) famously proposed a "two-turnover test" of democratic consolidation, in which "a democracy may be viewed as consolidated if the party or group that takes power in the initial election at the time of transition loses a subsequent election and turns over power to those election winners, and if those election winners then peacefully turn over power to the winners of a later election." At this limited remove from the so-called founding elections in Egypt, Tunisia, and Libya, we might be able to identify those that have definitively failed Huntington's test (as in Egypt, where a democratically elected government gave way to military coup), but not those that might yet pass it. We therefore shift our focus from the *consolidation* of democratic transitions to their *completion*. According to Linz and Stepan (1996), a democratic transition is "completed" (which, in their view, is an outcome distinct from consolidation), when:

> Sufficient agreement has been reached about political procedures to produce an elected government, when a government comes to power that is the direct result of a free and popular vote, when this government *de facto* has the authority to generate new policies, and when the executive, legislative and judicial power generated by the new democracy does not have to share power with other bodies *de jure*.

In this chapter, we present our empirical perspective on the transition processes in each of our four cases of regime breakdown, with a particular focus on determining whether these countries meet (or at least look as if they are destined to meet) Linz and Stepan's criteria for completed democratic transitions. In particular, we focus on five features of the transitional processes that we think are important indicators of each country's trajectory, and on which there is variation among our cases. First, we ask who controls the interim government after the dictator's removal? Are oppositionists and civil society activists (i.e., groups that were excluded from government under authoritarianism) accorded a formal role in interim governance structures? And, if so, how expansive is this role? Second, does this interim government eventually give way to one in which both executive and legislative authorities are vested in freely elected bodies? In other words, is the dictator's overthrow eventually followed by the election of a new government? Third, and relatedly, who makes the rules regarding those elections? Is it oppositionists and civil society (operating, for example, through an independent electoral commission), or is rulemaking controlled by components of the old regime (such as judiciaries and interior ministries)? The answer to this question allows us to determine the extent to which the new elected government is the democratically legitimate outcome of a genuinely competitive process, rather than simply a continuation of the distorted electoral practices of Arab autocrats. Fourth, is this duly-elected government possessed of the requisite state capacity and legitimacy among relevant groups in society to actually govern, or is its tenure marked by violence and separatism? In other words, is the elected government *actually* the government, or does it have to contend with subnational actors who challenge its monopoly over the legitimate means of violence? Fifth, and finally, if executive and legislative branches are duly elected, do they come to be replaced in anything other than an election? In other words, do the results of elections hold?

In the ideal scenario, the answers to all of these questions might be yes: a country that is on its way to democracy might be one in which oppositionists and civil society are able to assume control of government upon the flight of the dictator, constitute a new government through a free and fair election (whose rules they participate in shaping), are able to govern effectively without armed challenges to their authority, and are eventually replaced in an election.

As we shall see in the narratives of each country, however, the answers to these questions differ for each of our four cases. In Egypt, the interim government was controlled by the military, with oppositionists given a minimal role in transitional governance. Though free and fair elections for the legislature and the presidency were held, at no time were both of these bodies controlled by separate, duly-elected bodies. Moreover, the rules governing these elections were made, not by the parties that had to contest them, but by the same state bodies that controlled elections under Mubarak. And, although the elected government was not forced to contend with subnational challenges to its authority, neither was it able to hold onto power in the face of a military–civil society coalition that ousted the elected president in 2013.

In Tunisia, as in Egypt, the interim government was *de jure* controlled by remnants of the former governing coalition (in this case, the ruling party). However, a civilian-led forum of oppositionists and civil society gave these groups what amounted to *de facto* legislative powers. When elections were held to generate a constituent assembly, that assembly also formulated the government, replacing the old regime figures who had helmed government during the first months of the transition. Moreover, the rules governing those elections were made in an independent forum constituted and wholly controlled by oppositionists and civil society actors. The government has faced no serious challenge to its authority over Tunisia's territory or the state bureaucracy, and, as of this writing, the country's elected institutions have held.

In Yemen, the interim government has been controlled by components of the old regime; elections have not yet been held; the rules governing future elections will be made by a Constitutional Drafting Committee whose composition is determined largely by allies of the old regime (in the form of the interim president and his ruling-party parliamentary majority); and the government contends with separatist movements in the north and the south of the country. In Libya, in contrast, foreign intervention has meant that oppositionists have controlled the interim government, generated a democratically legitimated legislature and executive, and set the rules of elections free from interference of the Qaddafi regime. However, though elected institutions in Libya have so far held together, they have not necessarily held power. The proliferation of tribal and regional militias has meant that the entire Libyan state, let alone Libyan democracy, is far from consolidated.

Below, we document each of these transition cases in greater detail.

Egypt

From Mubarak to the Military

When Vice President Omar Suleiman took to the airwaves on the evening of Friday, February 11 to announce Mubarak's resignation, power in Egypt was assumed, not by the Speaker of the People's Assembly (as called for by article 84 of the country's constitution), nor by an interim government of national salvation (as called for by many of the protesters), but by the Supreme Council of the Armed Forces (SCAF), a conclave of twenty senior military officers led by the minister of defense, Muhammad Ḥussayn al-Ṭanṭāwī.[8] On February 13, 2011, two days after Mubarak's resignation, the SCAF dissolved the parliament that had been elected in December 2010, and suspended the constitution, pending revisions to that document and the construction of a roadmap for a transition to democratic government. Today, more than three years later, Egypt has still not effected that transition.

The political landscape of post-Mubarak Egypt was populated by two groups of actors. The first group comprised pillars of the old order: Foremost among these was the military establishment, which in the eyes of many had long ruled Egypt behind the scenes ever since a group of officers dethroned King Farūq in 1952.[9] Also included in this group was the former ruling National Democratic Party (NDP), an agglomeration of local notables and state bureaucrats cemented by Mubarak's patronage (Brownlee 2007; Blaydes 2010), and whose corruption figured prominently in the motivating discourse of the Tahrir Square protests. And finally there was what the scholar Nathan Brown has called Egypt's "wide state"—most notably the ministry of the interior and the judiciary, both of which had been the focus of calls for reform during the Mubarak era.[10]

Arrayed against the old order was a second group which comprised the oppositionists whose activism had unseated Mubarak. Foremost among these were the assorted youth organizations and movements—such as the Revolutionary Socialists and the

April 6 Youth Movement—who had ostensibly catalyzed the revolution. Equally important were the Islamists, led by the Muslim Brotherhood, widely considered the largest and most potent political movement in Egypt. And finally there were non-Islamist political parties (from Mubarak-sanctioned opposition parties such as the Wafd and the leftist Tagammu' to unrecognized groups such as the nationalist Dignity Party or the liberal Democratic Front party) and political leaders (such as former International Atomic Energy Agency Chairman Mohamed ElBaradei) who had also played a role in the Tahrir Square protests.

If the first group (the SCAF, the NDP, and the state apparatchiks) had an interest in limiting the pace of change, the second group (the Islamists, the revolutionaries, and non-Islamist political parties) was ostensibly interested in accelerating it. And yet there were divisions *within* these camps. The SCAF, which was now formally in charge of Egypt, appeared disinclined to ally with the NDP after Mubarak's resignation. That party had been the focus of popular anger during the eighteen days of revolution, and the SCAF seemed intent on responding to mass antipathy toward it. For example, Ahmed Ezz, the NDP's former organizational secretary and the owner of the country's largest steel manufacturer, was arrested on corruption charges the week after Mubarak's resignation, along with other prominent party members and allies of Mubarak's son Gamal.[11] In April 2011, the Supreme Administrative Court decided to dissolve the party entirely (ruling that it had been an instrument of a corrupt and repressive regime), and ordered the state to seize its assets.[12] These actions suggested that the military-ruling party coalition that had undergirded the Mubarak regime was at an end. However, the SCAF continued to rely on Mubarak-era officials to handle the day-to-day business of running the state. Mubarak's last cabinet was retained after he left office, and key state institutions, such as the judiciary, were largely untouched. For example, both the president of the supreme constitutional court, Farūq Sulṭān (appointed by Mubarak in 2009) and the attorney general, ʿAbd al-Magīd Maḥmūd (appointed in 2006), remained in their posts.[13] When the SCAF appointed a new prime minister on March 3, 2011, it selected Essam Sharaf, a former minister of transportation under Mubarak (who in turn kept on twenty of the twenty-six ministers in Mubarak's last cabinet).[14]

Although oppositionists may have been united in their demand for an end to Mubarak's rule, they had different priorities the day after Mubarak's departure. Revolutionary youth groups focused on eradicating remnants of the old regime. For example, in a meeting with the SCAF in February 2011, the Revolutionary Youth Coalition (*'I'tilāf shabāb al-thawra*)—described by the Egyptian analyst Alaa Bayoumi as "the main body coordinating between youth leaders in Egypt after the January 25 revolution"[15]—demanded (among other things) the resignation of Prime Minister Ahmad Shafiq (who had been installed by Mubarak shortly before his resignation), and the disbanding of the country's secret police, the State Security Investigation Service (*Mabāḥith amn al-dawla*).[16] Islamists, in contrast, seemed most interested in moving rapidly to electoral politics, which would enable them to seize control of the levers of the state. For example, on February 12, 2011, ʿIṣām al-ʿIryān, a member of the Muslim Brotherhood's governing council, called on the SCAF to enact "a peaceful transition of power as quickly as possible through free and fair elections."[17] This was not the view of the most prominent non-Islamist political parties and leaders. Given the Muslim Brotherhood's previous successes in Mubarak-era elections, non-Islamists feared that moving to elections too hastily would enable the Muslim Brotherhood to dominate Egypt's fledgling democracy (and, to some, smother it in the cradle).[18] For example, Usāma al-Ghazālī Ḥarb, a leading opposition intellectual and the founder of the Democratic Front Party, called for the SCAF to stay in power for two years while overseeing the writing of a new constitution by an independent constituent assembly.[19] Mohamed ElBaradei tweeted on March 4 that a "new constitution must precede all elections," and concluded by asking, "Why the rush?"[20]

Balancing Revolutionaries and Islamists

Faced with these conflicting demands, the SCAF appeared most attentive to the youth and the Islamists, both of whom commanded the ability to rally the kinds of mass protests that had brought down Mubarak, and which the SCAF seemed keen to avoid. (Evidence of how averse the SCAF was to mass protest can be seen in a communiqué it issued three days after Mubarak's departure, declaring that ongoing protests harmed national security and disrupted "the wheel of production."[21]) In order to mute street activism, the SCAF made concessions. For example, the SCAF met the RYC's demands for Shafiq's ouster and for the dissolution of the hated State Security Investigations agency (Mabāḥith Amn al-Dawla): Shafiq resigned his position on March 3, 2011,[22] and on March 15, 2011, the SCAF dissolved the SSI (albeit after protesters managed to storm the organization's facilities in Cairo and Alexandria ten days earlier).[23] The SCAF appeared even more eager to accommodate the Muslim Brotherhood. Although the precise role of the Muslim Brotherhood in the January 25 revolution has been a subject of debate, there is little doubt that the Egyptian state (and, by extension, the SCAF) saw it as an important player, and perhaps even the prime mover, in that event.[24] For example, when, on February 6, 2011 a journalist asked then-vice President Omar Suleiman for his interpretation of the protests that were then rocking Egypt, he said, "This is the Islamic current that pushed these people."[25] Consequently, when it came time for the SCAF to lay down the roadmap for the transition, Islamists were granted disproportionate influence.

This was demonstrated most clearly on February 14, 2011, when the SCAF announced the formation of an eight-member committee to amend the Egyptian constitution. To chair the committee, the SCAF selected an Islamist intellectual, jurist, and historian named Tariq al-Bishri, who, according to the scholar Ellis Goldberg, was widely considered a "'bridge' between secular political figures and the Muslim Brothers."[26] The only formal representative of any political party that the SCAF appointed to the committee was the Muslim Brotherhood's Ṣubḥī Saleh, who from 2005 to 2010 had served as a member of parliament from the Mediterranean coastal city of Alexandria. Other members of the committee were all drawn from the country's legal establishment: Ḥātim Bagātū, a commissioner of the Supreme Constitutional Court, Ḥassan al-Badrāwī, vice president of the Supreme Constitutional Court, Sāmī Yūsif, a technical advisor to the president of the Supreme Constitutional Court, Cairo University law professors Muḥammad Ḥassanayn Abd al-ʿāl and ʿāṭif al-Bannā, and Alexandria University law professor Muḥammad Bāhī Abū Yūnis.[27]

The SCAF's mandate for al-Bishrī and his colleagues further cemented the impression that the military was seeking a power-sharing arrangement with the Islamists. The decree that established the committee specifically called on it to make amendments to the constitution that it "deem[ed] necessary to ensure democracy and the *fairness of elections* for the presidency of the republic" and the two houses of parliament.[28] After fewer than two weeks of work, the committee produced a set of nine amendments that were designed to do just that.[29] These amendments strengthened oversight of elections (although this was placed in the hands of judicial bodies with no representation for parties or civil society), limited presidential terms, liberalized the rules for candidate entry into presidential elections, and trimmed some of the president's emergency powers.[30] Most important, however, was article 189—which specified that the constitution would be written by a 100-member committee that was to be chosen by an elected parliament.[31] This meant that parliamentary elections were to come first, thus encoding into law the transitional sequence that the Islamists had demanded from the outset.

The amendments were put to a popular referendum on March 19, 2011. They passed with 77% of the vote, with approximately 41% turnout. Observers of the referendum interpreted the result as an indication of Islamist popularity (since the Muslim Brotherhood and its allies campaigned vigorously for the their passage).[32] But if the referendum's passage was a sign of the Brotherhood's strength, what happened next was a sign of the military's. Instead of amending the 1971 constitution, as voters had agreed, the SCAF instead abrogated it and replaced it with a "constitutional declaration" (*ʾiʿlān dtstūrī*). The March 30, 2011 document contained the nine amended articles, in addition to fifty-four new articles added since the referendum.[33] Among these was article 56, which arrogated to the SCAF a set of sweeping prerogatives that rendered it more powerful than the autocrat Egyptians had overthrown a little more than a month prior. In sum, the constitutional declaration gave the SCAF full legislative and executive powers, essentially formalizing the generals' role as both president and parliament until elections for these offices could be held.

Opposition Polarization Deepens

The spring and summer saw the formation of new political parties to contest the upcoming parliamentary elections, continued protests against the SCAF by youth groups seeking punishment for police officers implicated in the killing of protesters, and increasing tensions between Islamists and non-Islamists. These tensions came to a head on July 29, 2011, when a planned protest that had, according to the late Anthony Shadid, "been billed as a show of national unity," came to be dominated by Islamists calling for the application of the *sharīʿa*.[34] In June 2011, twenty-eight parties, led by the Muslim Brotherhood, and including the Wafd, the leftist Tagammu, and several new and old parties, joined together to form a "Democratic Alliance" with the intention of contesting parliamentary elections as part of a unified list. However, this alliance soon cleaved along ideological lines.[35] Non-Islamists began to call for the SCAF to establish "supra-constitutional principles" that would limit the ability of Islamists to craft a theocratic constitution. Muhammad ElBaradei proposed adopting a Bill of Rights prior to the writing of the constitution, arguing that, "We do not know what will happen in the future. If any faction comes [to power] like in [Nazi] Germany, or if there is a military coup, my rights would still be preserved."[36]

In what was billed as an attempt to generate consensus, in May 2011 the SCAF convened a National Accord Conference (Muʿtamar al-Wifāq al-Waṭanī), inviting representatives of the country's political parties to a non-binding dialogue over the shape of the country's future constitution.[37] The Muslim Brotherhood, however, rejected participation in the initiative, deeming it a "conspiracy" against the will of the Egyptian people.[38]

As electoral competition between Islamists and non-Islamists loomed nearer, each side attempted to court the military. In July 2011, the Brotherhood's general guide, Muhammad Badīʿ, called for Egyptians to stand by the SCAF and to "appreciate its role in the defense of the revolution instead of criticizing it." He went on to point out how the Egyptian military was morally superior to those in "neighboring countries in which the army kills its people."[39] Similarly, the liberal Egyptian politician Mirvet al-Tilawi, who had served as minister of social affairs under Mubarak, explained the need for "the military to exercise oversight over all those who have power."[40] In short, both Islamists and their partisan rivals were "more likely to look to the SCAF as the neutral arbiter or referee in their fight, as opposed to the last vestige of a regime they fought to uproot" (Masoud 2011a: 126).

One group that seemed not to partake of this dynamic was the revolutionary youth. Though the scholar Kristen Stilt is probably overstating matters when she declares that "Egyptians in large numbers no longer viewed the Supreme Council of the Armed Forces (SCAF) as the guardian of the revolution and even considered it the revolution's antagonist," this statement is certainly true of groups such as the Revolutionary Youth Coalition.[41] On July 8, 2011, the RYC declared that the government should resign and that "a revolutionary government, endowed with plenary powers, be forcibly established by the will of the Square."[42] Reports of the military's abuse of female protesters, including subjecting them to so-called "virginity tests," and the army's assault on peaceful Christian demonstrators on October 9, 2011, would only reinforce this view (Stilt 2012).

In August 2011, as parliamentary elections loomed, the SCAF-appointed cabinet attempted to alter the political roadmap that had been laid out in the constitutional declaration of the previous spring. The deputy prime minister ʿAlī al-Silmī—who had also served as chairman of the SCAF's National Accord Conference—announced the cabinet's intention to put forward a new document that would guide the constitution-writing process after the November elections.[43] The document, finally circulated on November 1, 2011, contained twenty-two articles and reflected the preference of non-Islamists for supra-constitutional principles that would shape the constitution.[44] These included a declaration that Egypt is a "civil, democratic state based upon citizenship and the rule of law, which respects pluralism, and provides freedom, justice, equality, and opportunity to all citizens without discrimination or differentiation." (The principles also included an Islamist-friendly provision declaring Islamic law the principal source of legislation, while retaining for non-Muslims the right to be governed by their own religious law in their family or liturgical affairs). For Islamists, any attempt to limit the scope of the future constituent assembly was nothing less than a violation of the democratic process. Yāsir Burhāmī, the leader of the Salafī Nūr party, declared that "we reject the supra-constitutional principles categorically, and affirm that they do not apply to the Egyptian people, and we reject any attempts to patronize the Egyptian people in which a minority tries to impose its secular and liberal affiliations over the wishes of the nation."[45]

More objectionable to Islamists than the supra-constitutional principles, however, were the provisions of the document that attempted to tie the future parliament's hands by specifying the precise makeup of the council that would write the constitution. The document declared that only twenty of the constituent assembly's one hundred members could be selected from the parties in parliament, and they must be drawn in proportion to each party's share of seats in the legislature. The remaining eighty members were to be selected by national bodies outside the parliament, many of which remained dominated by remnants of the former ruling party. For example, fifteen members were to be university professors nominated by the High Council for Universities, another fifteen were to be representatives of professional syndicates; five were to be workers nominated by labor unions; five were to be farmers nominated by the farmers' union; and one each was to come from the police, businessmen's unions, armed forces, sporting unions, student unions, and churches, among corporate entities. Since these bodies retained much of their pre-revolutionary leadership (which, by definition, was non-Islamist), affording them an outsized role in determining the makeup of the body guaranteed not only that Islamists could not control the constitution-writing process, but that political elites of the Mubarak regime would have a place at the table as well.

It is not known whether the Silmī document was an independent initiative of the cabinet, or a product of the SCAF itself. However, the document did include provisions for ensuring the military's continued independence from civilian oversight. Article 9 declared that,

> The Supreme Council of the Armed Forces alone will be competent to oversee the affairs of the armed forces and discuss the terms of its budget to be listed as a single number in the state budget, it must also approve any legislation relating to the armed forces. The President of the Republic is the Commander-in-Chief of the Armed Forces and Minister of Defense is the commander of the armed forces, and President of the Republic may declare war after approval of the Supreme Council of the Armed Forces and the people.

Predictably, non-Islamist parties offered their assent to the document, finding military autonomy a small price to pay for protection from the designs of the Islamists. However, youth groups such as the April 6 movement joined the Muslim Brotherhood in condemning it. Many of the revolutionary groups were at that moment engaged in pitched street battles against the SCAF (whose rule they deplored) and the ministry of the interior (which had not yet been held to account for crimes against protesters), most notably on Muḥammad Maḥmūd street near Tahrir Square in downtown Cairo.[46] The Brotherhood made common cause with these groups by emphasizing that its opposition to the Silmī document was based on its provisions regarding military autonomy, and not solely on the fact that the declaration would have stripped the Islamists of the ability to determine the shape of the new constitution.

For example, Muhammad Morsi, then leader of the Brotherhood's Freedom and Justice Party, declared that his movement rejected the document because "it places one of the institutions of the state above the constitution and above the people."[47] After large protests in November 2011, the al-Silmī document was withdrawn, and the Muslim Brotherhood dedicated itself fully to the task of winning that month's parliamentary elections, and thus wrestling legislative power away from the SCAF. According to the Egyptian researcher Sameh Fawzi, the Brotherhood's pivot to elections was experienced by many in the revolutionary camp as an act of abandonment: "[T]he revolutionaries continued to look to Tahrir Square and mass protests as the only means of achieving revolutionary legitimacy. [...] The Brotherhood's focus on the parliamentary polls [...] opened the group up to criticism that its only concern was with attaining political power."[48]

Islamists Win Elections but not Power

Parliamentary elections eventually took place over six weeks from November 28, 2011 to January 11, 2012. Although opposition parties across the spectrum had demanded that elections be conducted according to a system of closed list proportional representation, the SCAF, acting with little input from political actors, chose a hybrid system in which only two thirds of the legislature's 498 elected seats would be chosen in this manner, with the remaining one third elected through a majoritarian system (which, it was believed, would enable local notables attached to the old regime to earn a measure of representation in the new legislature).[49]

If the SCAF's initial cooperation with Islamists had been based on the calculation that the Muslim Brotherhood and their fellow Islamists represented the largest political force, the results of Egypt's founding election seemed to bear that assessment out (Table 4.1). The Muslim Brotherhood's political wing, the Freedom and Justice Party (*Ḥizb al-Ḥurriya wa al-ʿAdālah*), captured almost 42% of the seats in parliament. Including seats from other parties on the Brotherhood's "Democratic Alliance" electoral list

Table 4.1. Egyptian Election Results, November 28, 2011 to January 11, 2012

	Vote*	%*	Seats	%
Democratic Alliance	10,138,134	37.5	235	46.2
Freedom and Justice (MB)			213	41.9
Dignity (Karāma)			6	
Tomorrow Revolution (Ghad al-Thawra)			2	
Civilization			2	
Islamic Labor			1	
Egyptian Arab Socialist			1	
Egyptian Reform			1	
Affiliated Independents			9	
Islamic Alliance	7,534,266	27.8	123	24.2
Al Nour			107	21.1
Building and Development			13	
Authenticity Party			3	
Egyptian Bloc	2,402,238	8.9	35	6.9
Social Democratic Party			16	
Free Egyptians			15	
Progressive Unionists			4	
New Wafd Party	2,480,391	9.2	38	7.5
Al Wasat	989,003	3.7	10	2.0
Reform and Development	604,415	2.2	9	1.8
Revolution Continues	745,863	2.8	7	1.4
National Party of Egypt**	425,021	1.6	5	1.0
Freedom Party**	514,029	1.9	4	0.8
Egyptian Citizen Party**	235,395	0.9	4	0.8
Union Party**	141,382	0.5	2	0.4
Conservative Party**	272,910	1.0	1	0.2
Democratic Peace Party	248,281	0.9	1	0.2
Justice Party	184,553	0.7	1	0.2
Arab Egyptian Unity Party	149,253	0.6	1	0.2
Independents			21	4.1
Total	27,065,134			

* PR vote; ** NDP offshoots.

Source: Compiled from data at <http://www.jadaliyya.com> and <http://egyptelections.carnegieendowment.org>, accessed June 6, 2014.

(*al-Taḥaluf al-Dumūqrāṭī*)—including the Dignity (Karāma) party of Nasserist writer and activist Ḥamdīn Ṣabbāḥī and the Tomorrow (Ghad) party of liberal lawyer and activist Ayman Nour—the total rises to 46.2%. The second largest bloc in parliament belonged to an Islamic Alliance Bloc (*Taḥāluf al-Kutla al-Islāmiyya*), led by the Party of Light (*Ḥizb al-Nūr*), which the Alexandria-based Salafi Preaching Society (*Jamāʿat al-Daʿwa al-Salafiyya*) established in May 2011 as their political arm.[50] Together, this Salafist bloc captured 24% of the seats in the legislature, bringing the Islamist total to more than 70%.

In contrast, the largest non-Islamist party in the legislature was the Wafd Party, with 7.5% of the seats. In third place, with approximately 7% of the seats, was the Egyptian Bloc (*al-Kutla al-Miṣriyya*), which was an alliance of three parties: the Free Egyptians Party (*Ḥizb al-Miṣriyīn al-Aḥrār*) established in May 2011 by the Egyptian telecommunications magnate Naguib Sawiris; the Egyptian Social Democratic Party (al-*Ḥizb al-Miṣrī al-Dimuqrāṭī al-Ijtimāʿī*), a center-left party established after Mubarak's overthrow by Egyptian intellectuals including AUC economics professor Samer Soliman; and the National Progressive Unionist Rally (*al-Tajammuʿ al-Waṭanī al-Taqaddumī al-Waḥdawī*) established in 1978 as the main leftist opposition party under then-president Anwar al-Sadat. Finally, ruling party offshoots such as the Union Party (*Ḥizb al-Ittiḥād*) of former NDP chairman Ḥusām Badrāwī, and the Conservative Party (*Ḥizb al-Muḥafiẓīn*) of former NDP member of parliament Akmal Qurṭām, together captured approximately 6% of the vote, a function, perhaps, of the NDP's post-breakdown fragmentation and the stigma of association with the former dominant party.[51]

Though the Muslim Brotherhood and its fellow Islamists had demonstrated that they were the most powerful electoral force in Egypt, the SCAF continued to entrust the day-to-day business of government to Mubarak-era officials. In December 2011, the SCAF appointed Kamāl al-Ganzūrī, prime minister under Mubarak from 1996 to 1999, to serve as interim prime minister. The Brotherhood in turn demanded the appointment of a government that represented the parliamentary majority, but the SCAF demurred.

In March 2012, Muḥammad Badīʿ, the Brotherhood's general guide, explained that the movement was therefore likely to renege on its earlier pledge not to seek the presidency. "The current parliament," he declared, "has no powers to hold the government to account, and there are those who threaten to call for the dissolution of the parliament."[52] Only a Muslim Brotherhood presidency could defend the gains of the revolution. On March 31, the Brotherhood announced that it too would seek the nation's highest office, and nominated Khayrat al-Shāṭir, a successful businessman and the movement's deputy general guide, as its candidate.[53]

It was not simply the need to capture a share of executive power that motivated the Brotherhood's pursuit of the presidency. The movement and its allies also pointed to the fact that representatives of the *ancien régime* were organizing to capture the office for themselves. As early as October 2011, former prime minister Ahmad Shafiq had intimated his intention to seek the presidency, and formally announced his candidacy in February 2012.[54] Rumors swirled that Omar Suleiman, Mubarak's former head of the General Intelligence Directorate and Egypt's vice president during Mubarak's last days in office, was also planning to run—which was finally announced in April 2012.[55] Alarmed at the prospect of a return of the *fulūl* (a term that has been taken to refer to the remnants of the old order) through the ballot box, the Islamist-dominated parliament in April 2012 passed law 17 of 2012 (also known as the "political exclusion law" (*qānūn al-ʿazl al-siyāsī*), which stipulated the suspension of all political rights until 2021 for "everyone who has worked, during the decade prior to February 11, 2011 as president of the republic or vice president or prime minister or president or secretary general of the dissolved National Democratic Party or who was a member of its political bureau or general secretariat."[56]

But as the Brotherhood angled for a greater share of power and for the exclusion of its rivals, the Mubarak-appointed judiciary became increasingly active in confronting the group's ambitions. The political exclusion law was immediately suspended by the courts (clearing the way for former NDP members to run for the presidency) and was ultimately ruled unconstitutional in June 2012.[57] In April

2012, the High Judicial Elections Commission—a body headed by the Mubarak-appointed chair of the Supreme Constitutional Court, Fārūq Ṣulṭān—disqualified the Brotherhood's al-Shāṭir from the presidential race. The legal rationale for the ruling was a reflection of the considerable legal continuity that existed with the Mubarak era: al-Shāṭir had been convicted in 2008 by a military court for membership of a banned organization, and the necessary ten years had not elapsed for the restoration of his political rights.[58] (The Brotherhood had also submitted candidacy papers for Muhammad Morsi, the head of its Freedom and Justice Party, in anticipation of this outcome.) That same month, the judiciary struck at the Brotherhood again when an administrative court dissolved the hundred-member committee that was then drafting the country's constitution (*al-Jam'iyya al-ta'sīsīya al-dustūriya*). The court reasoned that since the relevant article (60) of the SCAF's interim constitution did not explicitly say that the parliament could appoint its own members to the constituent assembly, the inclusion of any parliamentarians on the body rendered it unconstitutional.[59] This ruling was welcomed by non-Islamists, liberals, and Coptic leaders who, in March and April of 2012, had walked out on the assembly to protest Islamist dominance.[60]

The 2012 Presidential Elections: A Pyrrhic Victory

Despite dominating the parliamentary elections that concluded in January 2012, the Brotherhood's performance in the presidential elections a mere five months later revealed a significant reconfiguration of the balance of political forces. The first round of the election, held on May 23 and 24, 2012, featured thirteen candidates. Though Morsi received the most votes, at approximately 25%, close behind was Aḥmad Shafīq at 24%. Shafīq was a well-known protégé of Mubarak's who had commanded the Egyptian Air Force from 1996 to 2002, and then served as minister of civil aviation until being appointed prime minister in the last two weeks of Mubarak's presidency. That someone so closely associated with the ousted president could do so well in the contest to replace him suggested that the coalition undergirding the Mubarak regime had begun to regroup. Also surprising were the strong electoral performances posted by Ḥamdīn Ṣabāḥī, a dissident parliamentarian under Mubarak who had founded a small Nasserist political party, and ʿAbd al-Munʿim Abū al-Futūḥ, a former Muslim Brotherhood leader who had broken away from the group and styled himself a liberal.[61] Both candidates had earned the support of activists associated with the Revolutionary Youth Coalition, and their combined vote share of almost 40% (21% for Sabahi and 17% for Abū al-Futūḥ) revealed the continued importance of this constituency (although some of Abū al-Futūḥ's votes also came from the Salafi Nūr party, which had also endorsed him).[62] (Vote shares of the top five candidates, who together earned 98% of the vote, are presented in Figure 4.1). In the runoff election held on June 16 and 17, Morsi defeated Shafiq by 3.4% of the vote, but lost to the former air force general in most urban areas—including Cairo—and much of the Nile Delta.[63]

In the days prior to Morsi's election, the courts again intervened to trim Islamist sails. On June 14, the Supreme Constitutional Court, which had been considering a petition to dissolve the Islamist-dominated parliament elected in January 2012, finally

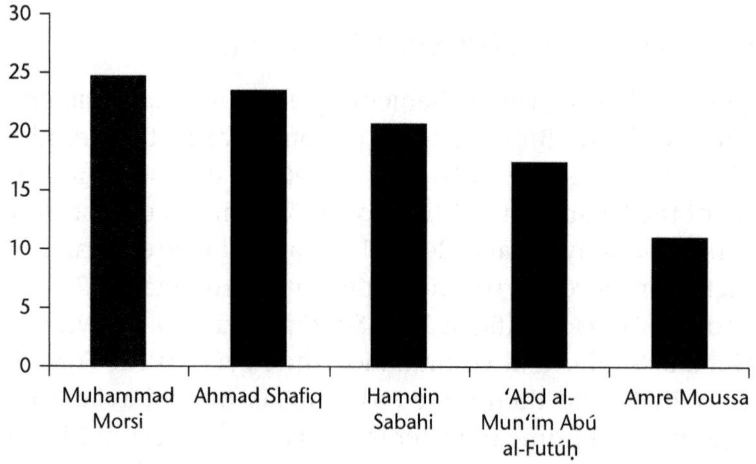

Figure 4.1. Results of First Round of 2012 Presidential Election

moved to disband the body.[64] The court ruled that the electoral system that had governed the November 2011 to January 2012 parliamentary elections was unconstitutional, as it allowed party members to compete for seats that should have been reserved for non-partisans.[65] This, the court decided, violated the constitutional principle of equal political opportunity (as it gave party-members more opportunities to get elected than non-party members).[66] The generals moved with alacrity to implement the ruling, stationing troops to prevent parliamentarians from entering the building.[67]

On June 17—the final day of the presidential election—the SCAF issued a constitutional declaration in which it assumed the vacated parliament's role as the country's legislative authority. The SCAF's decree also reinforced the military's autonomy from civilian oversight, gave the military an effective veto over presidential decisions in the realm of national security, and arrogated to the SCAF the right to choose a new constituent assembly if the courts decided to dissolve the current one.[68] The SCAF's decision was interpreted by some as an attempt to shore up its power in advance of what was expected to be Morsi's victory.[69]

Though the presidential election had concluded on the 17 June, it took the Presidential Elections Commission a week to certify the result in Mohamed Morsi's favor.[70] During that week, the Brotherhood once again made an effort to shore up support among the non-Islamist camp, inviting dozens of national leaders from across Egypt's political spectrum to a June 21 summit at Cairo's Fairmont hotel, to "discuss developments and changes in the political scene and the steps to be taken in the face of current challenges."[71] According to Wael Ghonim, the Egyptian online activist who had attended the meeting as part of a group calling itself the National Front for Completing the Revolution (al-Jabha al-Waṭaniyya li-istikmāl al-thawra), the outcome of the meeting (sometimes known as the "Fairmont Accord") was that Morsi made a number of promises intended to assure non-Islamists that they would be part of decision-making in Egypt. Notably, the president reportedly promised to include representatives of "all national trends" on his presidential team; to appoint a "national salvation government" headed by a prime minister who was a "political independent"; and "to strive for balance in forming the constituent assembly, in order to guarantee the writing of a constitution for all Egyptians."[72] The events that followed proved, at the very least, that Egypt's Islamist and non-Islamist oppositionists had very different interpretations of that agreement.

Morsi Takes Charge

When Morsi finally assumed office on June 30, 2012, it was almost a foregone conclusion that he would be locked in struggle with both a Mubarak-era judiciary intent on limiting Islamists' electoral gains, and a military determined not to cede any of its power or authority. One of the new president's first decisions was to reinstate the parliament that had been dissolved immediately prior to his election, but this was rejected by the court, and the president was forced to back down.[73] Egypt's new president did, however, manage to name his own cabinet—replacing Prime Minister al-Ganzūrī with a former irrigation minister named Hishām Qandīl.[74] Though Qandīl was not known to be a formal member of the Muslim Brotherhood, many felt that Morsi's decision to appoint this political unknown rather than a well-known non-Islamist figure meant that the president did not intend to hew to the power-sharing spirit of the so-called Fairmont Accord.[75] Similarly, though Morsi's cabinet was largely made up of technocrats, Muslim Brotherhood members were given the ministries of housing, communication, manpower, information, and higher education.[76] Control of the ministries of defense, foreign affairs, and the interior, however, remained in the hands of the professional bureaucracies that had controlled them in the Mubarak era.[77]

After little more than a month in office, Morsi appeared to move against the generals. On August 12, 2012, shortly after Islamist militants killed sixteen police officers in the Sinai peninsula, the president forced Defense Minister Ḥussayn al-Ṭanṭāwī and army chief of staff Sāmī ʿAnnān to resign.[78] Though some described the move as a "counter-coup," the fact that Tantawi and Annan's replacements hailed from the military, and that Morsi gave ʿAnnān and Tanṭāwī state honors and appointed them as presidential advisors, suggest that it was the product of an agreement between the president and the military.[79] To replace Ṭanṭāwī, Morsi chose military intelligence chief ʿAbd al-Fattāḥ al-Sīsī.[80] According to a later report by the *New York Times,* "General Sisi [had] cultivated Mr. Morsi and other leaders [...] including going out of his way to show that he was a pious Muslim."[81] But Morsi didn't just retire Mubarak's minister of defense. He also reduced the SCAF's political role, canceling the provisions of the June 17 constitutional declaration that had granted legislative authority to the military.[82] He now assumed these powers himself—becoming, in effect, both executive and legislature. Mohamed ElBaradei declared in an August 12 message that, while the "ending of the military's role is a step on the right path, a president with legislative and executive power contradicts the essence of democracy, and can only be an exceptional temporary measure."[83]

The Egyptian journalist Lina Attalah noted to the *Guardian* that Morsi's move would face opposition from the judiciary, and that the president consequently "need[ed] judicial figures on his team."[84] Perhaps in recognition of this, Morsi appointed a judge of the Court of Cassation, Maḥmūd Makkī, as his vice president.[85] Makkī had been an activist for judicial independence under Mubarak, and had been tried in 2005 for "defaming the judiciary" with his accusations of judicial complicity in the regime's electoral fraud.[86] It is not clear whether the appointment was intended to win over the judges, or to put them on notice that the reform of their institution was about to become the focus of the president's attentions. On October 11, 2012, the president attempted to remove the country's attorney general (al-nāʾib al-ʿām), ʿAbd al-Magīd Maḥmūd, from his post by naming him ambassador to the Vatican.[87] In doing so, Morsi was ostensibly responding to the demands of revolutionaries who felt that the attorney general had been lax in prosecuting those accused of violence against protestors during the January 25 revolution. However, the attorney general rejected the appointment, and the Supreme Judicial Commission (the state body responsible for judicial appointments and promotions) petitioned Morsi to rescind his decree.[88] On October 13, the president backed down and Maḥmūd kept his job.[89] The victorious attorney general declared that he insisted on defying the president's decision in order to "preserve the independence of the institution of the attorney general and the judicial branch."[90]

Morsi Overreaches

Though the judiciary appeared to have won that skirmish with the president, Morsi responded in dramatic fashion. On November 22, he issued a new constitutional declaration—something he was empowered to do as both Egypt's executive and legislature—in which he solved the problem of the judges' interference with his decisions by placing the office of the president above their authority entirely. According to article 2 of the document, everything the president did or said—from the moment of taking office until the completion of a new constitution—was to be taken as law:

> Previous constitutional declarations, laws, and decrees made by the president since he took office on 30 June 2012, until the constitution is approved and a new People's Assembly is elected, are final and binding and cannot be appealed by any way or to any entity. Nor shall they be suspended or canceled, and all lawsuits related to them and brought before any judicial body against these decisions are annulled.[91]

The stated aim of this move was to prevent the Supreme Constitutional Court from considering a complaint to dissolve the constituent assembly, which was then nearing completion on the draft constitution. However, the effect was to further heighten opposition to the president, providing a focal point around which previously scattered liberals, leftists, and Mubarak supporters could coalesce. On November 24, 2012, the president's opponents formed the National Salvation Front (*Jabhat al-inqādh al-waṭanī*).[92] The broad nature of the coalition now arrayed against the president was illustrated by the identities of the three leaders of the NSF: former International Atomic Energy Association Chairman Mohamed Elbaradei, leftist party leader and third-place presidential candidate

Ḥāmdīn Ṣabāḥī, and Mubarak-era foreign minister (and fifth-place presidential candidate) Amre Moussa. The front demanded the cancellation of the constitutional declaration, and the appointment of a new constituent assembly representing all Egyptians.[93] Shortly thereafter, it demanded that Morsi remove the Qandīl government and install instead a government of national unity, in keeping with what they took to be the spirit of the Fairmont Agreement made before Morsi took office.[94]

Protests raged throughout Egypt, including in front of the presidential palace, and demonstrators burned and vandalized several Muslim Brotherhood offices.[95] Muslim Brotherhood members and other Islamists in turn laid siege to the Constitutional Court, in a bid to prevent the judges from challenging the president's authority.[96] On December 8, the impasse was broken when Morsi withdrew the most controversial parts of the constitutional declaration, and the Court allowed the constituent assembly to continue its work.[97] On December 11, 2012, in an ostensible effort to smooth Egypt's turbulent political waters, Minister of Defense ʿAbd al-Fattāḥ al-Sīsī invited the president and his political opponents to a meeting "with the purpose of holding dialogue among all the nation's partners."[98] According to the scholar Yezid Sayigh, Morsi's response was "undisguised dismissal," prompting al-Sīsī "to cancel the proposed dialogue and to explain [...] that the [army] had merely sought 'a gathering of an Egyptian family.'"[99]

Throughout the crisis, the constituent assembly had worked round the clock to finalize the draft constitution, and had approved it in a vote of the body on November 29, 2012.[100] Several liberal members had by then withdrawn from the assembly and had been replaced by alternates, at least some of whom were drawn from the Islamist camp.[101] The document, which many criticized as deepening the religious character of the Egyptian state, was presented to the public in a referendum on December 15 and 22, 2012 (the referendum was held in two stages in order to facilitate judicial supervision of the balloting).[102] Though the new constitution passed with approximately 64% of the vote—allowing the Muslim Brotherhood to claim a healthy majority—turnout in the referendum was only 33%.[103]

This was far less than the 41% of eligible voters who had turned out in the previous referendum, and a potent indicator of just how many Egyptians had become alienated from their country's politics.

A Rebellion Emerges

If Morsi believed that the passage of the new constitution would bring stability to Egypt's fractious political order, he was to be disappointed. Dueling protests between Islamists and their rivals continued unabated. In March 2013, it was reported that citizens in three governorates had begun circulating petitions calling for the army to take over the management of the nation.[104] The following month, a group of young people calling themselves "Tamarrud" or "Rebel," began a nationwide signature drive calling for citizens to withdraw confidence from President Morsi and to gather for mass protests in front of the presidential palace on June 30, 2013.[105] By mid-May, Tamarrud's organizers claimed that they had collected more than two million signatures.[106] By late June, the number had ballooned to 15 million.[107]

As the protests scheduled for June 30 drew nearer, and the Muslim Brotherhood began to call for its own counter-protests, fears of violence intensified.[108] On June 23, Defense Minister Sīsī declared that the army would intervene to prevent civil war, and called on all political forces to come to an agreement, saying, "We have one week's time in which to achieve much."[109] On June 26, as crowds began to assemble in Tahrir Square, Morsi made a defiant speech, in which, according to one commentator, he "proceeded to place the blame for Egypt's current political and economic problems on all the traditional culprits: the media, the judiciary, the secular opposition, and the former Mubarak regime, and its supporters."[110] The speech did little to assuage the president's opponents.

On June 30, millions poured into squares throughout Egypt. Tamarud claimed that, all told, 33 million Egyptians took to the streets.[111] Though the reality was almost certainly more modest, the New York Times reported that "the scale of the demonstrations [...] appeared to exceed even the massive street protests in the heady final days of the uprising that overthrew President Hosni Mubarak in 2011."[112] On July 1, the military released a statement giving the president forty-eight hours to "meet the demands of the people," which it claimed it had heard with "the utmost respect and attention," and threatened to set forth its own roadmap for Egypt's future if Morsi did not comply.[113] On July 2, Morsi responded by telling Egyptians that the revolution was about to be stolen from them, warning that "the symbols of the old regime wish to return."[114] Though Morsi's supporters had begun to stage their own mass protest near the Rabʿa al-ʿAdawiya mosque in Naṣr city in northeast Cairo, the military made no indication that it was prepared to withdraw its ultimatum.[115] On July 3, al-Sisi—surrounded by some of the country's most prominent political and religious leaders—announced that Egypt's first democratically elected president had "failed to meet and conform to the demands of the people," and had been removed from office.[116] As if to preempt accusations that it had seized power for itself, the military replaced Morsi, not with a general, but with the president of the Supreme Constitutional Court, ʿAdlī Manṣūr, who would govern until presidential elections could be held. The 2012 constitution was suspended, and a new constituent assembly of fifty figures (and only two Islamists) was appointed to draw up a new national charter. Though the new constitution was eventually ratified in a public referendum, and a new president was eventually elected less than a year after Morsi's overthrow, it is safe to say—without passing judgment on Egypt's current institutions—that the country's first democratic experiment had ended. It remains to be seen whether what replaced it is a new attempt at democracy or a reversion to authoritarianism.

Tunisia

A Rump Regime Tries to Hold On

When both Tunisia's and Egypt's long-reigning presidents resigned within one month of each other, observers might have been forgiven for concluding that the country that launched the Arab protests and the region's most populous nation were on similar trajectories. In each country, broad opposition coalitions that encompassed labor unions, left-leaning but generally unaligned youth groups, established opposition parties, and Islamists overcame domestic security apparatuses and ruling parties. In both countries, teetering autocrats turned in desperation to their professional militaries—forces distinct from the police and security forces operated by the interior ministries—and in each case, the military declined to use force to rescue the regime (see Bellin 2004; 2012). Bereft of the means of suppression, in both Egypt and Tunisia, autocrats were left with no choice but to step down.

Here the similarities end, however.[117] In Egypt, as we have seen, the military seized power and suspended the constitution. In Tunisia, in contrast, the military returned to the barracks and everyone (initially) looked to the constitution to figure out what to do next. In the immediate aftermath of Ben Ali's departure, his prime minister, Ghannouchi, took to the airwaves to declare that he was now the interim president.[118] The prime minister claimed that his move was mandated by article 56 of the constitution, which stipulated that the president's powers could be delegated to the prime minister in case of his temporary incapacity. Others, however, argued that Ben Ali's departure was not temporary, but permanent, and therefore triggered a different constitutional provision (article 57), which empowered the speaker of parliament to take over until new presidential elections could be held.[119] The Constitutional Council (the judicial body responsible for adjudicating constitutional matters)[120] concurred with this latter interpretation, and on January 15—one day after Ben Ali's departure—Ghannouchi stepped aside in favor of the speaker of the parliament, Fouad Mebazaa.[121]

The protesters who had compelled Ben Ali's resignation did not take to the streets in order for either his prime minister or the speaker of his parliament to replace him, however. The exiled Islamist leader Rachid Ghannouchi (no relation to the then-prime minister) reportedly called on "all the [Tunisian] people to carry on picketing and protesting until declaration that this regime has fallen."[122] In an attempt to assuage dissenters, Prime Minister Ghannouchi named several members of the country's formal opposition parties to his new cabinet: Ahmad Najib al-Chebbi of the Progressive Democratic Party was appointed minister of development, the health ministry went to the Union of Freedom and Labor's Mustafa Ben Jaafar, and Ahmad Ibrahim of the Communist-offshoot Ettajdid party was named minister of higher education.[123] The prime minister also appointed a young online activist who had been jailed during the uprising against Ben Ali, Slim Amamou, to the post of minister of state for youth and sport.[124] However, the government's continued reliance on members of Ben Ali's ruling party did not escape notice. Moncef Marzouki, leader of the opposition party Congress for the Republic (al-Muʾtamar min ajl al-Jumhuriyya), declared on his return from twenty years in exile that the new government was illegitimate: "They have to leave. They don't represent anything. [...] It is the continuation of the dictatorship."[125] In an interview with the *Financial Times*, Ennahdha's Ghannouchi concurred, declaring that "the faces we see are the same faces of the old regime with some new faces from the official opposition."[126]

As protesters by the thousands called for the exclusion of members of the former Ben Ali regime from the new government, both President Mebezaa and Prime Minister Ghanouchi resigned their memberships in Ben Ali's political party, the RCD, on January 18, 2011.[127] The move was widely viewed as cosmetic. The following week, thousands in Sīdī Būzīd, the impoverished inland province that had sparked the revolution against Ben Ali, participated in a "march of freedom" (masīrat al-ḥurriya) to call for the dissolution of what they called Mohamed Ghannouchi's "counter-revolutionary government," declaring "we will not be silent until we achieve our goals and we will not give the traitors the chance to reorganize themselves in order to put us once again under their feet."[128] The marchers convened on the Qaṣba Square in Tunis, where the prime minister's office is located (Zemni 2014: 5).[129] On January 27, the prime minister appeared to respond to the protesters' demands by announcing a cabinet reshuffle, but this too proved insufficient for the opposition.[130] For instance, on January 30, Ennahdha leader Rachid Ghannouchi (who had just returned from exile) told an interviewer that "The Tunisian street can't be appeased with small and half-hearted gestures. [...] Until now the Tunisian elites have failed to reflect the people's will, namely to construct a democratic regime without the RCD apparatus."[131]

Inclusion of Civil Society in Transitional Governance

On February 15, 2011, twenty-eight opposition and civil society groups—including the Ennahdha movement, the Tunisian General Labor Union (UGTT), the Tunisian Communist Workers Party (Ḥizb al-ʿUmmāl al-Shīyūʿī al-Tūnisī), the Tunisian Judges Association (Jamʿiyyat al-Quḍāh an-Tūnisiyīn), the Tunisian Journalists' Syndicate (al-Niqāba al-Waṭaniyya lil-Ṣaḥafiyīn al-Tūnisiyīn), the National Lawyers' Association (al-Hayʾa al-Waṭaniiya lil-Muḥāmīn), and the Tunisian Association for Combatting Torture (al-Jamʿiyya al-Tūnissiya limuqāwamat al-taʿdhīb)—joined together to form the National Council to Protect the Revolution (al-Majlis al-Waṭanī li-Ḥimāyat al-Thawra).[132] The Council called on the interim president to grant it the power to issue new laws, cancel old ones, monitor the work of the government, and "take initiatives required by the transitional situation in all areas, especially the judiciary and the media."[133] Not all opposition parties supported this call, however. The leftist Ettajdid movement, for example, declared that the committee lacked the popular mandate to claim such sweeping powers.[134] Still, the new Council's goal of seizing control of government from the remnants of the old regime enjoyed broad popular support.

On February 20, protesters again took to the streets to demand fundamental change. These protests, labeled Qaṣba II (the moniker Qaṣba I is used to refer to the January 23 sit-in that compelled Prime Minister Ghannouchi's first cabinet reshuffle on January 27), called for the prime minister's resignation, the excision of all remnants of Ben Ali's regime from the country's government, and the election of a constituent assembly to write a new constitution.[135] A week later, Prime Minister Ghannouchi tendered his resignation.[136] His replacement was an eighty-four-year old politician named Beji Caid

Essebsi, who had served as foreign minister under Ḥabib Bourguiba, and later as speaker of the parliament under Ben Ali—chosen, according to President Mebezaa, "out of concern for the interests of Tunisia and to guarantee the continuity of the state and all its institutions."[137] In a March 4 press conference, the new prime minister expressed his concern for "the restoration of the prestige of the state that has largely been undermined in [the] recent period, [and] establishment of security in all provinces and institutions, because the country is about to collapse."[138] However, lest this sound like an intention to resurrect the Ben Ali regime, Essebsi also noted that his priorities included, "complete severance with the former regime and suspension of the 1959 constitution"—two key demands of the protesters.[139]

The appointment of a former RCD apparatchik, no matter how respected a statesman and how earnest his declarations of fealty to the revolution, was unlikely to alleviate fears of a return of the *ancien régime*. Ennahdha leader Rached Ghannouchi reportedly complained that Essebsi was just "dusted off and brought out of the archives" of Bourguiba and Ben Ali.[140] What the opposition wanted was a role in determining the course of the country's transition. This was to come in March of 2011. Though, as the Tunisian scholar Asmāʿ Nuwayra has written, the expansive demands of the National Council to Protect the Revolution were not met, its members were invited to join the government-appointed Higher Committee for Political Reform (al-Lajna al-ʿUlyā lil-Iṣlāḥ al-Siyāsī).[141] This was a body of legal experts, headed by the scholar al-ʿAyāḍ Bin ʿāshūr and established as part of Prime Minister Ghannouchi's first cabinet, tasked with "total and complete political reforms in all areas and institutions and laws, including the constitution."[142] Negotiations ultimately resulted in the merging of Bin ʿAshūr's committee with the National Council to Protect the Revolution into a new body called the High Commission for the Fulfillment of Revolutionary Goals, Political Reform, and Democratic Transition (al-Hayʿa al-ʿUlyā li-Taḥqīq Ahdāf al-Thawra wa al-Iṣlāḥ al-Siyāsī wa al-Intiqāl al-Dīmuqrāṭī, henceforth abbreviated HCFRG). This new entity included representatives of political parties, civil society groups, families of martyrs in the revolution against Ben Ali, and each of the country's twenty-four *wilāyāt* or governorates, among others.[143] According to the February 18, 2011 presidential decree establishing the new HCFRG, the new institution's mandate included: "studying legislative texts related to political organization and proposing reforms to ensure the achievement of the objectives of the revolution as they relate to the democratic process." The body was also empowered to "provide its opinion in coordination with the prime minister regarding the work of the government."[144]

Though the HCFRG's mandate was relatively limited, it soon became a pillar of the country's interim government, akin to a *de facto* legislature (Pickard 2011: 638).[145] As Bin ʿāshūr later testified, with the establishment of the HCFRG he found himself having gone "from being the head of a committee of legal scholars not exceeding 20 people to being the head of a parliament or something like a parliament," which eventually grew to 155 members "from the far right to the far left."[146] One of the HCFRG's first decisions was to abandon the political timetable mandated by the 1959 constitution.[147] As noted earlier, article 57 of that charter mandated that new presidential elections be held between forty-five and sixty days of a sitting president's incapacitation. On March 4, after consulting with the commission, interim president Fouad Mebazzaa announced that a new constitution would be drafted by a constituent assembly to be elected later that summer (although the election would ultimately take place in October 2011).[148] On March 23, 2011, this decision was enshrined in presidential decree number 14 of 2011, which also dissolved the country's existing legislature (which had been elected in 2009) and vested interim executive and legislative authority in the president until the new constituent assembly could be elected (at which time these authorities would pass to that body).[149]

The dismantling of the institutions of the Ben Ali regime also extended to the former ruling party, the Democratic Constitutional Rally (*al-Tajammuʿ al-Distūrī al-Dīmuqrāṭī*, or RCD after its French name). The party had already suffered a crippling blow shortly after the former president's escape to Saudi Arabia, as a string of senior party officials and government ministers resigned their memberships.[150] Scarcely three weeks later, on February 6, 2011, the interior ministry suspended the RCD and shuttered its offices.[151] On March 9, 2011, a court of the first instance ruled on a complaint brought before it by the interior ministry, which argued for "the dissolution of the RCD and the confiscation of its assets inside the country and outside of it, which have been obtained through theft of the people's money."[152] The court concurred, ordering the party dissolved and its assets seized.[153] The ruling was upheld on appeal later that month.[154] On April 11, the HCFRG went a step further and proposed a law that would have banned members of the former ruling party from participating in politics for twenty-three years—equivalent to Ben Ali's tenure in office.[155] However, Prime Minister Essebsi criticized the provision, declaring that banning RCD members would "lead to an imbalance in the political arena."[156] Instead, the government issued a modified version of the law, reducing the period of exclusion to only ten years, on the grounds that "there were officials from the RCD who were [also] victims of oppression by the previous regime."[157]

By simultaneously declaring his intention to dismantle the Ben Ali regime while also appearing to limit the scope of revolutionary change, Essebsi was attempting what the Tunisian scholar Hamadi Redissi labeled "the trick of both placating the impatient and not alarming those who want nothing to change."[158] In order to assuage the former, who lamented the continued presence of Ben Ali loyalists in the cabinet, Essebsi announced the formation of a new technocratic government shorn of these figures.[159] Meanwhile, the interior ministry announced the dissolution of the hated State Security Administration as well as "any shape or form of political police" out of respect for citizens' "freedoms and civil rights" and in order to achieve "democracy, freedom, and dignity."[160]

In April 2011, as the planned date for constituent assembly elections approached, the HCFRG (which, recall, was empowered by the February 18, 2011 presidential decree to propose laws regarding elections) took the unprecedented (for the Arab world) step of establishing an independent, non-governmental commission to oversee the coming elections.[161] The new High Independent Authority for Elections (al-hay'a al-'ulyā al-mustaqilla lil-intikhābāt, abbreviated ISIE after its French acronym) was to include sixteen members, all to be chosen by the HCFRG: three were to be judges chosen from among six candidates nominated by Tunisian judicial bodies and associations, three were to be selected from among six candidates nominated by the national bar association; one member was to be a notary ('adūl) selected from two candidates nominated by the national association of notaries; one was to be a bailiff ('adūl munafadh) selected from two candidates nominated by the national bailiffs association; one member was to be selected from two candidates nominated by national accountants' association; one member was to be selected from two candidates nominated by the journalists' syndicate; two members representing civil society in the domain of human rights were to be selected from among a list of individuals nominated by various human rights' associations; one member was to represent Tunisians abroad; another was to be a specialist in communications; and two were to be university professors (the law did not specify the nominating bodies for these last four members, merely saying that they would be selected from "among the list of nominees submitted to the commission)."[162] The new electoral commission was to be responsible for drawing up the electoral districts (in consultation with the interim government and the HCFRG), determining the eligibility of voters and candidates, guaranteeing the fairness of the electoral process, counting ballots, and deciding electoral disputes—functions that had previously resided in the ministry of the interior.[163]

From Cooperation to Competition

If the Tunisian narrative until this point is of a unified coalition of oppositionists acting in concert to pry power from the guardians of the state, fissures in this coalition began to appear as elections for the constituent assembly drew nearer. The critical issue was the timing of those elections. Although the elections were originally scheduled for July 24 2011, in May the ISIE proposed postponing them until October 16, arguing that there was simply not enough time to meet the administrative, financial, and technical requirements of organizing a free and fair election.[164] Some have interpreted the delay "as a way of countering the unfair advantage that the Islamists seemed to have over other parties."[165] For their part, Ennahdha opposed the delay, declaring in a June 1, 2011 press release that the ISIE's decision was "unilateral and unjustified."[166] Ennahdha leader Ghannouchi reportedly told Prime Minister Essebsi, that the ISIE was "overstepping its authorities and violating the consensus that is the only foundation for legitimacy in the country after the suspension of the [1959] constitution."[167] Nūr al-Dīn al-Buḥayrī, Ennahdha's official spokesman, reportedly cast doubt on the "technical and logistical reasons the [ISIE] gave for delaying elections," saying "it appears that there are entities that do not want to go to elections."[168] The head of the HCFRG, al-ʿAyāḍ Bin ʿāshūr, reportedly rejected accusations that the rationale for the delay was political, saying, "We can have elections in two weeks, but they will be like those of the past, without any meaning or credibility."[169] Ennahdha withdrew from the HCFRG in protest.[170]

However, it was not just Ennahdha that objected to the new timetable. Moncef Marzouki, head of the Congress for the Republic (which would also eventually pull out of the HCFRG), declared that the delay in the elections "does not serve the country, and will lead to a delay in the return of legitimacy to the state and consequently to a delay in solving the most urgent problems."[171] A spokesman for the leftist Ettajdid movement (which was then at the center of a newly formed coalition of secular parties) explained that the movement "has confirmed a number of times its commitment to the date of July 24 for the elections to the constituent assembly," and argued that instead of delaying elections, the ISIE should "call on the interim government to quickly put at its disposal all of the tools necessary to overcome the difficulties that have caused it to propose a postponement" in the first place.[172] Similarly, Ahmed Najib el-Chebbi of the Progressive Democratic Party explained that, although delayed elections might "serve narrow partisan interests," only a quick move to elected government would fill the "vacuum of authority, the constitutional vacuum, the unstable security situation, and the explosion in the demands of the society."[173] Even the Essebsi government seemed lukewarm. On May 18, the prime minister reportedly declared that "from our first day after forming the new government, we have said over and over again that these elections will take place on July 24."[174] However, Essebsi later appeared to backtrack, saying that elections would be delayed if the ISIE felt there was a compelling rationale for doing so.[175] The *New York Times* subsequently reported that Essebsi "was able to persuade the public and the parties to accept a postponement in the election for technical reasons."[176]

While most of Tunisia's larger parties and the transitional government were uneasy with the ISIE's decision to delay elections, the move was welcomed by the country's smaller parties. For example, Khaled Traouli of the Democratic Reform Meeting Movement (Ḥarakat al-Liqāʾ al-ʾIṣlāḥī al-Dīmuqrāṭī) explained that he supported the delay because it would afford small parties like his own more time to prepare for the country's first democratic election.[177] A more powerful argument was made by the Communist Workers Party, which welcomed the delay and rejected the framing of the antagonists as "those who hold to the date of July 24 'in service of the interests of the people and the nation' on one side, and those who want to delay [the election] 'in service of narrow partisan interests' on the other."[178] Instead, the party declared that "the true disagreement is not about the date [of the election] in itself, but about the nature and content of those elections. It is between those want it to be free and democratic and clean [...] and those who think of nothing but getting to the throne, even if this requires accepting elections that don't fulfill the conditions necessary to provide citizens with free democratic choice."[179]

Ultimately, the ISIE's decision carried the day, and elections were scheduled for October 23, 2011.[180] The elections were to be held according to a system of closed list proportional representation.[181] Seats were to be allocated according to the largest remainders formula, with no national threshold, a measure widely recognized to advantage smaller political parties.[182]

By June 2011, eighty-one political parties had been formally registered.[183] Foremost among these were Rachid Ghannouchi's Ennahdha Movement Party, which was widely tipped to perform well. According to Shadi Hamid, "caught up in a groundswell of support and Islamic sentiment, and with Tunisians hoping for a fundamental break from the old, secular regime, Ennahda found itself by far the most popular, best organized political party in the country."[184] Also important were two parties described as "centre-left": Moncef Marzouki's Congress for the Republic (al-Muʾtamar min ajl al-Jumhūriya), and the Democratic Forum for Labor and Liberties (al-Takatul al-Dīmqrāṭī min ajl al-ʿamal wa al-ḥuriyyāt, commonly called Ettakatol).[185] According to the scholars Khadija Mohsen-Finan and Malika Zeghal, these three parties—Ennahdha, the CPR, and Ettakatol "built their structures and ideas on a position of dissent against the previous regime."[186] Another important party was the Progressive Democratic Party of Ahmed Chebbi and Maya Jribi, which was established in 1983 as the Socialist Progressive Rally, and which had established itself as a principal opposition party during Ben Ali's reign.[187]

Though the former ruling party had by this time been dissolved, several parties emerged from its ruins to contest the upcoming elections. The most important of these was al-Mubādara al-Waṭaniyya (the National Initiative), founded by Kamel Morjane, Ben Ali's last minister of foreign affairs (and before that, his minister of defense). Another major RCD offshoot was al-Waṭan (Homeland), founded by Ahmed Friaa and Mohamed Jegham, two former ministers of the interior under Ben Ali.[188] Other RCD offshoots reportedly included Justice and Liberty (Ḥizb al-ʿAdālah wa al-Ḥurriya), founded by attorney and RCD member Suhayl al-Ṣālḥī, and the Independence for the Sake of Freedom (al-Istiqlāl min ajl al-ḥurriya), founded by a judge named Nabīl al-Qarjī.[189] According to one Tunisian observer, these RCD-descendant parties were expected to "present a united force [...] possessing know-how and experience with the tactics of the former regime."[190] By one account, the number of RCD offshoots exceeded forty, and many had coalesced into an electoral alliance called the "Republican Concord" (al-Ta'āluf al-Jumhūrī).[191]

As the parties headed toward elections to the constituent assembly, disagreement arose among the country's political forces over how long the body should serve and what precisely its powers should be. The March 2011 decree that served essentially as the country's interim constitution was nonspecific on these issues, stating only that the new constituent assembly would determine the structure of public authority (article 18).[192] In September 2011, a group of approximately fifty secular and leftist parties—including the PDP—proposed that the new assembly's term be limited to six months, after which it would become an oversight body supervising the work of the interim government for another six months until parliamentary and presidential elections could be held.[193] They called on the interim government to put these provisions to the public in a referendum to be conducted along with the constituent assembly election.[194] Ennahdha, the CPR, and several other parties, calling themselves the "October 23rd coalition," rejected any attempt to limit the incoming assembly's sovereignty as "a conspiracy against the revolution."[195] In fact, Moncef Marzouki of the CPR had argued that the new constituent assembly needed at least three years to complete its work, during which it would appoint a new president, form a government, and appoint a committee to prepare the constitution.[196]

This disagreement was not merely technical. According to many observers, some non-Islamists feared that Ennahdha was poised to capture a majority in the assembly, and therefore these non-Islamists wanted to limit both the assembly's term and its mandate, lest it prove the gateway to Islamist dominion.[197] As the secretary general of the Communist Workers Party—which opposed the referendum—put it, "Those who call for conducting a referendum are afraid of the Ennahda Movement."[198]

In order to break the impasse, the head of the HCFRG, Bin ʿāshūr, convened a dialogue of eleven political parties represented on the commission. On September 15, 2011 the parties signed a "declaration of transitional path," which represented a compromise of sorts.

This pact stated that the new constituent assembly's term "must not exceed one year at the most," (thus addressing the concerns of those who worried that the assembly would rule indefinitely), but also stated the assembly "would determine the new structure of public authority and would elect a new president" (thus fulfilling the demand of Ennahdha and its allies for the assembly to enjoy relatively unfettered power).[199] According to Bin ʿāshūr, the document did not have the force of law, but the signatories were "morally bound" by it.[200]

As if to demonstrate to non-Islamists what was at stake in the coming election, in early October, Islamist protesters attacked the offices of a television channel that had broadcast a film they deemed blasphemous for its depiction of God.[201] Shortly thereafter, the head of the television station was charged by the public prosecutor with "defaming Islam."[202] Many feared that the airing of the film would actually play into Ennahdha's hands by generating in voters' minds an impression that Islam was under threat and that they should therefore vote for parties that would defend it.[203] As one leftist activist put it, "it was nothing but free publicity for an Islamist party and since Ennahda is the only one that fits that description, people sought to relieve their conscience by believing in it."[204] PDP head Maya Jribi declared that "Tunisians will not be fooled by those who use religion to influence people."[205]

The results of the election confirmed the fears of those who believed that Islamists were on the rise, but also reflected the diversity of the Tunisian political landscape. Whereas in Egypt's elections, Islamists would win two-thirds of the vote, in Tunisia, it was non-Islamist parties that captured a majority. Table 4.2 details the results of Tunisia's constituent assembly election, held on October 23, 2011. The Islamist Ennahda party was the single largest party in parliament, with 37% of the ballots cast. But more Tunisians voted against the Islamists than for them. Marzouki's Congress for the Republic received almost 9% of the vote. In third place was an electoral list called The Popular Petition (al-ʿAriḍa al-Shaʿbiyya), headed by a businessman from Sīdī Būzīd named Moahmed Hechmi Hamdi, who campaigned on a mix of Islamism and populism.[206] The leftist

Table 4.2. Results of Tunisian Constituent Assembly Election, October 23, 2011

	Vote	%	Seats	%
Renaissance Movement (Ennahdha)	1,501,320	37.0	89	41.0
Congress for the Republic	353,041	8.7	29	13.4
The Popular Petition for Freedom. Justice and Development (al-ʿArīḍa al-Shaʿbiya)	273,362	6.7	26	9.6
Democratic Forum for Liberties and Labor (Ettakatol)	284,989	7.0	20	7.4
Progressive Democratic Party	159,826	3.9	16	5.9
Initiative Party	129,120	3.2	5	1.8
Modern Democratic Pole	113,005	2.8	5	1.8
Tunisian Horizons Party	76,488	1.9	4	1.5
The Revolutionary Option (The Tunisian Communist Workers' Party)	63,652	1.6	3	0.3
Peoples' Movement	30,500	0.7	2	0.1
Movement of Socialist Democrats	22,830	0.6	2	0.1
Free Patriotic Union	51,665	1.3	1	
Democratic Patriots Movement	33,419	0.8	1	
Magharibi Liberal Party	19,201	0.5	1	
Social Democratic Nation Party	15,534	0.4	1	
New Constitutional Party	15,448	0.4	1	
Social Struggle Party	9978	0.2	1	
Justice and Equality Party	7621	0.2	1	
Party of the Cultural Unionist Nation	5581	0.1	1	
Independent Lists	62,293	1.5	8	3.7
Unrepresented lists	1,290,293	31.8	0	
Total	4,053,148		217	

Source: <http://www.tunisia-live.net/2011/11/14/tunisian-election-final-results-tables>, accessed June 6, 2014.

movement Ettakatol, known for its opposition to Ben Ali, came in fourth place with approximately 7%. For all the fear of a resurgent RCD, the ruling-party's alleged descendants did poorly. The principal RCD-offshoot, the Initiative Party (*ḤizHb al-Mubādara*), came in fifth place with a little over 3% of the vote. In sixth place was a secularist alliance formed by the Ettajdid party called the Democratic Modernist Pole (*al-Quṭb al-Dīmqrāṭī al-Ḥadāthī*) with less than 3%. Another alleged RCD offshoot, Tunisia Horizon (*'āfāq Tūnis*) polled less than 2%.[207] The top ten parties in that first election were rounded out by two leftist parties—the Tunisian Communist Workers Party, with 1.6% of the vote, and the People's Movement (Ḥarakat al-Shaʿb) founded in March 2011 by a Nasserist politican named Muḥammad Brāhmī.[208]

Erecting the New Republic

The election of the constituent assembly signaled a definitive break with the Ben Ali regime. The interim government headed by President Mebezzaa and Prime Minister Essebsi, which in many ways was continuous with the previous administration and which derived its legitimacy from the now-suspended 1959 constitution, was finally to be replaced by a government legitimized by the elected constituent assembly. In the run-up to the assembly's first meeting, it was reported that Ennahdha, the CPR, and the left-wing Ettakatol Party had worked out a power-sharing agreement in which Ennahdha would form the cabinet, the CPR would get the presidency, and Ettakatol would fill the chairmanship of the constituent assembly.[209] In the assembly's first session, held on November 22, the secretary general of Ettakatol, Mustapha Ben Jaafar was elected chairman (raʾīs al-majlis) with 145 votes out of 217; his two elected vice presidents were Meherzia Labidi, a leading woman member of Ennahdha, and Larbi Abid of the CPR.[210] On December 13, 2011, the assembly elected CPR founder Moncef Marzouki to the presidency of the republic (153 votes), replacing interim president Fouad Mebezza.[211] The next day, Marzouki appointed Ennahdha's Secretary General, Hamadi Jebali prime minister and charged him with forming the new government.[212] Jebali's cabinet was approved by the constituent assembly in a vote of confidence on December 24, replacing the cabinet of interim prime minister Beji Caid Essebsi.[213] Tunisia's government was now completely controlled by former oppositionists to the Ben Ali regime.

In keeping with the power-sharing agreement among Ennahdha, the CPR, and Ettakatol, Jebali's cabinet was made up of these three parties.[214] The lion's share of ministries went to Ennahdha, including the all-important ministries of interior and foreign affairs.[215]

Ettakatol was granted the ministries of finance, tourism, education, and social affairs, while the CPR took control of the ministry of training and employment, the ministry of women's affairs, and the ministry of state property and real estate.[216] The ministries of youth and sports, the environment, culture, defense, and religious affairs were held by nominal political independents.[217] As if to signal that Tunisia's transition was complete, in April 2012, the constituent assembly passed legislation dissolving the HCFRG.[218]

Though the constituent assembly had now generated the executive and legislative branches of Tunisia's government, its main purpose was to write the country's new constitution. This began in February 2012. The assembly formed six 22-member committees, each responsible for a principal component of the constitution.[219] The first committee would work on the preamble, basic principles, and procedures for amendment (al-tawṭiʾa wa al-mabādiʾ al-asāsiyya wa taʿdīl al-dustūr); the second committee would address rights and freedoms (al-ḥuqūq wa al-ḥuriyāt); the third committee would address the "legislative and executive and the relationship between them" (al-sulṭa al-tashrīʿīya wa al_sulṭa al-tanfīdhiya wa al-ʿilāqa baynahumā); the fourth committee would address the criminal, administrative, financial, and constitutional courts (al-qaḍāʾ al-ʿadʿlī wa ʾidārī wa al-mālī wa al-dustūrī); the fifth committee would address so-called "constitiutional commissions" (al-hayʾāt al-dustūriya) such as an independent electoral commission, a commission for human rights, and a commission for anti-corruption;[220] and a sixth committee would be in charge of local and regional governance (al-jamāʿāt al-ʿumūmiyya wa al-jihawiyya wa al-maḥaliyya).[221]

The makeup of each committee reflected the partisan breakdown of the assembly at large: Ennahdha would appoint nine members of each committee; its coalition allies the CPR and Ettakatol would appoint three and two members respectively; the Democratic Bloc (al-Kutla al-Dimqrāṭiyya), a thirty-member parliamentary coalition composed of the PDP, the Democratic Modernist Pole, and Tunisia Horizon (*ʾāfāq Tūnis),* would appoint three members; two members would be appointed by the Liberty and Democracy Bloc

(Kutlat al-Ḥurriya wa al-Dīmqrāṭiyya) a thirteen-member coalition of independents; the Popular Petition (al-ʿArīḍa al-Shaʿbiya) and a twelve-member coalition of independents calling themselves Liberty and Dignity Bloc (Kutlat al-Ḥurriya wa al-Karāma) would each get one member; and one member would be drawn from unaffiliated independent members of the assembly.[222]

As noted earlier, prior to the election, political parties had disagreed over how long the constituent assembly should remain in place. Ennahdha and its allies resisted putting an expiration date on the country's first democratically elected body, while the PDP and other left-leaning and liberal parties worried that without one, the constituent assembly could govern without end. Though this disagreement had been ostensibly settled in the September 2011 "Declaration of the Transitional Process" brokered by the head of the HCFRG, in which the parties that were part of the HCFRG agreed to a tenure of twelve months, this proved difficult to enforce. In December 2011, Ennahdha and its coalition partners rejected an attempt within the assembly to impose a timeline on the body or otherwise restrict its powers.[223]

The procedural disagreements were matched by substantive ones. As in Egypt, one of the key issues was the role of Islamic jurisprudence in the making of the country's laws. Ennahdha had assured its liberal counterparts that it did not intend to introduce a constitutional article declaring shariʿa to be the principal source of legislation (as in Egypt), and would instead content itself with language merely identifying Islam as the religion of the state.[224] However, the party faced dissent on its right flank. On March 25, 2012, it was reported that "thousands of Tunisian Islamists took to the streets [...] to step up their demands for the creation of an Islamic state."[225] Later that year, the fears of secularists were further stoked by a video in which Ennahdha leader Ghannouchi allegedly mocked those afraid of the application of sharia and indicating a long-term plan for the Islamization of the state.[226] Ghannouchi reportedly also referred to Ennahdha's rivals as "enemies of Islam," and in June 2012 called for protests against an art exhibit that violated conservative sensibilities.[227] These and other actions helped chip away at any comity that might have existed between Islamists and their ideological adversaries in the early months of Ben Ali's departure.

Another key sticking point between Islamists and their rivals was whether Tunisia would be a presidential or parliamentary system. Islamists stated a clear preference for the latter.[228] In November 2011, Ghannouchi had declared his desire to "change the political system from a presidential one in which power is concentrated in one person, the president, to a parliamentary one in which power resides with the people. We want to bring power from on high down to the people, represented in parliament."[229] In August 2012, President Marzouki complained that "our brothers in Ennahda seek to control all administrative and political branches of the state." Under a pure parliamentary system, Marzouki said, "a party that earns a majority democratically gets to control both the executive and legislative powers, which will bring this country centuries of dictatorship, not democracy."[230] Though Marzouki, as sitting president, clearly had an institutional interest in the preservation of his office, other non-Islamist politicians echoed his reasoning. Fadhel Moussa, a member of the constituent assembly for the Democratic Modernist Pole, argued that the country needed a president "with the same legitimacy as parliament [...] so that he can effectively arbitrate disputes and guarantee the interests of the people."[231] It was difficult to read this demand for a separation of powers as driven by anything other than a fear of an Islamist monopoly over government.

Aside from substantive disagreements, parties outside the ruling coalition of Ennahdha, CPR, and Ettakatol expressed frustration with their inability to influence policy. As one member of the Tunisia Horizon party told a reporter:

> Decisions are not made by the whole Constituent Assembly, quite on the contrary, I don't know a single time the Constituent Assembly was consulted for a decision including this one. The three party leaders come together and agree on a policy that they know they have the votes for and then they use the Constituent Assembly to confirm their decision after it's been made.[232]

Challenging Islamists, Preserving Institutions

Throughout 2012, parties in opposition continued to press for the constituent assembly to complete its work and thus clear the way for new elections. Unsurprisingly, they also began to strike new alliances in order to increase their chances of toppling Ennahdha as the largest party in any new legislature. January 2012 saw a merger of the PDP, Tunisia Horizon (*'āfāq Tūnis*), and the Republican Party (al-Ḥizb al-Jumhūrī) into a new party (also called the Republican Party).[233] Similarly, in April, the Ettajdid Movement, the Tunisian Labor Party (Ḥizb al-ʿAmal al-Tūnisī), and independents associated with the Democratic Modernist Pole joined together to form a party called the Social Democratic Path (al-Masār al-Dīmqrāṭī al-Ijtimāʿī).[234] And in June, former interim prime minister Essebsi made a bid to gather some of the shards of the dismantled RCD under a new party named the Call of Tunisia Movement (Ḥarakat Nidāʾ Tūnis).[235] Noting Ennahdha's "hegemony," Essebsi declared that "the political scene is unbalanced, and the parties are unfortunately unable to unite themselves sufficiently."[236]

In January 2013, these three entities—the Republican Party, the Social Democratic Path, and the Call of Tunisia joined together in a new alliance called the Union for the Sake of Tunisia *(al-Ittiḥād min ajl Tūnis)* with the intention of jointly contesting the next legislative elections.[237] Maya Jribi, formerly of the PDP and then secretary general of the Republican Party, explained that "we're a party that tries to unify democratic forces to defeat Ennahda so we can eventually reach democracy."[238]

The impetus for the non-Islamists coalescence came not just from the makeup of parliament or the slow progress of constitution-writing, but from what they viewed as alarming developments on the Tunisian street. In October 2012, an activist for the Call of Tunisia Movement was killed in Tatouine during a clash with members of a vigilante group known as the National League for the Protection of the Revolution (al-Rābiṭat al-waṭaniyya li-ḥimāyat al-thawra), described as "an unofficial networks that supports the ruling Ennahdha party and aims to root out members of the former regime."[239] On

February 6, 2013, a leftist politician and opponent of Ennahdha named Chokri Belaid was felled by an assassin's bullet.[240] Protesters demanded the resignation of the government, in particular the minister of the interior, who had presided over what many came to view as the state's increasing tolerance of violent Islamist elements.[241]

In order to pacify widespread anger at Ennahdha, Prime Minister Jebali announced that he would form a new, national unity government to include members from outside the Islamist camp.[242] However, in declaring that "all the ministries will be independent, including the interior, justice and foreign affairs ministries," Jebali stoked the ire of members of his own party.[243] As it became clear that the Ennahdha bloc in parliament would not endorse Jebali's plan, the CPR pulled out of the governing coalition.[244] The prime minister resigned shortly thereafter, and Ennahdha stalwart (and former interior minister) Ali Larayedh was tasked with forming a new government.[245] In order to defuse tensions, Larayedh's new cabinet contained only eight Ennahdha ministers (out of twenty-four), and the key ministries of national defense, interior, justice, and foreign affairs were assigned to non-partisans.[246]

Tensions continued throughout the spring of 2013. A draft constitution, released in April 2013, aroused the ire of many with its subtle concessions to Islamism.[247] For example, the preamble to the draft constitution spoke of "enhancing [Tunisia's] cultural and civilizational affiliation to the Arab Islamic nation," and article 42 seemed to accept Islamist notions of female subordination, referring to the "different responsibilities" of men and women.[248] The international organization Human Rights Watch criticized the draft for "a provision recognizing universal human rights only insofar as they comport with 'cultural specificities of the Tunisia people,'" for failing "to affirm freedom of thought and conscience," and for what it called an "overly broad formulation of permissible limitations to freedom of expression."[249] Republican Party secretary general Jribi reportedly accused Ennahdha of trying to "push a constitution that [was] not backed by a general consensus of the deputies."[250] In order to soothe tensions, President Moncef Marzouki called a national dialogue in April, but this was boycotted by the UGTT (Tunisia's main labor union), a group of leftist parties (including Mūḥamad Brāhmī's People's Movement) calling themselves the Popular Front (al-Jabha al-Shaʿbiyya), and Essebsi's Call of Tunisia (the latter after initially saying it would participate in the talks).[251]

The need for political reconciliation and dialogue intensified in July 2013, when Muḥammad Brāhmī (of the People's Movement Party and the Popular Front coalition) was assassinated, allegedly with the same weapon that had killed Chokri Belaid six months prior.[252] As Brāhmī's funeral gave way to mass protests, dozens of opposition party members withdrew from the constituent assembly in protest.[253] Though some in the opposition, most notably the Call of Tunisia, demanded the dissolution of the assembly, the rest of the opposition merely reiterated its desire to see the constituent assembly complete its work and move to new elections. For example, on July 8, 2013, Maya Jribi of the Republican Party declared that the "dissolution of the National Constituent Assembly would lead directly to civil war," and that, while Ennahda should be rejected, rejections should take place at the ballot box.[254] Similarly, though the UGTT called a general strike for July 26, 2013 and demanded a government of national unity, it denied that it sought to disband the constituent assembly.[255] The head of the union, Ḥussayn ʿAbbāsī, explained "We propose maintaining the Constituent Assembly but with a time-frame to speed up completion of its work."[256] In late July, the two largest opposition party coalitions, the Union for the Sake of Tunisia and the Popular Front united around these demands in a National Salvation Front (al-Jabha al-Waṭaniyya lil-Inqādh).[257]

That month, in order to defuse the crisis, the UGTT, the Tunisian Union of Industry and Trade (al-Ittiḥād al-Tūnisī lil-ṣināʿa wa al-tijāra), the Tunisian Lawyers Union (Ittiḥad al-Muḥāmīn al-Tūnisiyīn), and the Tunisian League for the Defense of Human Rights (al-Rābiṭa al-Tūnisiyya lil-difāʿ ʿan ḥuqūq al-insān)—collectively called the quartet (al-lajna al-rubāʿiyya) sponsored their own national dialogue process.[258] Though the dialogue proceeded in fits and starts throughout the rest of that year, by October it had resulted in an agreement by Ennahdha to hand over the reins of government to a fully technocratic cabinet and to complete the drafting of the new constitution.[259] Prime Minister Larayedh resigned on January 9, 2014, handing over government to a non-partisan engineer and former minister of industry, Mehdi Jomaa.[260] And on January 26, Tunisia's new constitution was adopted by the constituent assembly by a vote of 200 to 12, with 4 abstentions.[261] Parliamentary elections were held without incident in October 2014, and by the time this book appears, presidential elections will have followed.[262] Early parliamentary election returns indicate that the secular Call of Tunisia (Nidāʿ Tūnis) has replaced Ennahdha as the largest party in the legislature, and will likely assume the reigns of government. Though Tunisia's democracy is far from consolidated, it has so far managed to pull off a feat that eluded Egyptians: taming Islamist power while preserving fledgling democratic institutions.

Yemen

A Top-Down Transition

One early indication of the likely trajectory of Yemen's transition was the fate of its dictator, Ali Abdullah Saleh, who resigned on November 23, 2011 after almost a year of protest and conflict.[263] Unlike Tunisia's Ben Ali, Egypt's Mubarak, or Libya's Qaddafi—who were, respectively, spirited out of the country, thrown into jail, and killed—Saleh suffered no such fate. In fact, when his vice president, ʿAbd Rabuh Manṣūr Hādī, was inaugurated as his successor, it was in a ceremony organized by Saleh's ruling party, (*al-Muʾtamar al-Shaʿbī al-ʿām*), and attended by the former dictator.[264] The absence of any kind of show of reckoning for the man that Yemenis ostensibly rose up to oust was a powerful signal of the boundedness of change in that country. As we saw in the cases of Egypt and Tunisia, satraps of the *ancien régime* always try to control the pace and scope of post-breakdown reform. But it is in Yemen that the attempt has proved most successful.

The modest nature of the Yemeni transition is in part encoded in the Gulf Cooperation Council-brokered transition plan signed by Saleh on November 23, 2011. This scheme was explicitly gradualist—calling for presidential elections within ninety days of Saleh's resignation, followed by a period of two years to write a new constitution, only after which would the country hold multi-party parliamentary and presidential elections.[265] Thus, unlike in Egypt or Tunisia, where constitutions put in place during the authoritarian period were quickly abrogated or transcended, Yemen has continued to consider the country's Saleh-era constitution to be the country's basic law.[266] Similarly, while legislatures elected under Mubarak and Ben Ali were dissolved, Yemen's 301-member Council of Representatives (*Majlis al-Nuwwāb*), which had been elected in April 2003, would continue its legislative functions. (On January 21, 2012, it granted Saleh and all of his deputies immunity from prosecution.[267]) Similarly, Saleh's ruling party—which controls more than two-thirds of the seats in the legislature, and of which Saleh is still president—has eluded the fate of Mubarak's NDP or Ben Ali's RCD, both of which were dismantled in the aftermath of the dictator's overthrow.[268] In fact, Yemen is the only Arab Spring country in which the dictator's resignation was not followed by multi-candidate or multi-party elections. President Hādī, elected in February 2012, ran unopposed as a "consensus candidate" endorsed by the GPC-dominated parliament.[269] It is worth noting that Hādī is the party's secretary general. (A year into the transition, the legislative opposition would boycott several parliamentary sessions, claiming that the GPC was violating the spirit of the GCC initiative by using its legislative majority to pass legislation instead of seeking consensus—indicating that the Arab Spring had not undone the fundamental mechanics of Yemen's dominant party system).[270]

In Egypt or Tunisia, old regimes found themselves bargaining with opposition actors who nonetheless remained committed to maintenance of the polity. The Yemeni regime, in contrast, contends with what we might call "loyal" and "disloyal" oppositions (Schedler 1996).[271] The latter is primarily composed of two distinct separatist movements in the north and south, as well as a violent al-Qaeda affiliated group called Guardians of Islamic Law (Anṣār al-Sharīʿa) headquartered in the southern governorate of Abyān.[272] The northern separatists—called Houthis after the name of their deceased leader, a Shiite tribal and religious figure named Ḥussayn Badr-al-Dīn al-Ḥūthī—have been engaged in a civil war with the

Yemeni state since 2004, which by one estimate has displaced more than 300,000 Yemenis.[273] In the south, the Yemeni state faces the so-called Southern Movement (al-Ḥirāk al-Junūbī), described as a loose confederation of groups with aims ranging from obtaining a greater share of the country's wealth at one end, to the restoration of the pre-unification state of the People's Democratic Republic of Yemen at the other.[274]

The principal loyal opposition actor in Yemen's ongoing transition is a coalition of parties called the Joint Meeting Parties (*Aḥzāb al-Liqāʾ al-Mushtarak*).[275] Founded in 2002, the JMP includes an Islamist party called the Yemeni Congregation for Reform (*al-Tajammuʿ al-Yamanī lil-Iṣlāḥ*), as well as the Yemeni Socialist Party (*al-Ḥizb al-Yamanī al-Ishtirākī*) which had governed southern Yemen until reunification in 1990, and three smaller parties, the Party of Truth (*Ḥizb al-Ḥaqq*), described as a party of "moderate Islamists" from the Shiite, Zaidi sect, the Popular Nasserist Unity Organization (*al-Tanẓīm al-Waḥdawī al-Shaʿbī al-Nāṣirī*), and the Union of Popular Forces (Browers 2007: 39). Together, the JMP controls fifty-seven seats in the parliament, or 19% of the total.[276] The majority of those seats (forty-six) belong to the Islamist Iṣlāḥ, which is ideologically related to the Egyptian Muslim Brotherhood, although not as cohesive as its Egyptian counterpart (Philbrick Yadav 2012). In fact, according to Schwedler (2006: 72) Iṣlāḥ is "far from a cohesive party at all," and is best described as "a confederation party of northern tribal leaders and a mix of Islamist groups" (p. 60). In addition to the JMP, the loyal opposition has included a vibrant if informally organized youth movement, rooted in part in a students' organization of one of the country's main institutions of higher learning, Sanaa University.[277]

To the extent that Saleh's ouster did result in greater inclusion of the opposition, it was of the loyal opposition. In accordance with the GCC plan, in December 2011, then acting-president Hadi appointed a so-called "National Unity" government intended to incorporate Saleh's opponents.[278] The new prime minister, Muḥammad Sālim Bāsindwa—who had served as minister of foreign affairs under Saleh (from 1993 to 1994), and had once been a member of the ruling party before resigning in 2000—was the nominee of the JMP.[279] Basindwa had also been the chief opposition member in a previous attempt at dialogue between the ruling party and the JMP in 2010.[280] But, while Basindwa's cabinet was reportedly "equally divided" between members of the opposition and Saleh's ruling GPC, several key Saleh ministers remained in place.[281] Most notably, the minister of foreign affairs, Abu Bakr Abdullah al-Qirbī, appointed in 2001, and the minister of defense, Muḥammad Nāṣir Aḥmad, appointed in 2006, held onto their jobs.[282] And though the interior ministry was assigned to a member of the Islamist Islah party named ʿAbd al-Qādir Qaḥṭān, it is worth noting that he was not a civilian, but rather a general in the Yemeni police force.[283]

Finally, another important set of actors in Yemen's transition are the country's tribes. Most Yemenis belong to one of two large agglomerations of tribes (often referred to as "tribal confederations"), the Ḥāshid and the smaller Bakīl.[284] Though former president Saleh hails from a branch of the Ḥāshid, that confederation is headed by a much larger and more powerful clan called al-Aḥmar.[285] The Aḥmar have long been an important pillar of support for the president. A 2005 US State Department cable on the problem of succession in Yemen pointed out that Saleh was "unable to govern the country single-handedly due to tribal and regional fractures," and was thus forced to rely on "a 'power sharing' arrangement with the country's leading tribal and military figures," especially those from the Ahmar.[286] According to the Yemen scholar Gregory Johnsen, the Aḥmar supported Saleh in both of his presidential elections.[287] However, this coalition began to fracture toward the end of Saleh's tenure. Sādiq al-Aḥmar, head of both the Aḥmar and the Hashid since 2007, emerged as a major opponent of the president and one of the principal organizers of the protests that eventually brought him low.[288] Sadiq al-Ahmar's brothers, too, had occupied major positions within the ruling GPC, although they broke with it during the revolution.[289] In May 2011, the conflict between the Saleh and the Ahmar turned bloody, as forces loyal to each side engaged in street battles for control of the capital.[290] The al-Ahmar are generally considered close to the Islamist Iṣlāḥ party, which was actually founded in 1990 by Abdullah al-Ahmar, who was then head of the clan and the leader of the Ḥāshid tribal confederation.[291]

The importance of tribe in Yemen has also meant that, unlike in Egypt, where the military has been a powerful force in shaping the post-breakdown period, Yemen's military has not been as important a corporate actor in that country's transition. According to the Yemeni scholar Khaled Fattah, "Yemen's military is heavily tribalized," which prevents it from acting in concert.[292] During the revolution, the military cleaved between those loyal to the president (particularly the presidential and republican guards), and those loyal to the Aḥmar clan (Noueihed and Warren 2012: 203).[293]

Demanding Change

Shortly after the appointment of the national unity government, youth groups began to chafe against what they considered the persistence of Saleh's clique in key positions of power, particularly in the armed forces. [294] On March 9, protesters took to the streets on a day they dubbed "Friday of restructuring the army" (Jumʿat iʿādat haykalat al-jaysh), calling on the regime to bring "justice to those who spilled the blood of the youth in the squares [of Yemen] and to try the killers from among the leftovers of the Saleh regime who still occupy high positions in the army."[295] After more than a month of protest, President Hadi appeared to respond to these demands in April with a series of decrees removing key Saleh loyalists from power.[296] Saleh's half brother, Muḥammad Ṣāliḥ al-Aḥmar, was removed as chief of the Air Force and Air Defense; his nephew, Ṭāriq Muḥammad ʿAbd Allāh Ṣāliḥ, was removed as commander of the presidential guards; and several other military commanders thought loyal to Saleh were reassigned.[297]

Though these moves were praised by the opposition, they were met with defiance by Saleh and his cronies. According to one report, in a meeting with a delegation of GPC youth in his home in April, Saleh declared that "no one is able to turn the GPC into a corpse."[298] Recalling the provisions of the GPC agreement that guarantee immunity for him and his family, he also warned that "if the Gulf initiative is not implemented, then no one must submit himself to death or liquidation."[299] Both Saleh's half brother and nephew initially refused to accept Hadi's order, and the ousted air force chief al-Aḥmar allegedly mounted an attack on the Sanaa Airport that prompted its closure.[300] However, after two weeks of defiance, both men eventually relented.[301] Al-Aḥmar's change of heart reportedly came after his half brother, the former president, personally asked him to step down.[302] In July, protesters turned their attentions to two other Saleh stalwarts—the president's son Aḥmad ʿAlī ʿAbdullāh, head of the Republican Guard, and his nephew, Yaḥyā Muḥammad ʿAbd Allāh Ṣāliḥ, chief of staff of the central security forces.[303] In December 2012, President Hadi purged these men as well.[304]

Despite the changes to the military, most of Yemen's structures have remained the same. For example, the body responsible for overseeing elections in Yemen, al-Lajna al-ʿUlyā lil-Intikhābāt wa al-Istiftāʾ (The Supreme Commission for Elections and Referendum, SCER), was established in 1992, and continues to function. Though new members were named in 2012, none of these represents civil society or political parties. Instead, all nine members are judges appointed by the president, as they were in Saleh's day.[305] Thus, as in Egypt, and unlike in Tunisia, oppositionists in Yemen have not managed to secure a place at the table when it comes to electoral governance.

An Inconclusive National Dialogue

One of the major provisions of the GCC-sponsored transition plan was the establishment of a Comprehensive Conference for National Dialogue (*Muʾtamar al-Ḥiwār al-Waṭanī al-Shāmil,* abbreviated NDC) including "all forces and political actors, including youth, the Southern movement, the Houthis, other political parties, civil society representatives, and women."[306] On March 18, 2013—more than two years after the start of the movement to oust Saleh—this process finally began, with more than 565 representatives from across the Yemeni political and social landscapes.[307] The largest bloc of seats (112) was accorded to the GPC, followed by the Southern Movement (85 seats), al-Iṣlāḥ (50 seats), various youth organizations (40 seats), the Yemeni Socialist Party (al-Ḥizb al-Ishtirākī al-Yamanī) which had been the ruling party in the south prior to unification (37 seats), and the Houthis (35 seats), with 64 seats going to various parties in the legislature, and another 62 to "tribal dignitaries, religious leaders, and representatives of religious minorities."[308]

Though praised by one writer as "the most inclusive political negotiation process in Yemen's modern history," the NDC was not without controversy.[309] Tawakol Karman, a civil society leader and Nobel Laureate, boycotted the dialogue, claiming that several key revolutionary demands—such as the exclusion of former president Saleh from political life—had not been met, although she later relented.[310] Similarly, according to one report, "most revolutionary youth [had] chosen to boycott the conference" as well, in protest at what was called an "organized marginalization policy practiced by Yemeni authorities."[311] Moreover, given the resilience of incumbents in post-Saleh Yemen, the Yemeni writer Samaʿa al-Hamdani has raised fears that "the outcome has been predetermined or that the solutions will be determined by the old ruling elites."[312]

Originally scheduled to end on September 18, 2013, the NDC was ultimately extended until January 25, 2014 when, according to one report, "participants failed to reach consensus on major issues, including what to do about unrest in the South and Saʿda [governorate], and Yemen's future form of government."[313] When the conference finally did conclude, it did so, as one observer put it, "without firm plans for a future government beyond general ideas of federalized parliamentary rule."[314]

Thus, almost three years after Saleh's ouster, Yemen has yet to complete its democratic transition. Though the end of the National Dialogue was originally supposed to be followed by presidential elections (scheduled for February 2014), these were postponed until 2015.[315] As of this writing, the drafting of the country's new constitution has only just commenced.[316] On March 8, 2014, President Hadi appointed a seventeen-member committee to draft the document; however, the makeup of this committee has been criticized for being unrepresentative of the full array of the country's political and social forces.[317] At the outset the President gave the committee a near open ended timetable, according to the Yemeni journalist Ahraf al-Falahi, the president has given the committee a near open-ended timetable, in a move "widely interpreted as a way for [him] to extend Yemen's interim period and remain in power longer than originally envisioned."[318] But after significant Houthi protests in the streets of Sana'a in September 2014 Hadi urged the CDC to finish up their drafting as quickly as possible.

But President Hadi's leisurely approach to the crafting of Yemen's democratic institutions may be the least of that country's problems. Jamal Ben Omar, the United Nations envoy to Yemen, reportedly explained that the postponement of elections was necessary because of "obstruction" from politicians close to ousted president Saleh.[319] According to one report, former president Saleh not only retains considerable influence in Yemen, he has also been accused by opponents of "orchestrating the attacks on oil and power lines that scourge Yemen's economy and cast an aura of incompetence on the new administration."[320] In April 2013, the *Yemen Post* reported that Saleh's nephew, Yaḥyā Muḥammad Ṣāliḥ (who, as we saw, had been removed by President Hadi as chief of central security in December 2012), claimed that "his family and party will be back in power in 2014."[321] Given how little has changed in that country since Saleh's ouster, this statement does not seem so outlandish.

Libya

A Fractured Landscape

In Chapter 3, we argued that the Libyan "transition" was unique among the four cases of regime breakdown in that it would not have been possible without foreign intervention. As a rentier state, the Libyan regime had significant resources available to repress or buy off dissenters. Unlike Egypt, Tunisia, or even Yemen (the most similar country in terms of tribal structure), Libyan civil society was weak, and political parties nonexistent. As Lisa Anderson (2011) has written, "Libya has no system of political alliances, network of economic associations, or national organizations of any kind." Political parties had been banned in Libya since the monarchy (Van de Walle 1998: 47), and Qaddafi muted civil society through a series of policies intended to "keep citizens atomized and their demands disaggregated" (Brownlee 2002: 46; see also Anderson 1995: 229). It is thus unlikely that the Libyan revolution would have succeeded had it not been for a sustained bombing campaign by the world's most powerful military alliance.

However, given that Libya's transition is the only one among our four cases of regime breakdown to have taken place against a backdrop of total defeat of the prior regime, it is the one that—on paper at least—most quickly fulfilled the institutional components of Linz and Stepan's (1996) conditions for a "completed" democratic transition. A mere 262 days elapsed between Qaddafi's capture on October 20, 2011 and the completion of the country's first democratic election on July 7, 2012. In contrast, Tunisia took 283 days from Ben Ali's departure to the completion of its constituent assembly election. But the most cursory examination of the Libyan transition reveals that a focus on formal institutions—elections, constituent assemblies, and constitution-writing processes—is insufficient when trying to assess the trajectory of a country's post-breakdown moment. In Libya, the struggle over the post-Qaddafi order is one that increasingly is taking place on the battlefield, something that risks rendering the country's formal political institutions irrelevant.

In Egypt, Tunisia, and Yemen, the narrative we have offered is one in which oppositionists bargain with elites of the prior regime over the shape of the new order, with the latter generally trying to limit the scope of reform. In Libya, however, Qaddafi left precious few satraps to play this role. According to Vandewalle (2012: 3), the Qaddafi regime "attempted to avoid the burdens of extending the mechanisms of the modern state," articulating a vision of "statelessness that was carefully wrapped in a cloak of nostalgia for earlier times when family and tribe provided solidarity, equity, and egalitarianism." Thus, where the Egyptian and Tunisian militaries were cohesive and professional, Qaddafi "repeatedly reshaped the army and prevented the emergence of a professional military by creating a popular army and popular militias" (Vandewalle 128). After high-ranking military officers from the Warfalla and Qadhādhfa tribes-both regime allies—attempted a mutiny in 1993, Qaddafi increased his reliance on mercenaries, particularly from sub-Saharan Africa (Joffe 2011). According to Joffe (2011), Qaddafi's main instrument of internal repression, the "Deterrent Batallion (32nd brigade)" largely consisted of such foreign fighters. Libya is thus the classic example of what Ayubi (1995: xi) called a "fierce" state—able to mete out swift violence to its opponents—but not a "strong" one: "lamentably feeble when it [came] to collecting taxes, winning wars, or forging a really 'hegemonic' power block or an ideology that [could] carry the state beyond the coercive." Once NATO airstrikes defeated the Qaddafi regime, there was little of it left to contest for power in the aftermath.

Given the endemic weakness of both state and society under Qaddafi, political competition after his departure has largely been dominated by cleavages of region and tribe. As Noueihed and Warren (2012: 192) put it, "the main fault lines in any new Libyan political structure will relate more to the distribution of power and money between different regions." The most important regional cleavage is between the oil-rich eastern province of Cyrenaica (known in Arabic as Barqa), the more populous coastal province of Tripolitania (Ṭrāblus), and the south-western province of Fezzan (Fazzān).[322] As we saw in Chapter 3, the uprising largely began in the east. One of the principal complaints of inhabitants of Cyrenaica was that Qaddhafi spent the region's oil revenues in other parts of the country, leaving cities like the regional capital of Beghazi without basic services.[323] It is thus not surprising that the so-called February 17 Coalition (ʾIʾtilāf 17 Fibrāyir), a group of "lawyers, professionals, and youth activists" that was one of the nuclei of the revolution against Qaddafi, got its start in Benghazi.[324]

Regional cleavages overlap with tribal ones. By some estimates, there are as many as 140 tribes in Libya, and one scholar has testified that "it will be the tribal system that will hold the balance of power [in Libya] rather than the military."[325] The country's largest tribe, the Warfalla, is estimated at around one million members and is centered in the southwestern Fezzan province.[326] The tribe had once been allied with Qaddafi, but according to one report, "many leading Warfalla figures around the country had defected to the rebels early on in the uprising—including for example Mahmoud Jibril, the wartime rebel prime minister."[327] Another large tribe, the Maqārḥa, was reportedly supportive of Qaddafi, and one of its leading members, Colonel ʿAbdullāh al-Sanūsī was a Qaddafi "loyalist and [the] powerful head of the Libyan internal and external security organizations."[328] Also loyal was Qaddafi's own tribe, the Qadhādhfa.[329] According to one report, the Qadhādhfa "ma[de] up the core eements of some of the 'regime protection units,'" although some peripheral branches of the tribe are thought to have defected during the rebellion.[330] The anchor of the anti-Qaddafi opposition was the Miṣrāta tribe (described as "the largest and most influential tribe in eastern Libya").[331] According to the scholar Bassam Tibi (2013, 143), the Miṣrāta were "characterized by a deep enmity toward the Warfalla that has existed since the Italian occupation of the country in the last century, when a leader of the Misrata was killed by some Warfalla warriors." Other eastern tribes that supported the uprising included the al-ʿAbaidāt, al-Burāʿṣa, and al-ʿAwāqīr.[332] However, despite frequent testimonies to the importance of tribal affiliations in determining Libya's future, the Libyan scholar Ali Ahmida has testified that, due to urbanization and increasing literacy "tribalism (exists) really just on the surface. It's now more about regional identities and dealing with the frustrations and consequences of what happened under the old regime."[333]

Though Qaddafi had deliberately kept civil society weak and had banned political parties, there was nonetheless an exiled opposition that would prove consequential once the dictator was overthrown. Foremost among them was the National Front for the Salvation of Libya (*al-Jabha al-Waṭaniya li-inqādh Lībyā*, NSFL), founded by former Qaddafi official Muḥammad al-Miqrīf in 1981 (Barger 1999: 64). According to Vandewalle, "the NSFL also had a military wing, the Salvation Forces, which, with French and US support, conducted a number of military actions against Qaddafi in the 1980s" (2012: 126). The NFSL's role in the Libyan uprising appears to have been limited, and its leader, al-Miqrīf, did not return to the country (from his exile in Atlanta, Georgia) until after Qaddafi was overthrown.[334] However, In May 2012, al-Miqrīf founded the National Front Party (*Ḥizb al-Jabha al-Waṭaniyya*) to contest the country's first legislative elections.[335]

Like Egypt, Tunisia, and Yemen, Libya also had an Islamist presence. The Muslim Brotherhood of Libya operated primarily in exile. According to the Libyan writer Abdel Sattar Hatita, (2011: 2) "the origins of the Muslim Brotherhood in Libya date back to the 1940s," but Qaddafi brutally suppressed the movement and dissolved it in 1973 (four years after he came to power). According to Joffe (1988: 629) Qaddafi ensured that "the Ikhwan was virtually eliminated from Libya. Those accused were imprisoned and often disappeared without trace after the late 1970s, while others were executed in public." By the 1980s, it had become, like the NFSL, primarily an opposition in exile (Pargeter 2009). In the latter years of the Qaddafi era the group had tried to "open channels with the regime in Tripoli [...] in the vain hope of being allowed some official presence in the country" (Pargeter 2009: 1042–1043). Nonetheless, in March 2012 the movement founded a political party, the Party of Justice and Construction (*Ḥizb al-ʿAdāla wa al-Bināʾ*).[336] The party's fate was momentarily thrown into doubt in April 2012 when the National Transitional Council issued a regulation banning parties based on religion; however, it was forced to withdraw this restriction shortly thereafter.[337]

More extreme than the Muslim Brotherhood was Libyan Islamic Fighting Group (*al-Jamāʿa al-Islāmiyya al-Muqātala bi-Lībyā*, LIFG), dedicated to overthrowing Qaddafi and establishing an Islamic emirate in Libya (Gambill 2005).[338] The group, which drew on Libyans who returned from fighting the Soviet presence in Afghanistan in the 1980s, was responsible for an almost-successful assassination attempt against Qaddafi in 1996.[339] According to researchers at the West Point Combatting Terrorism Center, the LIFG formally joined al-Qaida in, 2007.[340] After the revolution the head of the LIFG, ʿAbd al-Ḥakīm Balḥāj, founded the Nation Party (*Ḥizb al-Waṭan*) to contest the country's upcoming elections.[341]

A Blank Slate

When Qaddafi was killed, Libya already had a new government—in the eyes of the international community, at least—in the form of the National Transitional Council (al-Majlis al-Qaṭanī al-Intiqālī).[342] According to Ahmida (2011: 4), this was made up of a "combination of opposition forces that arose in the eastern region of the country" and "defectors and exile groups."[343] Perhaps reflecting its genesis, the leadership of the NTC was drawn from the east—the first president, Mustafa Abdul Jalil, was from the eastern coastal city of al-Bayḍā', and his deputy, Abdul Ḥāfiẓ Ghawqa was from Benghazi.[344] In March 2011, the NTC appointed Maḥmūd Jibrīl, a Warfalla born in Benghazi and a former technocrat under Qaddafi, to the "executive board," which was essentially equivalent to the post of prime minister.[345] In July 2011, the murder of General ʿAbd al-Fattāḥ Yūnis, described as "a former top Libyan commander who defected to the rebel side" generated dissension within the interim government as members of his ʿUbaidī tribe threatened to withdraw from the coalition.[346] The next month, Jibrīl's was tasked with forming a new cabinet, "in an effort by interest groups within the rebel movement, including homegrown leaders who helped start the uprising, to assert their power by sidelining leaders who had returned from exile and held key posts."[347]

In August 2011, the NTC promulgated an interim constitution (al-ʾIʿlān al-dustūrī) that laid out a roadmap for Libya's transition to multiparty democracy.[348] Article 30 stipulated that the NTC would continue to govern until the election of a 200-member General National Congress (al-Muʿtamar al-Waṭanī al-ʿām), which was "to take place within two hundred and forty days following the declaration of liberation."[349] Once the GNC was seated, it was to designate a prime minister and "choose a constitutive body for the formulation of a draft constitution [...] which shall present a draft constitution to the Congress within a period not exceeding sixty days following its first meeting."[350] The Congress would then have thirty days to approve the constitution and submit it to a national referendum, where it would require a two-thirds majority for passage.[351] After adoption of the new constitution, the GNC would then organize legislative elections (to take place within five months of the approval of the constitution), and which would be monitored by the judiciary, the United Nations, and "international and regional organizations."[352] The constitution also provided for a High National Commission on Elections (al-Mufawaḍiya al-Waṭaniyya al-ʿUlyā lil-Intikhābāt), which would be appointed by the NTC and made up of civilians.[353] Experts criticized the declaration for allocating insufficient time to the constitution drafting process, but lauded it for establishing an independent judiciary (article 32) and guaranteeing international oversight of elections (article 30).[354]

On October 23, 2011, three days after Qaddafi's death, NTC president Jalīl announced the country's liberation, starting the countdown to elections for the General National Congress.[355] The next day, Jibril—who had come under attack from Islamists as a "remnant of the old regime"—submitted his resignation and turned his attention to the upcoming contest.[356] In the runup to the election, which took place on July 7, 2012, 2.8 million of the country's 3.5 million eligible voters registered to cast ballots; more than 2,600 individuals registered to compete for the 120 constituency seats, and almost 400 parties competed for the 80 seats reserved for party lists.[357]

The National Forces Alliance (*Taḥāluf al-Quwā al-Waṭaniya*, or NFA), founded in February 2012 headed by Maḥmūd Jibrīl, won 48% of the vote and 39/80 party list seats.[358] The Muslim Brotherhood-aligned Justice and Construction Party won 10% of the vote and 17 party list seats. The Brotherhood performed particularly well in the East of the country, unsurprising given that the Libyan MB "originated in the [Eastern] region of Barqah" (Hattita 2011: 2) and that area of the country is described as "Libya's religious heartland" (Noueihed and Warren 2012: 177; see also Pargeter 2009: 1044). The National Front Party of former exiled opposition leader Muḥammad Al-Miqrīf won just 3 party list seats, and 18 smaller parties split the remaining 21 seats. Non-partisans with primarily tribal and local affiliations captured the majority of the 120 seats reserved for independents. However Lacher (2013) estimates that

National Force Alliance candidates won 25 of the "independent" seats, the Muslim Brotherhood's JCP won another 17, and the Salafi National front an extra 23 seats. Patterns of voting in the legislature for the prime minister in September 2012 provides further indication of the balance of parliament's factions. In the first round of balloting, Jibril (NFA) received the votes of 86 legislators (47%), while ʿAwaḍ Barāsi of the Brotherhood's Party of Justice and Construction won 41 votes (22%).[359] Assuming that all of the NFA's and MB's partisans voted for their respective prime ministerial candidates, this suggests that 47 of the 120 independents were NFA affiliates, and 24 were affiliates of the Brotherhood. We present the results of the election in Table 4.3.

As in Tunisia and Egypt, the role of Islam in public life was an important cleavage, albeit a muted one. Though the elections were billed as a success for the "secular" NFA, it is unlikely that the party's stance on political Islam was the party's main selling point.[360] NFA chief Jibrīl repeatedly rejected descriptions of his party as "secular" or "liberal."[361] In February 2012, he explained that his party believes that "the rulings (aḥkām) of sharīʿa are a principal source of legislation."[362] Similarly, the first article of the party's charter declares that "Islam is the religion of the society and its frame of reference and the adoption of the tolerant rulings and principles of Islamic jurisprudence are a principal source of legislation."[363] However, the fact that Jibrīl and the NFA refrained from declaring sharīʿa to be *the* (as opposed to *a*) principal source of legislation recalls debates in 1970s Egypt over the second article of their constitution, where Islamists successfully pushed to have the indefinite article replaced with the definite one.

The GNC came to be marked early on by competition between the NFA and the Islamist bloc. Though, as noted earlier, NFA chairman Jibril had earned the largest number of votes in the first round of balloting for the prime ministership, he was defeated in the second round by Musṭafā Abū Shāqūr, a former Rochester Institute of Technology engineering professor and political independent who had managed to garner the support of the Muslim Brotherhood.[364] When Abū Shāqūr was unable to secure GNC approval for his

Table 4.3. Results of Election for Libya's General National Congress, July 7, 2012

	PR Seats			Constituency Seats*		Total	
	Vote%	Seats	%	Seats	%	Seats	%
National Forces Alliance	48.1	39	48.7	25	20.8	64	32.0
Justice and Construction (MB)	10.3	17	21.2	17	14.2	34	17.0
National Front	4.1	3	3.7				
Salafi Aligned		2	2.5	23	19.2	27	*13.5*
Authenticity and Renewal		1	1.2				
Authenticity and Progress		1	1.2				
Wadi al-Hayah		2	2.5				
Union for Homeland	4.5	2	2.5				
National Centerist	4.0	2	2.5				
Libyan National Democratic		1	1.2				
The Message		1	1.2				
The Foundation		1	1.2				
Development and Welfare		1	1.2				
Nation and Prosperity		1	1.2				
Moderate Ummah Assembly		1	1.2				
Labaika National Party		1	1.2				
Wadi ash-Shati		1	1.2				
Centrist Youth Party		1	1.2				
Liberty and Development		1	1.2				
National Parties Alliance		1	1.2				
The Hope		1	1.2				
Wisdom		1	1.2				
Independents				55	45.8	55	27.5
Total		80		120			

*Partisan identifications for winners of constituency seats based on Lacher (2013).
Source: Libya High National Election Commission <http://www.hnec.ly/en/>.

proposed cabinet, he was replaced by Ali Zeidan, a former member of the National Front for the Salvation of Libya and a political ally of Jibril's.[365] Zeidan reportedly assumed a confrontational stance toward the Muslim Brotherhood: "strip[ing] Housing Secretary Ali Hussein al-Sharif, a Muslim Brotherhood figure, of a number of key powers," and "pass[ing] over a Muslim Brotherhood candidate for the post of religious affairs minister."[366] In October 2013, the prime minister declared that "The Muslim Brotherhood has been trying to undermine me for months."[367]

As we saw in both Egypt and Tunisia, Islamists championed laws that would exclude members of those countries' prior authoritarian regimes from participating in politics. This was also the case in Libya.[368] In June 2013, the GNC passed law 13 of 2013 on Political and Administrative Isolation, which banned twenty-two classes of people from "holding any public position."[369] Those excluded ranged from "anyone who served as the head of the interior and exterior security agencies, military intelligence, security brigades" to "anyone [who] served as an ambassador, secretary at any Public Office, held the position of a permanent representative of Libya at any International or Regional organization of any [type], [or] held the position of charge [d'affairs] or consul" to "anyone known for his/her constant praise and glorification of Gaddafi, his regime and his green book, whether through the media or through public talks."[370] According to the Libyan writer Mohamed Eljarh, passage of the law came as "the capital of Tripoli was effectively being taken over by armed supporters of the [political exclusion] law."[371] One of the first casualties of the new regulation was GNC chairman al-Miqrīf.[372] Though Miqrīf had spent 31 years in exile and was a co-founder of the National Front for the Salvation of Libya, he was forced to resign under the new law due to the fact that he had served as Qaddafi's ambassador to India for two years before breaking with the dictator in 1980.[373] The United Nations' special envoy for Libya declared that "many of the criteria for exclusion are arbitrary, far-reaching, at times vague, and are likely to violate the civil and political rights of large numbers of individuals."[374]

In September 2013, the GNC announced elections for the 60-member committee that would draft the country's new constitution.[375] Though the National Transitional Council's constitutional declaration of August 2011 had stated that this committee would be appointed by the GNC, one of the NTC's last acts was to amend the interim charter to specify that the constituent assembly would be elected, with 20 members from each of the country's three provinces.[376] The election, which took place on February 20, 2014, was marked by low turnout—according to one report, only 500,000 of Libya's 3.4 million eligible voters went to the polls.[377] According to reports, 13 seats remained vacant due to the disruption of the polling process, and the country's two non-Arab minorities—the Berber and Tuareg tribes—boycotted the process, claiming that it afforded them insufficient representation.[378] Islamist candidates reportedly performed poorly in the election.[379] Further suggestive of Islamists' limited presence on the committee was the committee's choice "liberal academic" and former leading member of the National Transitional Council, Ali al-Tarhouni, as its president in April 2014.[380]

Militia Politics

The role of militias in compelling the GNC to vote for the political isolation law underscores the precariousness of the Libyan state after Qaddafi's overthrow. A dramatic illustration of this fact came on September 11, 2012, when militants assaulted the United States mission office in Benghazi, Libya, killing four, including the American ambassador to Libya.[381] A further demonstration of the weakness of the Libyan state came in October 2013, when Prime Minister Zeidan was kidnapped briefly by a group of policemen calling themselves Gunmen of the Revolutionary Operations Room of Libya.[382] In December 2013, the GNC—which, according to the interim constitution would give way to a newly elected legislature in February 2014—voted to extend its mandate for an additional year, citing fears of a power vacuum in the country. [383] In February, an anti-Islamist Libyan general named Khalīfa Ḥiftar appeared on television and announced the suspension of the government and the dissolution of the GNC, but this claim was refuted by the prime minister, and the general proved either unable or unwilling to seize control of government facilities.[384]

In March 2014, amid a deteriorating security situation, the JCP orchestrated the collapse of Zeidan's government, bringing a vote of no-confidence against him for failing to retake oil terminals seized by Cyrenaican rebels.[385] Zeidan was replaced by his defense minister, Abdullah al-Thinnī, but the latter man resigned the post in April after an alleged militia assault on his family (although he declared that he would remain in office until a replacement was elected).[386] The JCP then nominated a forty-two-year-old businessman named Aḥmad Maʿtīq to take al-Thinnī's place, and his government won a vote of confidence on May 26, 2014.[387] However, opponents of the Brotherhood argued that the parliamentary vote for Maʿtīq failed to achieve the necessary quorum, and that al-Thinnī was consequently still the country's legitimate prime minister.[388] In June, the Libyan Supreme Court ruled that Maʿtīq's election had been illegal, forcing him to relinquish his office.[389]

As the legislature dickered over internal procedure, Ḥiftar's forces regrouped and launched "Operation Dignity" (ʿAmaliyat al-Karāma), attacking Islamist militants in Benghazi before laying siege to the GNC on May 18.[390] Claiming that he wished to "cleanse" Libya of Islamists, Ḥiftar declared that the "Muslim Brotherhood in Egypt is the driving force behind extremists arriving in Libya."[391] In an interview with a Saudi news agency (Okaz), Ḥiftar complained of Islamist dominance in the GNC, and declared that "everything the General National Congress does is a new disaster that not only continues Qaddafi's injustices but are worse than it. [...] Fundamentalists come from every corner to Libya, claiming to be supporters of Islam and Muslims [...] but the Islamic religion cannot become a means for cutting people's necks or assassinating them or kidnapping or terrorizing them."[392] However, the general once again did not seize the legislature, claiming only that "our operation is not a coup and we do not plan to seize power."[393]

As this book went to press, Libyans again went to the polls—this time to elect their chamber of deputies. Though the full results of that election are not yet available, preliminary reports indicate that only 630,000 of Libya's 3.4 million eligible voters went to the polls, only a slight uptick from the February constitutional assembly election, and a far cry from the 1.7 million who voted for the GNC in 2012.[394] Thus, while in August 2013 a group of insightful (if optimistic) analysts could write that "despite the ongoing violence, politics and elected institutions still matter" in Libya, the reality is that, almost a year later, the majority of Libyans seem to have concluded that elected institutions are but a sideshow.[395]

Conclusion: Distilling (Seemingly) Diverse Pathways

In this chapter, we have traced the transition process in each of our four cases of regime breakdown. Our aim here has been to identify where and how those processes diverged, with a view toward laying the groundwork for an explanation of that divergence in the next chapter. We focused on five features of the transition process that we believe are key markers of whether a transition is likely to culminate in democratic completion or authoritarian renewal. Those features are:

1. The role of oppositionists in interim governments.
2. The establishment of elected governments.
3. The role of oppositionists in determining and overseeing electoral process.
4. The de facto authority of the elected government over its territory.
5. The durability of the elected institutions in the face of non-electoral challenges.

Table 4.4 summarizes how each of our cases stacks up on each of these markers. As we can see, in Egypt, a democratic transition may have been initiated (and perhaps completed), but, was ultimately thwarted as elements of the Egyptian state intervened to abrogate the results of legitimate electoral processes. Though a new president was elected in May 2014, the cutting short of the previous president's term by force suggests that, at the very least, the Egyptian

Table 4.4. Features of the Transition Process in Four Cases of Regime Breakdown

	What Role Do Oppositionists Have in Interim Government?	Is Elected Government Established?	Do Oppositionists Have a Role in Determining Electoral Institutions?	Does the Elected Government Have *de facto* Authority?	Do Elected Institutions Hold?
Egypt	*Limited*. After Mubarak's overthrow, executive and legislative powers are claimed by the Supreme Council of Armed Forces	*Partially*. Parliamentary elections completed in January 2012. Abrogated in June 2012. Presidential elections completed in June 2012. Presidency claims legislative authority in August 2012	*Limited*. Electoral rules set by military-led interim government; oversight vested in judicial bodies	Yes.	*No*. June 2012 parliament dissolved by court order; military coup of July 3, 2013 brings end to democratically elected presidency
Tunisia	*Significant*. Though both legislative and executive power were claimed by the interim government that was headed by members of Ben Ali's ruling party, oppositionists claimed significant de facto (and later, de jure) power through the High Commission for the fulfillment of Revolutionary Goals	*Yes*. October 2011 elections to constituent assembly gave rise to democratically-legitimated legislature and executive	*Total*. High Authority for Elections (ISIE) constituted by oppositionist-dominated HCFRG	Yes.	*Yes*.

	What Role Do Oppositionists Have in Interim Government?	Is Elected Government Established?	Do Oppositionists Have a Role in Determining Electoral Institutions?	Does the Elected Government Have *de facto* Authority?	Do Elected Institutions Hold?
Yemen	*Limited*. After Saleh's overthrow, his vice president assumed the presidency, and the legislative power continues to be vested in the parliament elected in 2009. Oppositionists have been given a share of executive authority through ministerial portfolios	*No*. Though President Hadi was formally elected in February 2012, his elevation to the presidency was not the result of a multi-candidate election	*No*. Saleh-era structures for electoral oversight persist. Judiciary, not oppositionists, charged with electoral administration	Partially. Significant separatist challenges in north and south of country.	N/A
Libya	*Total*. Foreign-imposed regime change resulted in the total replacement of Qaddafi loyalists in government	*Yes*. July 2012 elections for the General National Congress give rise to democratically legitimated legislature and executive	*Yes*. National High Elections Commission a mix of judges, experts, and civil society representatives	Limited. Significant militia presence throughout the country; secessionist threat in the east.	*Yes*. Chamber of Deputies elected in June 2014 replaces General National Congress elected in July 2012

transition to democracy has been restarted, if not reversed entirely. In Yemen, as of this writing, it is difficult to see that a transition has even been initiated, as the power structures of the previous regime remain in place, and oppositionists—despite being allocated ministerial portfolios—are nonetheless subordinate to established elites. Only in Tunisia and Libya were oppositionists able to wrest a share of power from dictators, establish democratically elected institutions, and maintain those institutions. However, the inability of the Libyan government to establish what Max Weber considered the *sine qua non* of a modern state—the "monopoly over the legitimate use of physical force within a given territory"—underscores the insufficiency of institutional markers as indicators of a country's likelihood of establishing democracy.[396]

Having established variation in the Arab Spring's transitions, we now turn to explaining it. As we have done throughout this book, we ask whether post-breakdown successes and failures can be chalked up to contingent factors—such as the foresight of political actors and the fortuitousness of institutional choices—or were instead determined by deeper structures.

5

Why Breakdowns Did Not Always Produce Transitions

As we have seen in Chapter 4, oppositionists in Tunisia, Egypt, Yemen, and Libya may have all compelled their countries' dictators to leave office, but their fortunes in the aftermath of those watershed events could not have been more different. The most useful yardstick for assessing the ongoing transitions in the Arab world is whether they have been "completed" (Linz and Stepan 1996)—that is, whether they have resulted in a democratically elected government with de facto authority over the territory it ostensibly governs. Or, in the formulation offered by the scholars Bratton and Van de Walle (1997: 194), "A transition to democracy can be said to have occurred only when a regime has been installed on the basis of a competitive election, freely and fairly conducted within a matrix of civil liberties, with results accepted by all participants."

By this largely procedural definition, only Tunisia could be unambiguously said to have completed its transition by the time this volume went to press. In fact, Stepan (2012) points out that Tunisia's transition was completed in record time: once its constituent assembly was elected in October 2011 (a mere ten months after Ben Ali's resignation), the country had clearly achieved a government that was both legitimately-elected and possessed of the capacity to rule. Yemen represents the opposite outcome. More than three years after Saleh's departure, Yemen has yet to conduct multi-party or multi-candidate elections. Moreover, the limited role accorded to oppositionists in the country's interim governance suggests not only that the country has a long way to go to complete its transition, but that the trajectory of that transition is toward a renewed authoritarianism rather than a liberal democracy. As one analyst put it, "While Saleh's exit from office represents a major rupture in Yemeni political life, the future is best read in terms of the reassertion of pre-existing political dynamics, both domestic and international rather than in hopeful but unfounded expectations of democratic transformation."[1]

The other two cases of regime breakdown—Egypt and Libya—are more difficult to categorize. Does Egypt represent a completed transition that was then reversed by the military, or a transition that was never completed at all? As readers will recall, Egyptians freely elected a parliament in January 2012, but this body was dissolved by the country's Supreme Constitutional Court six months later, on the eve of Egypt's first free presidential election. When it appeared that the Muslim Brotherhood's Mohamed Morsi was poised to win that contest, the interim military government—the Supreme Council of the Armed Forces—issued a June 2012 "constitutional declaration" making itself the legislature to the soon-to-be democratically elected executive. This hybrid state of affairs—an elected president with a military "legislature"—persisted until August 2012, when Morsi—with the agreement of the army—arrogated legislative authority to himself. Only at that point could Egypt be said to have achieved a regime that was fully democratically constituted (inasmuch as both the legislature and the executive were elected). However, the fact that these two branches were vested in a single individual suggests that Egypt under Morsi met the standard of a "completed" transition in only the thinnest, most formalistic of senses.

The same can be said of Libya, albeit for different reasons. Though that country has completed not one but two democratic elections for parliamentary bodies (with fused executive and legislative powers), it is widely recognized that those parliaments have never truly governed that territory. According to the analyst Frederic Wehrey, Libya struggles with "the power and autonomy of the country's revolutionary armed groups (known in local parlance, depending on their size, as 'battalions,' 'brigades,' and 'companies') and the corresponding weakness of the official army and regular police."[2] Mieczystaw Boduszynski and Duncan Pickard testify to "the fatal weakness of [Libya's] central state institutions," most dramatically illustrated by the proliferation of "militias outside of state control."[3] As this book goes to press, reports from Libya indicate "intense fighting in Benghazi [...] and battles between rival militias in the capital Tripoli [that] have pushed the nation deeper into chaos."[4] As Linz and Stepan (2011: 27) have pointed out, "without a useable state there can be no safeguards for human rights, law and order, consolidated democracy, or effective governance" (see also Mansfield and Snyder 2007). That Libyan political elites have managed to hold elections thus seems almost irrelevant to any assessment of its democratic progress. In short, if both elected government and a functioning state are necessary for a completed transition, Libya has achieved only the former.

Figure 5.1 illustrates the divergent pathways taken by our four cases of regime breakdown. We are interested in two distinct outcomes—the first is transition *completion* (i.e., the establishment of elected and capable democratic regimes); the second is *maintenance* (i.e., the persistence of those regimes in the face of challenges). We code Tunisia and (more controversially) Egypt as completed transitions, since both at one point in their transition processes featured regimes that were both democratically elected (even if Egypt's came about through a flawed process that was ultimately reversed) and possessed of the capacity to govern. We code Yemen and Libya as incomplete—the former because of an absence of democratically elected government; the latter, despite many elections, due to pervasive state incapacity.

This chapter assesses some of the most prominent explanations for divergent outcomes in these two transition stages. We first explain why only Tunisia and Egypt *completed* a transition. This requires us to answer two questions: First, what explains variation in the occurrence of founding elections? And second, what determines whether a new regime would enjoy the requisite state capacity to actually administer the territory under its ostensible control?

The existing literature has generally answered the former question with reference to the relative power of oppositionists with respect to incumbents. That is, "founding elections" take place when oppositions are strong enough to force incumbents to conduct them. We concur with this literature, but try to explain the sources of opposition strength relative to their rivals. In the case of Libya, we argue, the strength of oppositionists was a function of international intervention on the opposition's behalf, but elsewhere we argue that opposition strength is a function of developmental factors long thought to influence the strength of civil society. This brings us to the second question, regarding variation in state capacity. We contend that the competence and reach of the states that oppositionists inherited from *ancién regimes* are functions of longue durée factors—rooted in geography, economic development, and even colonial history—that far precede the moments of revolutionary upheaval that mark the beginning of this study. Thus, we conclude that predictions of transition completion in the case of the Arab Spring could have been made with simple reference to the four countries' levels of economic development and measures of state effectiveness.

We then move from variation in *completion* to explaining divergence in transition *maintenance*. Honing in on Tunisia and Egypt, we ask why Islamists and secularists in the former managed to compromise over very real differences, while in Egypt their mutual intransigence provided a pretense for military intervention. The two most prominent explanations for this divergence are rooted in the actions and decisions of key political actors. On the one hand, it is argued that the preferences and capabilities of militaries were determinative: where armies long possessed political power, they were more likely to intervene to cut short democratic experiments (Bratton and Van De Walle 1997). On the other hand, it has been argued that the choices and decisions of political party leaders are what created the presence (or absence) of an opportunity for military intervention in the first place. Where Islamist and non-Islamist party leaders believed in the necessity of compromise (or were forced to do so by political circumstances), democratic institutions held.

Where they did not, or were overtaken by hubris, malice, or error, democratic institutions were abrogated. We shift the causal emphasis from actors and proximate causes to structures and distal ones. In particular, we locate the source of compromise in Tunisia and its absence in Egypt to economic and social structures that shaped political party leaders' electoral fortunes and thus their assessments of the *need* to reach across ideological lines and strike deals.

Ultimately, then, this chapter represents a contribution to the longstanding debate over the question of "sequencing" in democratic transitions. One strand of scholarship has argued that, as Huntington (1984: 211) put it, "the preferable overall process of development for a country is first to define its national identity, next to develop effective institutions of authority and then to expand political participation." In other words, in this view, democracy becomes possible only after certain developmental prerequisites have been met. An alternative strand of scholarship, emerging out of the study of so-called "third wave" (Huntington 1991) transitions in Latin America and elsewhere, has, as Bellin (2000: 175) puts it, "focused on the role of elites and leadership, the importance of political institutions, and the consequences of strategic choice for democratic reform." We come down solidly in the former camp. In this chapter, we demonstrate that close attention to the dynamics of transition processes in our four cases of regime breakdown demonstrate the limits of contingency and choice, and the importance of pre-existing structures in determining the ultimate dispositions of would-be democratic transitions.

Before proceeding, we note that the analytical challenge we faced in our explanation of protest success in Chapters 2 and 3—namely, the fact that we have multiple potential causal variables and few cases (i.e., what social scientists call "negative degrees of freedom")—becomes particularly acute when trying to explain the variation in outcomes in our four cases of breakdown. As the scholar James Fearon (1991: 172) has noted, "legitimate causal imputation cannot be made on the basis of negative degrees of freedom," a problem that in his view could be solved only by adding more cases or, more controversially, by using counterfactual thought experiments.

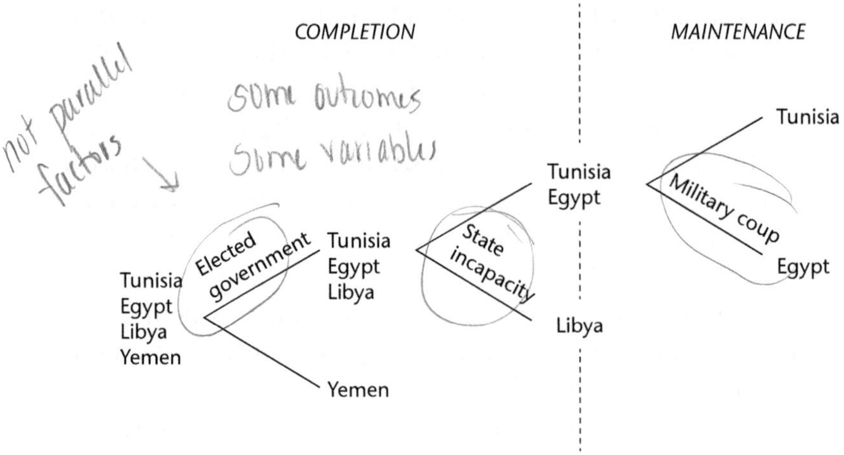

Figure 5.1. Transition Outcomes in Four Cases of Regime Breakdown

We deal with this problem in two ways. First, by situating our inquiry within the wider literature on democratic transitions, we implicitly compare the four Arab Spring transitions to those in Latin America, Eastern Europe, and elsewhere (on which that literature in based). Second, as in Chapter 3, we again turn to the method of "process tracing" (George and Bennett 2004)—defined by Bennett and Checkel (2014) as "the examination of intermediate steps in a process to make inferences about hypotheses on how that process took place and how it generated the outcome of interest." Each potential explanation for the varied outcomes in Tunisia, Egypt, Libya, and Yemen has observable implications in the form of "events that intercede between hypothesized causes and effects" (Bennett and Checkel 2014). When the intervening events expected under a particular theory are actually observed, this can be taken as evidence in support of that theory, just as their absence can be taken as evidence against it. Thus, even though we only have four "cases," each of these cases is a complex process that can be interrogated at multiple points in order to test the fit of alternative explanations.

This chapter proceeds as follows. First, we explain why only two of the four cases of regime breakdown have, as of the summer of 2014, yielded "completed" transitions. We argue that two factors—the strength of pre-existing state institutions, and the capacity of oppositionists and civic actors—were determinative. The former, we argue, is largely a historical legacy, while the latter is attributable to economic development. We then turn to the question of transition maintenance, asking why Tunisia's transition has so far held while Egypt's has collapsed. We explore two arguments: The first locates the source of divergence in differences in the two countries' histories of military intervention in politics. The second attributes it to differences in Tunisian and Egyptian political elites' belief in the need for compromise. We argue that, while both of these arguments capture important differences between the two cases, differences in the behaviors and beliefs of political actors have yet to be sufficiently explained. We contend that Tunisian party leaders' willingness to compromise (and the absence of such in Egypt), can be explained with reference to the configuration of the post-authoritarian party system in each country, which in turn can be endogenized to antecedent conditions of economic development and urbanization. Our argument thus validates a longstanding perspective that has emphasized the role of structure over agency in democratic transition and consolidation (Przeworski et al. 2000).

Completion: State and Society Strength after Regime Breakdown

As noted earlier, a completed transition is marked by two features, what Linz and Stepan (1996) call a "usable state," and the conduct of free and fair elections to choose the government that will run that state. Egypt and Tunisia featured both; Libya has had elections, but not much in the way of a state; and Yemen appears bereft of both: it has failed to conduct elections, and its long record of state weakness continues unchanged (and has perhaps even intensified) after Saleh's overthrow. In this section, we link variation in these two features to antecedent conditions.

The Capacity to Govern

In Chapter 2, we explored the distinction between "despotic" and "infrastructural" power (Mann 1984; see also Ayubi 1995). The former is the ability to mete out violence; the latter the ability to "reach into society" and enact policies. Though all Arab regimes were possessed of considerable despotic power, those that lacked sufficient material resources, or which lacked firmly cemented bonds between executives and agents of violence, experienced breakdowns in their ability to deploy that power in the face of popular challenges. Levels of infrastructural power enjoyed by Arab states—even within our four cases of regime breakdown—were even more varied. Figure 5.2 plots the World Bank's "state effectiveness" measure between 1995 and 2011 for Tunisia, Egypt, Yemen, and Libya. This measure, defined as the "quality of public services, the quality of the civil service and the degree of its independence from political pressures, the quality of policy formulation and implementation, and the credibility of the government's commitment to such

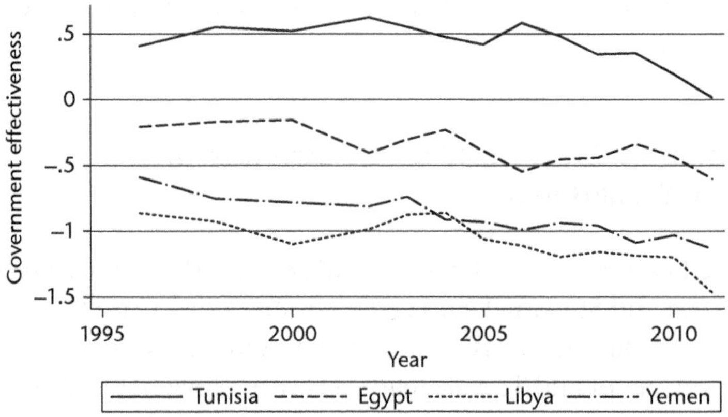

Figure 5.2. State Effectiveness in Four Cases of Regime Breakdown
Source: World Bank Governance Indicators.

policies," captures the construct of infrastructural power or state strength.[5] As we can see, Tunisia was deemed to possess the most effective state during the period (its 2012 score places it in the 56th percentile of all nations), followed by Egypt (25th percentile), then Yemen (9th percentile), with Libya at the bottom (5th percentile). It is thus easy to conclude that, inasmuch as stateness constitutes a definitional criterion of a completed transition, Libya never had a chance. Yemen exhibits a similar dearth of infrastructural power—wracked by a 1994 civil war and reeling from ongoing insurgencies in the north and south. All of which suggests that even if that country did manage to conduct a democratic election, it is highly unlikely that those whom the democratic process brought to power would actually be able to wield it.

But what accounts for this variance in state strength? As noted in Chapter 4, "Post-Breakdown Trajectories," Libya's chronically weak state is widely thought by scholars to be a function of Qaddafi's policy of "statelessness," which was designed to keep society fragmented and potential rivals at bay. Though the gifted student of Libya, Dirk Vandewalle (2012b), has declared that "a modern state has, against all odds, started to emerge" in Libya, the reality is that this process is not likely to be a speedy one. As Jaime Becker and Jack Goldstone (2005: 208) point out, "rapid state-building" is only possible "when a state can use a cadre of trained professional civil servants and military officers from the prior regime, when there is no sustained opposition to the new state from powerful autonomous elites, and where the state can secure financial resources to pay its officials and soldiers." Only one of these conditions—access to revenues—obtains in post-Qaddhafi Libya, and it appears to be a source of conflict among militias rather than a resource for potential state-builders.

Although the example of Libya demonstrates how the actions of the authoritarian state can certainly influence state capacity, the scholarly consensus has located the ultimate sources of state capacity in more distal causes. Tilly (1992) and Herbst (2000) have attributed the rise of the modern state to war-fighting, which requires leaders to hone their administrative and extractive apparatuses in order to generate the revenues needed for combat (see also Bates 2001). Roger Owen (2004) has pointed out that these processes have not operated in the Arab world, where modern states came about not through centuries of conflict, but at the whim of colonial powers as they carved up the former Ottoman Empire. "This gave many of the new states a somewhat artificial appearance," he writes evocatively, "with their new names, their new capitals, their lack of ethnic homogeneity and their dead-straight boundaries that were so obviously the work of a British or French colonial official using a ruler" (Owen 2004: 9). Though Dan Slater (2012) notes that colonial powers (at least in Southeast Asia) could play a role in building strong states when they wanted to, he validates the perspective that state strength is something modern-day autocrats largely inherit. As he puts it, autocrats "[do] not so much build their powerful state apparatuses as build them up" (Slater 2012: 20).

The importance of historical legacies of stateness is most keenly demonstrated in the case of Yemen. Unlike Egypt or Tunisia, which were both unitary states at the beginning of the twentieth century (Darwisheh 2014, 2), Yemen was for most of the twentieth century divided into two separate polities—a nominally Ottoman-controlled north and a British-controlled south (Brehony 2011, 3). Moreover, neither of the two halves of what is now Yemen enjoyed the kind of centralized authority that long obtained in Egypt and Tunisia. North Yemen was the site of a civil war throughout most of the 1960s between Egyptian-backed "republicans" on the one side, and "royalists" backed by Saudi Arabia on the other (Gerges 1995). Meanwhile, in South Yemen, the British—who administered the territory from 1839 to 1967—pursued what Halliday (2002, 108) described as a "pattern of [...] colonial control [...] that maintained the existing rulers in place in the hinterland under indirect rule and sought the cooperation of the merchants of [the capital city] Aden." According to Stork (1973: 3), "In order to pre-empt encroachment by competing European powers and resist Yemeni claims to sovereignty over the area, Britain followed a policy [of] [...] arming and subsidizing ruling families to preserve and accentuate tribal divisions and perpetuate an archaic and decaying social order." The form of indirect rule experienced by Yemen has long been thought by scholars to inhibit the development of strong states by dispersing (rather than centralizing) authority and by rendering leaders responsive to colonial powers rather than to their people (Acemoglu, Chaves, Osafo-Kwaako, and Robinson 2013).

One illustration of Yemen's historic lack of stateness (when compared to Egypt, Tunisia, and Libya) can be observed in the relative rates of urbanization observed in each of these countries as they emerged from the colonial period in the latter half of the twentieth century. Urbanization is of course an imperfect proxy for state strength, but Kirby and Ward (1992: 88) have identified a correlation "between the growth of the state apparatus and urbanization," and Kocher (2004) has posited a link between state strength and urban settlement as well. The World Bank's estimate of the share of each country's population in urban areas for 1960 (the earliest year available) shows Egypt and Tunisia tied at 38%, Libya at 27%, and Yemen at only 9%.[6] Thus, as Carapico (2001: 287) writes, "Even Yemenis refer to their society as *mutakhallif,* meaning 'backward.' Neither formal organizations nor legal guarantees are well institutionalized."

The upshot of this discussion is straightforward: Perhaps the most essential feature of a completed transition to democracy—the presence of what Linz and Stepan (1996) call a "usable state" apparatus—is independent of the political struggles that initiated that transition. Oppositionists who have managed to compel the flight of a strongman either find themselves at the helm of a genuine state or they do not. In the latter instance, the odds of generating and sustaining a functioning democratic system are long indeed.

Getting to Elections

The second feature of a completed transition—that is, the occurrence of free and fair elections—is generally attributed by scholars to the same factors that enable oppositionists to compel the resignation of the dictator: a balance of power between the *ancien régime* and its opponents that favors the opposition. According to Bratton (1997: 78), the conduct of founding elections depends on the ability of oppositions to "transform[...] loose urban protest movements into dominant political parties that could push effectively for elections and organize nationwide election campaigns." In their study of African transitions, Bratton and Vandewalle (1997: 18) find that the cohesion of oppositionists is the key explanatory factor: they argue that "fragmented opposition movements (with multiple leaders and weak organizations)" were generally unable to compel dictators to hold founding elections, whereas "relatively cohesive ones (with a dominant leader and relatively strong organization)" were most likely to achieve success in this regard.

The thesis that transition completion is a function of opposition strength and cohesion finds limited support in our four cases of regime breakdown, however. As we saw in Chapter 4, in none of the four cases did oppositionists cohere into what might be thought of as a "dominant political party." There were, of course, opposition coalitions in each country: In Tunisia, Islamists and non-Islamists joined together in an October 18th movement founded in 2005 to (in the words of Ennahdha leader Rachid Ghannouchi) "bring together political parties and civil society institutions, including [...] the Progressive Democratic Party, the Tunisian Communist Workers Party, and the Congress for the Republic and other human rights organizations [...] [around] one simple demand: to call for freedom of expression and association for everyone and recognizing the rights of all parties."[7] Egypt had a similar umbrella group called the National Association for Change (*al-Jamʿiyya al-Waṭaniyya lil-Taghyīr*)), founded by former International Atomic Energy Association chairman Mohamed ElBaradei in 2010, and which included representatives from across the Egyptian political spectrum, including the Muslim Brotherhood.[8] In Libya, as we saw in Chapter 4, oppositionists formed the National Transitional Council (*al-Majlis al-Waṭanī al-Intiqālī*) during the uprising against Qaddhafi.[9] And Yemeni oppositionists had in 2002 established the Joint Meeting Parties (*Aḥzāb al-Liqāʾ al-Mushtarak*) that brought together Islamists, socialists, and Nasserists (Browers 2007).

We are not able, a priori, to determine the cohesiveness of these coalitions and thereby link opposition cohesion to ultimate outcomes, but there are reasons to think that cohesion *qua* cohesion is less important that scholars have typically believed. It is notable that the most established of the opposition coalitions in our four cases of regime breakdown—the Yemeni JMP, founded three years before Tunisia's October 18th Movement, eight years before Egypt's NAC, and eleven years prior to Libya's NTC—has proven the least able to effect change (reflected in the fact that the country has not yet had an election, and in the circumscribed role oppositionists play in the country's interim governance). Furthermore, the least established of the four coalitions—the Libyan NTC, which only emerged during, not prior to, the anti-Qaddhafi uprising—was among the most successful (although this is less because of the cohesiveness or strength of the NTC than a natural product of the fact that the old regime was excised by a sustained bombing campaign by the world's most powerful military alliance).

The example of Yemen demonstrates that opposition cohesion and opposition strength are analytically distinct. That country may have had a cohesive opposition, but it was still not strong enough to compel the interim government to quicken the pace of change. Egypt represents the reverse of the Yemeni case—a fragmented opposition that nonetheless contained within it elements powerful enough to force the military to move toward elections. As we saw in Chapter 4, the Egyptian opposition was riven by deep cleavages among Islamists who wanted quick elections, non-religious oppositionists who wanted a period of military guardianship while they built up their organizational capabilities, and revolutionary youths who wanted transitional justice above all. These groups were unable to act in concert, and were only granted a limited role by the military in the country's interim governance (which remained dominated by the armed forces and Mubarak-era apparatchiks). However, the Islamists on their own possessed sufficient mobilizing power to influence the military's political calculus, at least with respect to the conduct of elections. Ultimately, it appears that Egypt's interim military rulers understood that deferring elections would generate significant opposition from the Muslim Brotherhood and its allies, and thus undermine the generals' ultimate goal of reducing street protests and restoring stability.

If opposition strength is a key determinant of transition completion, how do we measure it? In the accounts offered above, the best we have been able to do is to read opposition strength from features of the transition processes—the Tunisian opposition must have been strong because, as we saw in Chapter 4, it managed to emerge as a veto-player in Tunisia's interim government (in the form of the High Commission for the Fulfillment of Revolutionary Goals (HCFRG)), was able to dominate the process by which electoral institutions were chosen and administered (through the High Independent Authority for Elections (ISIE)), and ultimately triumphed over the leftovers of the old regime in free-and-fair founding elections. By contrast, the Yemeni opposition must have been weak because it managed to do none of these things. And, judging by the course of Egypt's transition, that country's opposition must have been weaker than Tunisia's (since it was accorded only a limited role in interim governance and institution-building) but stronger than Yemen's (since it was able to compel the military to hold elections). Clearly, a less *post-hoc* means of gauging opposition strength is needed, although we defer this task to future scholars.

Quite apart from the question of *measuring* variation in opposition strength is the matter of *explaining* it. If we accept that oppositionists in some countries were stronger, relative to incumbents, than others, what accounts for this variation? Again, existing theories only take us so far. In their study of African transitions, Bratton and Van De Walle (1997: 72) attribute opposition weakness to the machinations of so-called "neo-patrimonial" regimes, which, "tried to eliminate, weaken, or take over any nongovernmental institution that might contest their legitimacy and authority [...] includ[ing] opposition political parties, which were illegal in 32 states as late as 1989." Lust-Okar (2007) has similarly documented the ways in which Arab autocrats "manage and manipulate" their rivals in order to produce quiescent political landscapes. However, to the extent that our four cases of regime breakdown represent any variation in the extent to which autocrats enfeebled their oppositions, that variation appears negatively correlated with transition outcomes.

For example, despite allowing limited multiparty competition, Tunisia under Ben Ali had earned a reputation as being among the most repressive Arab regimes. The first multi-party parliamentary elections took place in 1981, but it was not until 1994 that a select few "official" parties were allowed to assume seats in the legislature, and this only because an electoral law accorded nineteen seats to parties that had lost in the regular elections.[10] In 2010, the year before the revolution, Freedom House gave Tunisia the worst possible score in terms of political rights (a 7), reserved for countries that "have few or no political rights because of severe government oppression" (Tunisia shared the bottom of the rankings with Qaddafi's Libya). In contrast, Egypt under Mubarak and Yemen under Saleh each scored a tick better at 6, a score assigned to countries with "very restricted political rights [that] allow a few political rights, such as some representation or autonomy for minority groups, and [. . .] tolerate political discussion."[11] In fact, from 2005 to 2009, Yemen had actually earned a Freedom House rating of 5 and a designation as "partly free," a label Tunisia and Egypt had not enjoyed since 1992 and which Libya had never merited. An indication of just how repressive Tunisia had been under Ben Ali is offered by the fact that the headquarters of the Council of Arab Interior Ministers, a yearly conclave of the chiefs of the repressive apparatuses of the Arab states, had been based in Tunis since 2003 (although its 2013 annual meeting was held not in the Tunisia capital, but in the Saudi one).[12]

Thus, we argue that opposition strength—and hence the ability of opposition actors to compel incumbents to hold founding elections—cannot be endogenized to variation in the policies of prior regimes. Instead, a better explanation for why only some oppositions were strong enough to see transitions through to completion lies in socio-economic conditions. Scholars have long recognized that the ability of citizens to challenge their leaders rests in part on the existence of a "dense" civil society that "establishes a counterweight to state power" (Rueschmeyer, Stephens, and Stephens 1992). The density of civil society, in turn, is largely thought to be a function of economic development. As Lipset (1959: 84) pointed out,

> Associated with greater wealth is the presence of intermediary organizations and institutions which can act as sources of countervailing power, and recruiters of participants in the political process in the manner discussed by Tocqueville and other exponents of what has come to be known as the theory of the mass society.

Similarly, Rueschmeyer, Stephens, and Stephens (1992: 6) explain that "Capitalist development furthers the growth of civil society—by increasing the level of urbanization, by bringing workers together in factories, by improving the means of communication and transportation, [and] by raising the level of literacy." By these lights, it is perhaps not surprising that Tunisia—which has the highest non-oil per capita income of our four cases of regime breakdown (see Figure 5.3)—gave rise to a capable and powerful opposition that ousted Ben Ali and earned a share of power immediately after his departure, despite the avidity with which the dictator had suppressed political activity during his rule. Similarly, it is unsurprising that oppositionists in Yemen, with less than half of Tunisia's per capita GDP, have lacked the organizational wherewithal to mount a sustained challenge to agents of the old regime (despite the fact that they had long been granted a measure of leeway). Again, Libya here is the exception that proves the rule. Though it boasts the highest per capita income of the four cases, it is a classic "rentier state," deriving most of its income from oil. As Ross (2001) points out, not only are the processes by which economic development strengthens civil society absent in such countries, but these regimes also use their oil windfall to stave off the development of civil society by buying off potential dissenters and obviating the need for collective action. As demonstrated in Chapter 3, without NATO's active intervention, that country would likely today remain in Qaddafi's grip.

The point of this discussion is simple: even when oppositionists were strong enough to compel coercive apparatuses to withdraw support from dictators, they were not all equally able to force

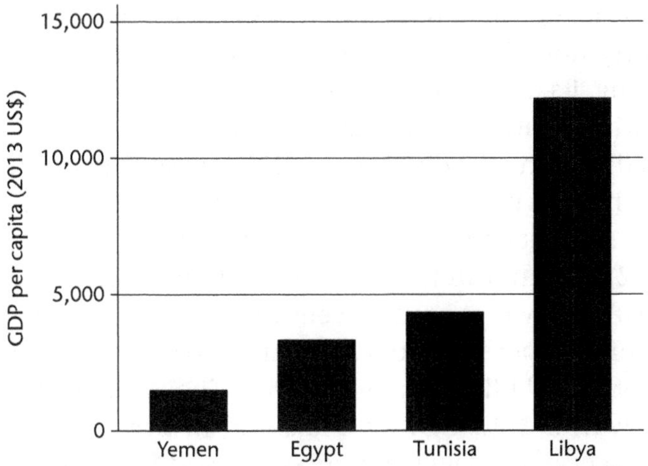

Figure 5.3. Per Capita Income in Four Cases of Regime Breakdown
Source: World Bank Development Indicators.

incumbents to hold the elections that are the hallmark of completed democratic transitions. The inability of oppositions to do this is less a function of prior regime strategies of repression than of more fundamental socio-economic forces that determined the strength of civil society and thus the power of mass actors to shape the political landscape after the fall of the strongman.

Maintenance: Explaining Divergence between Egypt and Tunisia

Although both Tunisia and Egypt are coded as "completed" transitions, we know that they did not both remain so. As we saw in Chapter 4, elected institutions in Egypt were the subject of constant challenge from agents of the so-called "deep state." In June 2012, the judiciary dissolved the democratically elected parliament. And a little more than a year later, the military ejected from power the country's first democratically elected president. Though the tensions between so called "secularists" and Islamists that ostensibly animated the Egyptian drama were also extant in Tunisia, the latter country nonetheless managed to avoid Egypt's fate, and as of this writing, its democratically elected governing assembly, and its democratically ratified constitution, remain in place.

When discussing the divergent paths between Egypt and Tunisia, scholars have tended to adopt the voluntaristic pose we first observed in explanations of uprising occurrence and success (see Chapter 2). In part, this is due to the fact that structural differences between those two countries seem minor, especially when compared to oil-rich but state-poor Libya and tribal Yemen. Both Tunisia and Egypt are middle-income countries: The World Bank classifies Tunisia, with a 2013 GDP of $4,329 as an *upper* middle-income country (per capita GDPs between $4,126 and $12,745), and Egypt, with a per capita GDP of $3,314 as a *lower* middle-income country (per capita GDPs of $1,046 to $4,125).[13] As Barbara Geddes (1999: 119) has argued, middle-income countries are where "human choices and serendipitous events—*virtu* and *fortuna*—could most easily affect outcomes, since underlying structural causes are fairly evenly balanced."

There are two powerful, agent-centric, narratives advanced for Tunisia's democratic continuity and Egypt's military coup. The first is that the decisions of generals were paramount. On the one hand are accounts that see the Egyptian military as having made a number of primarily technical errors regarding institutional design. For example, Tamir Moustafa (2012: 3), argued that "the Egyptian transition is shaping up to be a case study in how not to initiate a constitution writing process." Moustafa identified several "procedural deficits" and departures from "best practices" in the transition process designed by the Supreme Council of the Armed Forces—most notably a lack of transparency in its decisionmaking, a compressed timeline for the drafting of a new charter, and an inattention to the need to generate an "inclusive" process (Moustafa 2012: 3–6). Similarly, Nathan Brown has argued that the SCAF scuppered Egypt's transition with a series of bad and poorly-thought-out decisions that were, in his words, "politically and legally incoherent." He tells us that the generals "laid out a series of procedures for rebuilding the Egyptian political order. Those procedures have largely been followed. But they have led Egypt into a state of complete confusion."[14] Neither of these scholars argues that the SCAF's decisions were *calculated* to produce democratic failure, but rather that they were made hastily, without input from relevant actors, and were thus especially prone to error and unintended consequences.[15]

However, as important as questions of institutional design are, we concur with the scholar Jay Ulfelder, who has noted that such critiques of the SCAF's alleged errors "assume the existence of powerful but disinterested overseer–a manager rather than a politician."[16] An alternative account of the derailing of Egypt's transition is that the military was not simply a benign-but-befuddled actor, but instead an active spoiler. In this telling, Egypt's transition was doomed by a military that was long used to political supremacy and which had never seen its way clear to sharing power with democratically elected authorities. The gifted scholar of Egypt Joshua Stacher, has offered a forceful articulation of this view. Writing shortly after Mubarak's resignation, he contended that the interim military government, the Supreme Council of the Armed Forces, was even in those early days after the opposition victory in Tahrir Square carefully constructing a return to authoritarianism:

> The SCAF is disproportionately in charge and it is disproportionately to blame for how the transition has been structured. Whether by initiating new laws against protests, strategically deploying military trials against activists and opponents, continuing to apply Emergency Law, devising electoral laws that encourage social fragmentation, framing clashes with a sectarian hue, or intimidating and censoring the press, Egypt under the SCAF represents an attempt to continue the practices of the Mubarak era despite the social changes unleashed by the revolution's popular mobilization.[17]

The Tunisian military's behavior is thought to offer a sharp contrast to that of the Egyptian one. If the Egyptian military was conspiring to undo the January 25 revolution from the outset, the Tunisian military, by all accounts, was refraining from politics altogether. Thus, as Stepan wrote in 2011, Tunisia's "military is not complicating the transition to democracy."[18] Similarly, the Economist recently testified that, in Tunisia, "The army prefers to keep out of both politics and business," thus enabling that country's democratic success.[19] In sum, according to this narrative, Tunisia has maintained its transition because it lacked Egypt's overweening military.

The second explanation for the divergence in Tunisia's and Egypt's fates focuses on the behaviors of its political party leaders. Specifically, we are told that Tunisia evaded Egypt's fate because "Ennahda's leaders understood that compromise was essential to their own future political prospects."[20] As Eva Bellin (2013: 3) puts it, Tunisia "was blessed with elites committed to democratization," to "dialogue," and to "the principle and practice of inclusiveness." In contrast, we read that, in Egypt, "Morsi and the Brotherhood made almost every conceivable mistake [...] they alienated potential allies, ignored rising discontent, focused more on consolidating their rule than on using the tools that they did have, and used rhetoric that was tone deaf at best and threatening at worst" (Brown 2013: 57). Stepan and Linz (2013: 23) attribute the relative happiness of the Tunisian experience to the fact that "secular liberals and Islamists began meeting regularly eight years *before* Ben Ali's fall to see whether they could reduce mutual fears and agree upon rules for democratic governance," resulting in the conclusion of "highly innovative 'pacts' [...] between secularists and Islamists" that put both parties at ease once the transition began. In contrast, according to Brumberg (2013: 93) Egyptian Islamists displayed "no sudden readiness to offer 'credible assurances' to their non-Islamist rivals," and thus "the chances for a consensus-based draft constitution—and indeed for accommodation in general—appeared slim."

Though there is much to commend both of these accounts, they raise new questions. If the Egyptian military conspired to engineer a return to the pre-revolutionary status quo ante, how do we explain the Tunisian military's restraint in this regard? What was special about that country's men in uniform that caused them to resist claiming a share of power or working to resurrect the old order? Does the answer lie in different incentives, different capabilities, or both?

And if so, what was the source of those differences? Similarly, if the credit for Tunisia's success and blame for Egypt's failure belongs to opposition parties that compromised in the former case and squabbled in the latter, how do we explain that difference? Were Tunisians just smarter politicians or more virtuous people? Though it is perhaps plausible that Egyptian and Tunisian leaders did not possess the same degree of strategic acumen or the same belief in the necessity of compromise, there is little a priori evidence for that proposition, apart from the ultimate disposition of the two countries' transitions. As a more general matter, although Green and Shapiro (1996) have argued for greater attention to the strategic acumen of political actors as an explanatory factor in political outcomes, it is difficult to come up with credible reasons for why Tunisian political leaders might have been smarter than their Egyptian counterparts. If Tunisian politicians were more compromising than Egyptians, then we must look for the structures that incentivized them to be so.[21]

What we attempt to do in the remainder of this chapter is examine the structural causes behind the differing poses of the militaries and the differing incentives for compromise that confronted party leaders. We first ask why, as Brownlee (2012, 169) has written, "Tunisians were blessed with a military that was less entangled in politics than the Egyptian armed forces." We find that the countries' prior histories of military intervention in politics offered indications as to how those militaries would behave during the Arab Spring, and offer a provisional explanation that locates these differences in the different patterns of colonial control of each country's indigenous armed forces. Ultimately, however, we conclude that opportunities for military intervention are opened by political discord among mass actors, and closed (as in Tunisia) when those actors achieve political settlement. We therefore turn to explaining why Tunisian leaders compromised and Egyptian leaders did not. We argue (along with several others) that the difference is not a function of the relative depth of ideological disagreement or the relative foresight of political actors, but is a product of the particular partisan configuration that emerged in each country after founding elections. Specifically, the relative organizational parity between Islamists and non-Islamists in Tunisia rendered the former modest and kept the latter interested in playing the democratic game. In Egypt, in contrast, Islamist electoral dominance is thought to have given Islamists the delusions of a mandate and sent non-Islamists in search of extra-institutional means of redress. Our contribution is to push this further, and ask what caused these differences in the Islamist–secularist balance in our two cases. We provide evidence that suggests that the answer lies in antecedent socio-economic conditions that scholars have long considered key to democratic consolidation, and not in contingent factors such as the campaign strategies of parties or fortuitous choices of electoral institutions.

Military Inheritances

According to the great scholar of democratic transitions, Guillermo O'Donnell, "the central problem of democratic consolidation is to prevent a successful military coup."[22] When Egypt's minister of defense (and later field marshal) ʿAbd al-Fattāḥ al-Sīsī took to the airwaves to announce the end of Morsi's presidency on July 3, 2013, it was difficult not to see in that event the confirmation of this perspective. According to Nikolay Marinov and Hein Goemans (2013), the Egyptian experience is not unique. They have found that "three out of every four failures of democracy are the result of a successful coup d'état. This makes forceful power seizures the biggest single danger to democracy" (Marinov and Goemans 2013: 3).

To the extent that scholars have been able to explain the incidence of military violations of democratic institutions, they have attributed it to historical legacies. According to Bratton and Van de Walle (1997: 215), most coups "occur in countries with a previous history of military coups and rule." Examining failed transitions in Africa, they conclude that, "an institutional legacy of military involvement in politics seemed to predispose security forces to intervene during transitions and to incline subsequent transition outcomes to fall short of democracy" (Bratton and Van de Walle 1997: 215).

Jenkins and Kposowa (1990: 862) argue that "postcolonial military establishments that control a large share of state resources possess a strong corporate identity, a tradition of domestic control, and harbor political aspirations are politically central and therefore more likely to intervene." In other words—militaries that have a history of being in control are likely to wish to remain so.

That Egypt's military has historically been more politically central than Tunisia's cannot be in doubt. Table 5.1 contains indicators of military strength and centrality in both countries. As we can see, Egypt's military has almost twenty times the number of personnel as Tunisia's (over two times more on a per-capita basis) and its budget is almost ten times the size of Tunisia's (or close to double as a share of GDP). The Bonn International Center for Conversion has constructed a measure of "militarization" that includes not only the military's share of GDP and the number of military personnel as a share of the total population, but also military expenditures compared to government spending on healthcare, the ratio of military personnel to the number of physicians, and the number of heavy weapons (including armored vehicles, artillery, fighter aircraft, and ships) in relation to the population.[23] According to this measure, Egypt ranks in the top 20% of nations in terms of militarization (27 out of 150 countries) while Tunisia ranks in the bottom half (at 79th).

These quantitative indicators reflect the scholarly wisdom regarding the role of the militaries in each of these two countries.

Table 5.1. Indicators of Military Centrality in Egypt and Tunisia

Measure	Egypt	Tunisia
Size of armed forces	835,500	47,800
Total military spending (millions of USD)	4,560	534
Military spending as share of GDP	2.0%	1.3%
Military spending per capita	57.8	50.9
Soldiers per 1,000 inhabitants	10.6	4.6
Global Militarization Index Rank (150 countries, 2012)	27	79

Sources: World Bank Development Indicators, 2010; International Institute for Strategic Studies, *The Military Balance*, 2010; Bonn International Center for Conversion Global Militarization Index, 2012.

Egypt prior to the January 25 revolution long exemplified what Abdel Malek (1968) called the "military society." For example, Harb (2003: 270) argued that, "Throughout [...] periods of changing political roles, the Egyptian military remained the loyal repository of political power answerable only to a strong executive leadership in the person of a former military officer (the President) and sure of its privileged position within the polity." Similarly, in his study of the dynamics of Middle Eastern authoritarianism, Cook (2007: 8) argued that the Egyptian military, after seizing power in a 1952 coup, oversaw "the development of an institutional setting—a system—that ensures the predominance of the officers," allowing them to rule "without ever having to step beyond the boundaries of their barracks." Thus, both the Supreme Council of the Armed Forces' assumption of control after Mubarak's resignation and the later military coup against Mubarak's successor are easily seen as functions of a long legacy of military predominance in Egypt.

In contrast, the political quiescence of Tunisia's military appears to have deep historical roots. As Alfred Stepan (2011) has testified: "since independence, in 1956, [Tunisia] has been led by two party-based non-democratic leaders who strove to keep the military out of politics."[24] According to one scholar,

> Of the military establishments in the Arab world, Tunisia is almost unique. It is a non-praetorian, highly professional body of officers and men which, as an armed force, never mounted a coup or fomented revolution against the state, never involved itself directly in the Arab-Israeli crisis, has never been the instrument of national emancipation except as the adjunctive arm of civilian policy, and has always answered to the authority of the state through the intermediary of a civilian minister of defense (Ware 1985: 37).

In this telling, when the chief of Tunisia's armed forces, General Rachid Ben Ammar, threw his support behind the protesters, and then withdrew to the barracks after the dictator had been ousted, he was merely acting on values that were deeply ingrained within the Tunisian military. Presumably, those same values are what also kept the Tunisian military from following in the footsteps of its Egyptian counterpart and inserting itself in the tussles between Islamists and their opponents, instead remaining a neutral bystander and allowing them to achieve a political settlement that has preserved Tunisian democracy.

There is much to be said for this argument. Given the centrality of the Egyptian military throughout its authoritarian history and the post-Mubarak period, it seems obvious that any explanation for the reversal of the Egyptian democratic experiment must take into account the history and motivations of what was perhaps its principal *dramatis persona*. However, this attention to the differing histories of the Egyptian and Tunisian militaries ultimately cries out for more research. Once we endogenize outcomes to historical legacies, we must then explain those legacies, otherwise our explanations risk becoming tautological: "coups are conducted by militaries that conduct coups."

What accounts for the Egyptian military's legacy of interventionism and the Tunisian military's legacy of quiescence? This requires us to reach back into each country's post-colonial period, when the divergence first appears. After all, the autocracy inaugurated in Egypt in the 1950s was led by officers, while the dictatorship established at the same time in Tunisia was led by a lawyer. Was this merely a historical accident? We certainly could not have explained the 1952 "Free Officers" coup with reference to notions of military centrality. In fact, when Nasser and his allies seized power in 1952, the army was smaller relative to Egypt's population than the Tunisian one was in 2011. According to the scholar Hazem Kandil (2012: 9) the Egyptian army in 1952 contained approximately 36,000 men (out of a population of approximately 22 million).[25] McDermott (1988: 16) offers a larger, but still modest, estimate of 65,000. An intermediate estimate is offered by Pollak (2002: 15) who tells us that in 1948, "Cairo never succeeded in putting more than 40,000 men into the field." Regardless of the precise size, it is clear that before Egypt's military became "politically central," it was as peripheral as Tunisia's would later be described. This suggests "military centrality" is less an explanation for the coup of 2013 than (at best) an intermediate variable in a longer causal chain.

One potential explanation for the difference in military power between Egypt and Tunisia lies in colonial policy. Tunisia's French occupiers (who controlled the country from 1881 to 1956), dismantled the indigenous military and conscripted Tunisians into the French national army as *tirailleurs Tunisiens* (Tunisian skirmishers) along with other subject peoples (DeGeorges 2006: 26; Fogarty 2008: 82). It was not until 1956 that a Tunisian national army was established by Bourguiba (Moore 1965: 66). In contrast, the Egyptian army dates to the early nineteenth century, when it was created by the Ottoman Viceroy Mehmet Ali (Fahmy 2002), although briefly disbanded in the late 1800s. Though Kandil (2012: 7) tells us that Egypt's British occupiers "kept the army understaffed, unequipped, and trained for little more than parade ground marches," Egypt nonetheless had its own military prior to the final ejection of the British from the Canal Zone in 1956. Thus, if we take the 1950s as our starting point, Tunisia enters modern statehood with a brand new military created by civilians, while Egypt enters with one that had a much longer history and which had never been meaningfully subject to civilian authority. We leave it to future scholarship to determine whether the divergent behaviors of the two armies during the Arab Spring was inscribed in these different colonial legacies, but the evidence is suggestive.

The Islamist-Secularist Balance

Though the military's actions were (almost by definition) a central feature of the democratic collapse in Egypt, it could be argued that the men with guns would have been unable to intervene were it not for the conflict among Egypt's political parties. In this telling, the opportunity for the military to flex its muscles derived from the fact that the Muslim Brotherhood-backed government of Mohammed Morsi and its political rivals (most notably the National Salvation Front led by Mohamed Elbaradei, Amre Moussa, and Hamdin Sabahi) could not come to an agreement over the distribution of power in the post-Mubarak era. Morsi's opponents demanded that he submit to a new presidential election (in which they felt a non-Islamist could be successful), while Morsi and his allies instead called on them to participate in parliamentary elections (which the Islamists were reasonably certain they could win). As Masoud (2014: 14) put it, "The resulting chasm was just wide enough for the military to roll their tanks through."

It might be argued that the inability of Islamists and secularists in Egypt to come to a power-sharing agreement reflects the depth of the ideological gulf that separated the two sides. However, there is little evidence that this is the case. For example, the principle point of disagreement between Islamists and secularists in Tunisia—that of the role of Islamic law in the constitution—was not as great a source of conflict among Egyptian parties as it was among Tunisian ones. The majority of voters and parties (including secular parties such as the Free Egyptians Party and the Wafd) agreed that Islamic law should be the principal source of legislation, as had been specified by the country's constitution since 1980 (Masoud 2014: 140). In Tunisia, by contrast, there seems to have been far more disagreement over the question of sharīʿa, and suspicion by liberals that Ennahdha was composed of "Salafis in disguise, smarter and more cunning, perhaps, but with the same ultimate, obscurantist goals" (Hamid 2014: 196).

For others, the explanation for Egypt's collapse and Tunisia's democratic maintenance is less a function of ideological differences than of political fortunes. In this telling, the Islamists' dominance of elections after Mubarak's overthrow is thought to have caused non-Islamists to conclude that the democratic process was unlikely to give them a share of power. In contrast, in Tunisia, as two writers have testified, Islamists and secularists "were relatively evenly matched, with the Islamists winning only a plurality in Tunisia's first free vote." [26] Consequently, "each side needed the other to govern."[27] According to Bellin (2013: 4), "The fact that no party enjoyed a majority provided an incentive for coalition building and accommodation." A similar argument is made by Lust and Khatib (2014), who declare that "the playing field in Tunisia has been relatively level, with neither Ennahda nor any of the political parties able to dominate as the Muslim Brotherhood did in Egypt. This has fundamentally shaped Tunisian and Egyptian activists' willingness to engage in political parties, as well as non-Islamists' fear of the Islamist parties' ability to change state and society."[28] Likewise, Stepan (2012: 91) has noted that Ennahda was kept modest by the fact that it "fell short of a majority in the Constituent Assembly. [...] Indeed, under the Assembly's parliamentary procedures, Ennahda could even find itself subjected to a vote of no confidence that could lead to the accession of a new ruling majority in that body."

Although the literature on democratic transitions has attended to the balance of power between "incumbents" and "oppositionists" (see Bermeo 1997, Karl 1990, McFaul 2002), the cases of Egypt and Tunisia suggests that more attention should be paid to the balance of power *within* the oppositionist camp once the incumbents have been toppled. After all, as several scholars have noted, democracy ultimately arises out of stalemate. Dankwart Rustow (1970: 352–355) argued that democratization is "set off by a prolonged and *inconclusive* political struggle" that culminates in "a deliberate decision on the part of political leaders to accept the existence of diversity in unity and, to that end, to institutionalize some crucial aspect of democratic procedure." Similarly, O'Donnell and C. Schmitter (1986: 43–44), declare that democracy emerges when "no social or political group is sufficiently dominant to impose its 'ideal project,'" settling instead for "a second-best solution which none of the actors wanted or identified with completely but which all of them can agree to and share in." The same logic was expressed during the Second World War by the columnist Walter Lippmann (1982 (1939): 234), who explained that:

> The national unity of a free people depends upon a sufficiently even balance of political power to make it impracticable for the administration to be arbitrary and for the opposition to be revolutionary and irreconcilable. *Where that balance no longer exists, democracy perishes. For unless all the citizens of a state are forced by circumstances to compromise, unless they feel that they can affect policy but that no one can wholly dominate it,* unless by habit and necessity they have to give and take, freedom cannot be maintained.

Comparing political outcomes in Tunisia and Egypt after the resignations of Ben Ali and Mubarak, it is evident that Rostow's "inconclusive" struggle and Lippmann's "sufficiently even balance of power" was in evidence in Tunisia but nowhere in sight in Egypt. Table 5.2 summarizes the results of founding elections in these two cases of democratic transition. Using the Laakso-Taagepera (1979) measure of parliamentary pluralism, Gallagher (2014) finds that Tunisia had "effectively" 4.62 political parties, while Egypt had only 3.38.[29] This is in part a function of the different Islamist election fortunes in each country. In Tunisia, though Ennahdha was the largest parliamentary bloc, the majority of seats went to assorted non-Islamist parties. In Egypt, however, more than 70% of seats were captured by just two Islamist alliances, one headed by the Muslim Brotherhood's Freedom and Justice Party, and the other headed by the Salafi Call Society's (Jamāʿat al-Daʿwa al-Salafiyya) Party of Light (Ḥizb al-Nūr). Consequently, as we saw in Chapter 4, Egypt's Islamists were able to ignore their opponents' preferences when it came to constitution writing and interim governance, while in Tunisia, Islamists were forced to compromise. The question this raises, however, is why this imbalance existed in the first place.

There are, of course, multiple explanations that have been advanced to explain the lopsidedness of the Egyptian political landscape and the relative balance of the Tunisian one. In the remainder

Table 5.2. Pluralism in Founding Elections, Tunisia and Egypt

	Tunisia	Egypt
Date of election	October, 2011	November–January 2011–12
Number of seats	217	498
Electoral system	List PR	Parallel (2/3rds list PR, 1/3rd majoritarian)
Number of parties elected	26	26
Islamist share of seats	41%	71% (67% of PR seats; 80% of majoritarian seats)
Effective Number of Political Parties (Gallagher 2014)	4.62	3.38

of this section, we address two that also reflect the voluntarism that characterizes much of the scholarship on the Arab Spring: the role of electoral institutions, and the lethargy of secular political parties. We then offer an alternative explanation that is more attentive to structural preconditions than has so far been the case with dominant accounts.

ELECTORAL RULES

Scholars have long argued that electoral rules shape party systems (see Cox 1997 for a review of the literature). In both Egypt and Tunisia, autocrats had manipulated electoral rules to guarantee supermajorities for ruling parties: in Tunisia, this was achieved through a party bloc vote (in which the party receiving the majority of the national vote received all the seats), and in Egypt through a majoritarian, two-round system with 222 dual-member districts and lax requirements for candidate entry (Pripstein-Posusney 2002; Lust-Okar and Jamal 2002; Masoud 2008: 97–111). Once the autocrats were overthrown and new elections were scheduled, amending electoral rules in order to avoid past excesses became a priority of oppositionists in both countries. In Tunisia, the HCFRG settled on a system of closed-list proportional representation, with twenty-seven districts with an average district magnitude of 8.[30] In Egypt, the Supreme Council of the Armed Forces, in negotiation with political parties, generated a hybrid electoral system, where two-thirds of the seats were allocated through the same closed list PR system as Tunisia, and one-third according to the majoritarian, two-round system that had obtained in Egypt prior to the January 25 revolution.[31]

According to some scholars, the different electoral rules chosen in each case go a long way toward explaining differences in the ultimate makeup of parliament. According to Bellin (2013: 4) Tunisia's relatively balanced parliament (which she calls an "auspicious result") was "in part the product of elite agency: the decision by the electoral commission to embrace a system of proportional representation rather than a majoritarian/first-past-the-post/single member district electoral rule." Carey (2013) goes even further, arguing that it was not just Tunisia's eschewing of a majoritarian system that was auspicious, but its selection of a particular *form* of closed list proportional representation. Specifically, he argues that the Tunisians' use of Hare Quota with Largest remainders, "had enormous consequences for the outcome, in which the largest party was awarded less than a majority of seats and therefore has had to negotiate with other groups in drafting a constitution."[32] Using district-level data to simulate what would have happened had a different form of PR (the D'Hondt method of vote aggregation) been used, he argues that Ennahdha "would have been awarded a super-majority in the Assembly and been in a position to impose a constitution." This finding is echoed by the Tunisian scholar Hādī Trabulsī (n.d., 12) who finds that Ennahdha would have won approximately 70% of seats (151 of 217) had the Tunisians adopted the D'Hondt method.[33]

In this narrative, had Tunisians picked a different set of rules, they might have indeed found themselves under the kind of dominion that Islamists were able to achieve in Egypt, and Tunisian secularists then might have found need to seek their military's protection. Similarly, if the Egyptian SCAF had chosen pure PR as the Tunisians had, they might have produced an electoral landscape that was as balanced as the Tunisian one, in turn generating the incentives for compromise. Prior to the Egyptian parliamentary election in November 2011, Trager (2011) argued that "Egypt's complicated new parliamentary laws [...] represent the latest setback for the country's democratic prospects" and would disproportionately advantage Islamists. According to Trager,

> By perpetuating the individual candidacy system for one-third of the parliament, the new laws virtually ensure that the former ruling party will be well-represented in the next legislature. Meanwhile, the proportional representation voting system, which will determine the other two-thirds of the parliament, will likely include a provision for a 'largest remainder system,' making it virtually impossible for small parties to compete with larger, mostly illiberal [i.e. Islamist] parties.[34]

However, there are reasons to think that institutions should be assigned limited causal weight in our explanations of ultimate outcomes (although there is no question that the shift away from pre-authoritarian majoritarian systems did improve chances for smaller political parties). In the case of Tunisia, the choice of proportional representation or of the Hare quota, which ostensibly staved off Islamist dominion, is probably best viewed as a *function* of the relative balance of political power in that country, rather than as a cause. After all, as we saw in Chapter 4, the HCFRG and the ISIE—the institutions responsible for the formulation and administration of the electoral framework in post-Ben Ali Tunisia—included healthy representation from parties and civil society groups that would have had an interest in mitigating the dominance of Islamists. Thus, it makes perfect sense that they would consciously choose an electoral system (PR with Hare Quota) that would improve the fortunes of smaller, non-Islamist parties.

Carey, in contrast, seems to suggest that the Tunisians' choice of Hare Quota was purely serendipitous, saying that, "whether the Commission considered various electoral formulas within the broader phylum of PR, and made a conscious choice of [Hare Quota with Largest Remainders] rather than others, is not explicit." But the limited evidence available suggests that the opposite is true. First, under elections to the chamber of deputies in the Ben Ali period, an alternative method of vote aggregation to the Hare quota (the highest averages method) was used for determining seats for opposition parties—suggesting that, far from being unaware of the "broader phylum of PR" or the ways in which electoral institutions can advantage or disadvantage parties, the framers of Tunisia's electoral rules had ample understanding of this fact.[35] Another suggestive bit of evidence comes in the form of an editorial penned in April 2011 (shortly after the adoption of the new rule) by a legal scholar lamenting the influence of political parties in the new Tunisia. Criticizing the choice of electoral rule, he declared, "it is clear that parties have established control over the HCFRG [...] The system of largest remainders serves the interests of small parties at the expense of big ones and therefore this method does not result in true representation of the voters."[36]

The evidence against the causal effect of electoral institutions in determining the broad contours of the partisan landscape is even stronger in the Egyptian case. Though Trager was correct that Egypt would settle on a largest remainder system for its PR tier, he was incorrect in arguing that this would benefit large parties. As Carey pointed out in his analysis of Tunisia, the Hare Quota largest remainder system generally *mitigates* the advantage of large parties. In fact, one writer has suggested that Egypt's interim military rulers chose this system explicitly in order to trim Islamist sails.[37] And yet, as is evidenced in Table 5.2, the Hare quota was unable to work any miracles for non-Islamists. Instead, Egypt's Islamists captured 67% of seats in the list tier, using the same electoral system that is supposed to have *limited* Islamist chances in the Tunisian case. The fact is that regardless of the electoral systems chosen by the SCAF in 2011, Islamists would likely have captured a supermajority in parliament.

The point here is simple: In the case of Tunisia, the electoral rule may have helped to avoid Islamist dominance, but the fact that it was chosen was in part due to the fact that Islamists were not dominant. In other words, the institutions were a *reflection* of the relative power of different political parties rather than a cause. Or, to paraphrase Przeworski (2004: 527), underlying balances of power shape institutions, and institutions only transmit the causal effects of these underlying balances of power. In the case of Egypt, in contrast, Islamists were so powerful relative to their opponents that the electoral institution ultimately mattered little in determining the overall balance of power in the legislature. Even an electoral system that should have limited Islamist fortunes was unable to slow their advance. What this suggests, then, is that any explanation of variation in Islamist electoral dominance must attend to the pre-existing distribution of power among Islamists and their rivals.

LAZY LIBERALS

An alternative explanation for Islamist dominance in Egypt, also in the voluntarist vein, is that the dominance of Islamist parties is somehow attributable to the inability or unwillingness of secular political movements to transition from street protests to electioneering. For example, in her recent memoir, former Secretary of State Hilary Clinton 2014 has testified that Egyptian "liberals" were uninterested in the hard work of campaigning and elections:

> I met with a number of the students and activists who had played leading roles in the demonstrations. I was curious to hear about their plans to move from protests to politics and how they planned to influence the writing of a new Constitution and contest the upcoming elections. I found a disorganized group not prepared to contest or influence anything. They had no experience in politics, no understanding about how to organize parties, run candidates, or conduct campaigns. They didn't have platforms and showed little interest in forming them. [. . .] I came away worried that they would end up handing the country to the Muslim Brotherhood or the military by default, which in the end is exactly what happened. (Clinton 2014: 346)

Similar testimonials can be found throughout the literature (see Masoud 2014: 156–158). One writer has described the Egyptian opposition as "feckless, lazy, and disorganized, happier sulking in Cairo than campaigning in the countryside."[38] The scholar Steven Cook has similarly painted the Egyptian opposition as "people who have turned fecklessness into a high art."[39] More charitable was the assessment of Egyptian intellectual and politician Amr Hamzawy, who explained that instead of "articulat[ing] and spread[ing] a political program, Egyptian political parties instead "like to stick to generalities, to avoid the hassle and the damage of taking a stand on issues."[40]

The scholar Thomas Carothers has argued that such assessments neglect the challenges of party-building in post-authoritarian periods: "Even under the best of circumstances building an extensive local party structure usually takes many years."[41] But more than that, attributing Islamist dominance to secularist indolence merely begs the question. What accounts for this indolence? And why did we not observe it in Tunisia, where, as we have seen, non-Islamic parties were able to capture a majority of votes and seats in that country's first post-authoritarian elections? Again, as with the argument from electoral institutions, the inexorable conclusion is that we are more likely to gain purchase on the sources of divergence between Egypt and Tunisia by attending to initial conditions and underlying structures rather than to proximate causes and contingent decisions.

Back to Structures

So far, we have asked why Egypt's democratic transition was reversed by coup while Tunisia's has so far proceeded apace. We have argued that attention to the actions of particular players should instead be refocused on the structures that shaped their choices. In particular, we focused on two intermediate differences between Egypt and Tunisia that scholars have deemed consequential for their ultimate transition outcomes. The first are differences in the degree of "military centrality"—that is, the political importance of the military. We have found that the military's political importance is most often explained with reference to vaguely defined "historical legacies" that must themselves be explained. Moreover, we have argued that, since a necessary condition for military intervention is the failure of civilian political forces to reach agreement over how to share power in the post-authoritarian period, we would do better to attend to the sources of political compromise in transitioning systems.

This brings us to the second difference between the Tunisian and Egyptian transitional environments: The relative balance among political forces in Tunisia (which, it is argued, fostered compromise), and the Islamist supermajority in Egypt (which rendered Islamists intransigent and non-Islamists irreconcilable). We have argued against perspectives that explain variation in Islamist dominance with respect to electoral rules or to differences in the energy and organizational skill of non-Islamist political parties. In this section, we instead argue that variation in party systems can be linked to socio-economic structures that can be observed long before the onset of the so-called Arab Spring.

Our argument is straightforward: Islamist dominance in Egyptian politics and the relative pluralism of Tunisian politics are functions of the differing structures of those countries' civil societies. In Egypt, a weak civil society dominated by Islamic institutions provided Islamist parties with far more resources for mobilizing voters in the country's founding elections than were available to their secular rivals (Wiktorowicz 2002). In Tunisia, in contrast, a relatively strong civil society with a mixture of religious, non-religious, and labor-based groups meant that political contestants from across the political spectrum possessed significant resources for mobilizing voters into the country's first democratic elections. And, as Cohen and Arato (1994: 18) summarize decades of social science scholarship, "a highly articulated civil society with cross-cutting cleavages, overlappomg memberships of groups, and social mobility is the presupposition for a stable democratic polity, [and] a guarantee against permanent domination by any one group..."[42]

These differences in the relative pluralism of civil society in Egypt and Tunisia, we contend, are functions of differences in their underlying levels of economic development. So-called "modernization" theorists have long argued that processes of economic development lead to diversity and pluralism in a country's civic landscapes (Lerner 1958; Lipset 1959; Inglehart and Welzel 2009). Though both Egypt and Tunisia are middle-income countries, and as we argued earlier possessed of sufficient civil society capacity to compel incumbent autocrats to initiate democratic transitions, civil societies in the two nonetheless differed in important ways. In Egypt, as Masoud (2014) has argued, relatively low rates of urbanization and industrialization mean that the associational infrastructures on which leftist parties are based—such as labor unions—are not much in evidence. Instead, traditional forms of social organization prevail: When not "firmly bound by kinship and community" (Kornhauser 1998 (1959): 40), Egyptian citizens were most often embedded in religious forms of communal organization, such as the mosque and the Islamic *jamʿiyya* or association. Tunisia, in contrast, is a highly urbanized society (nearly 70% of Tunisians live in cities compared to 45% of Egyptians), with a GDP per capita approximately 30% higher than Egypt's. Tunisia's higher levels of urbanization and economic development contribute to the political parity we observed in post-Ben Ali Tunisia by generating an associational landscape that is far more diverse than the monolithically Islamic one that obtained in Egypt.

The relative pluralism of the two countries' civil societies can be seen in Table 5.3, which contains the rates of current and past membership in eleven types of organizations as reported by Egyptian and Tunisian respondents to the 6th wave of the World Values Survey. Across all types of organizations, Tunisians report significantly higher membership than their Egyptian counterparts. Where under 1% of Egyptians report (present or past) membership in a labor union or professional syndicate, approximately 2% of Tunisians do. Similarly, nearly 4% of Tunisians reported membership in "artistic, musical, or educational" organizations, compared to just 0.3% of Egyptians. Tunisians also appeared more likely to participate in political parties (1.7% versus 1.3% in Egypt). Thus,

Table 5.3. Self-Reported Rates of (Present or Past) Organizational Membership in Tunisia and Egypt Compared (2013)

Type of Organization	Tunisia	Egypt
Church or religious	1.2	0.8
Sport or recreational	5.5	0.3
Artistic, musical, or educational	3.9	0.3
Labor Union	1.9	0.3
Political party	1.7	1.3
Environmental	0.8	0.3
Professional association	1.8	0.4
Humanitarian or charitable	1.0	0.5
Consumer	0.4	N/A
Self-help, mutual aid	0.4	0.3
Other	0.1	N/A

Source: World Values Survey 6th Wave.

when non-Islamists sought to erect political parties in both Egypt and Tunisia, they had a much larger foundation of pre-existing, non-religious associations on which to build in Tunisia than in Egypt. The upshot is that the Tunisians' more pluralistic "political society" (Linz and Stepan 1996) may be attributable to their more pluralistic civil one.

The starkest illustration of the difference between Egyptian and Tunisian civil society lies in the two countries' labor movements and their roles in their countries' respective transitions. Where Egypt's principal labor organization, the Egyptian Trade Union Federation (ETUF), has long been seen as limited in scope and supine in the face of state authority (Pripstein-Posusney 1997), Tunisia's main union, the Tunisian General Labor Union (UGTT), is considered well organized, capable of pressing its demands, and in the post-authoritarian period has provided a center of gravity for opposition to Islamists.[43] Claiming approximately 500,000 members, the UGTT is described by Bellin (2002: 106) as an organization "with nationalist credentials, a broad popular base, and a dynamic, ambitious leadership that could credibly claim the national mantle." As we have seen in Chapter 3, the UGTT played a critical role in the December 2010 and January 2011 protests that brought down the Ben Ali regime. According to Beinin and Vairel (2011: 239) "while the highest ranks of the UGTT were part of the regime, its local leaderships joined the movement, providing activists with resources and savoir faire on the ground." Some have attributed the UGTT's activism during the revolution to its democratic structure, in which local union leaders were selected through direct elections.[44] For others, the UGTT's militancy dates to Tunisia's independence. According to King (2009: 171–172) "the UGTT's independent streak is tied to its history: it became the first independent trade union federation in Africa when it [. . .] detach[ed] itself from French trade union organizations during the colonial era." Regardless, of the source of the UGTT's superior militancy, the fact is that its Egyptian counterpart could not play a similar role as a source of organizational ballast for the non-Islamist opposition (Toensing 2011).

If the differences in Egypt's and Tunisia's civil societies proved determinative for the outcome of founding elections, where did those differences come from? There is evidence that they were a long time in the making. Tunisia was already ahead of Egypt developmentally as both were throwing off the shackles of colonialism in the 1950s. In 1952, the year of the Free Officer's coup that inaugurated the Egyptian Republic, Egypt's country's per capita GDP (in 1990 international dollars) is estimated at $900. Tunisia's per capita income for that same year is estimated at $1220.[45] Although both countries enter the middle of the twentieth century with similarly low rates of urbanization, Tunisia's urban population grew at a much more rapid clip than Egypt's, as can be seen in Figure 5.4. This was likely a reflection of what Bellin (2002, 17) has called Bourguiba's "liberal, as opposed to etatist" industrialization policies, which generated a far more vibrant and independent private sector than was able to emerge in Egypt under Nasser and Arab Socialism.

Susan Waltz (1995) has testified that Tunisia possessed a "well-rooted indigenous political culture of civil society" even

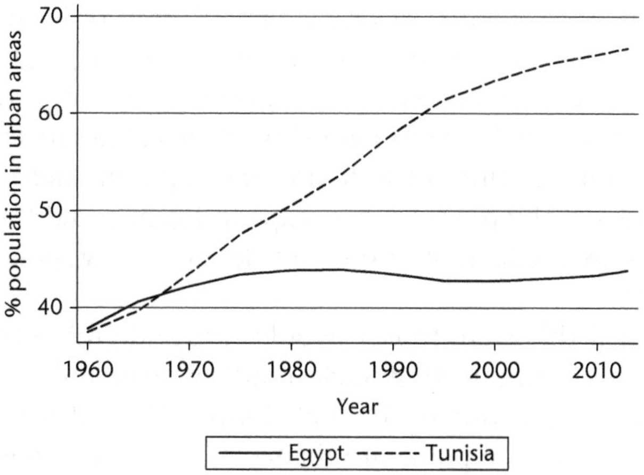

Figure 5.4. Historical Rates of Urbanization in Egypt and Tunisia
Source: World Bank Development Indicators.

prior to its independence. "Under French colonial tutelage," she writes, "Tunisians had participated in civic organizations as widely divergent as the scouts, the Women's International League for Peace and Freedom, Young Tunisians, the General Confederation of Workers (CGT), and, eventually, the General Union of Tunisian Workers (UGTT)" (Waltz 1995, 50). In Egypt during this period, by contrast, organized labor was so weak that President Nasser could "boast" in 1956 "that he had bought the working class for 4,000 [Egyptian pounds]," while it was the Muslim Brotherhood that was "the regime's most troublesome and potentially dangerous foe" (Gordon 1991, 135).

One might counter that our attention to the structure of civil society obscures a more basic explanation for why Islamists were more dominant in Egypt than in Tunisia—which is that Egyptians were simply more desirous than their Tunisian brethren of the application of Islamic law. This argument is difficult to dismiss. Evidence for this proposition is offered in Figure 5.5, which displays results from the Arab Barometer's 2011 surveys in both countries.[46] Citizens were asked to indicate the extent to which they agreed with the proposition that "government and parliament should enact laws in accordance with Islamic law (al-sharīʿa al-Islāmiyya)." Almost 47% of Egyptian respondents "strongly agreed" with the statement, in contrast to only 14% of Tunisians. It's worth noting that only 20% of Egyptians surveyed said they "disagreed" or "strongly disagreed" with the notion that government should enact laws to accord with shariah, while in Tunisia the figure was approximately 35%. The lopsidedness of the political landscape in Egypt could therefore be interpreted as a reflection of the lopsidedness of Egyptian political preferences.

But even if this were true, it would not undermine the central thesis of this chapter—that socio-political structures determined the ultimate disposition of the Arab Spring. After all, scholars have long argued that the political salience of religion wanes as countries industrialize and newly educated citizens cast aside religious superstition (Norris and Inglehart 2004; Gill 2001). Thus, whether Tunisia's pluralism stemmed from a pluralistic civil society or a

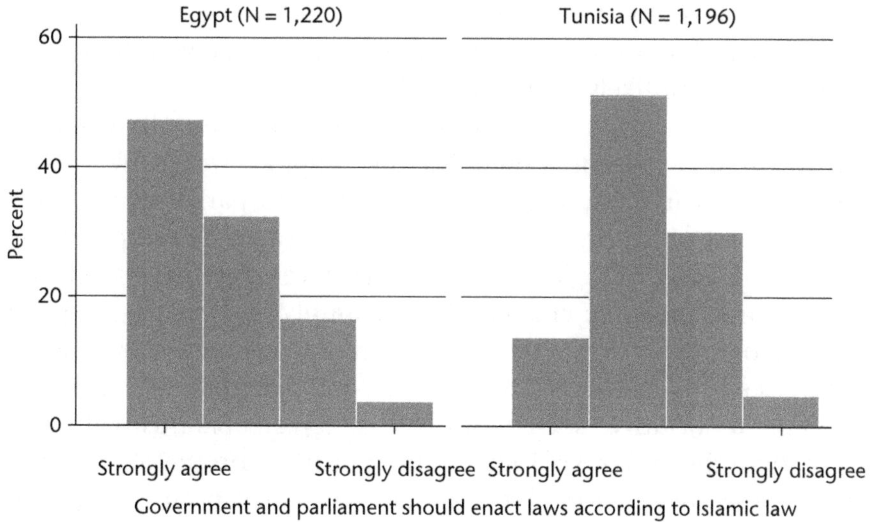

Figure 5.5. Egyptians' and Tunisians' Views on Sharia and Personal Status Laws
Source: Arab Barometer Project Second Wave, 2011.

smaller pool of believers, it is difficult to escape the conclusion that the ultimate cause of Tunisia's relative success, and Egypt's failure, is developmental.

Conclusion: Not Ready for Democracy?

On the eve of the January 25, 2011 revolution against Hosni Mubarak, the Egyptian scholar Amr Chobaki penned an essay entitled, "Egypt is not Tunisia." In it, he rehearsed a number of reasons why the ouster of Zine El Abidine Ben Ali would not be repeated on the banks of the Nile. "Tunisian workers and union leaders spoke out more eloquently than most Egyptian university professors," he declared. "The Tunisian education system may be the best in the Arab world," he said. "Tunisia does not have a Muslim Brotherhood that is intent on mobilizing thousands of people to defend its own agenda rather than the national interest," he wrote. "Tunisia [has] a healthy society," he argued, while "Egypt, on the other hand, has [. . .] a society that needs miracles to reform itself."[47] His sobering conclusion was that readers "should know that what happened in Tunisia is unlikely to happen in Egypt."

Of course, Chobaki was wrong: Mubarak, like Ben Ali, was overthrown—and in short order. But the Egyptian writer—who later went on to win a seat in Egypt's first democratic parliamentary election—was correct in a deeper sense. His error was not in emphasizing the importance of Egypt's and Tunisia's developmental trajectories for their democratic chances, it was simply in conflating regime breakdown with democratic transition. Regime breakdown, as we have seen in Chapter 3, "Breakdowns and Crackdowns," does not require a "healthy" society—only a coercive apparatus willing to cut loose the executive. Democratic transition, on the other hand, requires a highly particular confluence of state capacity and political pluralism that decades of scholarship have shown to be functions of long-term developmental factors. Analysts and historians will pore over the course of the transitions in Egypt, Tunisia, Libya, and Yemen, searching for critical junctures and momentous decisions that might have influenced each country's ultimate course. However, the simple—and perhaps, discouraging—fact is that if one had wished at the Arab Spring's outset to predict which of our four cases of regime breakdown would become a democracy, mere reference to gross developmental indicators (such as per capita income) would probably have been sufficient.

6

Limits and Legacies of the Arab Spring

After Tunisia's and Egypt's rulers resigned in quick succession in early 2011, nearly all observers of the Middle East sensed a tectonic shift in the region's politics. Every new act of defiance, no matter how small, suggested the Arabic-speaking world had changed irreovocably. For example, Marc Lynch (2012: 10), a gifted student of the Arab public sphere, wrote that, "The Arab uprisings are only the very earliest manifestations of a powerful change in the basic stuff of the region's politics." "The Arab people," he told us, "have been empowered."[1] In a March 2011 essay, the historian Rashid Khalidi marveled that the Arabs were "shaking off decades of cowed passivity under dictatorships that ruled with no deference to popular wishes."[2] The sentiment was echoed in the halls of power as well. When Mubarak stepped down on February 11, 2011, US president Barack Obama declared, "The people of Egypt have spoken, their voices have been heard, and Egypt will never be the same."[3]

However, three years after those uprisings began, the idea that the self-immolation of a frustrated fruitseller in a dusty Tunisian backwater could change the fundamental nature of Arab politics seems remarkably quaint, even naïve. After all, as we have seen in the preceding chapters, of the fourteen non-democratic Arab countries of the Middle East, only six—Tunisia, Egypt, Libya, Syria, Yemen, and Bahrain—experienced the kinds of regime-challenging protests that brought down autocrats.[4] Among these six cases of mass protest, only four—Libya, and the oil poor, non-hereditary regimes of Tunisia,

Egypt, and Yemen—actually unseated dictators and initiated democratic transitions. And of these four, only two countries—Tunisia and Egypt—could at any point have been said to have actually completed their transitions by produing elected governments with de facto authority over their territories. Libya, in contrast, produced an elected government whose actual power was tragically circumscribed by a proliferation of regional and tribal militias, and Yemen has featured neither an elected government nor a surfeit of the administrative capacity that is a democratic prerequisite. Finally, as of this writing, only Tunisia can be said to have *maintained* its transition, as Egypt's parliamentary elections were abrogated by court order and its elected president unseated by military coup.[5] Thus, like earlier political springtimes (1848, 1968) and the two prior "Arab Springs" of the late 1980s and the mid-2000s, the early rays of the third Arab Spring quickly yielded to a season far less agreeable.

One measure of the modesty of the Arab Spring's harvest is offered by the limited shift in the region's Freedom House scores of civil and political liberties over the past four years (Table 6.1).[6] Six of the fourteen countries of the Arab Spring have the same scores in 2013/14 that they had in 2010/11. Another six countries have scores that are worse (indicated by higher numbers). And only two—Libya and Tunisia—improved (that is, lowered) their scores during this period. Consistent with the narrative presented in Chapter 4, Egypt enjoyed a brief moment as a "partly free" country in 2012/13 before regressing to the "Not Free" designation that has stuck to the country ever since 1993. In fact, if we examine the Freedom House scores of just the six countries that experienced regime-challenging protests in the last three years (Bahrain, Egypt, Libya, Syria, Tunisia, and Yemen), three (Bahrain, Syria, and Yemen) are worse off at the time of this writing than they were before the Arab Spring began, one (Egypt) is exactly where it was, and only two (Tunisia and Libya) have posted improvements (although Libya's improvement, as we have shown, seems to exist only on paper).

This book comes to account for those trajectories, to explain why the hopes that attended the Arab Spring have not been fulfilled. All of these outcomes—the failures of uprisings in Syria and Bahrain,

Table 6.1. Freedom House Scores for the Countries of the Arab Spring, 2010–2014

Country	Popular Uprising?	Regime Breakdown?	Year 2010/11	2011/12	2012/13	2013/14
Algeria	No	No	11 (NF)	11 (NF)	11 (NF)	11(NF)
Bahrain	Yes	No	11 (NF)	12 (NF)	12 (NF)	12 (NF)
Egypt	Yes	Yes	11 (NF)	11 (NF)	10 (PF)	11 (NF)
Jordan	No	No	11 (NF)	11 (NF)	11 (NF)	11 (NF)
Kuwait	No	No	9 (PF)	9 (PF)	10 (PF)	10 (PF)
Libya	Yes	Yes	14 (NF)	13 (NF)	9 (PF)	9 (PF)
Morocco	No	No	9 (PF)	9 (PF)	9 (PF)	9 (PF)
Oman	No	No	11 (NF)	11 (NF)	11 (NF)	11 (NF)
Qatar	No	No	11 (NF)	11 (NF)	11 (NF)	11 (NF)
Saudi Arabia	No	No	13 (NF)	14 (NF)	14 (NF)	14 (NF)
Syria	Yes	No	13 (NF)	14 (NF)	14 (NF)	14 (NF)
Tunisia	Yes	Yes	12 (NF)	7 (PF)	7 (PF)	6 (F)
UAE	No	No	11 (NF)	12 (NF)	12 (NF)	12 (NF)
Yemen	Yes	Yes	11 (NF)	12 (NF)	12 (NF)	12 (NF)

*Shaded countries have worse Freedom House scores in 2013/14 than in 2010/11.

the successful transition in Tunisia, the coup in Egypt, the civil war in Libya, and the resilience of incumbent elites in Yemen—have been explained with reference to the strategies, choices, and idiosyncracies of each country's political actors. The literature on the Arab Spring is replete with narratives emphasizing the machinations of militaries, the sins (and virtues) of Islamists, the luck of institutional designers, and the pluck and savvy of protesters. However, this volume has attempted to make the case that close attention to the unfolding dynamic of the uprisings and their aftermaths reveals the overriding importance of structures, rather than agents, in determining outcomes.

Thus, we argue that the reason that quiescence rather than rebellion has been the norm for most Arab polities is that regimes were able to draw on structurally determined reserves of loyalty and repressive capacity to beat back challengers or to prevent them from emerging in the first place. The most resilient regimes were those that possessed oil wealth, which endowed them with the resources necessary to cement ruling coalitions and to bribe potentially restive populations. Also resilient were monarchies and other hereditary regimes, where decades (and in some cases, centuries) of fealty to the ruling family had cemented bonds between executives and coercive apparatuses, making defections of the sort observed in Egypt and Tunisia unlikely. It was only in regimes that lacked either of these attributes that oppositionists were able to compel the agents of despotic power to abandon rulers and initiate transitions. The one exception is Libya—an oil-rich regime that nonetheless broke down. However, Libya's defiance of our predictions was less due to inherent weaknesses in the ruling coalition than to the simple fact that even the strongest authoritarian regime would likely crumble before a sustained bombing campaign by the most powerful military alliance in human history.

The doleful outcomes in the Arab Spring's "success" cases also testify to the importance of inherited structures in determining ultimate trajectories. Democratic transitions do not begin from blank slates, after all. For three of the four cases of regime breakdown, the terrain faced by political elites was decidedly inhospitable to democratic projects. In their study of new democracies, the scholars Mansfield and Snyder (2007b: 8) summarized decades of social science wisdom on political development, noting that successful democratizers "tended to enjoy relatively high per capita income and literacy," featured citizenries with "the resources and skills to build the institutions and civil society organizations that democracy needs," and possessed "well-developed state institutions, particularly administrative bureaucracies that functioned in a reasonably efficient way to advance state objectives [...]" Only in Tunisia did some semblance of these things exist. Endemic state weakness in Libya has meant that elections in that country have not generated governments with the capacity to rule. In Yemen, a civil society fragmented by tribalism has proven unable to challenge incumbents for a share of power. Consequently, that country's transition increasingly seems cosmetic—a reshuffling rather than a revolution or even a reform.

Egypt is a more difficult case to account for. It has no deficit of stateness—in fact, it is famously possessed of thousands of years of centralized government. And its civil society was certainly strong enough to force the armed forces to defect from the executive, and to further compel incumbent elites to comply with popular demands for democratic elections. But what Egypt lacked was the kind of *pluralistic* civil society that has long been recognized to be a key ingredient for consolidated democracy. A poor, agrarian country, it had no equivalent of the powerful labor unions or confident secular groupings on display in more urban, developed Tunisia. Instead, Egyptian civil society was dominated by religious institutions, which Islamist parties mobilized to dramatic effect in the country's founding elections. Possessed of a supermajority in the country's legislature, Islamists seemed poised in the minds of some to erect a faith-based, one party regime in place of the patronage-based one over which Mubarak had presided. To roll back the Islamist juggernaut, non-religious parties and activists allied with agents of the state—the military and the judiciary—and endorsed a military coup that brought a decisive end not only to Islamist rule, but also to Egypt's first democratic experiment.

Our pessimistic assessment of the Arab Spring will almost invariably be met in some quarters with the rejoinder that democratic transitions take time, and that this book, coming as it does at the outset of what is a very long process, was destined to reach dismal conclusions. The scholar Sheri Berman has reminded us of the "inherent difficulty and complexity of building truly liberal democratic regimes."[7] "Getting rid of authoritarianism," she remarks, "is a long and nasty process; in the Middle East, at least that process has finally begun."[8] The scholar Eric Hobsbawm likewise cautions us to remember the long game of nineteenth- and twentieth-century Europe: "Two years after 1848, it looked as if it had all failed. In the long run, it hadn't failed. A good deal of liberal advances had been made. So it was an immediate failure but a longer term partial success—though no longer in the form of a revolution."[9] Similarly, the

Jack Goldstone (2014: 133) notes that "we should not expect most revolutions to suddenly create stable democracies. Revolutions create new dilemmas and unleash new struggles for power. Most revolutions, including even the American Revolution of 1776, went through more than one constitution, discriminated against minorities, and veered toward weak government or back toward authoritarian tendencies before achieving steady progress toward democracy."

We value these authors' optimism, even as we wonder precisely how much comfort can be taken in the conclusion that the Arab world today is where Europe was more than 165 years ago, or where the United States was almost 250 years ago. The more recent experience of other democratizing regions around the world teaches us that authoritarian breakdown does not have to be followed by resurgent dictatorships, military coups, or state collapse. Contrast the Arab Spring's discouraging report card with that of Eastern and Central Europe after the Berlin wall fell.[10] The year 1990 saw dramatic improvements in the Freedom House scores of every one of the eight members of the Warsaw Pact: Russia, Albania, Bulgaria, Czechoslovakia (now, of course, two countries), East Germany, Hungary, Poland, and Romania (see Table 6.2).[11] Today, all but the first two states are still considered democracies.

Table 6.2. Freedom House Scores for Warsaw Pact Countries, 1989–1992

Country	Year		
	1989/90	1990/91	1991/92
USSR/Russia*	11 (NF)	9 (PF)	6 (PF)
Albania	14 (NF)	13 (NF)	8 (PF)
Bulgaria	14 (NF)	7 (PF)	5 (F)
Czechoslovakia	12 (NF)	4 (F)	4 (F)
E. Germany**	12 (NF)	3 (F)	3 (F)
Hungary	7 (PF)	4 (F)	4 (F)
Poland	7 (PF)	4 (F)	4 (F)
Romania	14 (NF)	11 (NF)	10 (PF)

* 1989/90 score assigned to USSR, 1990/91 and 1991/92 to Russia.

** 1990/1, 1991/92 scores assigned to unified Germany.

Figure 6.1 helps us to begin understanding why the post-Cold War transitions in Eastern European countries proved more promising than those in the Arab world. The chart compares per capita incomes (PPP in 2005 constant dollars) between Eastern European cases in 1990 and the non-oil rich Arab regimes in 2010. The horizontal line is Argentina's estimated GDP per capita in 1975 on the eve of the coup that unseated Isabelle Peron, identified by Przeworski and Limongi (1996)[12] as the wealthiest democracy ever to have failed. Of the Eastern European cases, only Albania fell significantly below that threshold in 1990 (which might help explain why that country is not considered a democracy today). Of the Arab countries, in contrast, only Tunisia appears close to *meeting* the threshold.

One might expect that these developmental differences between Eastern European countries on the eve of the Velvet Revolution and Arab ones on the eve of the Spring are correlated with a constellation of other differences that would matter for the two regions' democratic fortunes. For instance, the states of Eastern Europe in 1990 appear to have been, on the whole, stronger than their contemporary Arab counterparts. To compare the two largest countries in each region—Russia's score on the World Bank's Government Effectiveness Index (which we use as a rough measure of state capacity) in 1996 (the earliest year available) was –0.5 on a scale from –2.5 to +2.5, while Egypt's 2012 score on the same index is –0.8.[13] To compare the two poorest countries from the two regions: Albania's 1996 government effectiveness score was -0.8, while Yemen's in 2012 was -1.3. The developmental differences are also likely to be reflected in the underlying pluralism of the two regions' respective societies: though Howard (2002) has argued that civil society in Eastern Europe was weak, the rates of organizational membership he reports for post-Communist countries in 1997 appear to outstrip those of the Arabic-speaking countries today, and aside from Tunisia's UGTT, there does not seem to be an Arab equivalent to the labor-based Solidarity movement that proved so decisive in ending Polish authoritarianism.[14] Though this is not the place to undertake a detailed comparison of post-Communist and Arab societies, our cursory comparison of their developmental differences suggests

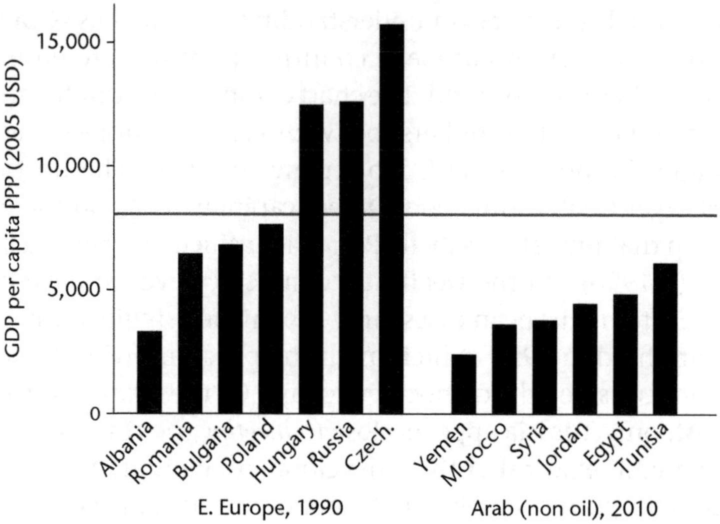

Figure 6.1. Per Capita GDPs of Eastern European (1990) and Arab Countries (2010) Compared

Source: Penn World Tables (7.1). Available at <https://pwt.sas.upenn.edu/php_site/pwt71/>.

that a principal reason most of the former Warsaw Pact countries are today members of the family of democracies is the same reason that only Tunisia seems poised to join them there: As the scholar Seymour Martin Lipset (1959: 75) put it so many years ago, "the more well to do a nation, the greater its chances of sustaining democracy."

In the remainder of this chapter, we explore the implications of our argument for future scholarship on the Middle East and democratic transitions more generally.

Personalism and Durability: A Curvilinear Relationship

Our first major implication concerns personal rule. When a capricious clique concentrates power in its own hands, comparativists have tended to expect violence and fragility. The textbook cases of modern "sultanism" regimes cruelly abused their peoples before collapsing like a house of cards. As a result, personalism has become synonymous with vulnerability.

The Arab uprisings have provided a rare test of this belief. In the span of a few months, mass movements challenged five non-monarchical regimes that were all personalistic, even sultanistic. Surprisingly, the regimes did not uniformly implode. In fact, one of the most corrupt, Syria, survived the wave of dissent. Personalism was not a structural flaw in the regime, but rather constituted a pillar of support. How did that phenomenon occur and what does it tell us about the general relationship between personalism and authoritarianism?

A sobering reality of the Arab uprisings is that non-violent opposition movements have not been able to defeat the coercive apparatus so long as it obeys the ruler (Chenoweth and Stephan 2014).[15] Clubs remained trumps and the best hope for breaking down authoritarianism was peeling off the top military commanders from the autocrat. Such defections occurred, to varying degrees, in Tunisia, Egypt, Yemen, and Libya, but in Syria, at the top echelons and in the innermost circles, the army and security forces cohered. In the core of authoritarian rule, personal fealty provided the backstop of repression. The corruption that had tied Syrian officers to the Asad clan did not doom the regime: it probably saved it.

The strength of this personalized coalition, however, was evident over a decade before the uprisings. If there is any event as unnerving for authoritarian elites as mass revolt, it is a top-level leadership transition. Succession moments are a breeding ground for factionalism and backstabbing. Syria passed through such a transition, more or less smoothly, when Bashar succeeded his father in 2000. The succession craft of prior years had cultivated deep commitments among officers to the regime's survival. This was not garden-variety personalism but dynasticism, and its regime-enforcing effects would devastate the regime's challengers in 2011. Regardless of the Syrian regime's ultimate fate, the immediate outcome—a military crackdown instead of authoritarian breakdown—was a remarkable departure from the trend elsewhere.

It is noteworthy that the other four non-monarchies hit by uprisings had been on some kind of path toward familial rule. In different ways, Tunisia, Egypt, Yemen, and Libya represented the rise of what the Egyptian scholar Saadeddin Ibrahim called "*gumlukiyyas*" ("republicarchies") in the Arab world. But they weren't there yet. Not one of their recent leaders had accomplished a father–son handover of power. Importantly, their armies had not sworn fealty to the heir apparent and, in Egypt and Yemen, privately balked at the prospect of hereditary succession. In sum, the repressive personnel were tied to a personalistic ruler, but they were not invested in a dynastic regime. When a crisis arose, the difference between this situation, on one hand, and Syria, on the other, was profound. Less intense personalism brought less, not more, stability.

Any broader lessons from this pattern are necessarily provisional. Nonetheless, the Arab uprisings suggest a curvilinear relationship between personalism and authoritarian durability, in which extreme personalization—through dynastic successions—actually fortifies regimes. If this pattern holds, it would substantially revise prior understandings. The literature on sultanism implies that rulers like Mubarak and Ben Ali would have been better off fortifying institutions and rooting out corruptions. Perhaps. The Asads' example, though, offers another survival strategy that may be far more brutal but just as effective: Instead of sharing power through legal-rational institutions, narrow the rulership to a family clique that enjoys the army's blessing.

This finding does not mean that dynastic regimes will never fall. In the twentieth century a number of regimes that resembled the Asads' Syria lost power. For example, regimes in Nicaragua and Haiti accomplished hereditary successions before crumbling before domestic unrest in 1979 and 1986 respectively. Still, even in those cases, regimes outlasted many other personalistic non-dynastic regimes. Further, when the opposition ultimately prevailed, authoritarian breakdown came through armed revolution (in Nicaragua) or through a rare combination of acute foreign pressure, domestic instability, and military discontent (in Haiti). In sum, the concentrated coercive power of dynastic rulers tends to extend their tenure compared to less personalized peers. Further, their embattled last years often entail large-scale repression as the security forces fight to save a system they helped establish.

Foreign Soldiers: The Agents that Change Structures

The second implication of our work concerns foreign intervention. We have shown that a structural framework based on oil rents and dynasticism accounts for variations between authoritarian breakdown and authoritarian survival across fourteen Arab states and, in particular, across the six states that faced uprisings in 2010–2011. The theory counters a tendency toward unwarranted voluntarism in the initial literature on the Arab Spring. The Arab world's autocracies are protected by an array of political and economic factors that suppress dissent in ordinary life and crush opposition when it emerges. If such fortified systems could be overturned by hastily formed social movements in a matter of months, the region would have witnessed far more successful uprisings in earlier periods. Therefore, while there is no denying that young activists helped catalyze the uprisings, their ultimate agency on questions of political change and continuity was circumscribed by the context in which they operated. Those antecedent contextual variables—not social networking or personal dignity—shaped the regime's response and determined whether rulers would fall or stand.

Such a structural account invites the question: Is there any role for human agency here? Can individuals undermine the structural supports of authoritarianism? Yes, in fact, they can. However, to find the agents of change, the people who shifted the structurally determined course of events in the Arab Spring, one must look beyond the local civilian opposition and consider the foreign soldiers who have periodically intervened on their side.

As we noted earlier, when the military remains loyal to the ruler, the dictator can execute a brutal crackdown on his opponents.

In this respect, the structural framework helps explains why Benghazi, Deraa, and Manama all suffered levels of armed repression that Tunis, Cairo, and Sanaa escaped. But the framework does not account for why Libya then experienced authoritarian breakdown and Qaddafi lost power—instead of remaining in office like his counterparts in Syria and Bahrain. At that point, human agency reenters the causal narrative. The Libyan regime was politically cohesive. It enjoyed dominance over its domestic opponents in terms of raw despotic power. But force could be overcome by greater force, drawn from outside the country's borders. When the foreign military forces of NATO and some members of the Gulf Cooperation Council imposed a no-fly zone, their airmen gradually tipped the military balance in favor of Libyan rebels.

To elaborate on this point, it is worth considering events before the Arab Spring. In essence, the triumph of foreign agents over authoritarian structures in Libya reprised the process of the Iraq invasion of 2003. Like Qaddafi, Saddam Hussein ruled an oil-rich (if internationally sanctioned) security state. Hussein's domestic opponents had failed to remove him during the 1990s. There was little expectation in 2003 that the agency and courage of local dissidents would topple the dictator in the near future. International events shattered this equilibrium. The US-led invasion ("Operation Iraqi Freedom") quickly broke the Iraqi army and Hussein's coercive control. In empirical terms, authoritarian breakdown through foreign-imposed regime change (FIRC) ushered in a turbulent decade of occupation and internecine war. In theoretical terms, the FIRC overrode Iraq's structural disposition to durable authoritarianism.

Foreign military interventions may be a kind of *deus ex machina* for saving countries gripped by durable authoritarianism, but they are no guarantee of happy endings or bright beginnings. The victory of indigenous opposition forces over authoritarianism can blaze a trail of optimism and promise, as in Tunisia. By contrast, the overthrow of Arab tyrants by foreign troops has paved the way to state collapse and militia rule. Analytically, it is not difficult to understand why this is the case. The same structures that held the regime together also kept violent sub-national actors in check. By razing the regime, the FIRC also shook the foundations of national political life. Normatively, however, this pattern raises a considerable problem. The only short-term treatment for durable authoritarianism may be a remedy — foreign military intervention — that carries harmful, and largely unmeasured, side effects for the presumptive beneficiaries.

This conundrum does not mean that some dictators do not "deserve" to lose power, because of their egregious moral or legal transgressions. It does imply, though, that the situation that comes after them may be no better, at least as far as large portions of the local population are concerned.

Development and Democracy

The third major implication of our argument concerns the relationship between economic development on the one hand, and democracy on the other. Scholars have long recognized, of course, that these two things are correlated, even as they have debated whether this correlation is evidence of causality, and whether the causal arrow runs from development to democracy or the other way around (see Przeworski et al. 2000 for a review). One strand of this literature, which has remained influential, holds that democracy emerges as a function of a modern, educated populace that is cognitively equipped for the give-and-take of a regime type founded on participation and compromise (Lipset 1959). Similarly, Lerner (1958: 25) in his study of modernization in the Middle East, hypothesized that "institutions of participation (e.g. voting)" grow out of the spread of literacy, which "equips [citizens] to perform the varied tasks required in [a] modernizing society."[16] More recently, Lankina and Getachew (2012) argued that subnational variation in democratic practice in India can be linked to variation in literacy rates, which they endogenize to the educational activities of foreign preachers during the colonial period: "Christian missionaires," they write, "have had a crucial bearing on democracy through literacy initiatives" (Lankina and Getachew 2012: 467).[17] This notion has also shaped public discourse. In 2012, the Egyptian novelist Alaa al-Aswany argued that voting should be restricted only to those who possessed basic literacy skills, as uneducated Egyptians were too susceptible to opportunistic politicians who "trade in religion" for the sake of achieving power.[18]

This book, while validating the perspective that development makes the emergence and survival of democracy more likely, has presented evidence that the causal pathway through which economic development strengthens prospects for democracy does not run through the preferences, values, and habits of individual voters. After all, it is worth noting that the literacy rate in Libya, according to the World Bank, is the highest of our four cases of regime breakdown—it hovers around 90%—and yet that has not enabled that country to complete a democratic transition and move politics from the battlefield to the ballot box. Tunisia's literacy rate, in contrast, is ten points lower, at 80%, and yet it is, as of this writing, the region's best performer (Egypt's adult literacy rate is 74%, and Yemen's 66%).[19]

Instead, the cases of regime breakdown and democratic transition in the Arab Spring direct our attentions to the ways in which developmental processes shape the resources available to oppositionists—both for compelling breakdowns in authoritarian regimes, and for competing with each other in the post-breakdown period. Industrialization generates new, class-based mass actors who can match older, religious-based ones. Increases in urbanization (and state capacity) mean that universal linkages based on class and citizenship supersede local ties based on sect, clan, and other ascriptive identities that fragment populations in the face of incumbents (Alexander 2010: 21; Arjomand 1988: 71–73; Richards and Waterbury 1998: 154–156; Charrad 2001: 4). Thus, we argue that it was the structure of political competition, rather than the alleged deficits of Arab voters, that constituted the link between development processes and democratic outcomes.

The "Arab" Democracy Deficit

The fourth implication of this book concerns the future study of regime durability and change in the object of social-scientific inquiry known as the "Arab" world. As noted in Chapter 1, Arabic-speaking countries have long been almost uniformly autocratic. It is thus natural that scholars would seek a unified explanation for why these lands remain stubborn holdouts agains the global tide of democracy. Earlier generations of scholars and writers located the fault in Islam. Writing in the eighteenth century, the French philosopher Montesquieu declared that "despotic government" was the special province of "Mohammedanism," while "the moderate government is better suited to the Christian religion."[20] The scholar Elie Kedouri (1992: 6) argued famously that Islam was profoundly bereft of the core democratic ideals of "representation, of elections, of popular suffrage, of political institutions being guarded and upheld by an independent judiciary, [of] the secularity of the state, [and] of society being composed of a multitude of self-activating, autonomous groups and associations." And Huntington (1991: 28) declared that "Islamic concepts of politics differ from and contradict the premises of democratic politics."

In an attempt to refute these claims, Stepan and Robertson (2003) note that Muslim countries such as Turkey and Indonesia have managed to sustain democracy for long periods, thus disproving the link between Islam and authoritarianism. Instead, they suggest that it is Arabs, and not Muslims, who have proven democratization-resistant. Diamond (2010) has argued that the answer to the riddle of Arab authoritarianism lies not in culture, but "political economy" and institutions—particularly, the dynamics of rentierism and the machinations of so-called "liberalized autocracies" to keep civil societies weak and oppositionists fragmented (see also Heydemann 2007). More recently, the economist Eric Chaney (2012: 393) has argued that the roots of Arab authoritarianism go back to the Muslim conquests of the seventh century: "The available evidence suggests that the region's democratic deficit is a product of the long-run influence of control structures developed under Islamic empires in the premodern era."

What this book has demonstrated, however, is that the quest to divine a single causal mechanism to explain authoritarianism throughout the Arabic-speaking countries is probably misguided.

As we have tried to show, there are multiple paths to authoritarianism, running through oil wealth, state incapacity, military centrality, the weakness of civil society, and other variables. Though we have argued that many of these are correlated with developmental factors, the fact remains that there is no identifiably "Arab" path to authoritarianism. Moreover, as the example of Tunisia demonstrates, not all of the countries of the region are bereft of resources for establishing democracies. Charles Kurzman (2007: 24) has noted that "the concept of a region called 'the Middle East' is a relatively recent and unstable construction," one that encompasses a diverse set of polities that sometimes share little in common. Our study suggests that this insight may also apply to the Middle East's Arab core, with its diversity of authoritarian forms and socio-economic structures.

The Future of the Arab Spring

As this book goes to press, the Arab world appears once again to be in the midst of a wave of change that is sweeping across borders and changing the lives of citizens. This new wave, however, is not one of democratic protest, of photogenic young people taking to the streets to reclaim their dignity, but of militant Islamists seizing control in the region's myriad ungoverned or weakly governed spaces. As Iraq and Syria contend with the rise of the so-called Islamic State in Iraq and the Levant (al-Dawla al-Islāmiyya fī al-ʿIrāq wa al-Shām), governments in Egypt, Libya, Tunisia, and Yemen also confront varying degrees of Islamist insurgency. In July 2014, Tunisian president Moncef Marzouki warned of "terrorist groups seeking to sow chaos and fear and trying to give excuses to postpone the elections and thus thwart the transition and the project of edifying a democratic state and pluralist society."[21] It is difficult to imagine a more sobering counterpoint to the expectations of democratic diffusion that attended the early days of the so-called Arab Spring.

Those looking for sources of optimism may wonder if they are to be found among the dogs that have not yet barked. Many think that it is only a matter of time before the doleful dynastic stability of

Jordan, Morocco, and Saudi Arabia gives way to popular demands for dignity and freedom. This may be so. But our theory predicts that these regimes will not respond to such challenges by turning in on themselves, packing the autocrat off to exile, and negotiating the dismantling of the old order. Monarchies that have ruled for the better part of 250 years in Saudi Arabia, 400 in Morocco, or 100 in Jordan, and gathered into their hands all the threads of power and privilege, will not go quietly. The Arab Spring's low-hanging fruit have fallen. If democracy does come to other countries in the region, it will likely be through a process far more evolutionary than revolutionary.

What of the four instances of regime breakdown? There is little reason to believe that surprises are in store, that dismal trajectories can be righted. Libyans completed a second parliamentary election in July of 2014, which by all accounts resulted in a reduction of Islamist representation in the legislature. Though some might believe this is an outcome to be celebrated, turnout was approximately one-fifth of what it had been in the country's first parliamentary elections, and Islamists reportedly responded to their loss by "attacking the airport, hoping that the conflict would prevent the new parliament from convening."[22] Increasingly, it seems that politics in the new Libya will be settled on the battlefield rather than at the ballot box.

Yemen, as of this writing, remains without a constitution or multiparty elections, although presidential and parliamentary contests are scheduled for February 2015.[23] Whether these will result in a dramatic break from authoritarianism remain to be seen, but the course of Yemen's transition thus far has given us little reason to expect that a liberal democracy will take root in that country. Similarly doleful is the outlook for Egypt. Though proponents of the July 3, 2013 military coup portray that event as a rescue of a fledgling democracy hijacked by radical Islam—US secretary of state John Kerry has declared that the Egyptian military "was asked to intervene by millions and millions of people: and that it was "restoring democracy"—the evidence suggests a more complex picture.[24] The country's new constitution includes promising provisions for gender equality, but also enshrined in the document are the military's prerogatives and effective independence from civilian oversight.[25]

A new law restricts political protests, and a new electoral system moves away from the limited proportional representation that Egyptian oppositionists had earned after Mubarak's overthrow.[26] In May 2014, in an uncomfortable echo of the Mubarak period, the general who overthrew Egypt's first democratically elected president was himself elevated to the presidency, with an official vote share of more than 95%.[27]

This leaves us with Tunisia. That country conducted its second parliamentary elections in October 2014. The result saw Ennahdha lose its plurality, replaced by the anti-Islamist Call of Tunisia party. Early indications suggest that Tunisia is managing its first elected alternation of governmental power without incident. Presidential elections, which will have been completed by the time this book goes to press, will provide another test of Tunisia's fledgling democracy.[28] A February 2014 survey of 1,232 Tunisians conducted by the International Republic Institute seems to indicate that Tunisians are ambivalent about their country's fledgling democracy. Healthy majorities of the citizens surveyed declared that they were satisfied with the new constitution and the new government. However, when asked if their country was headed in the right direction, only 47% answered affirmatively. Only time will tell if the pessimistic majority is on to something.[29]

The Tunisian exception, if it continues to be one, only underscores the modest harvest of the Arab Spring—a bitter litany of failed uprisings, brutal crackdowns, flawed elections, and endemic violence. If this book is any guide, the Arab Spring will be remembered not as a fundamental change in the dynamics of the region's politics, but as a reminder of the importance of inherited structures in determining the durability of autocrats and the prospects for democratic government. The uprisings may have opened a new chapter of contentious politics in the Arab world, but did not efface the social and economic structures impeding democratic development. It is thus difficult to escape the conclusion that, when the definitive history of the Arab Spring of 2011–2013 is finally written, it will be remembered less as a momentous change in the region's political makeup than as a momentary break in a longer, more dismal story.

Notes

Introduction

1. On the post hoc democratization argument for invading Iraq, see the memoirs of Douglas J. Feith (2008). Bush's Undersecretary of Defense for Policy from 2001 to 2005, *War and Decision: Inside the Pentagon at the Dawn of the War on Terror*. New York: Harper, 475–477.
2. See Charles Krauthammer (2005). "The Arab Spring of 2005," *Seattle Times*, March 21, <http://seattletimes.com/html/opinion/2002214060_krauthammer21.html>, accessed June 2, 2014; cf. Jon B. Alterman (2005). "Arab Spring into Long, Hot Summer," *CSIS: Middle East Notes and Comment*, 3.6 (June): 1.
3. *Why They Died: Civilian Casualties in Lebanon During the 2006 War* (New York: Human Rights Watch, 2007), 4.
4. "Secretary Rice Holds a News Conference," *Washington Post*, July 21, 2006. Available at <http://www.washingtonpost.com/wp-dyn/content/article/2006/07/21/AR2006072100889.html>, accessed July 6, 2014.
5. Joseph Massad has problematized the phrase "Arab Spring" as a US construct that carries ideological baggage from the Cold War. However, the Arabic version of the phrase (al-rabīʿ al-ʿarabī) enjoys nearly universal use in the Arab press and academe. In the United States, scholars appear to be split between talking about the Arab Spring and the Arab "uprisings." By contrast, the latter term is almost never heard in Arabic (*al-intifāḍāt al-ʿarabiyya*). See Joseph Massad (2012). "The 'Arab Spring' and Other American Seasons," *Al Jazeera*, August 29. Available at <http://www.aljazeera.com/indepth/opinion/2012/08/201282972539153865.html>, accessed March 19, 2014.
6. Our account of European "springs" from 1848 to 1968 relies heavily on John Merriman's excellent *A History of Modern Europe: From the Renaissance to the Present* (New York: W.W. Norton, 2010, 3rd ed.), 613–643.
7. For book-length treatments see, for example, Mohamed Althani (2012). *The Arab Spring and the Gulf States: Time to Embrace Change*.

London: Profile Books; Hamid Dabashi (2012). *The Arab Spring: The End of Post Colonialism*. London: Zed Books; John Davis, ed. (2013). *The Arab Spring and Arab Thaw: Unfinished Revolutions and the Quest for Democracy*. Farnham: Ashgate; James L. Gelvin (2012). *The Arab Uprisings: What Everyone Needs to Know*. New York: Oxford University Press; Mark L. Haas and David W. Lesch, eds. (2012). *The Arab Spring: Change and Resistance in the Middle East.* Boulder, CO: Westview; Clement Henry and Jang Ji-Hyang, eds. (2013). *The Arab Spring: Will it Lead to Democratic Transition?* New York: Palgrave Macmillan; Efraim Inbar, ed. (2013). *The Arab Spring, Democracy and Security: Domestic and International Ramifications*. New York: Routledge; Farhad Khosrokhavar (2013). *The New Arab Revolutions That Shook the World.* Boulder: Paradigm; Bahgat Korany and Rabab El-Mahdi, eds. (2012). *Arab Spring in Egypt: Revolution and Beyond.* Cairo: American University in Cairo Press; Marc Lynch (2012). *The Arab Uprising: The Unfinished Revolutions of the New Middle East.* New York: Public Affairs; David McMurray (2013). *The Arab Revolts: Dispatches on Militant Democracy in the Middle East.* Bloomington: Indiana University Press; Marwan Muasher (2014). *The Second Arab Awakening: And the Battle for Pluralism.* New Haven: Yale University Press; Carlo Panara (2013). *The Arab Spring: New Patterns for Democracy and International Law*. Leiden: Brill 2013; and Vijay Prashad (2012). *Arab Spring, Libyan Winter.* New York: AK Press.

Chapter 1

1. Marc Lynch (2011). "Will the GCC Stay on Top," *Foreign Policy*, December 15. Available at <http://mideastafrica.foreignpolicy.com/posts/2011/12/15/will_the_gcc_stay_on_top>, accessed July 7, 2014.
2. The survey asked respondents to report whether they obtained information from the Internet "daily, weekly, monthly, less than monthly, or never." Questionnaire and data are available at <http://www.worldvaluessurvey.org/WVSContents.jsp>, accessed July 8, 2014.
3. For a selected bibliography of social science research in this area, consult the list compiled by the Project on Middle East Political Science (POMEPS) at <http://pomeps.org/category/academic-works/arabuprisings>, accessed June 25, 2014.

Chapter 2

1. Website, US Naval Forces Central Command, US Fifth Fleet Combined Maritime Forces, <http://www.cusnc.navy.mil/command/history.html>, accessed June 4, 2014.
2. James Calderwood (2011). "Kuwait Gives Each Citizen Dh13,000 and Free Food," *The National* (Abu Dhabi), January 18. Available at <http://www.thenational.ae/news/world/middle-east/kuwait-gives-each-citizen-dh13-000-and-free-food>, accessed June 4, 2014.
3. "Saudi King Promises Reforms, Wage Increases, and Anti-Corruption Panel," Associated Press, March 18, 2011. Available at <http://www.thenational.ae/news/world/middle-east/saudi-king-promises-reforms-wage-increases-and-anti-corruption-panel>, accessed 4 June, 2014.
4. Habib Toumi (2011). "Public Sector in Qatar to Get 60% Pay Rise," Gulf News (Dubai), September 7. Available at <http://gulfnews.com/news/gulf/qatar/public-sector-in-qatar-to-get-60-per-cent-pay-rise-1.862595>, accessed July 8, 2014.
5. For Saudi Arabia's global ranking in terms of arms purchases, see Stockholm International Peace Research Institute, "The 15 Countries with the Highest Military Expenditure in 2011." Available at <http://www.sipri.org/research/armaments/milex/resultoutput/milex_15/the-15-countries-with-the-highest-military-expenditure-in-2011-table/view>, accessed 4 June, 2014.
6. Summer Said (2005). "Mubarak to Name Vice President after September Elections," *Arab News*, June 16. Available at <http://www.arabnews.com/node/268587>, accessed June 4, 2014; see also "I Will Not Succeed my Father," *News24*, November 6, 2007. Available at News24Archives <http://www.news24.com/Africa/News/I-will-not-succeed-my-father-20071105>, accessed June 4, 2014; and "Gamal Mubarak Denies Desire to Succeed Father," *Agence France Presse (AFP)*, March 29, 2006. Available at <http://dailystar.com.lb/Article.aspx?id=69415#axzz2Vv7CWjp4>, accessed June 4, 2014.
7. American Embassy in Cairo, Egypt (2009). "Scenesetter: President Mubarak's Visit to Washington." *Cablegate Search*, Cable Reference ID: #09CAIRO874. <http://www.cablegatesearch.net/cable.php?id=09CAIRO874&q=gamal%20mubarak>.
8. We thank Al Stepan for encouraging us to narrow the range of "sultanism." Note that this definition would set aside such corrupt but

non-hereditary regimes as the Philippines under Ferdinand Marcos and the Dominican Republic under Rafael Trujillo, while still including the Somozas' Nicaragua and the Duvaliers' Haiti.

9. An earlier version of this argument appeared in our essay "Tracking the 'Arab Spring': Why the Modest Harvest?" Journal of Democracy 24 (October 2013): 29–44.

Chapter 3

1. For an alternate view that Tunisian civilians, not the Tunisian military, determined the outcome, see Angrist (2013). "Understanding the Success of Mass Civic Protest in Tunisia," 550–551.
2. White House 2011. Press Release, "Statement by the President on Events in Tunisia." Available at <http://www.whitehouse.gov/the-press-office/2011/01/14/statement-president-events-tunisia>, accessed June 5, 2014.
3. Steven Erlanger (2011). "France Seen Wary of Interfering in Tunisia Crisis," *New York Times,* January 16. Available at <http://www.nytimes.com/2011/01/17/world/africa/17france.html>, accessed July 8, 2014.
4. Office of the Press Secretary (2011). "Remarks by the President in State of Union Address," January 25, Washington, DC. Available at < http://goo.gl/X0zpLahttp://goo.gl/X0zpLa>.
5. "Meet Asmaa Mahfouz and the Vlog that Helped Spark the Revolution," YouTube. <http://www.youtube.com/watch?v=SgjIgMdsEuk &feature=player_embedded>, accessed June 4, 2014.
6. "President Hosni Mubarak's Speech, January 28 (Arabic)," <http://www.youtube.com/watch?v=nE5wuvCyjNM>, accessed June 4, 2014.
7. Scott Shane and David D. Kirkpatrick (2011). "Military Caught between Mubarak and Protesters," *New York Times,* February 10.
8. Anthony Shadid (2011a). "Mubarak Won't Run Again, but Stays: Obama Urges a Faster Shift of Power," *New York Times,* February 2, 2011.
9. "US Urges Restraint in Egypt, Says Government Stable," Reuters, January 25, 2011. Available at <http://af.reuters.com/article/topNews/idAFJOE70O0KF20110125>, accessed June 5, 2014.
10. Mark Landler (2011). "Clinton Calls for 'Orderly Transition' in Egypt," *New York Times,* January 31. Available at <http://www.nytimes.com/2011/01/31/world/middleeast/31diplo.html?_r=0>, accessed June 5, 2014.
11. Peter Nicholas and Christi Parsons (2011). "Obama's Advisors Split on When and How Mubarak Should Go," *Los Angeles Times,* February

10. Available at <http://articles.latimes.com/2011/feb/10/world/la-fg-obama-team-20110210>, accessed June 5, 2014; Helene Cooper, Mark Landler, and David E. Sanger (2011). "Policy Rift Muddled U.S. Signals about the Departure of Mubarak," *New York Times,* February 13.

12. Sherif Tarek (2011). "Bosses, Enforcers, and Thugs in Egypt's Battle of the Camel to See Harsh Retribution," *Ahram Online,* April 19. Available at <http://english.ahram.org.eg/NewsContent/1/64/10293/Egypt/Politics-/Bosses,-enforcers-and-thugs-in-Egypts-Battle-of-th.aspx>, accessed July 8, 2014.
13. Ryan Lucas and Paul Schemm (2011). "Cairo's Anti-Mubarak Activists Bruised, Battered, Sleep-Deprived and Hungry," *Associated Press,* February 5.
14. "Egyptian Generals Speak About the Revolution, Elections," *Washington Post,* May 18, 2011,< http://www.washingtonpost.com/world/middle-east/egyptian-generals-speak-about-revolution-elections/2011/05/16/AF7AiU6G_print.html>, accessed May 26, 2011.
15. International Crisis Group (2011). "Popular Protests in the Middle East and North Africa (III): The Bahrain Revolt," *Middle East Report No. 105,* April 6.
16. "Yemen 'Day of Rage' Draws Tens of Thousands," *Reuters,* February 3, 2011. Available at <http://www.reuters.com/article/2011/02/03/us-yemen-protest-idUSLDE71206M20110203>, accessed June 5, 2014.
17. International Crisis Group (2011). "Popular Protests."
18. Houthis follow the Zaydi branch of Shi'ism.
19. See Steven Erlanger (2010). "In Yemen, U.S. Faces Leader Who Puts Family First," *New York Times,* January 4. <http://www.nytimes.com/2010/01/05/world/middleeast/05.html?_r=0>, accessed June 5, 2014.
20. "US urges Yemen's Saleh to Transfer Power", *Reuters,* January 25, 2011. Available at <http://www.aljazeera.com/news/middleeast/2011/07/201171016636884366.html >, accessed June 4, 2014.
21. Ariel Zirulnick (2011). "Egypt's Protests Told by# Jan25," *The Christian Science Monitor.* Available at <http://www.csmonitor.com/World/Global-News/2011/0125/Egypt-s-protests-told-by-Jan25>, accessed June 5, 2014.
22. "Security Council Condemns Human Rights Violations by Yemeni Authorities, Abuses by 'Other Actors', after Months of Political Strife," *United Nations Security Council Department of Public Information,* October 21, 2011. <https://www.un.org/News/Press/docs/2011/sc10418.doc.htm>, accessed June 11, 2014.
23. International Crisis Group (2011). "Popular Protests."

24. "Founding Statement of the Interim Transitional National Council," *The Interim National Transitional Council* website, March 5, 2011. Available at <http://tinyurl.com/lcen8fv>, accessed June 5, 2014.
25. While recognizing the relative power of the Libyan military over domestic dissidents, we do not overestimate the capacity of the Libyan armed forces for traditional war against other states. Despite its oil wealth, Libya met defeat in 1987 in the much poorer state of Chad. Rex Brynen, Pete W. Moore, Bassel F. Salloukh, and Marie-Joëlle Zahar (2012). *Beyond the Arab Spring: Authoritarianism & Democratization in the Arab World.* Boulder, CO: Lynne Rienner Press, 28.
26. "Security Council Approves 'No-Fly Zone' Over Libya," United Nations Security Council Department of Public Information, March 17, 2011. Available at <http://www.un.org/News/Press/docs/2011/sc10200.doc.htm>, accessed June 5, 2014.
27. White House (2011b). "Remarks by the President in Address to the Nation on Libya," National Defense University, Washington D.C., March 28, <http://whitehouse.gov/the-press-office/2011/03/28/remarks-president-address-nation-libya>, accessed June 24, 2014.
28. As Secretary of Defense Gates, an initial opponent of intervention, explained in early March: "A No-Fly Zone Begins with an Attack on Libya to Destroy the Air Defenses. That's the Way You Do a No-Fly Zone. And Then You Can Fly Planes around the Country and Not Worry about the Other Guys Being Shot Down. But That's the Way it Starts. So it's a Big Operation in a Big Country," David E. Sanger (2012). *Confront and Conceal: Obama's Secret Wars and Surprising Use of American Power.* New York: Broadway Books, 301.
29. "Muammar Gaddafi: How He Died," *BBC News*, October 31, 2011. Available at <http://www.bbc.co.uk/news/world-africa-15390980>, accessed June 5, 2014).
30. See, for example, Ziad Abu-Rish (2011). "All Sorts of Interventions," *Bitter Lemons* 10.9 (March 24). Available at <http://www.bitterlemons-international.org/previous.php?opt=1&id=333#1365>, accessed June 5, 2014.
31. International Crisis Group (2011). "Popular Protests."
32. *The World Factbook: Bahrain* (n.d.). Washington, DC: CIA. Available at <https://www.cia.gov/library/publications/the-world-factbook/geos/ba.html>, accessed June 5, 2014.

33. Bumiller (2011), 'Egypt Stability Hinges on a Divided Military,' *New York Times,* 5 February 2011. Available at <http://www.nytimes.com/2011/02/06/world/middleeast/06military.html>, accessed June 5, 2014.
34. A more intriguing counterfactual comes from Marc Lynch's discussion of the crisis. His account indicates that the Saudi influence was most significant for tipping the political balance in elite negotiations away from a pacted transition to constitutional monarchy and toward a political impasse that would be resolved through violence. In this telling, the Saudi-led security action served mainly to enforce the political consensus among Saudi and Bahraini hard-liners, and squelch deal making between Bahraini soft-liners and moderate oppositionists (Lynch 2012: 137).
35. US Department of State, Office of the Spokesperson (2011). "Clinton at National Democratic Institute's Award Dinner" 7 November. Available at <tunisia.usembassy.gov/clinton-ndi-nov-7-2011.html>, accessed June 5, 2014.
36. Ian Black (2011a). "Six Syrians Who Helped Bashar al-Assad Keep Iron Grip after Father's Death," *Guardian,* April 28, 2011. Available at <http://www.guardian.com/world/2011/apr/28/syria-bashar-assad-regime-members> (March 30, 2014).
37. Rania Abouzeid (2011). " Syria's Revolt: How Graffiti Stirred an Uprising," *Time,* March 22. Available at <http://tinyurl.com/lzvv49a>, accessed June 5, 2014.
38. "A Timeline of Some Key Events in the Syrian Uprising," *Associated Press,* March 16, 2012, <http://english.alarabiya.net/articles/2012/03/16/200987.html>, accessed June 6, 2014.
39. "A Timeline of Some Key Events in the Syrian Uprising," *Associated Press,* March 16, 2012, <http://english.alarabiya.net/articles/2012/03/16/200987.html>, accessed June 6, 2014.
40. Despite months of bullish commentary in US media implying the Syrian opposition was gaining ground, in summer 2013 the rebels controlled only one of sixteen provincial capitals, and that foothold was in an area where demography (a Sunni-dominated population) was particularly unfavorable for the Assad regime. Interview with Patrick Cockburn, *Democracy Now,* June 5, 2013. Available at <http://www.democracynow.org/2013/6/5/as_us_deploys_patriot_missiles_and>, accessed June 6, 2014.

Chapter 4

1. "Sisi Sworn in as President of Egypt," Egyptian State Information Service, June 8, 2014. Available at <http://www.sis.gov.eg/En/Templates/Articles/tmpArticles.aspx?CatID=2848#.U6rwFo1dXGE>.
2. For example, the Yemen expert Gregory Johnsen declared in June 2011 that if the Yemeni military became involved in the struggle for power between his rivals, "then we could have something that really drags Yemen into a civil war." See Bernard Gwertzman (2011). "Yemen Tensions at the Tipping Point," Council on Foreign Relations, June 2.
3. For an excellent account of how a new political elite emerged out of the chaos in the early days of the Libyan revolution, see Duncan Pickard (2014). "Forging Legitimacy: Abdel Hafiz Ghoga and the Founding Weeks of Libya's National Transitional Council," Harvard Kennedy School Case Program.
4. Patrick Markey and Ulf Laessing (2014). "Armed Militias Hold Libya Hostage," Reuters, March 30.
5. "Libyan Major General Khalifa Haftar Claims Government Suspended in Apparent Coup Bid," *CBS*/Reuters, February 14, 2014; Abdullah Kamal (2014). "Libya's Conflict: Between Coup and State Restoration," *al-Arabiyya*, June 4.
6. For an optimistic take on Libya's prospects, see Lindsay Benstead, Ellen M. Lust, and Jakob Wichmann (2013). "It's Morning in Libya: Why Democracy Marches On," Foreignaffairs.com, August 6.
7. Zaid al-Ali and Donia Ben Romdhane (2012). "Tunisia's New Constitution: Progress and Challenges to Come," Opendemocracy.net, February 16.
8. This account draws on material from Tarek Masoud (2011a). "The Road to (and from) Liberation Square," *Journal of Democracy*, July 2011: 20–34; Masoud (2011b). "Liberty, Democracy, and Discord in Egypt," *Washington Quarterly*, August 2011: 117–129; and Masoud (2014). "Egyptian Democracy: Smothered in the Cradle, or Stillborn?" *Brown Journal of World Affairs*, Summer/Fall: 3–19.
9. See Steven Cook (2007). *Ruling But Not Governing: The Military and Political Development in Egypt, Algeria and Turkey* (Council on Foreign Relations).
10. Nathan Brown (2013). "Egypt's Wide State Reassembles Itself," *Foreign Policy*, July 17. Available at <http://mideastafrica.foreignpolicy.com/

posts/2013/07/17/egypt_s_wide_state_reassembles_itself>, accessed August 14, 2014.

11. "Egypt after Mubarak: Three Ex-Ministers Arrested," *BBC News*, February 17, 2011.
12. Shaymā' al-Qarnshāwī and Basant Zayn al-Dīn and ʿĀdil al-Darjalī (2011). "Tawābiʿ ḥal al-Ḥizb al-Waṭanī (Effects of the Dissolution of the NDP), *al-Miṣrī al-Yawm* (Cairo), April 17. Available at <http://www.almasryalyoum.com/node/404437>.
13. Clark Lombardi (2009). "Egypt's New Chief Justice," www.comparativeconstitutions.org, September 30, 2009. Available at <http://www.comparativeconstitutions.org/2009/09/egypts-new-chief-justice.html>, accessed August 14, 2014.
14. This count does not include the three non-ministerial positions of cabinet rank: Governor of the Central Bank; director of the General Intelligence Directorate; and the Chairman of the Suez Canal Authority (all of whom were also retained by Sharaf). Cabinet lists available at <http://en.wikipedia.org/wiki/Shafik_Cabinet> and <http://en.wikipedia.org/wiki/Sharaf_Cabinet>, accessed August 14, 2014.
15. Alaa Bayoumi (2013). "Lack of Unity Stalls Egypt's Youth Revolution," *al-Jazeera*, February 21.
16. "In Translation: The Revolutionary Youth Coalition's Final Report," *Jadaliyya Reports*, July 18, 2012. Available at <http://www.jadaliyya.com/pages/index/6480/in-translation_the-revolutionary-youth-coalitions>, accessed August 14, 2014.
17. "al-ʿIryān: al-kura fī malʿab al-quwwāt al-mislaḥa (al-ʿIryān: The Ball is in the Armed Forces' Court)," Shabakat Raṣd (Raṣd News Network), February 12, 2011. Available at <https://www.facebook.com/RNN.NEWS/posts/188587671176234>, accessed August 14, 2014.
18. See Michele Dunne (2011). "Egypt: Elections or Constitution First," Carnegie Endowment for International Peace, June 21. Available at <http://carnegieendowment.org/2011/06/21/egypt-elections-or-constitution-first/2rad>.
19. Ḍuḥā al-Gindī and Muḥammad Khayāl (2011). "Usāma al-Ghazālī Ḥarb fī ḥiwār maʿ al-Shurūq Atmanā an yabqā al-ʿaskarī fi al-sulṭa liʿāmayn, li'anahu mish qāʿid ʿalā nafasnā (Usāma al-Ghazālī Ḥarb in an interview with al-Shurūq (I Hope the Army Stays in Power for Two Years, Because It's Not Inconveniencing Us)," *al-Shurūq* (Cairo), September 29. Available at <http://www.shorouknews.com/news/view.aspx?cdate=29092011&id=703e808f-86d4-47ba-a0d5-758d6a7e8dcd>.

20. Available at <https://twitter.com/ElBaradei/status/43809276766076928>, accessed August 14, 2014.
21. "Al-bayān raqam 5 lil-majlis al-ʾaʿlā lil-quwwāt al-misalaḥa (Statement number 5 of the Supreme Council of the Armed Forces)," Egyptian State Information Service, February 14, 2013. Available at <http://www.sis.gov.eg/Ar/Templates/Articles/tmpArticles.aspx?ArtID=44125#.U6smwo1dXGE>.
22. Steve Hendrix and William Wan (2011). "Egyptian Prime Minister Ahmad Shafiq Resigns Ahead of Protests," *Washington Post*, March 4.
23. Amro Hassan (2011). "Thousands of Protesters Storm into State Security Headquarters," *Los Angeles Times*, March 5, 2011; "Egypt Security Building Stormed," *al-Jazeera*, March 5; Neil MacFarquhar (2011). "Egypt Ends Domestic Spying Agency, but Creates New One," *New York Times*, March 15.
24. For a review of the debate surrounding the extent of the Muslim Brotherhood's role in the January 25, 2011 revolution, see Hisham Hellyer (2014). "Faking Egypt's Past: The Brotherhood and Jan. 25," *al-Arabiyya*, January 20. Available at: <http://english.alarabiya.net/en/views/news/middle-east/2014/01/20/Faking-Egypt-s-past-the-Brotherhood-and-Jan-25.html>, accessed August 14, 2104.
25. See "Omar Suleiman on the Crisis," *ABC News*, February 6, 2011. Available at <http://abcnews.go.com/ThisWeek/video/omar-suleiman-crisis-12852023>, accessed August 14, 2104; and Christiane Amanpour (2011). "Suleiman: Egypt Will Not Be Anything Like Tunisia," *ABC News*, February 3, 2011. Available at <http://abcnews.go.com/International/egypt-abc-news-christiane-amanpour-exclusive-interview-vice/story?id=12836594>, accessed August 14, 2014.
26. Ellis Goldberg (2011). "Tariq al-Bishri and Constitutional Revision," February 15. Available at <http://nisralnasr.blogspot.com/2011/02/tariq-al-bishri-and-constitutional.html>, accessed August 14, 2014.
27. "al-Bishrī raʾīsan li-lajnat taʿdīl al-dustūr (al-Bishrī is President of Constitutional Amendment Committee)," *al-Wafd* (Cairo), February 15, 2011.
28. "Qarār al-Majlis al-ʾAʿlā lil-quwwāt al-misalaḥa raqm 1 lisanat 2011 (Supreme Council of the Armed Forces decree #1 of the year 2011), February 14, 2011. Available at <http://www.sis.gov.eg/Newvr/rev25th3/html/link12x.htm>. (Emphasis is the author's.) Although the committee's mandate was broad, the decree did single out specific articles for possible cancellation or amendment, including article 179 (which had eliminated due process for so-called "terror

suspects"), article 77 (which allowed the president to serve an unlimited number of six-year terms), article 88 (which had limited judicial oversight of elections), article 93 (which limited the ability of parliamentary candidates to appeal electoral decisions), and article 189 (which specified procedures for constitutional amendment).

29. "Key Constitutional Amendments Announced, Egypt," *Ahram Online*, February 27, 2011. Available at <http://english.ahram.org.eg/NewsContent/1/64/6537/Egypt/Politics-/Key-constitutional-amendments-announced,-Egypt.aspx>, accessed August 14, 2014.
30. For the text of the proposed amendments (eventually passed on March 19, 2011), see: "Al-Naṣ al-kāmil lil-taʿdīlāt al-dustūriyya alatī sayujrī al-istiftāʾ ʿalayhā fī Miṣr (The Complete Text of the Constitutional Amendments that Will Be Put to a Referendum in Egypt)," *al-Arabiyya*, March 8, 2011. Available at <http://www.alarabiya.net/articles/2011/03/08/140716_1.html>; For helpful English-language summaries of the amendments, see Michele Dunne and Mara Revkin (2011). "Overview of Egypt's Constitutional Referendum," Carnegie Endowment for International Peace, March 16; and James Feuille (2012). "Reforming Egypt's Constitution: Hope for Egyptian Democracy?" *Texas International Law Journal*, 47(1): 237–259. Ultimately, the committee proposed the cancellation of article 179 and amendments to all of the articles specified in the SCAF's February decree as well as to articles 75, 76, 77, 139, and 148. See also discussion in Masoud (2014: 133–134).
31. This new legislature would then have six months to select a one-hundred member constituent assembly, which would then have another six months to craft a new constitution, which would then be put to a popular referendum.
32. Raḍwā Silāwī (2011). "al-Ikhwān yadʿūn al-shaʿb al-liltaṣwīt liṣāliḥ al-taʿdīlāt al-dustūriyya (The Brothers Call the People to Vote for the Constitutional Amendments)," *Ikhwan Online* (Cairo), March 12. Available at <http://www.ikhwanonline.com/new/print.aspx?ArtID=80460&SecID=0>.
33. The English-language text of the declaration is available at <http://www.egypt.gov.eg/english/laws/constitution/>, accessed on May 1, 2014.
34. Anthony Shadid (2011). "Islamists Flood Square in Cairo in Show of Strength," *New York Times*, July 29.
35. "Democratic Alliance (Freedom and Justice)," *Ahram Online*, November 18, 2011. Available at <http://english.ahram.org.eg/NewsContent/33/

103/26895/Elections-/Electoral-Alliances/Democratic-Alliance.aspx>, accessed August 15, 2014.

36. Heba Saleh (2011). "ElBaradei to Launch Bill of Rights for Egypt," *Financial Times*, June 19. Available at <http://www.ft.com/cms/s/0/13acd2c8-9a91-11e0-bab2-00144feab49a.html#ixzz1T66Q77Kf>, accessed August 15, 2014.
37. "Yaḥyā al-Gamal: Muʿtamar al-Wifāq al-Waṭanī yaʿqid jalsatahu al-ʿāma althāniya ghadan (The National Accord Conference Holds its Second General Meeting Tomorrow)," Egypt State Information Service, May 25, 2011. Available at <http://www.sis.gov.eg/Ar/Templates/Articles/tmpArticles.aspx?ArtID=47502#.U8q7W4BJfiM>.
38. Usāma ʿAbd al-Salām (2011). "Khubarā': Mu'tamar al-Wifāq al-Waṭanī Mu'āmara (Experts: The National Accord Conference is a Conspiracy)," *Ikhwanonline*, May 23, 2011. Available at <http://www.ikhwanonline.com/Article.aspx?ArtID=84824&SecID=0>.
39. Aḥmad Raḥīm, "Miṣr: Murshid al-Ikhwān yudāfaʿ ʿan al-ʿaskar wa al-jamāʿa lam tatakhidh mawqifan min jumʿa al-indhār al-akhīr (Egypt: The Brotherhoods Guide defends the military and the Society has not taken a stance regarding the Friday of Last Warning)," al-Hayāt (London), July 14, 2011. Available at: <http://www.daralhayat.com/portalarticlendah/287835>, accessed August 15, 2014.
40. Nawāra Fakhrī and Nirmīn ʿAbd al-Ẓāhir, "Mamdūḥ Shahīn: al-dustūr al-jadīd yajib an yaḥmī al-jaysh min hawā al-ra'īs al-qādim (Mamdūḥ Shahīn: The new constitution must defend the army from the whims of the next president," al-Yawm al-Sābiʿ (Cairo), May 26, 2011. Available at: <http://www.youm7.com/News.asp?NewsID=421567&SecID=12>.
41. Kristen Stilt (2012). "The End of One Hand: The Egyptian Constitutional Declaration and the Rift between the 'People' and the Supreme Council of the Armed Forces," Northwestern Public Law Research Paper No. 12-10, April 8, 2012. Available at <http://papers.ssrn.com/sol3/papers.cfm?abstract_id=2037563>, accessed August 15, 2014.
42. "In Translation: The Revolutionary Youth Coalition's Final Report." Available at: <http://www.jadaliyya.com/pages/index/6480/in-translation_the-revolutionary-youth-coalitions->, accessed August 15, 2014.
43. "Cabinet to Announce Charter of 'Governing' Constitutional Principles," *Daily News* Egypt, August 18, 2011. Available at <http://thedailynewsegypt.com/2011/08/18/cabinet-to-announce-charter-of-governing-constitutional-principles.html>.

44. The text of the so-called Silmī document can be viewed here: <http://www.youm7.com/News.asp?NewsID=533327#.U6uW641dXGE>.
45. Yasser Burhāmi statement, August 13, 2011. Available at <https://www.facebook.com/yasserborhamy/posts/268753966475177>.
46. Nada Hussein Rashwan (2012). "Mohamed Mahmoud Street, 1 Year On: Changing the Course of Egypt's Revolution," *al-Ahram Online*, November 21. Available at <http://english.ahram.org.eg/NewsContent/1/64/58526/Egypt/Politics-/Mohamed-Mahmoud-Street,--year-on-Changing-the-cour.aspx>, accessed August 15, 2014.
47. "Mursī: Rafaḍnā wathīqat al-Silmī i'anahā taḍ' al-jaysh fawq al-dustūr (Morsi: We Refused the Silmī Document Because it Puts the Army above the Constitution," *Maṣrāwī* (Cairo), November 17, 2011. Available at <http://www.masrawy.com/news/egypt/politics/2011/november/17/4601062.aspx>.
48. Quoted in Rashwan (2012). "Mohamed Mahmoud Street, 1 Year On: Changing the Course of Egypt's Revolution," *al-Ahram Online*, November 21.
49. See ʿAmrū Hāshim Rabīʿ (2011). "al-asbāb al-ḥaqīqiyya warāʾ qānūn al-intikhāb (The True Reasons Behind the Electoral Law)," *al-Miṣrī al-Yawm* (Cairo), August 14. Available at <http://www.almasryalyoum.com/news/details/209957>; For details of the Egyptian electoral system used in 2011, see "Elections in Egypt: Analysis of the 2011 Parliamentary Electoral System," Middle East and North Africa, International Foundation for Electoral Systems, November 1, 2011.
50. "Nour Party," Carnegie Endowment for International Peace, September 21, 2011. Available at <http://carnegieendowment.org/2011/09/21/nour-party?reloadFlag=1>, accessed August 15, 2014.
51. For a description of NDP-successor parties, see "NDP Offshoots," *al-Ahram Online*, November 18, 2011. Available at <http://english.ahram.org.eg/NewsContent/33/104/26897/Elections-/Political-Parties/NDP-Offshoots.aspx>, accessed June 6, 2014.
52. Ḥamdī Dabsh, Hānī al-Wazīrī, Ghāda Muḥammad al-Sharīf, Majdī Abū al-ʿAynayn (2012). "Shūrā al-Ikhwān yaḥsim murashaḥ al-riʾāsa al-thulathāʾ (MB Consultative Council Decides Presidential Candidacy on Tuesday)," *al-Miṣrī al-Yawm* (Cairo), March 26. Available at <http://www.almasryalyoum.com/node/735301>, accessed June 6, 2014.
53. Video of the March 31, 2012 press conference nominating Khayrat al-Shāṭir can be seen here: <http://www.youtube.com/watch?v=nX3-y_l6_iE>.

54. For an early report of Shafiq's intention to seek the presidency, see Aḥmad Abū Ṣāliḥ (2011). "Video: Shafīq ladā al-niyya liltarashuḥ lil-riʾāsa (Video: Shafīq Intends to Run for the Presidency)," *al-Wafd* (Cairo), October 25, 2011. Available at <http://www.masress.com/alwafd/113683>; For a report on Shafiq's official announcement, see Amīra Hishām (2012). "Aḥmad Shafīq Yaʿlan Tarashaḥuh rasmiyan li-riʾāsat al-jumhūriya (Ahmad Shafiq Officially Announces his Candidacy for the Presidency)," *Bawābat al-Ahrām*, February 14, 2012. Available at <http://www.masress.com/ahramgate/172313>.
55. Ashraf Badr, "ʿUmar Sulaymān yaʿlan tarashaḥuh lil-riʾāsa khilāl sāʿāt (Sources: Omar Suleiman to Announce his Presidential Candidacy within Hours)," *al-Ahrām* (Cairo), April 2, 2012. Available at <http://gate.ahram.org.eg/NewsContent/13/105/1922272/>.
56. The law was an amendment to law 73 of 1956 governing the exercise of political rights. The text is available at <http://kenanaonline.com/users/lawing/posts/419293>.
57. "Ḥaythiyāt ḥukm al-dustūriyya bibuṭlān mawād fī qānūn mubasharat alḥuqūq al-siyasiya 'al-ʿazl' (Rationale of the Constitutional Court's Decision to Invalidate Articles in the Law on the Exercise of Political Rights 'Exclusion')," *al-Waṭan* (Cairo), June 14, 2012. Available at <http://www.elwatannews.com/news/details/15643>.
58. "Al-Shater Reinstated Deputy Chairman of Muslim Brotherhood in Egypt," *Ikhwanweb.com*, April 19, 2012. Available at <http://www.ikhwanweb.com/article.php?id=29907>, accessed June 6, 2014.
59. "Maḥkama al-qaḍāʾ al-idārī tuwaḍaḥ asbāb ḥal al-jamʿiyya al-taʾsīsīya (Administrative Court Explains Reasons for Dissolving Constituent Assembly)," *alFajr* (Cairo), April 10, 2012. Available at <http://new.elfagr.org//?option=com_content&view=article&id=158757#>, accessed June 6, 2014.
60. See "al-Librāliyūn fī al-barlamān al-miṣrī yansaḥibūn min jalsat al-dustūr al-jadīd (Liberals in the Egyptian Parliament Withdraw from Session on New Constitution)," *al-Wasaṭ*, March 25, 2012. Available at <http://www.alwasatnews.com/3487/news/read/645567/1.html; and "Aqbāṭ Miṣr yansaḥibūn min lajnat ṣiyāghat al-dustūr> (Copts of Egypt Withdraw from the Constitution Drafting Committee)," *al-Waṭan al-ʿArabī*, April 2, 2012. Available at <http://www.alwatanalarabi.com/article/4264/#.U6yKmY1dXGE>; and Tarek Masoud (2012). "Egypt's Spymaster Candidate for President," *Newsweek*, April 16.

61. For two takes on Abū al-Futūḥ, see Shadi Hamid (2012). "A Man for All Seasons," *Foreign Policy*, May 9, and Eric Trager (2012). "The American Media Gets an Egyptian Presidential Candidate All Wrong," *New Republic*, May 3.
62. For evidence that Sabāḥī and Abū al-Futūḥ were seen by activists of the RYC as the two most congenial candidates, see "In Translation: The Revolutionary Youth Coalition's Final Report."
63. Results for both rounds of the 2012 presidential election are available at <http://pres2012.elections.eg/>.
64. David D. Kirkpatrick (2012a). "Blow to Transition as Court Dissolves Egypt's Parliament," *New York Times*, June 14, 2012. Available at <http://www.nytimes.com/2012/06/15/world/middleeast/new-political-showdown-in-egypt-as-court-invalidates-parliament.html?pagewanted=all>, accessed August 14, 2014.
65. "Ḥaithīyāt al-Dustūriyya fi ḥukm ḥal majlis al-sha'b (Rationale of the Constitutional Court's Decision to Dissolve the People's Assembly)," *al-Waṭan* (Cairo), June 14, 2012. Available at <http://egyptelections.carnegieendowment.org/2012/06/19/the-constitutional-declaration-with-june-17-2012-annex-addedhttp://www.elwatannews.com/news/details/15636>, accessed June 6, 2014.
66. See Masoud (2014: 216–217, fn19) for a critique of the legal rationale behind the ruling.
67. "Military Shuts down Egypt's Parliament," *CNN*, June 15, 2012. Available at <http://www.cnn.com/2012/06/15/world/meast/egypt-ruling/>, accessed August 15, 2014.
68. Text of June 18. 2012 constitutional declaration available at <http://english.ahram.org.eg/NewsContent/1/64/45350/Egypt/Politics-/English-text-of-SCAF-amended-Egypt-Constitutional-.aspx>, accessed August 15, 2014.
69. For example, on June 17, 2012 the noted analyst of Arab affairs Issandr al-Amrani concluded that the constitutional declaration was "a plan for living with Morsi." See <https://twitter.com/arabist/status/214496661391675392>.
70. David D. Kirkpatrick (2012b). "Named Egypt's Winner, Islamist Makes History," *New York Times*, June 24, 2012. Available at <http://www.nytimes.com/2012/06/25/world/middleeast/mohamed-morsi-of-muslim-brotherhood-declared-as-egypts-president.html?pagewanted=all&_r=0>, accessed August 14, 2014.

71. "Morsi Campaign Press Conference at Fairmont Hotel to Discuss Latest Developments," *Ikhwanweb*, June 22, 2012. Available at <http://www.ikhwanweb.com/article.php?id=30125>, accessed August 14, 2014.
72. Sāmī Majdī (2012a). "Wā'il Ghunaym yuṭālib al-ra'īs Mursī bitaṣḥīḥ al-masār wa taḥqīq al-wu'ūd al-sita (Wael Ghonim Demands President Morsi to Right the Path and Fulfill his Six Promises)," *Maṣrāwī* (Cairo), July 28, 2012. Available at <http://www.masrawy.com/news/egypt/politics/2012/july/28/5216953.aspx?ref=moreclip>.
73. Steve Hendrix and Ernesto Londono (2012). "Egypt's Morsi Makes Bid to Reinstate Islamist Parliament," *Washington Post*, July 8. Available at <http://articles.washingtonpost.com/2012-07-08/world/35488975_1_morsi-islamists-supreme-constitutional-court>, accessed June 6, 2014.
74. "Choice of New PM Hisham Qandil Divides Egypt's Political Class," *Ahram Online*, July 24, 2012. Available at <http://english.ahram.org.eg/NewsContent/1/64/48570/Egypt/Politics-/Choice-of-new-PM-divides-Egypts-political-class.aspx>, accessed August 14, 2014.
75. Sāmī Majdī (2012b). "Wathīqat al-Fairmont wa musalsal al-khidā' al-Ikhwānī (The Fairmont Document and the Series of Brotherhood Deceptions)," *Maṣrāwī* (Cairo), July 29, 2012. Available at <http://www.masrawy.com/News/Writers/General/2012/july/29/5219555.aspx>.
76. Aḥmad 'Abd al-'Aẓīm 'Āmir (2012). "Bawābat al-Ahrām tanshur biṭāqa ta'rīfiya bi'abraz wuzarā' ḥukūmat Qandīl wa khalfiyātihim al-siyāsiya (Ahram Gate Publishes Biographical Sketches of the Most Prominent Ministers of Qandīl's Cabinet and Their Political Backgrounds)," *al-Ahrām*, August 3, 2012. Available at <http://gate.ahram.org.eg/News/237222.aspx>.
77. 'Abd al-'Aẓīm 'Āmir, "Bawābat al-Ahrām tanshur biṭāqa ta'rīfiya . . . "
78. "Morsi Retires Egypt's Top Army Leaders." *Al-Ahram Online* (Cairo), August 12, 2012. Available at <http://english.ahram.org.eg/NewsContent/1/64/50239/Egypt/Politics-/UPDATE--Morsi-retires-top-army-leaders;-amends--Co.aspx>, accessed June 6 2014.
79. Michele Dunne (2012). "Egyptian President Morsi's Counter-Coup, Move Three," Atlantic Council, August 12. Available at <http://www.acus.org/egyptsource/egyptian-president-morsis-counter-coup-move-three>, accessed June 6, 2014.
80. It has been reported that Sīsī was not the passive recipient of Morsi's favor in August 2012, but an active player in the so-called

"counter-coup" who allegedly shared "the aggravation of officers who watched huge amounts of money squandered on projects that lined the pockets of the high command but left the soldiers unable to fight effectively." See Christopher Dickey (2012). "Egypt's New Defense Minister Abdel Fatah al-Sisi," *Newsweek*, August 20. Available at <http://www.newsweek.com/egypts-new-defense-minister-abdel-fatah-al-sisi-64401>, acessed August 12, 2014.

81. David D. Kirkpatrick and Mayy El Sheikh (2013). "Morsi Spurned Deals, Seeing Military as Tamed," *New York Times*, July 6. Available at <http://www.nytimes.com/2013/07/07/world/middleeast/morsi-spurned-deals-to-the-end-seeing-the-military-as-tamed.html?pagewanted=all>, accessed August 14, 2014.
82. Avi Issacharoff (2012). "Egypt's President Morsi Removes Defense Minister Tantawi, Chief of Staff," *Haaretz*, August 12, 2012. Available at <http://www.haaretz.com/news/middle-east/egypt-s-president-morsi-removes-defense-minister-tantawi-chief-of-staff-1.457696>.
83. <https://twitter.com/ElBaradei/status/234763863990620162>.
84. Abdel-Rahman Hussein (2012). "Egyptian Military Bows to Morsi's Orders," *The Guardian*, August 13. <http://www.theguardian.com/world/2012/aug/13/egyptian-military-shakeup-not-personal-morsi>, accessed August 14, 2014.
85. "Morsi Appoints Mahmoud Mekki as Vice President," *al-Ahram*, August 12, 2012. Available at <http://english.ahram.org.eg/NewsContent/1/64/50241/Egypt/Politics-/-Morsi-appoints-Mahmoud-Mekki-as-vice-president.aspx>, accessed August 14, 2014.
86. "Profile: Egypt's Vice-President Mahmoud Mekki," *BBC News*, December 22, 2012. Available at <http://www.bbc.com/news/world-middle-east-19255836>, accessed August 14, 2014.
87. Aḥmad Ḥāfiẓ (2012). "Bil-ʾams nāʾib ʿām wa ghadan safīr Mursī bil-fātīkān (Yesterday the Attorney General and Tomorrow Morsi's Ambassador to the Vatican)," *al-Ahrām*, October 11. Available at <http://gate.ahram.org.eg/News/260554.aspx>.
88. ʿĀdil al-Sirūgī (2012). "al-Nāʾib al-ʿām yarfuḍ qubūl manṣib safīr Miṣr bil-fātīkān wa yufaḍal al-istimrār fi ʿamalih (The Attorney General Rejects the Position of Egypt's Ambassador to the Vatican and Prefers to Stay in his Job)," *al-Ahrām* (Cairo), October 14. Available at <http://digital.ahram.org.eg/articles.aspx?Serial=1060125&eid=1387>.

89. "Update: Public Prosecutor to Stay after Morsy Agreement," *Egypt Independent*, October 13, 2012. Available at <http://www.egyptindependent.com/news/update-public-prosecutor-stay-after-morsy-agreement>, accessed August 14, 2014.
90. Muḥammad Waṭanī (2012). "Baqā᾽ al-nā'ib al-ʿām fi manṣibuhu intiṣār lil- qaḍā᾽ ʿalā al-ri'āsa . . . wa tarājāʿ than li-Mursī amām al-sulṭa al-qaḍā'iyya (The Continuation of the Attorney General in His Post is a Victory for the Judges Against the Presidency . . . and Morsi Backs Down Before the Judicial Branch a Second Time)," *al-Ahrām*, October 13. Available at <http://gate.ahram.org.eg/NewsContent/13/70/261187/أخبار/الشارع-السياسي/بقاء-النائب-العام-في-منصبه-انتصار-للقضاء-على-الرئا.aspx>.
91. Text of constitutional declaration available at <http://english.ahram.org.eg/News/58947.aspx>, accessed June 6, 2014.
92. "Egypt's Baraei to Address Tahrir Rally, List Demands of New 'National Front,'" *Ahram Online*, November 30, 2012. Available at <http://english.ahram.org.eg/NewsContent/1/64/59510/Egypt/Politics-/Egypts-Baradei-to-address-Tahrir-rally,-list-deman.aspx>, accessed August 14, 2014.
93. "Egypt's Baraei to Address Tahrir Rally."
94. Kareem Fahim and Nicholas Kulish (2013). "Opposition in Egypt Urges Unity Government," *New York Times*, January 30. Available at <http://www.nytimes.com/2013/01/31/world/middleeast/egypt-protests.html>, accessed August 14, 2014.
95. Reza Sayah, Michael Pearson, and Laura Smith-Spark (2012). "Morsi to Address Egyptians Amid Mounting Violence," *CNN*, December 5. Available at <http://www.cnn.com/2012/12/05/world/meast/egypt-protests>.
96. Heba Saleh (2012)."Egypt's Constitutional Court Halts work," *Financial Times*, December 2, 2012. Available at <http://www.ft.com/intl/cms/s/0/f08f7efc-3c75-11e2-86a4-00144feabdc0.html#axzz365iWrfEW>, accessed August 14, 2014.
97. Randa Ali and Hatem Maher (2012). "Morsi's Decree Cancelled, Constitution Referendum to Take Place on Time," *al-Ahram Online*, December 9. Available at <http://english.ahram.org.eg/NewsContent/1/64/60092/Egypt/Politics-/Morsis-decree-cancelled-constitution-referendum-t.aspx>, accessed June 6, 2014.

98. Zeinab El Gundy (2012). "Egypt's Defence Minister Calls for 'Dialogue Meeting' Wednesday," *Ahram Online*, December 11. Available at <http://english.ahram.org.eg/NewsContent/1/64/60316/Egypt/Politics-/Egypts-defence-minister-calls-for-dialogue-meeting.aspx>, accessed June 6, 2014.
99. Yezid Sayigh (2013). "Morsi and Egypt's Military," *Al Monitor*, January 8. Available at <http://www.al-monitor.com/pulse/originals/2013/01/morsi-army-egypt-revolution.html#>, accessed August 14, 2014.
100. Abdel-Rahman Hussein (2012). "Egyptian Assembly Passes Draft Constitution Despite Protests," *The Guardian*, November 29. Available at <http://www.theguardian.com/world/2012/nov/30/egypt-constitution-morsi>, accessed August 14, 2014.
101. "Beleaguered Constituent Assembly Votes on Egypt's Draft Constitution," *Ahram Online*, November 29, 2012. Available at http://english.ahram.org.eg/NewsContent/1/64/59447/Egypt/Politics-/Beleaguered-Constituent-Assembly-votes-on-Egypts-d.aspx, accessed August 14, 2014.
102. For an analysis of the 2012 constitution and the role it carves out for Islamic law, see Clark Lombardi and Nathan Brown (2012). "Islam in Egypt's New Constitution," *Foreign Policy Middle East Channel*, December 13. Available at <http://mideastafrica.foreignpolicy.com/posts/2012/12/13/islam_in_egypts_new_constitution>, accessed August 14, 2014.
103. Salma Abdelaziz (2012). "Morsi Signs Egypt's Constitution into Law," *CNN*, December 26.
104. Hend Kortam (2013a). "More Governorates Call on Army to Manage State," *Daily News Egypt*, March 4. Available at <http://www.dailynewsegypt.com/2013/03/04/more-governorates-call-on-army-to-manage-state/>, accessed August 14, 2014.
105. Hend Kortam (2013b). "No-Confidence Petition Launched against Morsi," *Daily News Egypt*, April 28. Available at <http://www.dailynewsegypt.com/2013/04/28/no-confidence-petition-launched-against-morsi/>, accessed August 14, 2014.
106. Eman El-Shenawi (2013). "Sign up for Mursi's Ouster, Urges Egypt 'Rebellion' Group," *al-Arabiyya*, May 14. Available at <http://english.alarabiya.net/en/News/middle-east/2013/05/14/Sign-up-for-Mursi-s-ouster-urges-Egypt-rebellion-group-.html>, accessed August 14, 2014.

107. Patrick Kingsley (2013). "Tamarod Campaign Gathers Momentum among Egypt's Opposition," *The Guardian*, June 27, 2013. Available at <http://www.theguardian.com/world/2013/jun/27/tamarod-egypt-morsi-campaign-oppsition-resignation>, accessed August 14, 2014.
108. Haitham el-Tabei (2013). "Fears Grow of Clashes between Morsi Supporters, Foes," Agence France Press, June 25, 2013. Available at <https://uk.news.yahoo.com/fears-grow-clashes-between-morsi-supporters-foes-022155676.html#tvu9Tk0>, accessed August 14.
109. Dāliā ʿUthmān (2013a). "Fīdīū . . . Al-Sīsī: lan nasmaḥ bitarwīʿ al-shaʿb al-Miṣrī wa sananmnaʿ al-iqtitāl al-dākhilī wa amāmnā usbūʿ lil-muṣālḥa (Video . . . Al-Sīsī: We Won't Allow the Intimidation of the Egyptian People and Will Prevent Domestic Slaughter and We Have One Week for Reconciliation)," *al-Miṣrī al-Yawm* (Cairo), June 23. Available at <http://www.almasryalyoum.com/news/details/ 224875>.
110. Heba F. El-Shazli (2013). "Should Egyptians Believe Morsi?" *Jadaliyya*, June 28. Available at <http://www.jadaliyya.com/pages/index/12479/should-egyptians-believe-morsi->, accessed August 14, 2014.
111. Mike Giglio (2013). "A Cairo Conspiracy," *Daily Beast*, July 12. Available at <http://www.thedailybeast.com/articles/2013/07/12/a-cairo-conspiracy.html>, accessed August 14, 2014.
112. David Kirkpatrick, Kareem Fahim, and Ben Hubbard (2013). "By the Millions, Egyptians Seek Morsi's Ouster," *New York Times*, June 30.
113. Dālyā ʿUthmān (2013b). "Al-jaysh: muhla 48 sāʿa li-talbiyat maṭālib al-shaʿb wa ʿilā sanusharaf ʿalā khāriṭat ṭarīq lil-mustaqbal (Army: 48 Hours to Respond to the Demands of the People Or Else We Will Supervise a Roadmap to the Future)," *al-Miṣrī a-Yawm* (Cairo), July 1. Available at <http://www.nytimes.com/2013/07/01/world/middleeast/egypt.html?pagewanted=allhttp://www.almasryalyoum.com/news/details/229197#>, accessed August 14, 2014>; Gregg Carlstom (2013). "Army Delivers Ultimatum to End Egypt Crisis," *Al-Jazeera*, July 1. Available at <http://www.aljazeera.com/news/middleeast/2013/07/201371145513525182.html>, accessed June 6, 2014.
114. "Morsi: Ḥayātī thaman lilḥifāẓ ʿalā al-sharʾiyya wa atbāʿ al-niẓām al-sābiq lan yaʿūdū, wa hunāk man yastaghil ghaḍab al-shabab (Mursi: My Life is the Price of Maintaining Legitimacy, and the Followers of the Old Regime Must Not Return, and There Are Those

Who Exploit the Anger of the Youth)," *al-Ahrām*, July 2, 2013. Available at <http://gate.ahram.org.eg/News/367671.aspx>.

115. Khālid al-Shāmī (2013). "Tamarrud taṣur ʿalā raḥīl Mursī wa tuhadid bimuḥakamatihi wa anṣārahu wāṣlū al-ʿitiṣām fī Rābʿa (Tamarrus Insists on Morsi's Departure and Threatens to Try Him as His Supporters Continue Their Protest in Rābʿa)," *al-Quds al-ʿArabī* (London), July 1. Available at <http://www.alquds.co.uk/?p=59332>.
116. Tarek El-Tablawy and Mariam Fam (2013). "Egypt Interim Leader Sworn in as Islamists Targeted," *Bloomberg*, July 4. Available at <http://www.bloomberg.com/news/2013-07-03/Morsi-proposes-power-sharing-as-egypt-army-deadline-approaches.html>.
117. The EUSpring project of the Department of Politics and International Studies of the University of Warwick has compiled a timeline of the Tunisian transition from 2010 to 2013 that proved useful in structuring this narrative. The timeline is available at <http://www2.warwick.ac.uk/fac/soc/pais/research/clusters/irs/euspring/advisoryboard/tunisia_timeline_2010-2013.pdf>, accessed August 14, 2014.
118. David Kirkpatrick (2011b). "Tunisian Leader Flees and Prime Minister Claims Power," *New York Times*, January 14. Available at <http://www.nytimes.com/2011/01/15/world/africa/15tunis.html?pagewanted=all&_r=0>, accessed August 14, 2014.
119. "Constitutional Debate," *al-Jazeera*, January 14, 2011. Available at <http://www.aljazeera.com/news/africa/2011/01/201111420494248476.html>, accessed August 14, 2014.
120. For background information on the Tunisian constitutional council, see "Constitutional History of Tunisia," Constitutionnet. Available at <http://www.constitutionnet.org/country/constitutional-history-tunisia>, accessed August 14, 2014.
121. Amy Fallon (2011). "Tunisia Gets Third Leader in 24 Hours," *The Guardian*, January 15, 2011. Available at <http://www.theguardian.com/world/2011/jan/15/tunisia-third-leader-speaker-parliament>, accessed August 14, 2014.
122. "Tunisian Opposition Factions to Unite," *PressTV* (Iran), January 19, 2011. Available at <http://edition.presstv.com/detail/160953.html>, accessed August 14, 2014.

123. "Tunisia's Mohammed Ghannouchi Defends New Government," *BBC News*, January 18, 2011. Available at <http://www.bbc.co.uk/news/world-africa-12213284>, accessed August 15, 2014.
124. "Tunisian Minister and Ex-Dissident Defends Cabinet," *BBC News*, January 19, 2011. Available at <http://www.bbc.co.uk/news/world-africa-12223043>, accessed August 15, 2014.
125. "Tunisian Minister and Ex-Dissident Defends Cabinet."
126. "Interview Transcript: Rachid Ghannouchi," *Financial Times* (London), January 18, 2011. Available at <http://www.ft.com/intl/cms/s/0/24d710a6-22ee-11e0-ad0b-00144feab49a.html#axzz36EiHDRLr>, accessed August 15, 2014.
127. "Tūnis: Istiqālat al-Ghanūshī wa al-Mibazaʿ min al-ḥizb al-ḥākim (Tunis: Resignation of Ghannouchi and Mebezaa from the Ruling Party)," *BBC News Arabic*, January 18, 2011. Available at <http://www.bbc.co.uk/arabic/middleeast/2011/01/110118_ghannouchi_tunisia.shtml>.
128. "Masīrat al-ḥurriya tuṭālib biʾisqāṭ ḥukūmat ijhāḍ al-thawra fī Tūnis (March of Freedom Demands the Fall of the Counterrevolutionary Government in Tunis)," *al-Ahrām al-Masāʾī* (Cairo), January 24, 2011. Available at <http://massai.ahram.org.eg/issue/Inner.aspx?IssueId=411&typeid=27&ContentID=26639>.
129. Sami Zemni (2014). "The Extraordinary Politics of the Tunisian Revolution: The Process of Constitution Making," Taylor and Francis Online, *Mediterranean Politics*, 1–17.
130. Makeup of the first and second cabinets of Mohamed al-Ghannouchi can be found at "Ḥukūmatā al-Wazīr al-awwal Muḥammad al-Ghanūshī (Two Cabinets of Prime Minister Mohamed al-Ghannouchi)," al-Qaṣba (Tunis), n.d. Available at <http://www.alkasbah.tn/حكومتا-الوزير-الأول-محمد-الغنوشي>.
131. Mahan Abedin, "Tunisia: Islamist Leader Returns from Exile—An Interview with Rashid al-Ghannoushi," *Le Monde Diplomatique* English Edition, January 2011. Available at <http://mondediplo.com/openpage/tunisia-islamist-leader-returns-from-exile-an>, accessed August 14, 2014.
132. Īhāb al-Tūnisī (2011). "Jadal fī Tūnis Ḥawl Majlis Ḥimāyat al-Thawra (Debates in Tunisia around the Committee to Protect the Revolution," *Maghārbiyya*, February 22. Available at <http://magharebia.com/ar/articles/awi/features/2011/02/22/feature-03>, accessed August 15, 2014.
133. "Tūnis: Taʾsīs al-Majlis al-Waṭanī li-Ḥimāyat al-Thawra (Tunis: Establishment of National Council to Protect the Revolution)," *al-Fajr*

News, February 16, 2011. Available at <http://www.turess.com/alfajrnews/45748>.

134. "Ḥarakat al-Tajdīd: Majlis Ḥimāya al-Thawra. Izdiwājiya fī al-sulṭa qad takhlaq azma siyasiya tuʿarqil taḥqīq al-intiqāl al-dīmqrāṭī wa injāz mahām al-thawra (Ettajdid Movement: Committee to Protect the Revolution . . . Dualism of Power Could Create a Political Crisis and Delay the Achievement of Democratic Transition and the Goals of the Revolution)," *al-Ṭarīq al-Jadīd*, February 22, 2011. Available at <http://attariq.org/spip.php?article1123&debut_articles_rubrique=195>.
135. Eymen Gamha (2011b). "Tunisia's Constituent Assembly: How Long Will it Last?" *Tunisialive*, October 10, 2011. Available at <http://www.tunisia-live.net/2011/10/10/constituent-assembly-what-about-its-duration/>, accessed August 15, 2014.
136. "Tunisian PM Mohammed Ghannouchi Resigns Over Protests," *BBC News*, February 27, 2011. Available at <http://www.bbc.co.uk/news/world-africa-12591445>, accessed August 15, 2014.
137. "Taʿyīn al-Bājī Qāʾid al-Sibsī wazīran ʾawwal (Appointment of Beji Caid Essebsi as Prime Minister)," *al-Ṣabāḥ al-Yawm* (Tūnis), February 28, 2011. Available at <http://www.turess.com/assabah/50124>.
138. Iheb Ettounsi (2011). "Tunisia Unveils Political Roadmap, New Cabinet," *Magharebia*, March 7. Available at <http://magharebia.com/en_GB/articles/awi/features/2011/03/07/feature-01>, accessed August 15, 2014.
139. Ettounsi, "Tunisia Unveils Political Roadmap, New Cabinet."
140. Rajaa Basly, "The Future of al-Nahda in Tunisia," Sada (Carnegie Endowment for International Peace), April 20, 2011. Available at <http://carnegieendowment.org/2011/04/20/future-of-al-nahda-in-tunisia/fel7>, accessed August 24, 2014. For Ghannouchi's full statement (and Essebsi's riposte), see <https://www.youtube.com/watch?v=6akJ2E7CGIM>, accessed August 15, 2014.
141. Asmāʿ Nuwayra (2011). "Ṣuʿūbāt fī masār al-taḥawwul al-dīmuqrāṭī fī Tūnis (Difficulties of Democratic Transition in Tunis)," Ṣadā (Carnegie Endowment for International Peace), March 30. Available at <http://carnegieendowment.org/2011/03/30/صعوبات-في-مسار-التحول-الديمقراطي-في-تونس/flut>. For Ghannouchi's full statement (and Essebsi's riposte), see <https://www.youtube.com/watch?v=6akJ2E7CGIM>, accessed 15 August, 2014.
142. "Nadwa ṣaḥafiyya li-ruʾasāʾ al-lijān al-waṭaniyya al-thalāth al-mukalafa bil-ʾiṣlāḥ al-siyāsī wa bil-naẓar fī al-tajāwuzāt wa al-fasād

(Press Conference of Heads of the Three National Committees Charged with Political Reform and Investigating Abuses and Corruption)," Bawābat Riʾāsat al-Ḥukūma (Cabinet Portal, Government of Tunisia), January 22, 2011. Available at <http://www.pm.gov.tn/pm/actualites/actualite.php?id=2016&lang=ar>, accessed August 15, 2014. This body was one of three independent commissions promised by Ben Ali during his last days in office—the other two being committees to investigate police abuses and corruption. See "Tūnis: Rudūd faʿl khiṭāb al-raʾīs Ben Ali (Tunisia: Responses to Ben Ali's speech)," *Babnet Tunisie*, January 13, 2011. Available at <http://www.babnet.net/cadredetail-31939.asp>.

143. "Qāʿimat ʾaʿḍāʾ Majlis al-Hayʿa al-ʿUlyā lil-Taḥqīq Ahdāf al-Thawra wa al-Iṣlāḥ al-Siyāsī wa al-Intiqāl al-Dīmqrāṭī (List of Members of the Council of the High Commission for the Fulfillment of Revolutionary Goals, Political Reform, and Democratic Transition)," Bawābat al-Ḥukūma al-Tūnisiyya (Tunisian Government Portal), April 7, 2011. Available at <http://www.tunisie.gov.tn/index.php?option=com_content&task=view&id=1488&Itemid=518>.
144. "Marsūm ʿadad 6 lisanat 2011 muʾarikh fī 18 fīfrī 2011 yataʿlaq bi-ʾiḥdāth al-hayʾa al-ʿulyā li-taḥqīq ahdāf al-thawra wa al-iṣlāḥ al-siyāsī wa al-intiqāl al-dīmqrāṭī (Decree Law No. 6-2011 dated 18 March, Related to the Establishment of the Higher Commission for the Achievement of Revolutionary Goals and Political Reform and Democratic Transition)." Available at <http://ar.jurispedia.org/index.php/مرسوم_عدد_6_لسنة_2011_مؤرخ_في_18_فيفري_2011_يتعلق_بإحداث_الهيئة_العليا_لتحقيق_أهداف_الثورة_والإصلاح_السياسي_والانتقال_الديمقراطي_(tn)>.
145. Duncan Pickard (2011). "Challenges to Legitimate Governance in Post-Revolution Tunisia," *Journal of North African Studies*, 16.4: 637–652.
146. Kārim Yaḥyā, "al-Ahrām tastaṭlʿ masār al-thawra fī Tūnis (al-Ahram Explores the Course of Revolution in Tunisia)," *al-Ahrām* (Cairo), October 6, 2011. Available at <http://www.ahram.org.eg/archive/Journalist-reporters/News/105201.aspx>.
147. Arabic, English, and French translations of the 1959 constitution are available at the website of the World Intellectual Property Organization: <http://www.wipo.int/wipolex/en/details.jsp?id=7201>, accessed August 15, 2014.

148. Eileen Byrne (2011). "Tunisia Opts to Reform Constitution," *Financial Times*, March 4, 2011. Available at <http://www.ft.com/intl/cms/s/0/36fb0cfa-4671-11e0-aebf-00144feab49a.html?siteedition=intl#axzz36pxgshW1>, accessed August 15.
149. "Marsūm ʿadad 14 lisanat 2011 mu'arikh fī 23 Māris yataʿlaq bil-tanẓīm al-mu'aqat lilsulaṭ al-ʿumūmiyya (Decree law No. 14-2011 dated 23 March, related to the temporary organization of the public authorities)," Available at <http://www.wipo.int/wipolex/en/details.jsp?id=11175>, accessed August 15, 2014.
150. "Tunisia's Leaders Resign from Ruling Party," National Public Radio, January 20, 2011. Available at <http://www.npr.org/2011/01/20/133083002/tunisias-leaders-resign-from-ruling-party>, accessed June 6, 2014.
151. "Tunisia Suspends Ben Ali's RCD Party," *BBC News*, February 6, 2011. Available at <http://www.bbc.co.uk/news/world-africa-12378006>, accessed June 6, 2014.
152. "Tūnis: Ḥal al-Ḥizb al-Ḥākim al-sābiq 'al-tajamuʿ al-dustūrī al-dīmqrāṭī (Tunisia: Dissolution of Former Ruling Party, Democratic Constitutional Rally)," *al-Wasaṭ*, March 9, 2011. Available at <http://www.alwasatnews.com/3106/news/read/531425/1.html>.
153. "Ḥal al-Tajamuʿ al-dustūrī al-dīmqrāṭī (Dissolution of the Democratic Constitutional Rally)," Bawābat al-'Idhāʿa al-Tūnisiyya (Tunisian Radio Portal), March 9, 2011. Available at <http://www.radiotunisienne.tn/index.php?option=com_content&view=article&id=12371:2011-03-09-09-24-47&catid=148:2010-03-19-16-52-43>.
154. "Tunis Court Confirms Dissolution of Ben Ali Party," Reuters, March 28, 2011. Available at <http://uk.mobile.reuters.com/article/worldNews/idUKTRE72R2HY20110328>, accessed June 6, 2014. See also, "'Iqrār ḥal al-Tajamuʿ al-dustūrī al-dīmqrāṭī bishakl nihā'ī wa qāṭiʿ (Final Confirmation of Dissolution of RCD)," *al-Ṣaḥafa al-Yawm* (Tunis), March 29, 2011 Available at <http://www.essahafa.info.tn/index.php?id=128&tx_ttnews%5Btt_news%5D=13112&tx_ttnews%5BbackPid%5D=5&cHash=3b1bf9f3fa>.
155. Mona Yahia (2011a). "L'interdiction du RCD lors des élections suscite un débat en Tunisie (Prohibition of RCD in Elections Stirs Debate in Tunisia)," *Magharebia*, April 19, 2011. Available at http://magharebia.com/fr/articles/awi/features/2011/04/19/feature-01, accessed August 15, 2014.

156. Yahia, "L'interdiction du RCD lors des élections."
157. Muḥammad al-Hadaf (2011). "Tūnis tu'addil qānūn ḥaẓr Ḥizb al-Tajamu' al-Dustūrī al-Dimuqrāṭī min al mushāraka fī al-intikhābāt (Tunisia Amends the Policy of Excluding the RCD from Participation in Elections)," *Magharebia*, April 29. Available at <http://magharebia.com/ar/articles/awi/features/2011/04/29/feature-03>.
158. Hamadi Redissi (2011). "The Revolution Is Not Over Yet," *New York Times*, July 15, 2011. Available at <http://www.nytimes.com/2011/07/16/opinion/16redissi.html?_r=0>, accessed August 15.
159. Monia Ghanmi (2011). "Tunisia Forms New Government," *Magharebia*, March 8. Available at <http://magharebia.com/en_GB/articles/awi/features/2011/03/08/feature-01>, accessed August 15, 2014.
160. "Tūnis: 'Ilghā' 'idārat amn al-dawla wa kul shakl min 'askāl al-shurṭa al-siyāsiyya (Cancellation of the State Security Administration and All Forms of Political Police)," *al-'Alam* (Rabat), March 10, 2011. Available at <http://www.alalam.ma/def.asp?codelangue=23&id_info=38924&date_ar=2011-4-9>.
161. "Inshā' hay'a 'ulyā mustaqilla lil-intikhābāt fī Tūnis (Establishment of Independent High Commission for Elections in Tunisia)," *'Īlāf*, April 6, 2011. Available at <http://www.elaph.com/Web/news/ 2011/4/644799.html>.
162. "Marsūm 'adad 27 lisanat 2011 mu'arrikh fī 18 Ifrīl 2011 yata'alq bi-'iḥdāth hay'a 'ulyā mustaqilla lil-intikhābāt (Decree 27 of 2011 dated April 18 2011 related to establishment of Independent High Elections Commission)." Available at <http://www.legislation-securite.tn/ar/node/30374>.
163. Additional background material on the ISIE (Instance Supérieure Indépendante pour les Élections) is drawn from Mohamed Chafik, "Tunisia: The Independent High Authority for the Elections," ACE Project Electoral Knowledge Network. Available at <http://aceproject.org/ace-en/topics/em/electoral-management-case-studies/tunisia-the-independent-high-authority-for-the#ref1>, accessed August 15, 2014, and "Elections in Tunisia: The 2011 Constituent Assembly:Frequently Asked Questions," International Foundation for Electoral Systems, July 13, 2011. Available at <http://www.ifes.org/~/media/Files/Publications/White%20PaperReport/2011/Tunisia_FAQs_072011.pdf>, accessed August 15,2014.

164. "Tūnis . . . Al-hay'a al-'ulyā li-intikhāb al-majlis al-ta'sīsī taqtaraḥ al-ta'jīl ilā 'uktūbar (Tunisia: The High Commission for Electing the Constituent Assembly Proposes Delaying until October)," al-'Arabiyya, May 22, 2011. Available at <http://www.alarabiya.net/articles/2011/05/22/150130.html>.
165. Erik Churchill (2011). "Tunisia's Electoral Lesson: The Importance of Campaign Strategy," Sada (Carnegie Endowment for International Peace), October 27. Available at: <http://carnegieendowment.org/2011/10/27/tunisia-s-electoral-lesson-importance-of-campaign-strategy/6b7g>, accessed August 15, 2014.
166. "Bayān Ḥizb Ḥaraka al-Nahḍa Ḥawl Ta'jīl Intikhābāt al-Majlis al-Ta'sīsī (Statement of the Ennahdha Movement Party on the Delay of Constituent Assembly Elections)," June 1, 2011. Available at <https://www.facebook.com/notes/حركة-النهضة-التونسية/بيان-حزب-حركة-النهضة-حول-تاجيل-انتخابات-المجلس-التاسيسي/164843880246819>, accessed August 15, 2014.
167. "Bayān Ḥizb Ḥaraka al-Nahḍa."
168. "Al-Nahḍa fī Tūnis ta'lan tamasukhā bi'ijrā' intikhābāt al-majlsi al-ta'sīsī fī maw'id tawāfuqī (Ennahdha in Tunisia Announces its Commitment to Holding Elections for the Constituent Assembly at a Mutually Agreed upon Time)," al-'Arabiyya, June 2, 2011. Available at <http://www.alarabiya.net/articles/2011/ 06/02/ 151511.html>.
169. "'Ayāḍ bin 'āshūr ra'īs hay'at taḥqīq 'ahdāf al-thawra . . . ḍarūrat taqniya wa mādiya fariḍat al-ta'jīl ('Ayāḍ bin 'āshūr, Head of the Committee for Fulfillment of Revolutionary Goals . . . Technical and Financial Imperatives Forced the Delay)," *al-Ittiḥād al-Ishtirākī* (Rabat), May 25, 2011. Available at <http://www.maghress.com/alittihad/129273>.
170. "Tūnis: Al-Nahḍa tu'alliq 'uḍwiyatihā fī hay'at ḥimāyat al-thawra (Ennahdha Suspends its Membership in the Commission to Protect the Revolution)," *al-Tajdīd* (Casablanca), June 1, 2011. Available at <http://www.maghress.com/attajdid/66857>.
171. Amīna al-Najjār, "Jadal ḥawl maw'id intikhābāt al-majlis al-ta'sīsī fī Tūnis (Debate Around the Timing of Elections of the Constituent Assembly in Tunisia," *al-Qāhira*, June 7, 2011. Available at <http://www.masress.com/alkahera/2367>. For information on the CPR's withdrawal from the HCFRG, see "Al-Marzūqī yasḥab ḥizbahu min al-hay'a al-'ulyā lil-thawra al-Tūnisiyya (Marzouki Withdraws his Party from the

High Commission of the Tunisian Revolution)," *al-Ḥiwār*, July 1, 2011. Available at <http://www.alhiwar.net/PrintNews.php?Tnd=19562>.

172. ʿAlī Laʿbīdī Manṣūr, "Taʾjīl al-Intikhābāt fī Tūnis qad yufham naẓariyan wa lakinahu yaqsim al-sāḥa al-siyāsisyya wa yuthīr al-makhāwif (Delaying the Elections in Tunisia Might Be Understandable in Theory but it Divides the Political Science and Raises Fears)," *al-Maṣdar* (Tunis), May 23. Available at <http://ar.webmanagercenter.com/2011/05/23/4631/ تأجيل-الانتخابات-في-تونس-قد-يفهم-نظريا-ولكنه-يقسم-الساحة-السياسية-ويثير-المخاوف/>.
173. "Aḥmad Najīb al-Shābī: Rafaḍna ḥal al-tajammuʿ . . . istakhdamnā al-ḥāfilāt li-ḥashd al-jamāhīr . . . wa taḥaṣalnā ʿalā amwāl min rijāl al-ʾiʿmāl (We Rejected the Dissolution of the RCD . . . We Used Buses to Mobilize the People . . . and We Received Funds from Businessmen)," *al-Tūnisiyya*, June 2, 2011. Available at <http://www.attounissia.com.tn/details_article.php?t=42&a=27277>.
174. "Al-Ḥukūma al-Tūnisiyya turīd tanẓīm al-ʾintikhābāt fī mawʿidha fī 24 Julyū (The Tunisian Government Wishes to Hold Elections on July 24)," *al-Nahār al-Jadīd* (Algiers), May 18, 2011. Available at <http://www.ennaharonline.com/ar/latestnews/dernieres_nouvelles_monde/79830--الحكومة-التونسية-تريد-تنظيم-الإنتخابات-في-موعدها-في-يوليو24-html#.VEr2DUvxVR1>.
175. "Qāʾid al-Sibsī yulamaḥ bil-muwāfaqa ʿalā taʾjīl al-ʾintikhābāt al-Tūnisiyya (Caid Essebsi Hints at Agreement to Delay the Tunisian Elections)," *al-Khalīj* (Sharjah), May 28, 2011. Available at <http://www.alkhaleej.ae/alkhaleej/page/644de9cb-a9a2-4632-a95a-94b346e88abd>.
176. David D. Kirkpatrick (2011c). "Interim Tunisian Leader with Ties to Old Ruler Defends Gradual Path," *New York Times*, October 3. Available at <http://www.nytimes.com/2011/10/04/world/africa/tunisias-interim-leader-essebsi-defends-gradualist-path.html?pagewanted=all&_r=0>, accessed August 15, 2014.
177. Khālid al-Ṭrāwlī (2011). "Limādhā nurīd taʾjīl mawʿid al-intikhābāt (Why Do We Want a Delay in the Date of Elections)," *al-Ḥiwar Net*, April 5. Available at <http://www.turess.com/alhiwar/16587>.
178. "Bayān Ḥizb al-ʿUmmāl al-Shīyūʿī al-Tūnisī ḥawl taʾjīl al-ʾintikhābāt wa mawqif al-ḥukūma wa al-hayʾa (Statement of Tunisian Communist Workers Party on the Postponement of Elections and the Stance of the Government and the Commission)," May 26, 2011. Available at http://goo.gl/5xurM3

179. "Bayān Ḥizb al-ʿUmmāl al-Shīyūʿī al-Tūnisī."
180. Tarek Amara (2011b). "Tunisia Election Delayed until October 23," Reuters, June 8, 2011. Available at <http://www.reuters.com/article/2011/06/08/us-tunisia-election-idUSTRE7571R020110608>, accessed August 15, 2014.
181. Article 32, decree Law 35 on Election of the National Constituent Assembly, May 10, 2011. Available at <http://aceproject.org/ero-en/regions/africa/TN/tunisia-decree-no.-35-dated-10-may-on-the-election/view>, accessed August 15, 2014.
182. Akram Balḥāj Raḥūma (2011). "al-Marsūm al-mutaʿlaq bi-intikhāb ʾaʿḍāʾ al-majlis al-taʾsīsī: ʿuyūb bil-jumla (The Decree Law Relating to Election of Members of the Constituent Assembly: Wholesale Flaws)," *al-Mashhad al-Tūnisī*, April 23, 2011. Available at <http://www.machhad.com/1709>. Also see John Carey's unpublished 2013 manuscript, "Electoral Formula and the Tunisian Constituent Assembly," for a very useful discussion of the precise method of seat allocation (Hare quota) and a hypothesis about the effect of this system on the final outcome. Available at <http://sites.dartmouth.edu/jcarey/files/2013/02/Tunisia-Electoral-Formula-Carey-January-2013.pdf>, accessed August 15, 2014.
183. "Tūnis: ʾAy mustaqbal lil-aḥzāb al-siyāsiyya baʿd intikhābāt al-majlis al-taʾsīsī? (What Future for Political Parties After the Constituent Assembly Elections?)," *al-Ḥiwār*, June 3, 2011. Available at <http://www.alhiwar.net/ShowNews.php?Tnd =18567#.U8K8UI1dXGE>.
184. Shadi Hamid, *Temptations of Power*, Oxford University Press, 2014, 196.
185. Sam Bollier, "Who are Tunisia's Political Parties?" *Al-Jazeera*, October 27, 2011. Available at <http://www.aljazeera.com/indepth/features/2011/10/20111061457939O256.html>.
186. Khadija Mohsen-Finan and Malika Zeghal (2011). "The Day After: First Readings of the Tunisian Election," October 24. Available at <http://onislamandpolitics.wordpress.com/2011/10/24/the-day-after-first-readings-of-the-tunisian-election/>, accessed August 15, 2014.
187. Eymen Gamha (2011d). "Progressive Democratic Party," *Tunisialive*, October 9, 2011d. Available at <http://www.tunisia-live.net/2011/10/09/parti-democratique-progressiste-الحزب-الديمقراطي-التقدمي/>.
188. Eymen Gamha (2011c). "al-Watan," October 8, 2011. Available at <http://www.tunisia-live.net/2011/10/08/profile-party-al-watan-الوطن/>.

189. Sam Bollier, "Who Are Tunisia's Political Parties?".
190. Wiem Melki (2011a). "Political Parties' Arena: Which Is the Most Popular? Why?," *Tunisialive*, September 26, 2011. Available at <http://www.tunisia-live.net/2011/09/26/political-parties-arena-which-is-the-most-popular-why/#sthash.F6EwCvLQ.dpuf>, accessed August 15, 2014.
191. Nizār Maqnī (2011). "Tūnis: Al-Wasaṭiyya . . . Wa ḍiyā' al-'Aydīūlūjiyya (Tunisia: Centrism and the End of Ideology)," al-Akhbar, October 20. Available at <http://www.al-akhbar.com/node/24046>.
192. "Decree Law 14 of 2011, Dated March 23 2011, Relating to the Provisional Organization of Public Authorities." Available at <http://www.wipo.int/edocs/lexdocs/laws/en/tn/tn052en.pdf>, accessed August 15, 2014.
193. "Khilāfāt siyāsiyya ḥawl mahām al-majlis al-ta'sīsī al-muqbil fī Tūnis (Political Differences over the Responsibilities of the Constituent Assembly in Tunisia)," *Wikālat al-Maghrib al-'Arabī* (Agence Maghreb Arabe Presse), September 6, 2011. Available at <http://www.maghress.com/map/41590>.
194. "Khilāfāt siyāsiyya."
195. Mona Yahia (2011b). "Tunisia Debates Constituent Assembly Powers," *Magharebia*, September 13, 2011(b). Available at <http://magharebia.com/en_GB/articles/awi/features/2011/09/13/feature-04>, accessed August 15, 2014; See also "I'tilāf 23 Uktūbur: al-da'wa li-'ijrā' istiftā' kharq lil-īṭār al-qānūni wa tashwīsh 'alā al-istiḥqāq al-intikhābī (Coalition of October 23: The Call for a Referendum is a Violation of the Legal Framework and a Disruption of Electoral Integrity)," *al-Tūnisiyya*, September 7, 2011. Available at <http://www.attounissia.com.tn/details_article.php?t=64&a=36403>
196. "Al-Marzūqī: Yajib 'an lā laqil mudat al-majlis al-ta'sīsī al-zamaniyya 'an 3 sanawāt," *Tūnis al-Yawm* (*Tunis Today TV*), August 25, 2011. Available at <http://tunisiatodaytv.blogspot.com/2011/08/3_25.html>.
197. Ghassen Ben Kahlifa (2011). "Tunisia: The Ballot Box Obsession," *al-Akhbar*, September 14. Available at <http://english.al-akhbar.com/node/588>.
198. Yahia (2011b). "Tunisia Debates Constituent Assembly Powers."
199. "al-'Aḥzāb al-Tūnisiyya al-mumathala fī al-hay'a al-'ulyā litaḥqīq ahdāf al-thawra tuwaqa' 'alā 'i'lān al-masār al-intiqālī (Tunisian Parties Represented in the High Commission to Fulfill Revolutionary Goals

Sign Declaration of Transitional Path)," *al-Sharq al-Awsaṭ* (London), September 16, 2011. Available at <http://classic.aawsat.com/details.asp?section=4&issueno=11980&article=640642&feature=#.U8Mfjo1dXGE>.

200. "al-ʾAḥzāb al-Tūnisiyya al-mumathala."
201. "Protesters Attack TV Station over Film Persepolis," *BBC News*, October 9, 2011. Available at <http://www.bbc.com/news/world-africa-15233442>, accessed August 15, 2014.
202. Hoda Trabelis (2011). "Persepolis Screening Stirs Passions in Tunisia," *Magharebia*, October 14, 2011. Available at <http://magharebia.com/en_GB/articles/awi/features/2011/10/14/feature-04>, accessed August 15, 2014.
203. Wiem Melki (2011b). "The 'Affaire Persepolis:' Free publicity for Ennahda?" Tunisialive, October 31. Available at <http://www.tunisia-live.net/2011/10/31/persepolis-a-gratuous-publicity-for-ennahda/>, accessed August 16, 2014.
204. Melki (2011b). "The 'Affaire Persepolis'."
205. Anthony Shadid (2011c). "Islamist Imagines a Democratic Future for Tunisia," *New York Timesi*, October 20, 2011. Available at <http://www.nytimes.com/2011/10/20/world/africa/rachid-al-ghannouchi-imagines-democratic-future-for-tunisia.html?pagewanted=all>, accessed 16 August, 2014.
206. Issandr El Amrani and Ursula Lindsey (2011). "Tunisia Moves to the Next Stage," MERIP, November 8. Available at <http://www.merip.org/mero/mero110811Z>, accessed June 10, 2014.
207. The party's leaders have denied connections to the RCD. See Sophie-Alexandra Aiachi, "Afek Tounes, un parti politique bourgeois constitue cols blancs? Interview d'Emna Menif, membre fondateur et porte parole du parti (Afaq Tunis: A bourgeoisie political party of white collars? Interview with Emna Menif, founding member and party spokesperson)," *Nawaat* (Tunis), August 16, 2011. Available at <http://nawaat.org/portail/2011/08/16/tunisie-afek-tounes-un-parti-politique-bourgeois-constitue-de-cols-blancs-interview-demna-menif-membre-fondateur-et-porte-parole-du-parti-afek-tounes/>, accessed August 16, 2014.
208. See <http://www.partistunisie.com/mp.html>.
209. Sana Ajmi (2011a). "Ongoing Negotiations between Ennahda, CPR and Ettakatol," *Tunisialive*, November 13, 2011. Available at <http://www.tunisia-live.net/2011/11/13/ongoing-negotiations-

between-ennahdha-cpr-and-ettakatol/>, accessed August 16, 2014; "Tunisian Parties Formalize Power-Sharing Deal, Defense and Finance Ministers to Keep their Jobs," *al-Arabiyya*, November 21, 2011. Available at http://english.alarabiya.net/articles/2011/11/21/178459.html>, accessed August 16, 2014.

210. Myriam Ben Ghazi (2011). "Day of Tunisia's Historic Democratic Transition," *Tunisialive*, November 23, 2011. Available at <http://www.tunisia-live.net/2011/11/23/mustapha-ben-jaafar-president-of-the-constituent-assembly>, accessed August 15, 2104/; "Tunisia: Elected Constituent Assembly Holds Inaugural Session," Global Voices Online, November 24, 2011.
211. "Moncef Marzouki Tunisia's New President," *News24*, December 13, 2011. Available at <http://www.news24.com/Africa/News/Moncef-Marzouki-Tunisias-new-president-20111212>, accessed August 16, 2014.
212. Houda Mzioudet (2011). "Ennahda's Jebali Appointed as Tunisian Prime Minister," *Tunisialive*, December 14. Available at <http://www.tunisia-live.net/2011/12/14/ennahdas-jebali-appointed-as-tunisian-prime-minister/>, accessed August 16, 2014.
213. Asma Ghribi (2011). "Jebali's Cabinet: 29 Ministers and 12 Deputy Ministers will be Approved in a Vote of Confidence by the Constituent Assembly," *Tunisialive*, December 22, 2011. Available at <http://www.tunisia-live.net/2011/12/22/jebalis-cabinet-29-ministers-and-12-deputy-ministers-will-be-approved-in-a-vote-of-confidence-by-the-constituent-assembly/>, accessed August 16, 2014.
214. Cabinet makeup from Tunisian Government Portal: <http://www.tunisie.gov.tn/index.php?option=com_content&task=view&id=145&Itemid=183&lang=arabic>, accessed June 6, 2014; and "Get to Know the Tunisian Government," *Tunisia Live*, December 22, 2011. Available at <http://www.tunisia-live.net/2011/12/22/tunisia-new-government>, accessed June 6, 2014.
215. Cabinet makeup from Tunisian Government Portal, and "Get to Know the Tunisian Government," *Tunisia Live*.
216. Cabinet makeup from Tunisian Government Portal, and "Get to Know the Tunisian Government," *Tunisia Live*.
217. Cabinet makeup from Tunisian Government Portal, and "Get to Know the Tunisian Government," *Tunisia Live*.

218. "Ḥal al-hay'a al-ʿulyā litaḥqīq ahdāf al-thawra wa al-iṣlāḥ al-siyāsī wa al-intiqāl al-dīmqrāṭī (Dissolution of the High Commission for the Fulfillment of Revoliutionary Goals and Political Reform and Democratic Transition)," *Shams FM* (Tunis), April 20, 2012. Available at <http://www.shemsfm.net/ar/actualite/حل-الهيئة-العليا-لتحقيق-أهداف-الثورة-والإصلاح-السياسي-والانتقال-الديمقراطي-14518>.
219. Muḥammad ʿAlī Khalīfa (2012). "Al-Shurūq tanshur qā'imat 'aʿḍā' al-lijān al-ta'sīsīya: Hā'ulā' sayaktibūn dustūr Tūnis (Al-Chourouk Publishes the Lists of Members of Constituest Assembly Commissions: These Are the Ones Who Will Write Tunisia's Constitution," *Al-Chourouk* (Tunis), February 7. Available at <http://www.turess.com/alchourouk/522084>.
220. Chapter 6 of the 2014 Tunisian constitution contains provisions for five independent constitutional commissions: an electoral commission (article 126), an audio-visual communication commission charged with guaranteeing freedom of expression and fairness in the media (article 127), a human rights commission (article 128), a commission on "sustainable development and the rights of future generations" to play a role in making "economic, social, and environmental" laws (article 129), and a commission on good governance and anti-corruption (article 130). The Tunisian constitution can be found at <http://www.marsad.tn/constitution>. An unofficial English translation was prepared by the Tunis-based Jasmine Foundation for Research and Communication, and is available here: http://www.jasmine-foundation.org/doc/unofficial_english_translation_of_tunisian_constitution_final_ed.pdf.
221. The final reports of each of the six commissions can be found on the website of the Constituent Assembly: <http://www.anc.tn/site/main/AR/docs/rapport_final/liste_rapports.jsp#>, accessed August 16, 2014.
222. Wafa Ben Hassine (2012). "Process of Writing Tunisia's New Constitution Begins," Tunisialive, February 13. Available at <http://www.tunisia-live.net/2012/02/13/process-of-writing-tunisias-new-constitution-begins/>. Information on the parliamentary blocs that formed in the Constituent Assembly shortly after the election can be found at "al-'Iʿlān ʿan sabʿ kutal niyābiyya dākhil al-majlis al-ta'sīsī (Announcement of 7 Parliamentary Blocs inside the Constituent Assembly)," *alMasdar* (Tunis), February 2, 2012. Available at <http:/ar.webmanagercenter.com/2012/02/02/8313/الإعلان-عن-سبع-كتل-نيابية-داخل-المجلس-التأسيسي/>.

223. Kouichi Shirayanagi (2012)."Constituent Assembly Members Disagree on Scheduling An End to Their Mandate," *Tunisialive*, March 25.Availableat<http://www.tunisia-live.net/2012/03/25/constituent-assembly-members-disagree-on-scheduling-an-end-to-their-mandate/>, accessed August 16, 2014.
224. Tarek Amara (2011a). "Tunisia's Ennahda to Oppose Sharia in the Constitution," Reuters, March 26, 2011. Available at <http://www.reuters.com/article/2012/03/26/us-tunisia-constitution-idUSBRE82P0E820120326>, accessed August 16, 2014.
225. Tarek Amara (2012). "Tunisian Islamists Step Up demand for Islamic State," Reuters, March 25, 2012. Available at<http://www.reuters.com/article/2012/03/25/us-tunisia-salafis-protest-idUSBRE82O0D120120325>, accessed August 16, 2014.
226. Hoda Trabelsi (2012). "Leaked Ghannouchi Tape Raises Salafism Concerns," *Magharebia*, October 15. Available at <http://magharebia.com/en_GB/articles/awi/features/2012/10/15/feature-01>, accessed August 16, 2014.
227. Jeremy Farrell (2012). "Tunisian Constitution: Text and Context," *Jadaliyya*, August 23, 2012. Available at <http://www.jadaliyya.com/pages/index/6991/tunisian-constitution_text-and-context>, accessed August 16, 2014.
228. "Al-Nahḍa bi-Tūnis tafriḍ al-nizām al-barlamānī wa al-mūʿāraḍa tarfud," *al-Arabiyya*, April 24, 2013. Available at <http://www.alarabiya.net/ar/north-africa/tunisia/2013/04/24/النهضة-بتونس-تفرض-النظام-البرلماني-
والمعارضة-ترفض.html>, accessed June 6, 2014.
229. "Al-Ghanūshi: Hadafnā taghyīr al-niẓām fī Tūnis min riʾāsī ilā barlamānī (Ghannouchi: Our Goal is to Change the System in Tunisia from Presidential to Parliamentary)," *al-Riyāḍ* (Saudi Arabia), November 28, 2011. Available at <http://www.alriyadh.com/2011/11/28/article686636.html>, accessed June 6, 2014.
230. This and previous quote from "Munṣif al-Marzūqī yatahim ḥarakat al-nahḍa bilsaʿī ilā al-sayṭara ʿalā mafāṣil al-dawla al-Tūnisiyya (Moncef Marzouki Accuses Ennahdha of Striving to Control the Branches of the Tunisian State)," Anfa Press (Morocco), August 25, 2012. Available at <http://www.anfapress.net/الواجهة/منصف-المرزوقي-يتهم--حركة-النهضة-بالسع/>, accessed June 7, 2014.

231. Thierry Brésillon (2012). 'Which Political System for Tunisia?' *Nawaat*, July 30. Available at <http://nawaat.org/portail/2012/07/30/which-political-system-for-tunisia/>, accessed June 7, 2014.
232. Shirayanagi, "Constituent Assembly Members Disagree."
233. AsmaGhribi(2012a)."MajorTunisianSecularPartiesAnnounceMerger," *Tunisialive*, January 11, 2012. Available at <http://www.tunisia-live.net/2012/01/11/major-tunisian-secular-parties-announce-merger/>, accessed August 16, 2014.
234. Asma Ghribi (2012b). "Fusion of Centrist Parties to Create a New Force in Tunisian Politics," *Tunisialive*, April 2, 2012. Availableat<http://www.jadaliyya.com/pages/index/6991/tunisian-constitution_text-and-context>, accessed August 16, 2014; Emine M'tiraoui, "Mawlūd siyāsī jadīd taḥt ʿunwān al-masār al-dīmqrāṭī al-ijtimāʿī: ṣidq al-irādāt yudhalil al-ṣuʿūbāt (Newborn Political Entity under the Title of Social Democratic Path: Can Sincerity of Belief Overcome Obstacles?)," *Nawaat*, April 2, 2012. Available at <http://nawaat.org/portail/2012/04/02/الندوة-الوطنية-التاسيسية-التوحد-صدق/>.
235. "Al-Sibsī yaʿlan ʿan taʾsīs ḥizb Nidāʾ Tūnis (Essebsi Announces Formation of Call of Tunisia Party)," *Tunisien FM*, June 16, 2012. Availableat<http://www.tunisien.tn/تونس/السبسي-يعلن-عن-تأسيس-حزب-نداء-تونس.
236. "Al-Bāji al-Sibsī yaʿlan taʾsīs ḥarakat Nidāʾ Tūnis lil-taṣadī lihaymanat al-Nahḍa (Beji Essebsi announces formation of Call of Tunisia movement to challenge Ennahdha's hegemony)," *al-Fajr News*, June 16, 2012. Available at <http://www.turess.com/alfajrnews/105857>.
237. ʿAbd al-Ruʾūf Bālī, "Ḥāmilan al-ʾAmal: a-ʾIʿlān rasmiyan ʿan taʾsīs al-Ittiḥād min ajl Tūnis (Bearing Hope: Formal Announcement of Formation of Union for the Sake of Tunisia)," *Al-Shurūq* (Tunis), January 30, 2013. Available at <http://www.turess.com/alchourouk/613710>.
238. Monica Marks and Omar Belhaj Salah (2013). "Uniting for Tunisia," *Sada*, March 28. Available at <http://carnegieendowment.org/sada/2013/03/28/uniting-for-tunisia/fu2q>, accessed June 6, 2014.
239. Houda Mzioudet (2012). "Hearings Continue for Suspects in Death of Nidaa Tounes Tatouine Coordinator," *Tunisialive*, November 13. Available at <http://www.tunisia-live.net/2012/11/13/hearings-continue-for-suspects-in-death-of-nidaa-tounes-tataouine-

coordinator/>; For an alternative account of the Leagues' makeup and relationship with Ennahdha, see Ian Patel and Safa Belghith (2013). "Leagues for the Protection of the Tunisian Revolution," *OpenDemocracy*, June 25, 2013. Available at <http://www.opendemocracy.net/ian-patel-safa-belghith/leagues-for-protection-of-tunisian-revolution>, accessed August 16, 2014.

240. Monica Marks and Kareem Fahim (2013). "Tunisia Moves to Contain Fallout after Opposition Figure is Assassinated," *New York Times*, February 6.
241. Tarek Amara (2013a). "Tunisia's New Premier Promises Inclusive Government," Reuters, February 22, 2013a. Available at <http://www.reuters.com/article/2013/02/22/us-tunisia-politics-idUSBRE91L0F720130222>, accessed August 16, 2014.
242. Dan Rivers and Laura Smith-Spark (2013). "Jebali Vows to Press On with Plans for Caretaker Government in Tunisia", February 9, 2013. Available at <http://www.cnn.com/2013/02/08/world/africa/tunisia-unrest>, accessed June 6, 2014.
243. "No Role for Islamists in Tunisia's Next Cabinet: PM Jebali," *al-Arabiyya*, February 9, 2013. Available at <http://www.alarabiya.net/articles/2013/02/09/265348.html>, accessed June 6, 2014.
244. "Tunisian President's Party Pulls Out of Islamist-Led Government," *al-Arabiyya*, February 10, 2013. Available at <http://english.alarabiya.net/articles/2013/02/10/265490.html>, accessed August 16, 2014.
245. "Tunisia: Ali Larayedh Named New Prime Minister," *BBC News*, February 22, 2013. Available at <http://www.bbc.com/news/world-africa-21550375>, accessed August 16, 2014.
246. The new foreign minister, Othman Jerandi, was a veteran diplomat: "New Permanent Representative of Tunisia Presents Credentials," United Nations Security Council Department of Public Information, August 23, 2011. Available at <http://www.un.org/News/Press/docs/2011/bio4311.doc.htm>, accessed June 6, 2014.
247. Sana Ajmi, "Final Draft of Tunisia's New Constitution Released," *Opendemocracy*, April 30, 2013. Available at http://www.opendemocracy.net/sana-ajmi/final-draft-of-tunisia%E2%80%99s-new-constitution-released>, accessed August 16, 2014.
248. Tunisian draft constitution of April 2013 is available here: http://constitutionaltransitions.org/wp-content/uploads/2013/05/Tunisia-third-draft-Constitution-22-April-2013.pdf. Please note that the document is mis-translated in at least one place. Article 111

(page 29) says that "The court of audit shall have jurisdiction to supervise the sound spending of public funds in accordance with the principles of *Shariah*, effectiveness, and transparency." However, reference to the Arabic text reveals that the proper translation is, "The court of audit shall have jurisdiction to supervise the sound spending of public funds in accordance with the principles of *legitimacy*, effectiveness, and transparency." The word in the Arabic text was not sharīʿa (Islamic jurisprudence) but sharʿiyya (legitimacy).

249. "Tunisia: Revise the Draft Constitution: An Analysis of Human Rights Concerns," Human Rights Watch, May 13, 2013. Available at <http://www.hrw.org/news/2013/05/13/tunisia-revise-draft-constitution>, accessed August 16, 2014.
250. "Third Draft Constitution To Be Presented before the NCA," *Tunis Times*, April 30, 2013. Available at <http://www.thetunistimes.com/2013/04/third-draft-constitution-to-be-presented-before-the-nca-60797/>, accessed August 16, 2014.
251. Mona Yahia, "Tensions Mar Tunisia Political Dialogue," *Magharebia*, April 24, 2013. Available at <http://magharebia.com/en_GB/articles/awi/features/2013/04/24/feature-03>; Mona Yahia (2013b). "Tunisia Reaches Power Sharing Deal," *Magharebia*, May 8, 2013(b). Available at <http://magharebia.com/en_GB/articles/awi/features/2013/05/08/feature-03>, accessed August 16, 2014.
252. Peter Beaumont, "Tunisian Opposition Figures Killed with Same Gun," *The Guardian*, July 26, 2013. Available at <http://www.theguardian.com/world/2013/jul/26/tunisian-opposition-killed-same-gun>, accessed August 16, 2014.
253. "Tens of Thousands Attend Funeral of Slain Tunisian Politician," July 27, 2013. Available at <http://english.al-akhbar.com/node/16550>, accessed August 16, 2014.
254. "Maya Jribi: La dissolution de l'ANC menera tout droit a la guerre civile," *African Manager*, July 8, 2013. Available at <http://www.africanmanager.com/152998.html>, accessed June 6, 2014.
255. Robert Joyce (2013). "NCA Member Mohamed Brahmi Assassinated," *Tunisia Live*, July 25, 2013. Available at <http://www.tunisia-live.net/2013/07/25/nca-member-mohamed-brahmi-assassinated>, accessed July 9, 2014.
256. Tarek Amara (2013b). "Tunisia's Biggest Union Tells Islamist-Led Government to Quit," Reuters, July 30, 2013. Available at <http://

www.reuters.com/article/2013/07/30/us-tunisia-protests-idUSBRE96T0WM20130730>, accessed June 6, 2014; see also, al-Ḥabīb al-Aswad, "Wazīr al-dākhiliya al-Tūnisī mustaʿid lil-istiqāla (The Tunisian Interior Minister is Ready to Resign)," *al-Bayān*, July 30, 2013. Available at <http://www.albayan.ae/one-world/arabs/2013-07-30-1.1932963>, accessed June 6, 2014.

257. "al-ʾIʿlān ʿan taʾsīs jabha lil-ʾinqādh al-waṭanī fī Tūnis (Announcement of Formation of National Salvation Front in Tunisia)," *Mosaique FM* (Tunis), July 26, 2013. Available at <http://www.mosaiquefm.net/ar/index/a/ActuDetail/Element/26151-الإعلان-عن-تأسيس-جبهة-للإنقاذ-الوطني-في-تونس>; "Tunisia: Political Parties and Civil Society Components Announce Formation of National Salvation Front," Tunis Afrique Presse (Tunis), July 26, 2013. Available at <http://allafrica.com/stories/201307291665.html>, accessed August 16, 2014.

258. Mokhtar Awad (2013). "Tunisia's Troubled Talks," *Foreign Policy*, November 13, 2013. Available at <http://mideastafrica.foreignpolicy.com/posts/2013/11/13/tunisias_troubled_talks>, accessed August 16, 2014.

259. "Siyāsī: Al-Mushārikūn fi al-ḥiwār al-waṭanī al-Tūnisī yuwaqaʿūn mubādarat al-lajna al-rubāʿiyya li-inhāʾ al-azma al-siyāsiyya fī Tūnis (Politics: Participants in the Tunisian National Dialogue Sign the Initiative of the Quartet to End the Political Crisis in Tunisia)," *Wikālat al-Anbāʾ al-Suʿūdiyya* (Saudi Press Agency), October 5, 2013. Available at <http://www.spa.gov.sa/details.php?id=1154190>.

260. Carlotta Gall (2014). "Tunisia's Premier Resigns, Formally Ending His Party's Rule," *New York Times*, January 9, 2014. Available at <http://www.nytimes.com/2014/01/10/world/middleeast/tunisias-leader-resigns.html?_r=0>, accessed August 16, 2014.

261. "Tunisian Constitution Officially Ratified," *Tunis Times*, January 26, 2014. Available at <http://www.thetunistimes.com/2014/01/tunisian-constitution-officially-ratified-31532/#>, accessed August 16, 2014.

262. Caroline Abader (2014). "Elections Scheduled for Tunisia," *Muftah*, June 29, 2014. Available at <http://muftah.org/elections-scheduled-tunisia/#.U8lKrIBJfiM>.

263. Tom Finn (2011). "Yemen President Quits after Deal in Saudi Arabia," *The Guardian*, November 23. Available at <http://www.theguardian.com/world/2011/nov/23/yemen-president-quits?guni=Article:in%20body%20link>, accessed August 16, 2014.

264. Yasser Ezzi (2013). "JMP to Boycott Hadi's Inauguration," *Yemen Times*, February 27, 2012. Available at <http://www.yementimes.com/en/1550/news/470/JMP-to-boycott-Hadi%E2%80%99s-inauguration-ceremony.htm>, accessed August 16, 2014.
265. Yemen transition agreement, 2011. Unofficial translation by the Yemen Peace Project. Available at <http://www.al-bab.com/arab/docs/yemen/yemen_transition_agreement.htm>, accessed August 2014>; see also Brian Whitaker (2011). "Yemen's Ali Abdullah Saleh Resigns—but It Changes Little," *The Guardian*, November 24. Available at <http://www.theguardian.com/commentisfree/2011/nov/24/yemen-ali-abdullah-saleh-resigns>, accessed August 16, 2014.
266. "Constitution of the Republic of Yemen, 1994). Available at <http://www.al-bab.com/yemen/gov/con94.htm>, accessed August 16, 2014.
267. Laura Kasinof (2012). "Yemen Legislators Approve Immunity for the President," *New York Times*, January 21, 2012. Available at <http://www.nytimes.com/2012/01/22/world/middleeast/yemens-parliament-approves-immunity-for-president-saleh.html?_r=0>, accessed August 16, 2014.
268. As this book went to press in the summer of 2014, the official website of the GPC (www.almotamar.net) continued to refer to former president Saleh as "the leader" (al-zaʿīm). See, for example, "Turkiyā tushīd bimawāqif al-zaʿīm ʿAlī ʿAbd Allāh Ṣāliḥ (Turkey Praises the Positions of the Leader Ali Abdullah Saleh)," almotamar.net (Sanaa), June 2, 2014. Available at <http://www.almotamar.net/news/117221.htm>.
269. "Parliament Endorses Immunity Law," *Saba* (Sanaʿāʾ), January 21, 2012. Available at <http://www.sabanews.net/en/news258543.htm>, accessed August 16, 2014.
270. <http://www.yementimes.com/en/1690/news/2563/Hadi-resolves-Parliamentary-dispute.htm>; Lassad Ben Ahmed (2013). "The Troika Falters," *al-Ahram Weekly*, February 6, 2013. Available at <http://weekly.ahram.org.eg/News/1309/19/The-troika-falters.aspx>, accessed August 16, 2014.
271. Andreas Schedler (1996). "Anti-Political-Establishment Parties," Party Politics, 2.3: 291–312.
272. "Interview with Ansar al-Shariah Leader in Abyan, Jalal Baleedi al-Murqashi," *Yemen Times*, May 17, 2012. Available at <http://www.yementimes.com/en/1573/intreview/869/Interview-with-Ansar-A

l-Sharia-Leader-in-Abyan-Jalal--Baleedi-Al-Murqashi.htm>, accessed August 16, 2014.

273. Madeleine Wells (2012). "Yemen's Houthi Movement and the Revolution," *Foreign Policy*, February 27. Available at: <http://mideastafrica.foreignpolicy.com/posts/2012/02/27/yemen_s_houthi_movement_and_the_revolution>. accessed August 16, 2014.
274. Stephen Day (2010). "The Political Challenge of Yemen's Southern Movement," Carnegie Papers, Middle East Program, Number 108, March. Available at <http://carnegieendowment.org/files/yemen_south_movement.pdf>, accessed August 16, 2014.
275. "Who's Who in Yemen's Opposition?" *al-Jazeera*, February 28, 2011. Available at <http://www.aljazeera.com/indepth/spotlight/yemen/2011/02/2011228141453986337.html>
276. "Who's Who in Yemen's Opposition?"
277. Shatha al-Harazi (2011). "All You Need to Know about the Youth Movement," *Yemen Times*, December 29. Available at <http://www.yementimes.com/en/1533/report/154/All-you-need-to-know-about-the-Youth-Movement.htm>, accessed 16 August 2014.
278. Hakim Almasmari and Mohammed Jamjoom (2011). "Yemen National Unity Government Named," *CNN*, December 7. Available at <http://www.cnn.com/2011/12/07/world/meast/yemen-unrest/>, accessed August 16, 2014.
279. "Yemen's VP Asks Opposition Leader Basindwa to Form Government," *al-Arabiyya*, November 27, 2011. Available at <http://english.alarabiya.net/articles/2011/11/27/179470.html>, accessed August 16, 2014.
280. Muḥammad Sālim Bāsindwa (2010). "ʿAlā ṭarīq al-ḥiwār al-shāmil (On the Road to Complete Dialogue)," al-Ṣaḥwa net (Sanaa), June 3. Available at: <http://www.yemeress.com/alsahwa/1207>.
281. Ahmed Al-Haj (2011). "Yemen Forms National Unity Government," *Huffington Post*, December 7. Available at <http://www.huffingtonpost.com/2011/12/07/yemen-national-unity-government_n_1133767.html>, accessed August 16, 2014.
282. Biographies of Yemeni ministers available at the National Information Center, Presidency of the Republic of Yemen: <http://www.yemen-nic.info/english_site/government/government/present_gov/main.php>, accessed August 16, 2014.
283. National Information Center, Presidency of the Republic of Yemen.

284. Charles Schmitz (2011). "Yemen's Tribal Showdown," *Foreign Affairs*, June 3. Available at <http://www.foreignaffairs.com/articles/67877/charles-schmitz/yemens-tribal-showdown>, accessed 16 August, 2014.
285. Sheila Carapico (2011). "No Exit: Yemen's Existential Crisis," University of Richmond, Department of Political Science, September 28. Available at <http://blog.richmond.edu/poliscidept/category/faculty/sheila-carapico/>; "Al-Ahmar Versus Saleh: When Yemen Power Houses Stand at Odds," *Yemen Post*, February 17, 2014. Available at <http://yemenpost.net/Detail123456789.aspx?SubID=7565>.
286. "Will Saleh's Successor Please Stand Up," Embassy Sanaa, U.S. Department of State, September 17, 2005. Available at <http://wikileaks.org/cable/2005/09/05SANAA2766.html>, accessed August 16, 2014.
287. Gregory Johnsen (2011). "The al-Ahrmar Family: Who's Who," Waq al-Waq: A Blog on Yemen, June 3, 2011. Available at <http://bigthink.com/waq-al-waq/the-al-ahmar-family-whos-who>, accessed August 16, 2014.
288. Ginny Hill (2011). "Yemen Unrest: Saleh's Rivals Enter Elite Power Struggle," *BBC News*, May 26. Available at <http://www.bbc.com/news/world-middle-east-13560514>, accessed August 16, 2014.
289. Hill, "Yemen Unrest."
290. "Street Battles in Sana'a between Saleh Loyalists and Tribal Guards," *The National*, May 25, 2011. Available at <http://www.thenational.ae/news/world/middle-east/street-battles-in-sanaa-between-saleh-loyalists-and-tribal-guards>, accessed August 16, 2014.
291. Leslie Campbell, "Yemen: The Tribal Islamists," *The Islamists are Coming* (blog), Woodrow Wilson International Center for Scholars. Available at <http://www.wilsoncenter.org/islamists/yemen-the-tribal-islamists>, accessed August 16, 2014.
292. "Yemen's Hadi in No Position to Confront Tribal Politics," *World Politics Review*, March 27, 2013. Available at <http://www.worldpoliticsreview.com/trend-lines/12826/global-insider-yemen-s-hadi-in-no-position-to-confront-tribal-politics>, accessed August 16, 2014.
293. "Top Yemeni General, Ali Mohsen, Backs Opposition," *BBC News*, March 21, 2011. Available at <http://www.bbc.co.uk/news/world-middle-east-12804552>, accessed August 16, 2014.
294. A helpful timeline of unrest in Yemen after Hādī's inauguration, which proved useful for this chapter, was compiled by the United Nations Office for the Coordination of Humanitarian

Affairs and is available at <http://www.irinnews.org/report/95362/yemen-timeline-of-key-events-under-new-president>, accessed August 16, 2014.

295. ʿAdnān Hāshim (2012). "Masīra lil-shabāb tadʿū al-ḥukūma wa Hādī ilā surʿat iʿādat haykalat al-jaysh (Rally of the Youth Calls on the Government and Hadi to Speed up the Restructuring of the Army)," *Akhbār al-Yawm* (Sanaa), March 2, 2012. Available at <http://www.akhbaralyom.net/news_details.php?sid=51269>, accessed August 16, 2014.

296. Adam Baron (2012). "Yemen's President Hadi Surprises Pessimists with Moves Toward Reform," *Christian Science Monitor*, April 27. Available at http://www.csmonitor.com/World/Middle-East/2012/0427/Yemen-s-President-Hadi-surprises-pessimists-with-moves-toward-reform>, accessed August 16, 2014.

297. Ali Saeed (2012a). "Fundamental Changes in the Yemeni Army," *Yemen Times*, April 7, 2012. Available at <http://www.yementimes.com/en/1561/news/680/Fundamental-changes-in-the-Yemeni-army.htm>, accessed August 16, 2014.

298. "Ṣāliḥ: Lā aḥad yasalim nafsahu lil-mawt aw al-taṣfiya (No One Must Submit Himself to Death or Liquidation)," Yemen Press, April 17, 2012. Available at <http://yemen-press.com/news8440.html>.

299. "Ṣāliḥ: Lā aḥad yasalim."

300. Ahmed Dawood (2012). "Dismissed General Closes Sana'a Airport," *Yemen Times*, April 7. Available at <http://www.yementimes.com/en/1561/news/681/Dismissed-general-closes-Sana'a-airport.htm>, accessed August 16, 2014.

301. "Saleh Nephew Quits as Yemen Presidential Guard Chief," *BBC News*, April 27, 2012. Available at <http://www.bbc.com/news/world-middle-east-17868326>, accessed August 16, 2014.

302. Ali Saeed (2012b). "Dismissed General al-Ahmar Finally Leaves Office," *Yemen Times*, April 26, 2012. Available at <http://www.yementimes.com/en/1567/news/762/Dismissed-general-Al-Ahmar-finally-leaves-office.htm>, accessed August 16, 2014.

303. "ālāf al-Yamaniyīn yuṭālibūn al-raʾīs Hādī bi-ʾiqālat aqārib Ṣāliḥ min qiyādat al-jaysh (Thousands of Yemenis Call on President Hadi to Remove Saleh's Relatives from the Army)," *al-Khabar*, July 19, 2012. Available at <http://www.yemeress.com/alkhabar/3416>.

304. Hakim Almasmari, "Saleh Cronies Sacked in Yemen," *The National* (UAE), December 21, 2012. Available at <http://www.thenational.ae/news/world/middle-east/saleh-cronies-sacked-in-yemen>, accessed August 16, 2014.
305. "al-lajna al-ʿulyā al-ḥālia (the current Supreme Commission)," al-Lajna al-ʿUlyā lil-Intikhābāt wa al-Istiftāʾ (The Supreme Commission for Elections and Referendum), 2012. Available at <http://www.scer.gov.ye/ar-page.aspx?show=37>.
306. GCC Transition Plan, Part IV: Second phase of the transfer of power; article 20. Available at <http://www.al-bab.com/arab/docs/yemen/yemen_transition_agreement.htm>.
307. Atiaf Alwazir (2013). "Yemen's Independent Youth and Their Role in the National Dialogue Conference," German Institute for International and Security Affairs, August 23. Available at <http://www.swp-berlin.org/en/publications/swp-comments-en/swp-aktuelle-details/article/yemens_independent_youth.html>, accessed August 16, 2013.
308. "Yemen National Dialogue Conference Participants," *The National*, March 18, 2013. Available at <http://www.thenational.ae/news/world/middle-east/yemen-national-dialogue-conference-participants>, accessed August 16, 2014.
309. Philip Barrett Holzapfel (2014). "Yemen's Transition Process: Between Fragmentation and Transformation," *Peaceworks #95*, March, United States Institute of Peace.
310. Sadeq al-Wesabi (2013). "Tawakkol Karman: Saleh and His Aides Obstruct the Transitional Process, their Immunity will be Annulled," *Yemen Times*, June 10, 2013.
311. Fawaz Traboulsi (2013). "Yemen's National Dialogue off to a Rough Start," *al-Monitor*, March 20. Available at <http://www.al-monitor.com/pulse/politics/2013/03/yemen-dialogue-rough-start.html#>.
312. Samaʿa al-Hamdani, "Yemen's National Dialogue Behind Closed Doors," Atlantic Council MENASource, June 17, 2013. Available at <http://www.acus.org/viewpoint/yemens-national-dialogue-behind-closed-doors>, accessed August 16, 2014.
313. Ali Ibrahim Al-Moshki (2014). "National Dialogue Conference Concludes," *Yemen Times*, January. Available at <http://www.

yementimes.com/en/1750/news/3398/National-Dialogue-Conference-concludes.htm>, accessed August 16, 2014.

314. Stephen W. Day (2014). "The 'Non-Conclusion' of Yemen's National Dialogue." *Foreign Policy*. January 27 2014. Available at <http://mideastafrica.foreignpolicy.com/posts/2014/01/27/the_non_conclusion_of_yemen_s_national_dialogue_0>, accessed August 16, 2014.

315. Joseph Kechichian (2014). "Yemen in Transition—and Turmoil," *alJazeera*, February 6. Available at <http://www.aljazeera.com/indepth/opinion/2014/02/yemen-transition-turmoil-2014264255740696.html>, accessed August 16, 2014.

316. Mohammed Al-Hassani (2014). "Constitutional Drafting Committee to be Established in Coming Days," *Yemen Times*, February 13, 2014. Available at <http://www.yementimes.com/en/1755/news/3474/Constitutional-Drafting-Committee-to-be-established-in-coming-days.htm>, accessed August 16, 2014.

317. Ashraf al-Falahi (2014). "Yemen's Fraught Constitution Drafting Committee," Sada (Carnegie Endowment for International Peace), May 2. Available at <http://carnegieendowment.org/sada/2014/05/02/yemen-s-fraught-constitution-drafting-committee/h9tn>

318. al-Falahi, "Yemen's Fraught Constitution Drafting Committee."

319. "UN Envoy to Yemen Says Country's President Will Stay on for Longer than Two Years," Associated Press, November 18, 2013. Available at <http://www.foxnews.com/world/2013/11/18/un-envoy-to-yemen-says-country-president-will-stay-on-for-longer-than-2-years/>, accessed August 16, 2014.

320. Robert F. Worth (2014). "Even Out of Office, a Wielder of Great Power in Yemen," *The New York Times*. January 31, 2014. Available at <http://www.nytimes.com/2014/02/01/world/middleeast/even-out-of-office-a-wielder-of-great-power-in-yemen.html>, accessed August 16, 2014.

321. "General People's Congress to Stage a Comeback in 2014?" *Yemen Post*, April 3, 2013. Available at <http://yemenpost.net/Detail123456789.aspx?SubID=6747>, accessed August 16, 2014.

322. Gabriel Gatehouse (2012). "Benghazi's Bid for Cyrenaica Autonomy Divides Libyans," *BBC News*, March 9. Available at <http://www.bbc.com/news/world-africa-17316264>, accessed August 16, 2014.

323. Andrew Lee Butters (2011). "Dispatch from Libya: Why Benghazi Rebelled," *Time*, February 22. Available at <http://content.time.com/

time/specials/packages/printout/0,29239, 2045328_2045338_2056521,00.html>, accessed August 16, 2014.

324. Ahmad Shokr (2011a). "Benghazi: The Birthplace of Libya's Revolution," *Egypt Independent*, February 26. Available at http://www.egyptindependent.com//news/benghazi-birthplace-libyas-revolution>, accessed August 16, 2014.
325. Stephen Kurczy and Drew Hinshaw (2011). "Libya's Tribes: Who's Who?" *Christian Science Monitor*, February 24. Available at, http://www.csmonitor.com/World/Backchannels/2011/0224/Libya-tribes-Who-s-who>.
326. "al-Qabā'il al-Lībīya (Libyan Tribes)," *al-Jazeera*, February 24, 2011. Available at <http://www.aljazeera.net/news/arabic/2011/2/24/القبائل-الليبية>.
327. Oliver Holmes and Taha Zargoun (2012). "Tribal Ties Tangle Post-Gaddafi Libya," Reuters, Feburary 14. Available at <http://uk.reuters.com/article/2012/02/14/uk-libya-tribes-idUKTRE81D19Q20120214>, accessed August 16, 2014.
328. Ranj Alaaldin (2011). "How Libya's Tribes Will Decide Gaddafi's Fate," *The Telegraph* (London), March 4. Available at <http://www.telegraph.co.uk/news/worldnews/africaandindianocean/libya/8361279/How-Libyas-tribes-will-decide-Gaddafis-fate.html>, accessed August 16, 2014.
329. Hadeel al-Shalchi and Lee Keith (2011). "Gadhafi Rule Relies on Wavering Tribal Support," Associated Press, March 31, 2011. Available at <http://www.nbcnews.com/id/42365946/ns/world_news-mideast_n_africa/t/gadhafi-rule-relies-wavering-tribal-support/#.U803tYBJfiM>, accessed August 16, 2014.
330. Peter Apps (2011). "Libya's Tribal, Cultural Divisions," Reuters, August 25. Available at <http://www.reuters.com/article/2011/08/25/us-libya-tribes-idUSTRE77O43R20110825>, accessed August 16, 2014.
331. "Libyan Tribal Map: Network of Loyalties that Will Determine Gaddafi's Fate," February 22, 2011. Available at <http://www.aawsat.net/2011/02/article55247429>, accessed August 17, 2014.
332. "al-Qabā'il al-Lībīya (Libyan Tribes)," *al-Jazeera*, February 24, 2011.
333. William Maclean (2011). "In Libya's New Politics, Localism May Trump Tribes," Reuters, September 27. Available at <http://english.alarabiya.net/articles/2011/09/27/168944.html>, accessed August17, 2014.

334. "After Decades in Exile, Libya President Magarief Ready to Die for Democracy," *NBC News*, September 29, 2012. Available at <http://worldnews.nbcnews.com/_news/2012/09/29/14142378-after-decades-in-exile-libyan-president-magarief-ready-to-die-for-democracy?lite>, accessed August 17, 2014.

335. "Al-Iʿlān ʿan taʾsīs Ḥizb al-Jabha al-Waṭaniya fī Lībyā (Announcement of Formation of National Front Party in Libya)," *Al-ān TV* (Libya), May 8, 2012. Available at <http://www.youtube.com/watch?v=y4WL8UXiAPA>, accessed August 17, 2014.

336. "Intikhāb ʿikhwānī raʾīsan li-ḥizb al-ʿadāla wa al-bināʾ bi Lībyā (Election of a Brotherhood Member as President of Justice and Construction Party in Libya)," *al-Muslim*, March 3, 2012. Available at <http://www.almoslim.net/node/161483>, accessed August 17, 2014.

337. See "Libya Bans Religious, Tribal, or Ethnic Parties," Reuters, April 25, 2012. Available at <http://www.reuters.com/article/2012/04/25/us-libya-election-idUSBRE83O0Y620120425>, accessed August 17, 2014; and "Libya Drops Ban on Religious Parties," *al-Jazeera*, May 2, 2012. Available at <http://www.aljazeera.com/news/africa/2012/05/2012522304234970.html>, accessed August 17, 2014.

338. Martin Bright (2002). "MI6 Halted Bid to Arrest bin Laden," *The Guardian*, November 9. Available at http://www.theguardian.com/politics/2002/nov/10/uk.davidshayler; Ian Black (2011b) "The Libyan Islamic Fighting Group—From al-Qaida to the Arab Spring," *The Guardian*, September 5, 2011. Available at <http://www.theguardian.com/world/2011/sep/05/libyan-islamic-fighting-group-leaders>, accessed August 17, 2014.

339. Gary Gambill (2005b). "The Libyan Islamic Fighting Group (LIFG)," *Terrorism Monitor*, 3.6.

340. Joseph Felter and Brian Fishman (2007). "Al-Qaʿida's Foreign Fighters in Iraq: A First Look at the Sinjar Records," Combatting Terrorism Center at West Point, p. 12. Available at <http://tarpley.net/docs/CTCForeignFighter.19.Dec07.pdf>, accessed August 17, 2014.

341. Frederic Wehrey (2012). "The Wrath of Libya's Salafis," Sada (Carnegie Endowment for International Peace), September 12. Available at <http://carnegieendowment.org/2012/09/12/wrath-of-libya-s-salafis/dtdn>, accessed August 17, 2014.

342. This section draws on some details provided in what may be the finest English-language account of the formation of the

NTC: Duncan Pickard (2013). "Forging Legitimacy: Abdel Hafiz Ghoga and the Founding Weeks of Libya's National Transitional Council." Case Study, John F. Kennedy School of Government, Harvard University.

343. Ali Abdullatif Ahmida (2011). "The Libyan National Transitional Council: Social Bases, Membership and Political Trends," AlJazeera Center for Studies, October 30.
344. Ahmida, "The Libyan National Transitional Council."
345. Vivenne Walt (2012). "Meet Mahmoud Jibril: The Man Who May Be Libya's First Elected Leader," *Time*, July 11, 2012. Available at <http://world.time.com/2012/07/11/meet-mahmoud-jibril-the-man-who-may-be-libyas-first-elected- leader/>, accessed August 16, 2014; Basheer al-Baker (2011). "Mahmoud Jibril: Libya's Touted Statesman," *al-Akhbar*, September 7. Available at <http://english.al-akhbar.com/node/528>, accessed August 17, 2014.
346. David D. Kirkpatrick (2011a). "Death of Rebel Leader Stirs Fears of Tribal Conflict," *New York Times*, July 28, 2011.
347. Kareem Fahim (2011). "Libya Rebels Dissolve Cabinet Amid Discord," *New York Times*, August 8. Available at <http://www.nytimes.com/2011/08/09/world/africa/09libya.html?_r=0>, accessed August 17, 2014.
348. A timeline of the Libyan transition, which proved useful in the writing of this section, is available here: <http://www.aljazeera.com/indepth/interactive/2014/02/timeline-three-years-after-libya-uprising-201421691755192622.html>, accessed August 17, 2014.
349. Libya interim constitution, Article 30. An English translation of Libya's 2011 constitutional declaration can be found at the website of the Comparative Constitutions Project <https://www.constituteproject.org/constitution/Libya_2011.pdf>.
350. Comparative Constitutions Project.
351. Comparative Constitutions Project.
352. Comparative Constitutions Project.
353. As in Tunisia, electoral governance was placed in the hands of oppositionists. Article 8 of Law 3 of 2012 "On the Establishment of the National High Elections Commission" stipulated that the NHEC would be comprised of 17 members—including three judges, two professors, two men, and two women "from civil society institutions," an administrative expert, and one representative each of the youth

and Libyan diaspora. See <http://pomed.org/wordpress/wp-content/uploads/2012/07/Law-No-3-2012-en.pdf>, accessed August 17, 2014.

354. Zaid al-Ali, "Libya's Interim Constitution: An Assessment," *OpenDemocracy*, October 5, 2011. Available at <https://www.opendemocracy.net/zaid-al-ali/libya%E2%80%99s-interim-constitution-assessment>, accessed August 17, 2014.

355. "Libya's New Rulers Declare Country Liberated,"*BBC News*, October 23, 2011. Available at <http://www.bbc.com/news/world-africa-15422262>, accessed 17 August, 2014.

356. Emma Farge, "Libyan Islamist Says NTC Executive Committee Should Resign," Al-Arabiyya, September 4, 2011; Vivian Salama and Lara Setrakian, "Libya's Jibril to Resign Tomorrow After Liberation is Declared," Bloomberg News, October 22, 2011. Available at <http://www.businessweek.com/news/2011-10-22/libya-s-jibril-to-resign-tomorrow-after-liberation-is-declared.html>, accessed August 17, 2014.

357. Wyre Davis (2012). "Libya Election: High Turnout in Historic Vote," *BBC News*, July 7. Available at: http://www.bbc.com/news/world-africa-18749808

358. For profiles of Libyan political parties and alliances in the July 2012 elections, see: "Libya's Political Parties,"*alJazeera*, July 3, 2012. Available at: <http://www.aljazeera.com/news/africa/2012/06/2012626224516206109.html>, accessed August 17, 2014.

359. Ashraf Abdul Wahab and Michel Cousins (2012). "Abushagur To Be New Libyan Prime Minister," *Saudi Gazette*, September 14. Available at <http://www.saudigazette.com.sa/index.cfm?method=home.regcon&contentid=20120914136108>, accessed August 17, 2014.

360. "Libya Election Success for Secularist Jibril's Bloc," *BBC News*, July 18, 2012. Available at <http://www.bbc.com/news/world-africa-18880908>, accessed August 17, 2014.

361. ʿAlī Qarbūsī (2012). "Maḥmūd Jibrīl: Taḥāluf al-quwā al-waṭaniyya lays ʿilmāniyan wa al-ḥukūma al-Lībīya satakūn iʾtilāfiya (Mahmud Jibril: The NFA Is Not Secular and the Government of Libya Will Be Coalitional)," *al-Sharq* (Saudi Arabia), July 7. Available at <http://www.alsharq.net.sa/2012/07/10/386763>.

362. "Maḥmūd Jibrīl: Aḥkām al-Sharīʿa al-Islāmiyya haya maṣdar raʾīs lil-tashrīʿ fī Lībyā (Mahmud Jibril: Islamic Jurisprudence Is a Principal Source of Legislation in Libya), *Elnashra* (Beirut), February 24, 2012. Available at <http://www.elnashra.com/news/show/443353/

محمود-جبريل-أحكام-الشريعة-الإسلامية-مصدر-رئيسي-للتشريع>. See also, "Jibrīl: 'Al-Taḥāluf al-Lībī istiḥqāq waṭanī lā siyāsī (Jibril: The Libyan alliance is a national not political right)," al-Arabiya, February 24, 2012. Available at: <http://www.alarabiya.net/articles/2012/02/24/196734.html>.

363. "Lībyā: Mashrūʿ mīthāq taḥāluf al-Quwā al-Waṭaniyya (Libya: Draft Charter of the National Forces Alliance)," *Ṣaḥifat al-Ḥurriya* (Libya), February 19, 2012. Available at <http://www.lawoflibya.com/mag/2012/02/19/ليبيا-مشروع-ميثاق-تحالف-القوى-الوطنية/>.
364. Ashraf Abdul Wahab and Michel Cousins, "Abushagur to be New Libyan Prime Minister," *Saudi Gazette*, September 14, 2012; Abushagur's academic homepage can be viewed here: <http://www.rit.edu/kgcoe/microsystems/faculty/Abushagur.html>, accessed August 17, 2014.
365. "Ali Zeidan Elected Libyan Prime Minister," *Telegraph*, October 15, 2012. Available at <http://www.telegraph.co.uk/travel/destinations/africaandindianocean/libya/9608420/Ali-Zeidan-elected-Libyan-prime-minister.html>, accessed August 17, 2014.
366. Karim Mezran, Fadel Lamen, and Eric Knecht (2013). "Post Revolutionary Politics in Libya: Inside the General National Congress," *Atlantic Council*, May 21, 2013, p. 4. Available at <http://www.atlanticcouncil.org/images/publications/postrevolutionary_politics_libya.pdf>, accessed August 17, 2014.
367. Chris Stephen (2013). "Libyan PM Ali Zeidan Says His Kidnap Was Coup Attempt," *The Guardian*, October 11. Available at <http://www.theguardian.com/world/2013/oct/11/libyan-pm-ali-zeidan-kidnap-coup-attempt>, accessed August 17, 2014.
368. Kamel Abdallah (2013). "Libya Passes Controversial Political Isolation Law," *al-Ahram Weekly* (Cairo), May 16. Available at <http://weekly.ahram.org.eg/News/2596/19/Libya-passes-controversial-political-isolation-law.aspx>, accessed August 17, 2014.
369. An English translation of the law is available at <http://muftah.org/full-text-libyas-political-isolation-law/#.U81tcIBJfiM>, accessed August 17, 2014.
370. Law No 13-2013.
371. Mohamed Eljarh (2013a). "Isolation Law Harms Libya's Democratic Transition," *Foreign Policy*, May 8, 2013a. Available at <http://transitions.foreignpolicy.com/posts/2013/05/08/isolation_law_harms_libya_s_democratic_transition>, accessed August 17, 2014; See also Mezran, Lamen, and Knecht, ""Post Revolutionary Politics in Libya," p. 5.

372. "Libya GNC Chairman Muhammad al-Magarief Resigns," *BBC News*, May 28, 2013. Available at <http://www.bbc.com/news/world-africa-22693963>, accessed August 17, 2014.
373. "Libya GNC Chairman Muhammad al-Magarief Resigns."
374. Michelle Nichols, "UN Says Libya Political Exclusion Law Likely Violates Rights," Reuters, June 18, 2013. Available at <http://www.reuters.com/article/2013/06/18/us-libya-un-idUSBRE95H15Y20130618>, accessed August 17, 2014.
375. Mohamed Eljarh (2013b). "One Step Closer to a New Libyan Constitution," *Foreign Policy*, September 26, 2013. Available at <http://transitions.foreignpolicy.com/posts/2013/09/26/one_step_closer_to_a_new_libyan_constitution>, accessed August 17, 2014.
376. Saʿīd Faraḥāt, "Jadal ḥawl intikhāb lajna kitābat al-dustūr fī Lībyā (Debate on the election of the constitution drafting committee in Libya)," *al-Ahram*, April 13, 2013. Available at http://arabi.ahram.org.eg/NewsQ/25704.aspx; Valerie Stocker (2013). "The Constituent Assembly Will Be Elected and the Political Isolation Law Is Constitutional, Rules Congress," *Libya Herald*, April 11. <http://www.opemam.org/node/999>, accessed August 17, 2014.
377. "Low-Key Vote for Libya's Constitution Panel," *alJazeera*, February 20, 2014. Available at <http://www.aljazeera.com/news/africa/2014/02/low-key-vote-libya-constitution-panel-2014220132815676510.html>, accessed August 17, 2014; Ulf Laessing and Ghaith Shennib, "Poor Turnout in Libyan Vote for Constitution-Drafting Body," Reuters, February 20, 2014. Available at <http://www.reuters.com/article/2014/02/20/us-libya-vote-idUSBREA1J0ZP20140220>, accessed August 17, 2014.
378. "Constititional Assembly Electoral Law Blow to Inclusivity in Post Revolution Libya," *Libya Herald*, July 23, 2013. Available at <http://www.opemam.org/node/1652?language=en>; and "Libya's Constitution-Drafting Body Holds First Meeting," April 21, 2014. Available at <http://www.middleeasteye.net/news/libyas-constitution-drafting-body-holds-first-meeting-1236768923>, accessed August 17, 2014.
379. Mohamed Eljarh (2014). "Democracy Fatigue in Libya," February 26, 2014. Available at <http://transitions.foreignpolicy.com/posts/2014/02/26/democracy_fatigue_in_libya>.

380. Mohamed al-Nagem, "Liberal Academic Heads Libya Constitution Panel," *Turkish Press*, April 22, 2014. Available at <http://www.turkishpress.com/news/402838/>, accessed August 17, 2014.
381. "The Facts About Benghazi," *New York Times*, December 30, 2013.
382. Chris Stephen (2013). "Libyan PM's Kidnapping Deepens Fears for Country's Disintegration," *The Guardian*, October 10. Available at <http://www.theguardian.com/world/ 2013/oct/10/libyan-pm-kidnapping-zeidan>, accessed August 17, 2014.
383. Mohamed Eljarh (2013c) "Citizens Versus Lawmakers in Libya," *Foreign Policy*, December 29, 2013. Available at <http://transitions.foreignpolicy.com/posts/2013/12/29/citizens_versus_lawmakers_in_libya>, accessed August 17, 2014.
384. "Libya Major General Khalifa Haftar Claims Gov't Suspended in Apparent Coup Bid," *CBS News*, February 14, 2014. Available at <http://www.cbsnews.com/news/libya-major-general-khalifa-haftar-declares-govt-suspended-in-apparent-coup-bid/>, accessed August 17, 2014.
385. Chris Stephen (2014). "Ousting of Libyan PM Ali Zeidan Brings Threat of Civil War," *The Guardian*, March 13, 2014. Available at <http://www.theguardian.com/world/2014/mar/13/libya-ali-zeiden-threat-civil-war>, accessed August 17, 2014.
386. "Libya's Interim Prime Minister Resigns," *al-Arabiyya*, April 13, 2014. Available at <http://english.alarabiya.net/en/News/middle-east/2014/04/13/Libya-interim-prime-minister-resigns.html>, accessed August 17, 2014.
387. "Man huwā Aḥmad Maʿtīq raʿīs al-wuzarāḥʾ al-lībī wa kayf tam intikhābahu (Who Is Aḥmad Maʿtīq the Libyan Prime Minister and How Was He Elected?)" *al-Maṣdar Online*, May 5, 2014. Available at http://almasdaronline.com/article/57384; "Libyan Premier Wins Congress Backing After Renegade General's Threats," Reuters, May 26, 2011. Available at <http://thecairopost.com/news/111915/news/libyan-premier-wins-congress-backing-after-renegade-generals-threats>, accessed August 17, 2014.
388. "Who's For Prime Minister?" *The Economist*, May 6, 2014. Available at <http://www.economist.com/blogs/pomegranate/2014/05/libya>, accessed August 17, 2014.

389. "Libyan Court: PM Maiteeq's Election was Illegal," *al-Arabiyya*, June 5, 2014. Available at <http://english.alarabiya.net/en/News/middle-east/2014/06/05/Libya-court-annuls-PM-election-.html>, accessed August 17, 2014.
390. "I Want to Cleanse Libya of Muslim Brotherhood," *al-Ahram*, May 20, 2014. Available at <http://english.ahram.org.eg/NewsContent/2/8/101760/World/Region/I-want-to-cleanse-Libya-of-Muslim-Brotherhood-Haft.aspx, accessed August 17, 2014>; Hassan Morajea and Abigail Hauslohner (2014). "Libyan Militias Led by Former General Attack Parliament and Declare it Dissolved," *Washington Post*, May 18, 2014. Available at <http://www.washingtonpost.com/world/middle_east/libyan-militias-led-by-former-general-attack-parliament-and-declare-it-dissolved/2014/05/18/579e18da-deb7-11e3-810f-764fe508b82d_story.html>, accessed August, 2014.
391. "I Want to Cleanse Libya of Muslim Brotherhood," *al-Ahram*, May 20, 2014
392. "Ḥiftar li-ʿUkāẓ: Lan nabqā aghrāban fi waṭaninā, wa la makān lil-ikhwān fī Lībyā wa nurīd dawla Islāmiyya ḍāmina lil-ʿadl (Hiftar to Okaz: We Won't Become Strangers in Our Homeland, and There Is No Place for the Muslim Brotherhood in Libya, and We Want an Islamic State that Guarantees Justice)," *al-Ahram* (Cairo), June 14, 2014.
393. "Libya's Rogue General Prepares to Renew Offensive amid Accusations of Attempted Coup," *The National* (UAE), May 18, 2014. Available at <http://www.thenational.ae/world/middle-east/libyas-rogue-general-prepares-to-renew-offensive-amid-accusations-of-attempted-coup>, accessed August 17, 2014.
394. "Libyan Elections: Low Turnout Marks Bid to End Political Crisis," *BBC News*, June 25, 2014. Available at <http://www.bbc.com/news/world-africa-28005801>, accessed August 17, 2014; GNC election figure from Inter-Parliamentary Union database, available at <http://www.ipu.org/parline/reports/2185_E.htm>, accessed August 17, 2014.
395. Lindsay Benstead, Ellen M. Lust, and Jakob Wichmann (2013). "It's Morning in Libya: Why Democracy Marches On," *Foreign Affairs*, August 6. Available at <http://www.foreignaffairs.com/articles/139628/lindsay-benstead-ellen-m-lust-jakob-wichmann/its-morning-in-libya>, accessed August 17, 2014.
396. Max Weber (1958). "Politics as a Vocation." In *Max Weber: Essays in Sociology*. Eds H. H Gerth and C. Wright Mills. Oxford: Oxford University Press: 78.

Chapter 5

1. Vincent Durac (2013). "Yemen's Arab Spring—Democratic Opening or Regime Maintenance?" *Mediterranean Politics 2012*; See also April Longley Alley, "Yemen Changes Everything . . . And Nothing," *Journal of Democracy, 24.4* (October): 74–85.
2. Frederic Wehrey (2013). "Building Libya's Security Sector," Carnegie Endowment for <International Peace. <http://carnegieendowment.org/2013/08/06/building-libya-s-security-sector/ghle#>, accessed August 19, 2014.
3. Mieczysław P. Boduszyński and Duncan Pickard (2013). "Libya Starts from Scratch," *Journal of Democracy, 24.4* (October): 86–96.
4. Ayman al-Warfalli (2014). "Libyan Militants Overrun Benghazi Special Forces Base as Chaos Deepens," Reuters, July 29. Available at <http://uk.reuters.com/article/2014/07/29/uk-libya-security-idUKKBN0FY1E420140729>, accessed August 19, 2014.
5. Description of the indicator and the components used to generate it available at <http://info.worldbank.org/governance/wgi/pdf/ge.pdf>, accessed June 6, 2014.
6. World DataBank World Development Indicators. Available at <http://databank.worldbank.org/data/>, accessed August 27, 2014.
7. "Interview transcript: Rachid Ghannouchi," *Financial Times*, January 18, 2011. Available at <http://www.ft.com/cms/s/0/24d710a6-22ee-11e0-ad0b-00144feab49a.html#axzz39FiDZQwm>, accessed August 20, 2014.
8. "ElBaradei To Form National Association for Change," *BBC News*, February 24, 2010. Available at <http://news.bbc.co.uk/2/hi/8534365.stm>, accessed August 20, 2014. The Muslim Brotherhood's representative on the NAC was Muḥammad al-Biltāgī, a former member of parliament from Shubrā al-Khayma who is as of this writing on trial for allegedly participating in acts of violence after the July 3, 2013 overthrow of President Mohamed Morsi. See "MB and NAC to Continue Anti-Power Inheritance Protests," *Ikhwanweb*, September 30, 2010. Available at <http://www.ikhwanweb.com/article.php?id=26584>, accessed August 20, 2014.
9. Duncan Pickard, "Forging Legitimacy: Abdel Hafiz Ghoga and the Founding Weeks of Libya's National Transitional Council." Case Study, John F. Kennedy School of Government, Harvard University, 2013.

10. Results of Tunisian elections from 1969 to 2009 available from Inter-Parliamentary Union's Parline database: <http://www.ipu.org/parline-e/reports/2392_arc.htm>, accessed June 6, 2014. For discussion of Tunisian 1994 electoral law, see Michael Collins Dunn (1994). "Tunisia's New Elections Law Guaranteed Opposition a Voice," Washington Report on Middle East Affairs, April/May, p. 20. Available at <http://www.wrmea.org/wrmea-archives/154-washington-report-archives-1994-1999/april-may-1994/7457-tunisias-new-elections-law-guaranteed-opposition-a-voice.html>, accessed June 6, 2014.
11. Discussion of Freedom House's methodology available at <http://www.freedomhouse.org/report/freedom-world-2010/methodology>, accessed June 6, 2014.
12. "Arab Interior Ministers Conclude Works of 30th Session 5 Riyadh," Saudi Press Agency, March 13, 2013. Available at: <http://www.spa.gov.sa/details.php?id=1087537>, accessed August 27, 2014.
13. World Bank income data available at <http://data.worldbank.org/indicator/NY.GDP.PCAP.CD/countries?order=wbapi_data_value_2013>, accessed August 20, 2014>; World Bank Income groups available at <http://data.worldbank.org/about/country-and-lending-groups>, accessed August 20, 2014.
14. Nathan Brown (2012b). "Egypt's Transition Imbroglio," Foreign Policy Middle East Channel, April 16, 2012.
15. Moustafa (2012); Brown (2012b).
16. Jay Ulfelder (2012). "Constitution-Writing in Egypt," March 16. Available at <http://dartthrowingchimp.wordpress.com/2012/03/16/constitution-writing-in-egypt/>, accessed August 27, 2014.
17. Joshua Stacher (2011). "Blame the SCAF for Egypt's Problems," *Foreign Policy*, October.
18. Alfred Stepan (2011). "Uprising in Egypt: Contrasting Progress on Democracy in Tunisia and Egypt," The Immanent Frame, Social Science Research Council, April 21. Available at <http://blogs.ssrc.org/tif/2011/04/21/contrasting-progress-on-democracy-in-tunisia-and-egypt/comment-page-1/>, accessed August 20, 2014.
19. "Transition in Tunisia: A Success Story?" *Economist*, January 14, 2014. Available at <http://www.economist.com/blogs/pomegranate/2014/01/transition-tunisia>, accessed August 27, 2014.

20. Mark Freeman and Seth Kaplan (2014). "Common Ground, Common Good: Tunisia's Model for Bridging Political and Social Divides," *Christian Science Monitor*, March 17. Available at <http://www.csmonitor.com/Commentary/Common-Ground/2014/0317/Tunisia-s-model-for-bridging-political-and-social-divides>, accessed August 20, 2014.
21. One potential answer is that the two cases are not independent of each other—that Tunisia's experience was shaped by the Egyptian one. After all, it was only after Morsi was overthrown in July 2013, that the ultimately-successful UGTT-brokered national dialogue process began. In this telling, Tunisia succeeded because Egypt failed. As one group of scholars put it, "The ripple effects of the Egyptian coup initially exacerbated tensions between Islamists and secularists in Tunisia, but then helped persuade Islamists to compromise to prevent the failure of the country's democratic experiment." (See Anouar Boukhars, Nathan J. Brown, Michele Dunne, Raphaël Lefèvre, Marwan Muasher, Frederic Wehrey, Katherine Wilkens, and Scott Williamson (2014) "The Egypt Effect: Sharpened Tensions, Reshuffled Alliances," Carnegie Endowment for International Peace, February 13.) Though this account is plausible, we believe that it ignores the fact that the differences between the Tunisian and Egyptian transition processes appeared well before the coup that ousted Morsi. As Stepan and Linz (2013) have testified, and as we saw in Chapter 4, from the outset, Tunisian oppositionists from across the political spectrum cooperated to a much greater extent than their Egyptian counterparts in shaping the course of their country's future. Morsi's overthrow may have focused Tunisians' minds, but it was evident long before then that Egypt and Tunisia were on two different trajectories.
22. Quoted in Timothy Power, "Theorizing a Moving Target: O'Donnell's Changing Views of Postauthoritarian Regimes." In *Reflections on Uneven Democracies: The Legacy of Guillermo O'Donnell*. Eds. Daniel Brinks, Marcelo Leiras, and Scott Mainwaring. Baltimore: Johns Hopkins University Press.
23. A fuller description of the Global Militarization Index and the full country rankings are available here: <http://gmi.bicc.de/>, accessed August 21, 2014.

24. Alfred Stepan (2011). "Uprising in Egypt: Contrasting Progress on Democracy in Tunisia and Egypt," The Immanent Frame, Social Science Research Council, April 21. Available at: <http://blogs.ssrc.org/tif/2011/04/21/contrasting-progress-on-democracy-in-tunisia-and-egypt/comment-page-1/>, accessed August 21, 2014.
25. Estimate of 22 million based on Khalid Ikram (2007). *The Egyptian Economy, 1952–2000: Performance Policies and Issues*. London, New York: Routledge, p. 86, who pegs the population in 1947 at 19 million and in 1960 at 26 million.
26. David D. Kirkpatrick and Carlotta Gall (2014). "Arab Neighbors Take Split Paths in Constitutions," *New York Times*, January 14. Available at <http://www.nytimes.com/2014/01/15/world/middleeast/arab-neighbors-take-split-paths-in-constitutions.html?_r=0>, accessed August 21, 2014.
27. Kirkpatrick and Gall (2014). "Arab Neighbors."
28. Ellen Lust and Lina Khatib (2014). "The Transformation of Arab Activism," *POMED Policy Brief Series*, May.
29. Michael Gallagher, "Election Indices," March 2014. Available at <http://www.tcd.ie/Political_Science/staff/michael_gallagher/ElSystems/Docts/ElectionIndices.pdf>, accessed August 21, 2014.
30. There were also six districts for expatriates. Details of Tunisia's electoral institutions for its 2011 constituent assembly election can be found at the International Foundation for Election Systems' White Paper: <http://www.ifes.org/~/media/Files/Publications/White%20PaperReport/2011/Tunisia_FAQs_072011.pdf>, accessed August 21, 2014.
31. Mazen Hassan (2011). "The Effects of Egypt's Election Law," Foreign Policy Middle East Channel, November 1, 2011. Available at <http://mideastafrica.foreignpolicy.com/posts/2011/11/01/egypts_electoral_cunundrum>, accessed August 21, 2014.
32. John Carey (2013). "Electoral Formula and the Tunisian Constituent Assembly," Dartmouth College, January 17. Available at <http://sites.dartmouth.edu/jcarey/files/2013/02/Tunisia-Electoral-Formula-Carey-January-2013.pdf>, accessed August 21, 2014.
33. Hādī Trabulsī n.d. "Hawl tatbīq nizām al-tamthīl al-nisbī fī Tūnis (On the application of the system of proportional representation in Tunisia," Available at <http://aceproject.org/ero-en/regions/africa/TN/Tunisian-electoral-systems>

34. Eric Trager (2011). "Egypt's New Election Laws Are Yet Another Setback for Democracy," Washington Institute for Near East Policy, October 3. See also Andrew Reynolds, "Egypt's Doomed Election," *New York Times*, November 22. Available at <http://www.nytimes.com/2011/11/23/opinion/egypts-doomed-election.html>, accessed August 21, 2014.
35. See "Tunisia, Majlis al-Nuwab (Chamber of Deputies)," Parline, Inter-Parliamentary Union. Available at <http://www.ipu.org/parline-e/reports/2321_B.htm>, accessed August 21, 2014.
36. ʾAkram Balḥāj Raḥūma (2011). "al-Marsūm al-mutaʿlaq bi-intikhāb ʾaʿḍāʾ al-majlis al-taʾsīsī: ʿuyūb bil-jumla (The Decree Law Relating to Election of Members of the Constituent Assembly: Wholesale Flaws)," *al-Mashhad al-Tūnisī*, April 23. Available at <http://www.machhad.com/1709>, accessed August 21, 2014.
37. David Jandura (2011). "Predicting the Results of Egypt's Elections: Why the Electoral Rules Do Not Actually Favor the Muslim Brotherhood," *The Monkey Cage*, November 29. Available at <http://themonkeycage.org/2011/11/29/predicting-the-results-of-egypts-elections-why-the-electoral-rules-do-not-actually-favor-the-muslim-brotherhood/>, accessed August 21, 2014.
38. James Traub, "Lost in the Desert," *Foreign Policy*, March 15, 2013. Available at: <http://www.foreignpolicy.com/articles/2013/03/15/lost_in_the_desert_obama_morsy_egypt>, accessed August 28, 2014.
39. Steven Cook (2013). "The High Art of Being Feckless," Council on Foreign Relations, March 7. Available at <http://blogs.cfr.org/cook/2013/03/07/egypt-the-high-art-of-being-feckless/>, accessed August 21, 2014.
40. Leslie T. Chang (2013). "Egypt's Petition Rebellion," *The New Yorker*, June 28. Available at <http://www.newyorker.com/online/blogs/newsdesk/2013/06/egypts-petition-rebellion.html>, accessed June 9, 2014.
41. Thomas Carothers (2013). "Egypt's Dismal Opposition: A Second Look," Carnegie Endowment for International Peace, May 14. Available at <http://carnegieendowment.org/2013/05/14/egypt-s-dismal-opposition-second-look/g3cf>accessed August 21, 2014.
42. Jean L. Cohen and Andrew Arato (1994). *Civil Society and Political Theory*. Cambridge, MA: MIT Press, 1994.
43. "Tunisia's Main Union a Secular Counterweight to Islamists," Agence France-Presse, February 8, 2013. Available at <http://www.globalpost.

com/dispatch/news/afp/130208/tunisias-main-union-secular-counterweight-islamists#1>, accessed June 6, 2014.

44. Jano Charbel (2011). "State's Union Control Keeps Egyptian Labor Quiet," *Al-Masry Al-Youm* English Edition (Cairo), January 21. Available at <http://www.egyptindependent.com//news/states-union-control-keeps-egyptian-labor-quiet>, accessed August 21, 2014.
45. Data drawn from the Maddison Project, Groningen Growth and Development Centre, 2013. Available at <http://www.ggdc.net/maddison/maddison-project/data.htm>, accessed August 21, 2014; J. Bolt and J. L. van Zanden (2013). "The First Update of the Maddison Project; Re-Estimating Growth Before 1820. Maddison Project Working Paper 4."
46. The Egyptian survey was conducted by the Ahram Center for Strategic Studies from June 16 to July 3, 2011, and encompassed 1,219 respondents drawn from throughout the country. The Tunisian survey was conducted from September 30 to October 11, 2011 by Sigma Conseil, and encompassed 1,196 respondents from across Tunisia. Details of the sample and the questionnaire are available in the project codebook, located on the Arab Barometer Project's website: <http://www.arabbarometer.org/sites/default/files/code_book/ADB%20II%20Master%20English%20Code_book.pdf>, accessed August 28, 2014.
47. Amr Chobaki (2011). "Egypt is not Tunisia," *al-Masry al-Youm* (English edition), January 17. Available at <http://www.egyptindependent.com//opinion/egypt-not-tunisia>, available August 21, 2014.

Chapter 6

1. Marc Lynch (2012). *The Arab Uprisings: The Unfinished Revolutions of the New Middle East*, PublicAffairs, p. 10.
2. Rashid Khalidi, "The Arab Spring," *The Nation*, March 21, 2011.
3. "Remarks by the President on Egypt," The White House, Office of the Press Secretary, February 2, 2011. Available at <http://www.whitehouse.gov/the-press-office/2011/02/11/remarks-president-egypt>, accessed August 28, 2014.
4. Our identification of six cases of regime-challenging protests is consistent with Yom and Gause's (2012) coding of protests in seventeen Arab countries plus the Palestinian territories during the period from December 2010 to August 2012. They identify Bahrain, Tunisia,

Egypt, Libya, Yemen, and Syria as having had "mass protests" featuring "radical demands" that included the removal of the leader. Four other countries—Morocco, Jordan, Kuwait, and Algeria—were coded as having had "significant protests but moderate demands," which did not extend to regime change.

5. There is a great deal of controversy in Egypt over the use of the term "military coup" (inqilāb ʿaskarī) to describe the July 3, 2013 ouster of President Mohamed Morsi. By using the term here, we are not making a political statement regarding the legitimacy of that event. Instead, we use it in keeping with decades of social science practice to denote instances where a country's chief executive is removed from office by members of the armed forces (Thompson 1980, p. 495).
6. This analysis echoes that of Diamond, Plattner, and Grubman (2014, xiii), who compared the Freedom House scores for fifteen Arab countries for a shorter time period (2010 and 2012) and found improvements only in Tunisia, Libya, and Egypt.
7. Sheri Berman (2013). "The Continuing Promise of the Arab Spring: Why Nostalgia for the Ancien Regime is Misguided," *Foreign Affairs*, July 17, 2013. Available at <http://www.foreignaffairs.com/articles/139586/sheri-berman/the-continuing-promise-of-the-arab-spring>, accessed August 28, 2014.
8. Berman (2013). "The Continuing Promise of the Arab Spring."
9. Andrew Whitehead (2011). "Eric Hobsbawm on 2011: 'It Reminds Me of 1848,'" BBC World Service News, December 22. Available at <http://www.bbc.com/news/magazine-16217726>, accessed August 28, 2014.
10. Jason Brownlee, Tarek Masoud, and Andrew Reynolds (2013). "Tracking the Arab Spring: Why the Modest Harvest?" *Journal of Democracy*, 24.4 (October): 29–44.
11. Freedom House scores are available at <http://www.freedomhouse.org/report-types/freedom-world#.U58xAo1dXGE>, accessed August 28, 2014. One observes the same pattern of democratic improvement in the Warsaw Pact countries if one uses the principal alternative measure of democracy, the "Polity IV" scores, for the same period. See <http://www.systemicpeace.org/polity/polity4.htm>, accessed August 28, 2014.
12. Adam Przeworski and Fernando Limongi (1997). "Modernization: Theories and Factsm" World Politics, 49.2 (January): 155–183.

13. Data available at <http://databank.worldbank.org/>, accessed September 2, 2014.
14. Marc M. Howard (2002). "The Weakness of Postcommunist Civil Society," *Journal of Democracy*, 13.1 (January): 157–169.
15. Erica Chenoweth and Maria J. Stephan, "Drop Your Weapons When and Why Civil Resistance Works," Foreign Affairs July/August 2014, <http://goo.gl/KhNsbV>, accessed August 11, 2014.
16. Daniel Lerner (1958). *The Passing of Traditional Society*. New York: Free Press.
17. Tomila Lankina and Lullit Getachew (2012). "Mission or Empire, Word or Sword? The Human Capital Legacy in Postcolonial Democratic Development," *American Journal of Political Science*, 56.2, April: 465–483.
18. Muṣtafā al-Aswānī, "ʿAlāʾ al-Aswānī: tujjār al-dīn yastaghilūn ummiya wa jahl al-nās min ajl al-sulṭa (Alla al-Aswany: Traders in Religion Take Advantage of Illiteracy and Ignorance of the People for the Sake of Power)," *al-Shurūq* (Cairo), December 9. Available at <http://www.shorouknews.com/news/view.aspx?cdate=09122012&id=430fad9c-be99-41bd-beda-febb9174129e>.
19. Literacy rate, adult total (% of people ages 15 and above), World Development Indicators, World Bank, available at <http://data.worldbank.org/>, accessed August 28, 2014.
20. Anne M. Cohler, Basia C. Miller, and Harold S. Stone, eds (1989). *Montesquieu: the Spirit of the Laws*. Cambridge: Cambridge University Press, Part 5, Book 24, Chapter 3, p. 461.
21. "Tunisia: Marzouki Accepts Resignation of General Hamdi," *Tunis Afrique Press*, July 31, 2014. Available at <http://allafrica.com/stories/201407311701.html>.
22. Mohamed Eljarh (2014). "Libya's Islamists Go For Broke." *Foreign Policy*, July 22. 2014. Available at <http://transitions.foreignpolicy.com/posts/2014/07/22/libyas_islamists_go_for_broke>. Turnout estimate drawn from Mustafa Fetouri, "Poor Election Turnout Sign of Libya's Despair," Al-Monitor, June 30. Available at <http://www.al-monitor.com/pulse/originals/2014/06/libya- elections-democracy-transition-chaos-war.html#>, accessed September 2, 2014.
23. Joseph A. Kechichian (2014). "Yemen in Transition, and in Turmoil," al-Jazeera,February6.Availableat<http://www.aljazeera.com/indepth/

opinion/2014/02/yemen-transition-turmoil-2014264255740696.html>, accessed September 2, 2014.

24. "Interview with Hamid Mir of Geo TV," United States Department of State, August 1, 2013. Available at <http://www.state.gov/secretary/remarks/2013/08/212626.htm>.
25. Mariam Rizk and Osman El Sharnoubi (2013). "Egypt's Constitution 2013 vs. 2012: A Comparison," Ahram Online, December 12, 2013. Available at <http://english.ahram.org.eg/NewsContent/1/0/88644/Egypt/0/Egypts-constitution--vs--A-comparison.aspx>, accessed September 2, 2014.
26. David D. Kirkpatrick (2013). "New Law in Egypt Effectively Bans Street Protest," New York Times, November 25, 2013. Available at <http://www.nytimes.com/2013/11/26/world/middleeast/egypt-law-street-protests.html?_r=0>, accessed September 2, 2014; The text of protest law can be viewed here: <http://english.ahram.org.eg/News/87375.aspx>, accessed September 2, 2014, and <http://www.almasryalyoum.com/news/details/346065>, accessed September 2, 2014; For a critique of Egypt's new electoral system, see Scot Williamson and Nathan Brown (2014). "Egypt's New Law for Parliamentary Elections Sets Up a Weak Legislature," Atlantic Council, June 24, 2014. Available at <http://www.atlanticcouncil.org/blogs/egyptsource/egypt-s-new-law-for-parliamentary-elections-sets-up-a-weak-legislature>, accessed September 2, 2014.
27. "Sisi Declared Egypt President with 96% of Votes," al-Arabiya, June 3. Available at <http://english.alarabiya.net/en/News/middle-east/2014/06/03/Egypt-to-officially-announce-Sisi-as-president.html>, accessed August 28, 2014.
28. Caroline Abadeer (2014). "Elections Scheduled for Tunisia," Muftah, June 29. Available at <http://muftah.org/elections-scheduled-tunisia/#.U-vtbYBJdMY>, accessed August 28, 2014.
29. International Republican Institute, Survey of Tunisian Public Opinion, February 12–22, 2014. Summary available at <http://www.iri.org/sites/default/files/2014%20April%2023%20Survey%20of%20Tunisian%20Public%20Opinion%2C%20February%2012-22%2C%202014.pdf>, accessed August 28, 2014.

Bibliography

Abdel-Malek, Anouar (1968). *Egypt. Military Society: The Army Regime, the Left, and Social Change under Nasser*. New York: Random House.

Acemoglu, Daron, Isafas N. Chaves, Philip Osafo-Kwaako, and James A. Robinson (2013). "Indirect Rule and State Weakness in Africa: Sierra Leone in Comparative Perspective," Africa Project, National Bureau of Economic Research, October. Available at <http://economics.mit.edu/files/9110>, accessed August 20, 2014.

Ackerman, Bruce (1994). "Political Liberalisms." *Journal of Philosophy*, 91: 364–386.

Ahmida, Ali Abdullatif (2011). "The Libyan National Transitional Council: Social Bases, Membership and Political Trends," AlJazeera Center for Studies, October 30.

al-Ali, Zaid (2011). "Libya's Interim Constitution: An Assessment," *OpenDemocracy*, October 5, 2011.

al-Ali, Zaid, and Donia Ben Romdhane (2012). "Tunisia's New Constitution: Progress and Challenges to Come," *Opendemocracy.net*, February 16, 2012.

Albrecht, Holger and Dina Bishara (2011). "Back on Horseback: The Military and Political Transformation in Egypt." *Middle East Law and Governance*, 3: 13–23.

Alexander, Christopher (2000). "Opportunities, Organizations, and Ideas: Islamists and Workers in Tunisia and Algeria." *International Journal Middle East Studies*, 32.04: 465–490.

Alexander, Christopher (2010). *Tunisia: Stability and Reform in the Modern Maghreb*. New York: Routledge.

Alexander, Christopher (2011). "Tunisia's Protest Wave: Where it Comes from and What it Means." Foreign Policy website, January 3, 2011, http://goo.gl/92l11Nhttp://goo.gl/92l11N.

Bibliography

Alley, April Longley (2013). "Yemen Changes Everything . . . And Nothing." *Journal of Democracy*, 24.4 (October): 74–85.

Alterman, Jon B. (2005). "Arab Spring into Long, Hot Summer." *CSIS: Middle East Notes and Comment*, 3.6: 1.

Althani, Mohamed (2012). *The Arab Spring and the Gulf States: Time to Embrace Change*. London: Profile Books.

Alwazir, Atiaf (2013). "Yemen's Independent Youth and Their Role in the National Dialogue Conference," German Institute for International and Security Affairs, August 23, 2013. <http://www.swp-berlin.org/en/publications/swp-comments-en/swp-aktuelle-details/article/yemens_independent_youth.html>, accessed August 16, 2013.

Andersen, Jørgen J. and Michael L. Ross (2014). "The Big Oil Change: A Closer Look at the Haber-Menaldo Analysis." *Comparative Political Studies*, 47.7: 993–1021.

Anderson, Lisa (1987). "The State in the Middle East and North Africa." *Comparative Politics*, 20.1: 1–18.

Anderson, Lisa (1995). "Democracy in the Arab World: A Critique of the Political Culture Approach." In *Political Liberalization and Democratization in the Arab World: Comparative Experiences*. Eds. Rex Brynen, Bahgat Korany, and Paul Noble. Boulder. CO: Lynne Rienner: 77–792.

Anderson, Lisa (2011). "Demystifying the Arab Spring: Parsing the Differences between Tunisia, Egypt, and Libya." *Foreign Affairs*, 90.7: 2–7.

Anderson, Margaret Lavinia (2000). *Practicing Democracy: Elections and Political Culture in Imperial Germany*. Princeton: Princeton University Press.

Angrist, Michele Penner (2013). "Understanding the Success of Mass Civic Protest in Tunisia." *The Middle East Journal*, 67.4 (Autumn): 547–564.

Arjomand, Said A. (1988). *The Turban for the Crown: The Islamic Revolution in Iran*. Oxford: Oxford University Press.

Awad, Mokhtar (2013). "Tunisia's Troubled Talks," *Foreign Policy*, November 13, 2013. Available at <http://mideastafrica.foreignpolicy.com/posts/2013/11/13/tunisias_troubled_talks>, accessed August 16, 2014.

Ayubi, Nazih N. (1995). *Over-Stating the Arab State: Politics and Society in the Middle East*. London: Tauris.

Bakry, Mustapha (2012). Al-Jaysh wa al-thawrah: Qiṣat al-ayām al-akhīrah (The Army and the revolution: The story of the final days), Cairo: Akhbar al-Yum.

Barany, Zoltan (2011). "Comparing the Arab Revolts: The Role of the Military." *Journal of Democracy*, 22.4: 27–39.

Barger, John (1999). "After Qadhafi: Prospects for Political Party Formation and Democratisation in Libya." *Journal of North African Studies*, 4.1, 62–77.

Bates, Robert H. (2001). *Prosperity and Violence: The Political Economy of Development*. New York, NY: W.W. Norton & Co.

Becker, Jaime and Jack A. Goldstone (2005). "How Fast Can you Build a State? State Building in Revolutions." In *States and Development: Historical Antecedents of Stagnation and Advance*. Eds. Matthew Lange and Dietrich Rueschemeyer. New York: Palgrave/Macmillan: 183–210.

Beinin, Joel and Frédéric Vairel (2011). *Social Movements, Mobilization, and Contestation in the Middle East and North Africa*. Stanford: Stanford University Press.

Bellin, Eva R. (1995). "Civil Society in Formation: Tunisia." In *Civil Society in the Middle East*. Ed. Augustus Richard Norton. Leiden: E. J. Brill: 120–147.

Bellin, Eva R. (2000). "Contingent Democrats: Industrialists, Labor, and Democratization in Late-Developing Countries." *World Politics*, 52: 175–205.

Bellin, Eva R. (2002). *Stalled Democracy: Capital, Labor, and the Paradox of State-Sponsored Development*. Ithaca, NY: Cornell University Press.

Bellin, Eva R. (2004). "The Robustness of Authoritarianism in the Middle East: Exceptionalism in Comparative Perspective." *Comparative Politics*, 36.2: 139–157.

Bellin, Eva R. (2012). "The Robustness of Authoritarianism Reconsidered: Lessons of the Arab Spring." *Comparative Politics*, 44: 127–149.

Bellin, Eva R. (2013). "Drivers of Democracy: Lessons from Tunisia, No. 75," August. Crown Center for Middle East Studies, Brandeis University.

Bennett, Andrew and Jeffrey T. Checkel (2014). "Process Tracing: From Philosophical Roots to Best Practices." In *Process Tracing in the Social Sciences: From Metaphor to Analytic Tool*. Eds. Andrew Bennett and Jeffrey T. Checkel. Cambridge: Cambridge University Press. Version quoted here available at <http://file.prio.no/files/projects/PT-MS-Chapter1.0212.pdf>, accessed August 19, 2014.

Benstead, Lindsay, Ellen M. Lust, and Jakob Wichmann (2013). "It's Morning in Libya: Why Democracy Marches On," Foreignaffairs.com, August 6, 2013. <http://www.foreignaffairs.com/articles/139628/lindsay-benstead-ellen-m-lust-jakob-wichmann/its-morning-in-libya>, accessed August 17, 2014.

Berman, Ilan (2002). "Israel, India, and Turkey: Triple Entente?". *Middle East Quarterly*, 9.4: 333–340.

Bermeo, Nancy (1997). "Myths of Moderation: Confrontation and Conflict during Democratic Transitions." *Comparative Politics*, 29.3: 305–322.

Blaydes, Lisa (2010). *Elections and Distributive Politics in Mubarak's Egypt.* New York: Cambridge University Press.

Bolt, J. and J. L. van Zanden (2013). "The First Update of the Maddison Project; Re-Estimating Growth Before 1820." Maddison Project Working Paper 4.

Bratton, Michael (1997). "Deciphering Africa's Divergent Transitions." *Political Science Quarterly*, 112.1 (Spring): 67–93, at p. 78.

Bratton, Michael and Nicolas van de Walle (1996). *Political Regimes and Regime Transitions in Africa: A Comparative Handbook.* No. 14, Dept. of Political Science, Michigan State University.

Bratton, Michael and Nicolas van de Walle (1997). *Democratization in Africa: Regime Transitions in Comparative Perspective.* Cambridge: Cambridge University Press.

Brehony, Noel (2011). *Yemen Divided: The Story of a Failed State in South Arabia*. London: I.B. Tauris & Co.

Browers, Michaelle (2007). "Origins and Architects of Yemen's Joint Meeting Parties." *International Journal of Middle East Studies*, 39.04: 565–586.

Brown, Harold (1980). "What the Carter Doctrine Means to Me." *MERIP Reports* 90 (September): 20–23.

Brown, Nathan J. (2002). *Constitutions in a Nonconstitutional World: Arab Basic Laws and the Prospects for Accountable Government.* Albany, NY: SUNY Press.

Brown, Nathan J. (2012a). "Egypt's Judges in a Revolutionary Age," Carnegie Endowment for International Peace. <http://carnegieendowment.org/2012/02/22/egypt-s-judges-in-revolutionary-age/9sri#>, accessed June 8, 2014.

Brown, Nathan (2012b). "Egypt's Transition Imbroglio," *Foreign Policy Middle East Channel*, April 16, 2012.

Brown, Nathan (2013). "Egypt's Failed Transition." *Journal of Democracy* (October), 24.4: 45–58.

Brown, Nathan (2014). "Egypt's Wide State Reassembles Itself," *Foreign Policy*, July 17, 2013. <http://mideastafrica.foreignpolicy.com/posts/2013/07/17/egypt_s_wide_state_reassembles_itself>, accessed August 14, 2014.

Brownlee, Jason (2002). ". . . And Yet They Persist: Explaining Survival and Transition in Neopatrimonial Regimes." *Studies in Comparative International Development*, 37.3: 35–63.

Brownlee, Jason (2007). "Can America Nation-Build?" *World Politics*, 59.2: 314–340.

Brownlee, Jason (2007a). *Authoritarianism in an Age of Democratization*. Cambridge: Cambridge University Press.

Brownlee, Jason (2009). "Portents of Pluralism: How Hybrid Regimes Affect Democratic Transitions." *American Journal of Political Science*, 53.3: 515–532.

Brownlee, Jason (2011). "Executive Elections in the Arab World: When and How Do They Matter?" *Comparative Political Studies*, 44.7: 807–828.

Brownlee, Jason (2012). *Democracy Prevention: The Politics of the U.S.-Egyptian Alliance*. New York: Cambridge University Press.

Brownlee, Jason, Tarek Masoud, and Andrew Reynolds (2013). "Tracking the Arab Spring: Why the Modest Harvest?" *Journal of Democracy*, 29.4 (October): 29–44.

Brumberg, Daniel (2002). "The Trap of Liberalized Autocracy." *Journal of Democracy*, 13.4: 56–68.

Brumberg, Daniel (2013). "Transforming the Arab World's Protection Racket Politics." *Journal of Democracy*, 24.3 (July): 88–103.

Brynen, Rex, Pete W. Moore, Bassel F. Salloukh, and Marie-Joëlle Zahar (2012). *Beyond the Arab Spring: Authoritarianism & Democratization in the Arab World*. Boulder, CO: Lynne Rienner Press.

Bunce, Valerie (1995). "Comparing East and South." *Journal of Democracy*, 6.3: 87–100.

Bunce, Valerie (1999). *Subversive Institutions: The Design and Destruction of Socialism and the State*. Cambridge: Cambridge University Press.

Bunce, Valerie J. and Sharon L. Wolchik (2010). "Defeating Dictators: Electoral Change and Stability in Competitive Authoritarian Regimes." *World Politics*, 62.1: 43–86.

Bunce, Valerie J. and Sharon L. Wolchik (2011). *Defeating Authoritarian Leaders in Postcommunist Countries*. Cambridge: Cambridge University Press.

Campbell, Leslie. "Yemen: The Tribal Islamists," *The Islamists are Coming* (blog), Woodrow Wilson International Center for Scholars. <http://www.wilsoncenter.org/islamists/yemen-the-tribal-islamists>, accessed August 16, 2014.

Carapico, Sheila (2001). "Yemen Between Civility and Civil War." In *Civil Society in the Middle East (Vol. 2)*. Ed. Augustus Norton. Leiden: Brill: 287–316.

Carapico, Sheila (2011). "No Exit: Yemen's Existential Crisis," *MERIP Online*, May 3, 2011. <http://www.merip.org/mero/mero050311-1>, accessed June 10, 2014.

Carey, John (2013). "Electoral Formula and the Tunisian Constituent Assembly." <http://sites.dartmouth.edu/jcarey/files/2013/02/Tunisia-Electoral-Formula-Carey-January-2013.pdf>, accessed August 15, 2014.

Carothers, Thomas (1991). *In the Name of Democracy: U.S. Policy Toward Latin America in the Reagan Years*. Berkeley: University of California Press.

Chaney, Eric (2012). "Democratic Change in the Arab World, Past and Present," Brookings Papers on Economic Activity, Spring.

Charrad, Mounira (2001). *States and Women's Rights: The Making of Postscolonial Tunisia, Algeria, and Morocco*. University of California Press.

Chehabi, Houchang E. and Juan J. Linz (1998). *Sultanistic Regimes*. Baltimore: The Johns Hopkins University Press.

Cheibub, José Antonio (2007). *Presidentialism, Parliamentarism, and Democracy*. Cambridge: Cambridge University Press.

Chenoweth, Erica and Maria J. Stephan (2014). "Drop Your Weapons: When and Why Civil Resistance Works," *Foreign Affairs* July/August. Available from <http://goo.gl/KhNsbV>, accessed August 11, 2014.

Chomiak, Laryssa (2011). "The Making of a Revolution in Tunisia." *Middle East Law and Governance* 3: 68–83.

Clark, William Roberts, Matt Golder, and Sona Nadenichek Golder (2009). *Principles of Comparative Politics*, Thousand Oaks, CA: CQ Press.

Clinton, Hilary Rodham (2014). *Hard Choices*, New York: Simon and Schuster.

Collier, Ruth Berins and David Collier (1991). *Shaping the Political Arena*. Princeton: Princeton University Press.

Cook, Steven (2007). *Ruling But Not Governing: The Military and Political Development in Egypt, Algeria and Turkey* (Council on Foreign Relations). Baltimore, Maryland: John Hopkins University Press.

Cox, Gary W. (1997). *Making Votes Count: Strategic Coordination in the World's Electoral Systems*. New York: Cambridge University Press, 1997.

Dabashi, Hamid (2012). *The Arab Spring: The End of Post Colonialism*. London: Zed Books.

Dahl, Robert (1971). *Polyarchy: Participation and Opposition.* New Haven: Yale University Press.

Davis, John, ed. (2013). *The Arab Spring and Arab Thaw: Unfinished Revolutions and the Quest for Democracy.* Farnham: Ashgate.

Day, Stephen (2010). "The Political Challenge of Yemen's Southern Movement," Carnegie Papers, Middle East Program, Number 108, March. <http://carnegieendowment.org/files/yemen_south_movement.pdf>, accessed August 16, 2014.

Day, Stephen W. (2014). "The 'Non-Conclusion' of Yemen's National Dialogue," *Foreign Policy.* January 27, 2014. <http://mideastafrica.foreignpolicy.com/posts/2014/01/27/the_non_conclusion_of_yemen_s_national_dialogue_0>, accessed August 16, 2014.

DeGeorges, Thomas Patrick (2006). "A Bitter Homecoming: Tunisian Veterans of the First and Second World Wars," Doctoral Dissertation, Department of History, Harvard University, May.

Diamond, Larry (2002). "Thinking about Hybrid Regimes." *Journal of Democracy*, 13.2: 21–35.

Diamond, Larry (2009). "Escaping the Development Impasse." *Journal of Democracy*, 20.4: 167–171.

Diamond, Larry (2010). "Why Are There No Arab Democracies." *Journal of Democracy*, 21.1 (January): 93–112.

Diamond, Larry, Marc F. Plattner, and Nate Grubman (2014). "Introduction." In *Democratization and Authoritarianism in the Arab World.* Eds. Larry Diamond and Marc F. Plattner. Baltimore: Johns Hopkins University Press.

Downes, Alexander B. and Jonathan Monten (2013). "Forced to Be Free?: Why Foreign-Imposed Regime Change Rarely Leads to Democratization." *International Security*, 37.4: 90–131.

Dresch, Paul and Bernard Haykel (1995). "Stereotypes and Political Styles: Islamists and Tribesfolk in Yemen." *International Journal of Middle East Studies*, 27.4: 405–431.

Dunne, Michele (2011). "Egypt: Elections or Constitution First," Carnegie Endowment for International Peace, June 21, 2011. <http://carnegieendowment.org/2011/06/21/egypt-elections-or-constitution-first/2rad>, accessed August 14, 2014.

Dunne, Michele (2012). "Egyptian President Morsi's Counter-Coup, Move Three," *Atlantic Council*, August 12, 2012. <http://www.acus.org/

egyptsource/egyptian-president-morsis-counter-coup-move-three>, accessed June 6, 2014.

Dunne, Michele and Mara Revkin (2011). "Overview of Egypt's Constitutional Referendum," Carnegie Endowment for International Peace, March 16, 2011.

Durac, Vincent (2012). "Yemen's Arab Spring—Democratic Opening or Regime Maintenance?" *Mediterranean Politics*, 17.2 (July): 161–178.

El Amrani, Issandr and Ursula Lindsey (2011). "Tunisia Moves to the Next Stage," *Middle East Research and Information Projecct (MERIP)*, November 8, 2011. <http://www.merip.org/mero/mero110811>, accessed June 10, 2014.

El-Ghobashy, Mona (2011). "The Praxis of the Egyptian Revolution," <http://stealthishijab.com/2011/05/31/the-praxis-of-the-egyptian-revolution>, accessed June 10, 2014.

El-Menawy, Abdel Latif (2012). *Tahrir—The Last 18 Days of Mubarak: An Insider's Account of the Uprising in Egypt*. London: Gilgamesh Publishing.

El-Shazli, Heba F. (2013). "Should Egyptians Believe Morsi?" *Jadaliyya*, June 28, 2013. <http://www.jadaliyya.com/pages/index/12479/should-egyptians-believe-morsi>, accessed August 14, 2014.

Eljarh, Mohamed (2013a). "Isolation Law Harms Libya's Democratic Transition," *Foreign Policy*, May 8, 2013. <http://transitions.foreignpolicy.com/posts/2013/05/08/isolation_law_harms_libya_s_democratic_transition>, accessed August 17, 2014.

Eljarh, Mohamed (2013b). "One Step Closer to a New Libyan Constitution," *Foreign Policy*, September 26, 2013. <http://transitions.foreignpolicy.com/posts/2013/09/26/one_step_closer_to_a_new_libyan_constitution>, accessed August 17, 2014.

Eljarh, Mohamed (2013c). "Citizens Versus Lawmakers in Libya," *Foreign Policy*, December 29, 2013. <http://transitions.foreignpolicy.com/posts/2013/12/29/citizens_versus_lawmakers_in_libya>, accessed August 17, 2014.

Eljarh, Mohamed (2014). "Democracy Fatigue in Libya," Foreign Policy, February 26, 2014. <http://transitions.foreignpolicy.com/posts/2014/02/26/democracy_ fatigue_in_libya>.

Elster, Jon (1999). "Arguing and Bargaining in Two Constituent Assem blies." *University of Pennsylvania Journal of Constitutional Law*. 2.2: 345–421.

Evans, Peter (1995). *Embedded Autonomy: States and Industrial Transfor mation*. Princeton, NJ: Princeton University Press.

Fahmy, Hazem (2012). "An Initial Perspective on 'The Winter of Discontent': The Root Causes of the Egyptian Revolution," *Social Research*, 79.2 (Summer): 349–376.

Fahmy, Khaled (2002). *All the Pasha's Men: Mehmed Ali, His Army, and the Making of Modern Egypt*. Cairo: New York American University in Cairo Press.

Farrell, Jeremy (2012). "Tunisian Constitution: Text and Context," *Jadaliyya*, August 23, 2012. <http://www.jadaliyya.com/pages/index/6991/tunisian-constitution_text-and-context>, accessed August 16, 2014.

Fearon, James D. (1991). "Counterfactuals and hypothesis testing in political science." *World Politics*, 43.02: 169–195.

Feith, Douglas, J. (2008). *War and Decision: Inside the Pentagon at the Dawn of the War on Terror*. New York: Harper.

Felter, Joseph and Brian Fishman (2007). "Al-Qaʿida's Foreign Fighters in Iraq: A First Look at the Sinjar Records," Combatting Terrorism Center at West Point, p. 12. Available at <http://tarpley.net/docs/CTCForeignFighter.19.Dec07.pdf>, accessed August 17, 2014.

Feuille, James (2012). "Reforming Egypt's Constitution: Hope for Egyptian Democracy?" *Texas International Law Journal*, 47.1: 237–259.

Fildis, Ayse Tekdal (2012). "Roots of Alawite-Suni Rivalry in Syria." *Middle East Policy*, 19.2: 148–156.

Fish, M. Steven (2002). "Islam and Authoritarianism." *World Politics*, 55.01: 4–37.

Fischer, David Hackett (1970). *Historians' Fallacies: Toward a Logic of Historical Thought*. New York: Harper & Row.

Fisher, Roger D. and Eugene V. Rostow (1970). "Legal Aspects of the Search for Peace in the Middle East." *The American Journal of International Law* 64.4: 64–71.

Fishman, Robert (1990). "Rethinking State and Regime: Southern Europe's Transition to Democracy." *World Politics*, 42.3: 422–440.

Fogarty, Richard S. (2008). *Race and War in France: Colonial Subjects in the French Army, 1914–1918*. Baltimore: Johns Hopkins University Press.

Freedom House (2010). "Freedom in the World: Methdology," <http://www.freedomhouse.org/report/freedom-world-2010/methodology>, accessed June 6, 2014.

Fukuyama, Francis (1989). "The End of History?" *The National Interest*, Summer 1989.

Gallagher, Michael and Paul Mitchell eds. (2008). *The Politics of Electoral Systems*, Oxford and New York: Oxford University Press.

Gambill, Gary C. (2005a). "Syria after Lebanon: Hooked on Lebanon." *Middle East Quarterly*, 12.4: 35–42.

Gambill, Gary (2005b). "The Libyan Islamic Fighting Group (LIFG)," *Terrorism Monitor*, 3.6.

Gandhi, Jennifer, and Adam Przeworski (2007). "Authoritarian Institutions and the Survival of Autocrats." *Comparative Political Studies*, 40.11: 1279–1301.

Gause, F. Gregory III (1995). "Regional Influences on Experiments in Political Liberalization in the Arab World." In *Political Liberalization and Democratization in the Arab World*, vol. 1, *Theoretical Perspectives*. Eds. Rex Brynen, Bahgat Korany, and Paul Noble. Boulder, CO: Lynne Rienner: 283–306.

Gause, F. Gregory III (2011). "Why Middle East Studies Missed the Arab Spring: The Myth of Authoritarian Stability." *Foreign Affairs*, 90.4: 81–90.

Gaventa, John (1980). *Power and Powerlessness: Quiescence and Rebellion in an Appalachian Valley*. Chicago, IL: University of Illinois Press.

Geddes, Barbara (1999a). "What Do we Know about Democratization after Twenty Years?" *Annual Review of Political Science*, 2.1: 115–144.

Geddes, Barbara (1999b). "Authoritarian Breakdown: Empirical Test of a Game Theoretic Argument." Paper presented at the Annual Meeting of the American Political Science Association, Atlanta, GA, 2–5 September.

Gelvin, James L. (2012). *The Arab Uprisings: What Everyone Needs to Know*. New York: Oxford University Press.

George, Alexander L. and Andrew Bennett (2004). *Case Studies and Theory Development in the Social Sciences*. Boston, MA: MIT Press.

Gerges, Fawaz A. (1995). "The Kennedy Administration and the Egyptian-Saudi Conflict in Yemen: Co-Opting Arab Nationalism." *Middle East Journal*, 49.2: 292–311.

Gerges, Fawaz A. (1999). *America and Political Islam: Clash of Cultures or Clash of Interests?* New York: Cambridge University Press.

Ghonim, Wael. 2012. *Revolution 2.0: The Power of the People Is Greater Than the People in Power: A Memoir*. New York: Houghton Mifflin Harcourt.

Gill, Anthony (2001). "Religion and Comparative Politics." *Annual Review of Political Science*, 4: 117–138.

Goldberg, Ellis (2011). "Tariq al-Bishri and Constitutional Revision," February 15, 2011. <http://nisralnasr.blogspot.com/2011/02/tariq-al-bishri-and-constitutional.html>.

Goldstone, Jack A. (2011). "Understanding the Revolutions of 2011: Weakness and Resilience in Middle Eastern Autocracies." *Foreign Affairs*, 90.3 (May/June): 8–16.

Goldstone, Jack A. (2014). "Bringing Regimes Back In: Explaining Success and Failure in the Middle East Revolts of 2011." In *The Arab Revolt of 2011*. Ed. Said Arjomand. Albany, NY: State University of New York Press.

Gordon, Joel (1991). *Nasser's Blessed Movement: Egypt's Free Officers and the July Revolution*. New York: Oxford University Press.

Green, Donald and Ian Shapiro (1996). *Pathologies of Rational Choice Theory: A Critique of Applications in Political Science*. New Haven:Yale University Press.

Grimmett, Richard F. (2010). "Conventional Arms Transfers to Developing Nations, 2002–2009," Washington, DC: Congressional Research Service, September 10, 2010: 44.

Haas, Mark and David W. Lesch, eds. (2012). *The Arab Spring: Change and Resistance in the Middle East*. Boulder, CO: Westview Press.

Haas, Mark and David W. Lesch, eds. (2013). *The Middle East and the United States: History, Politics and Ideologies*, 5th Ed. Boulder, CO: Westview Press.

Haber, Stephen and Victor Menaldo (2011). "Do Natural Resources Fuel Authoritarianism? A Reappraisal of the Resource Curse." *American Political Science Review* 105.1 (February): 1–26.

Haddad, Bassam (2012). "Syria's Stalemate: The Limits of Regime Resilience." *Middle East Policy* 19.1: 85–95.

Haggard, Stephan (1990). *Pathways from the Periphery: The Politics of Growth in the Newly Industrializing Countries*. Ithaca, NY: Cornell University Press.

Hamdi, Muhammed al-Hashimi (1998). *The Making of an Islamic Political Leader: Conversations with Hasan al-Turabi*. Boulder, CO: Westview Press.

Hamid, Shadi (2012). "A Man for All Seasons," *Foreign Policy*, May 9, 2012.

Hamid, Shadi (2014).*Temptations of Power*. Oxford: Oxford University Press.

Halliday, Fred (2002). *Revolution and Foreign Policy: The Case of South Yemen*, Cambridge: Cambridge University Press.

Harb, Imad (2003). "The Egyptian Military in Politics: Disengagement or Accommodation?" *Middle East Journal*, 57.2 (Spring): 269–290.

Hatita, Abdel Sattar (2011). "Libya, Searching for a Political Map." *Arab Reform Brief*, 48: 1–8.

Henry, Clement and Jang Ji-Hyang, eds. (2013). *The Arab Spring: Will it Lead to Democratic Transition?* New York: Palgrave Macmillan.

Herb, Michael (1999). *All in the Family: Absolutism, Revolution, and Democratic Prospects in the Middle Eastern Monarchies*. Albany, NY: SUNY Press.

Herbst, Jeffrey (2000). *States and Power in Africa: Comparative Lessons in Authority and Control.* Princeton, NJ: Princeton University Press,

Heydemann, Steven (2007). "Upgrading Authoritarianism in the Arab World." Analysis Paper Number 13. Washington, DC: Saban Center for Middle East Policy, Brookings Institution.

Heydemann, Steven (2013). "Syria and the Future of Authoritarianism." *Journal of Democracy* 24.4: 59–73.

Hilsum, Lindsay (2012). *Sandstorm: Libya in the Time of Revolution.* New York: Penguin Press.

Holtermann, Helge (2008). "Poverty and Civil War: An Assessment of Four Prominent Explanations of the Per Capita Income–Civil War Relationship." University of Oslo, November. Available at <https://www.duo.uio.no/bitstream/handle/10852/14771/Thesis6.pdf?sequence=2>, accessed August 20, 2014.

Holzapfel, Philip Barrett (2014). "Yemen's Transition Process: Between Fragmentation and Transformation," *Peaceworks #95,* March 2014, United States Institute of Peace.

Horowitz, Donald L. (2006). "Constitution-Making: A Process Filled With Constraint." *Review of Constitutional Studies,* 12: 1–17.

Horowitz, Donald L. (2011). "Writing the New Rules of the Game." *Wilson Quarterly,* 35: 52–54.

Housam, Darwisheh (2014). "Trajectories and Outcomes of the Arab Spring: Comparing Tunisia, Egypt, Libya and Syria." Institute of Developing Economies, Discussion paper No. 456, March. Available at <http://www.ide.go.jp/English/Publish/Download/Dp/pdf/456.pdf>.

Howard, Philip N. and Muzammil M. Hussain (2012). *Democracy's Fourth Wave? Digital Media and the Arab Spring.* New York: Oxford University Press.

Howard, Philip and Muzammil Hussain (2013). "What Best Explains Successful Protest Cascades? ICTs and the Fuzzy Causes of the Arab Spring." *International Studies Review 15.1*: 48–66.

Htun, Mala and G. Bingham Powell, Jr (2013). *Political Science, Electoral Rules, and Democratic Governance.* Washington DC: American Political Science Association.

Hudson, Michael C. (1991). "After the Gulf War: Prospects for Democratization in the Arab World." *Middle East Journal,* 45.3: 407–426.

Huntington, Samuel P. (1984). "Will More Countries Become Democratic?" *Political Science Quarterly,* 99.2 (Summer): 193–218.

Huntington, Samuel P. (1991), "Democracy's Third Wave." *Journal of Democracy,* 2.2 (Spring): 12–34.

Huntington, Samuel P. (1991). *The Third Wave: Democratization in the Late Twentieth Century*. Norman, OK: University of Oklahoma Press.

Ikram, Khalid (2007). *The Egyptian Economy, 1952–2000: Performance Policies and Issues*. London, New York: Routledge.

Inbar, Efraim ed. (2013). *The Arab Spring, Democracy and Security: Domestic and International Ramifications*. New York: Routledge.

Inglehart, Ronald and Christian Welzel (2009). "How Development Leads to Democracy," *Foreign Affairs* (March/April) 88.2: 33–48.

International Crisis Group (2011). "Popular Protest in North Africa and the Middle East: Egypt Victorious," *Middle East Report No 101*, February 24.

International Crisis Group (2011). "Popular Protests in the Middle East and North Africa (III): The Bahrain Revolt," *Middle East Report, No. 105*, April 6.

International Institute for Strategic Studies (2010). *The Military Balance*. 110:1

International Crisis Group (2012). "Conflicts, Threatened Transition," *Middle East Report No. 125*, July 3.

Ismail, Salwa (2011). "Civilities, Subjectivities and Collective Action: Preliminary Reflections in Light of the Egyptian Revolution." *Third World Quarterly*, 32.5: 989–995.

Jenkins. J. Craig and Augustine J. Kposowa (1990). "Explaining Military Coups D'état: Black Africa, 1957–1984." *American Sociological Review*, 55.6 (December): 861–875.

Joffe, George (1988). "Islamic Opposition in Libya." *Third World Quarterly*, 10.2: 615–631.

Joffé, George (2011). "The Arab Spring in North Africa: Origins and Prospects." *The Journal of North African Studies*, 16.4: 507–532.

Johnsen, Gregory D. (2013).*The Last Refuge: Yemen, al-Qaeda, and America's War in Arabia*. New York: W.W. Norton.

Jones, Toby Craig (2011). *Desert Kingdom: How Oil and Water Forged Modern Saudi Arabia*. Cambridge, MA: Harvard University Press.

Kamrava, Mehran (2000). "Military Professionalization and Civil-Military Relations in the Middle East." *Political Science Quarterly*, 115.1: 67–92.

Kandil, Hazem (2012). *Soldiers, Spies, and Statesmen: Egypt's Road to Revolt*. New York: Verso.

Karl, Terry Lynn (1990). "Dilemmas of Democratization in Latin America." *Comparative Politics*, 23.1: 1–21.

Karl, Terry Lynn (1995). "The Hybrid Regimes of Central America." *Journal of Democracy*, 6.3: 72–86.

Karl, Terry Lynn (1997). *The Paradox of Plenty: Oil Booms and Petro-States.* Berkeley: University of California Press.

Karl, Terry Lynn and Philippe C. Schmitter (1991). "Modes of Transition in Latin America, Southern and Eastern Europe." *International Social Science Journal*, 128.2: 267–282.

Katzenstein, Peter J. ed. (1978). *Between Power and Plenty: Foreign Economic Policies of Advanced Industrial States.* Madison, WI: University of Wisconsin Press.

Kedourie, Elie (1992). *Democracy and Arab Culture.* Washington Institute for Near East Policy.

Khosrokhavar, Farhad (2012). *The New Arab Revolutions That Shook the World.* Boulder: Paradigm.

King, Stephen Juan (2009). *The new authoritarianism in the Middle East and North Africa.* Bloomington: Indiana University Press.

Kirby, Andrew and Michael Don Ward (1992). "Modernity and Process of State Formation." In *The New Geopolitics*. Ed. Michael Don Ward. Abingdon: Taylor and Francis: 77–90.

Kocher, Matthew Adam (2004). "Human Ecology and Civil War." Doctoral Dissertation, University of Chicago Department of Political Science.

Kohli, Atul (2004). *State-Directed Development: Political Power and Industrialization in the Global Periphery.* New York: Cambridge University Press.

Korany, Bahgat and Rabab El-Mahdi, eds. (2012). *Arab Spring in Egypt: Revolution and Beyond.* Cairo: American University in Cairo Press.

Kornhauser, William (1998).*The Politics of Mass Society.* London: Routledge.

Kuran, Timur (1991). "Now Out of Never: The Element of Surprise in the East European Revolution of 1989." *World Politics*, 44.1: 7–48.

Kurzman, Charles (1996). "Structural Opportunity and Perceived Opportunity in Social Movement Theory: The Iranian Revolution of 1979." *American Journal of Sociology*, 61.1: 153–170.

Kurzman, Charles (2007). "Cross-Regional Approaches to Middle East Studies: Constructing and Deconstructing a Region," *Middle East Studies Association Bulletin*, 41.1: 24–29.

Laakso, Markku and Rein Taagepera (1979). "Effective Number of Parties: A Measure with Application to West Europe," *Comparative Political Studies*, 12.1 (April): 3–27.

Lacher, Wolfram (2013). "Fault Lines of the Revolution: Political Actors, Camps and Conflicts in the New Libya." Stiftung Wissenschaft und Politik (SWP), German Institute for International and Security Affairs :1–36.

Landis, Joshua (2012). "Why the Assad Regime Is Likely to Survive to 2013." *Middle East Policy* 19.1: 72–84.

Leenders, Reinoud (2012). "Collective Action and Mobilization in Dar'a: An Anatomy of the Onset of Syria's Popular Uprising." *Mobilization* 17.4: 419–434.

Lerner, Daniel (1958). *The Passing of Traditional Society: Modernizing the Middle East.* New York: Free Press.

Levitsky, Steven and Lucan Way (2002). "The Rise of Competitive Authoritarianism."*Journal of Democracy*, 13.2: 51–65.

Levitsky, Steven and Lucan Way (2010). *Competitive Authoritarianism: Hybrid Regimes After the Cold War.* New York: Cambridge University Press.

Linz, Juan J. (1975). "Totalitarianism and Authoritarianism." In *The Handbook of Political Science*. Eds. Fred I. Greenstein and Nelson W. Polsby. Reading: Addison Wesley: 336–350.

Linz, Juan J. (1992). "Change and Continuity in the Nature of Contemporary Democracies." In *Reexamining Democracy: Essays in Honor of Seymour Martin Lipset.* Eds. Gary Marks and Larry Diamond. Newbury Park, CA: Sage Publications: 184–190.

Linz, Juan J. and Alfred C. Stepan (1996). *Problems of Democratic Transition and Consolidation: Southern Europe, South America, and Post-Communist Europe*. Baltimore: Johns Hopkins University Press.

Lippmann, Walter (1939). "The Indispensable Opposition." *Atlantic Monthly*, 164; reprinted in Rossiter and Latre (eds.) (1982). *The Essential Lippmann: A Political Philosophy for Liberal Democracy.* Cambridge, MA: Harvard University Press: 232–234.

Lipset, Seymour Martin (1959). "Some Social Requisites of Democracy: Economic Development and Political Legitimacy." *American Political Science Review*, 53.1: 69–105.

Lombardi, Clark (2009). "Egypt's New Chief Justice," www.comparativeconstitutions.org, September 30, 2009. <http://www.comparativeconstitutions.org/2009/09/egypts-new-chief-justice.html>, accessed August 14, 2014.

Lombardi, Clark and Nathan Brown (2012). "Islam in Egypt's New Constitution," *Foreign Policy Middle East Channel*, December 13, 2012. <http://mideastafrica.foreignpolicy.com/posts/2012/12/13/islam_in_egypts_new_constitution>, accessed August 14, 2014.

Luong, Pauline Jones and Erika Weinthal (2001). "Prelude to the Resource Curse: Explaining Oil and Gas Development Strategies in the Soviet Successor States and Beyond," *Comparative Political Studies* 34.4: 367–399.

Lukes, Steven (1974). *Power: A Radical View*. London: MacMillan Press.

Lust, Ellen and Lina Khatib (2014). "The Transformation of Arab Activism," *POMED Policy Brief Series*, May.

Lust, Ellen (2007). Structuring Conflict in the Arab World: Incumbents, Opponents, and Institutions. Cambridge University Press.

Lust-Okar, Ellen (2011). "Missing the Third Wave: Islam, Institutions, and Democracy in the Middle East." *Studies in Comparative International Development*, 46.2: 163–190.

Lust-Okar, Ellen and Amaney Ahmed Jamal (2002). "Reassessing the Influence of Regime Type on Electoral Law Formation." *Comparative Political Studies*, 35.3: 337–366.

Lynch, Marc (2011). "After Egypt: The Limits and Promise of Online Challenges to the Authoritarian Arab State." *Perspectives on Politics*, 9.2: 301–310.

Lynch, Marc (2012).*The Arab Uprising: The Unfinished Revolutions of the New Middle East*. New York: Public Affairs.

Mahdavy, Hossein (1970). "The Patterns and Problems of Economic Development in Rentier States: The Case of Iran." In *Studies in the Economic History of the Middle East*. Ed. M. A. Cook. Oxford: Oxford University Press: 428–467.

Mainwaring, Scott and Timothy Scully, eds. (2003). *Christian Democracy in Latin America: Electoral Competition and Regime Conflicts*. Stanford: Stanford University Press.

Mann, Michael (1984). "The Autonomous Power of the State: Its Origins, Mechanisms and Results." *European Journal of Sociology*, 25.2: 185–213.

Mansfield, Edward D. and Jack Snyder. (2007a). "The Sequencing 'Fallacy.'" *Journal of Democracy*, 18.3 (July): 5–10.

Mansfield, Edward D. and Jack Snyder (2007b). *Electing to Fight: Why Emerging Democracies Go to War*. Cambridge, MA: MIT Press.

Marinov, Nikolay and Hein Goemans (2013). "Coups and Democracy." *British Journal of Political Science*, August 28: 1–27.

Marks, Monica and Omar Belhaj Salah (2013). "Uniting for Tunisia," *Sada*, March 28, 2013. <http://carnegieendowment.org/sada/2013/03/28/uniting-for-tunisia/fu2q>, accessed June 6, 2014.

Masoud, Tarek El-Miselhy (2009). "Why Islam Wins: Electoral Ecologies and Economies of Political Islam in Contemporary Egypt." Doctoral Dissertation, Yale University.

Masoud, Tarek (2011a). "The Road to (and from) Liberation Square." *Journal of Democracy*, 22.3: 20–34.

Masoud, Tarek (2011b). "Liberty, Democracy, and Discord in Egypt." *Washington Quarterly*, 34.4: 117–129.

Masoud, Tarek (2014a). "Egyptian Democracy: Smothered in the Cradle, or Stillborn?" *Brown Journal of World Affairs*, Summer/Fall 2014: 3–19.

Masoud, Tarek (2014b). *Counting Islam: Religion, Class, and Elections in Egypt*. Cambridge: Cambridge University Press.

Massad, Joseph (2012). "The 'Arab Spring' and Other American Seasons," *Al Jazeera*, August 29, 2012. <http://www.aljazeera.com/indepth/opinion/2012/08/201282972539153865.html>, accessed March 19, 2014.

McAdam, Doug (1982). *Political Process and the Development of Black Insurgency, 1930–1970*. Chicago, IL: University of Chicago Press.

McAdam, Doug, Sidney Tarrow, and Charles Tilly (2001). *Dynamics of Contention*. Cambridge: Cambridge University Press.

McDermott, Anthony (1988). *Egypt from Nasser to Mubarak*. London: Routledge.

McFaul, Michael (2002). "The Fourth Wave of Democracy and Dictatorship: Noncooperative Transitions in the Postcommunist World." *World Politics*, 54.2: 212–244.

McMurray, David (2013). *The Arab Revolts: Dispatches on Militant Democracy in the Middle East*. Bloomington: Indiana University Press.

Merriman, John (2010). *A History of Modern Europe: From the Renaissance to the Present*. 3rd ed. New York: W.W. Norton.

Mezran, Karim, Fadel Lamen, and Eric Knecht (2013). "Post Revolutionary Politics in Libya: Inside the General National Congress," *Atlantic Council*, May 21, 2013, p. 4 <http://www.atlanticcouncil.org/images/publications/postrevolutionary_politics_libya.pdf>, accessed August 17, 2014.

Migdal, Joel (1988). *Strong Societies and Weak States: State-Society Relations and State Capabilities in the Third World*. Princeton, NJ: Princeton University Press.

Mohsen-Finan, Khadija and Malika Zeghal, "The Day After: First Readings of the Tunisian Election," October 24, 2011. <http://onislamandpolitics.wordpress.com/2011/10/24/

the-day-after-first-readings-of-the-tunisian-election/>, accessed August 15, 2014.

Moore, Clement Henry (1965). *Tunisia Since Independence: the Dynamics of One Party Government.* Berkeley: University of California Press.

Moustafa, Tamir (2012). "Drafting Egypt's Constitution: Can a New Legal Framework Revive a Flawed Transition?" Brookings Institution, March.

Muasher, Marwan (2014). *The Second Arab Awakening: And the Battle for Pluralism.* New Haven: Yale University Press.

Nettl, J. P. (1968). 'The State as a Conceptual Variable'. *World Politics*, 20.4: 559–592.

Norris, Pippa and Ronald Inglehart (2004). *Sacred and Secular: Religion and Politics Worldwide*. Cambridge, UK: Cambridge University Press.

Noueihed, Lin and Alex Warren (2012). *The Battle for the Arab Spring: Revolution, Counter-Revolution and the Making of a New Era.* New Haven: Yale University Press.

Nouira, Asma (2011). "Obstacles on the Path of Tunisia's Democratic Transformation," Carnegie Endowment for International Peace. *Arab Reform Bulletin*, March 30, 2011.

O'Donnell, Guillermo A. and Philippe C. Schmitter (1986). *Transitions from Authoritarian Rule: Tentative Conclusions about Uncertain Democracies.* Baltimore: Johns Hopkins University Press.

O'Donnell, Guillermo, Philippe C. Schmitter, and Laurence Whitehead, eds. (1986). *Transitions from Authoritarian Rule: Comparative Perspectives*, Vol. 3. Baltimore: Johns Hopkins University Press.

Ottaway, Marina (2011). "The Limits of Women's Rights." In *Uncharted Journey: Promoting Democracy in the Middle East.* Eds. Thomas Carothers and Marina Ottaway. Washington, DC: Carnegie Endowment for International Peace: 115–129.

Owen, Roger (2004). *State, Power and Politics in the Making of the Modern Middle East* 3rd Edition. London: Routledge.

Panara, Carlo (2013). *The Arab Spring: New Patterns for Democracy and International Law.* Leiden, Brill.

Pargeter, Alison (2009). "Localism and Radicalization in North Africa: Local Factors and the Development of Political Islam in Morocco, Tunisia and Libya." *International Affairs*, 85.5: 1031–1044.

Philbrick Yadav, Stacey (2012). "Opposition to Yemen's Opposition." In *Yemen's Stalemate.* Ed. Marc Lynch. Washington DC: POMEPS Briefings: 9–12.

Pickard, Duncan (2011). "Challenges to Legitimate Governance in Post-Revolution Tunisia." *Journal of North African Studies*, 16.4: 637–652.

Pickard, Duncan (2014). "Forging Legitimacy: Abdel Hafiz Ghoga and the Founding Weeks of Libya's National Transitional Council," Harvard Kennedy School Case Program.

Pierson, Paul (2003). "Big, Slow-Moving, and . . . Invisible." In *Comparative Historical Analysis in the Social Sciences*. Eds. James Mahoney and Dietrich Rueschemeyer. Cambridge: Cambridge University Press: 177–207.

Pipes, Daniel (1989). "The Alawi Capture of Power in Syria." *Middle Eastern Studies*, 25.4: 429–450.

Pollak, Kenneth Michael (2002). *Arabs at War: Military Effectiveness, 1948–1991*, Lincoln, NE: University of Nebraska Press.

Posusney, Marsha Pripstein (1997). *Labor and the State in Egypt, 1952–1994: Workers, Unions, and Economic Restructuring, 1952-1996*. New York: Columbia University Press.

Posusney, Marsha Pripstein (2002). "Multi-Party Elections in the Arab World: Institutional Engineering and Oppositional Strategies." *Studies in Comparative International Development*, 36.4 (Winter); 34–62.

Posusney, Marsha Pripstein (2004). "Enduring Authoritarianism: Middle East Lessons for Comparative Theory." *Comparative Politics*, 36.2: 127–138.

Posusney, Marsha Pripstine and Michelle Penner Angrist, eds. (2005). *Authoritarianism in the Middle East: Regimes and Resistance*. Boulder, CO: Lynne Rienner Publishers.

Power, Timothy (2014). "Theorizing a Moving Target: O'Donnell's Changing Views of Postauthoritarian Regimes." In *Reflections on Uneven Democracies: The Legacy of Guillermo O'Donnell*. Eds. Daniel Brinks, Marcelo Leiras, and Scott Mainwaring. Baltimore: Johns Hopkins University Press.

Prashad, Vijay (2012). *Arab Spring, Libyan Winter*. New York: AK Press.

Przeworski, Adam (2004). "Institutions Matter?" *Government and Opposition*, 2004, 39.2: 527–540.

Przeworski, Adam, Michael E. Alvarez, Jose Antonio Cheibub, and Fernando Limongi (2000). *Democracy and Development: Political Institutions and Well-Being in the World 1950–1990*. Cambridge: Cambridge University Press.

Quandt, William (2002). "Algeria's Uneasy Peace." *Journal of Democracy*, 13. 4: 15–23.

Quandt, William B. (2002a). "Democratization in the Arab World?" *Journal of Democracy*, 13.4: 15–23.

Remmer, Karen L. (1985). "Exclusionary Democracy." *Studies in Comparative International Development*, 20.4: 64–85.

Reynolds, Andrew and John M. Carey (2012). "Getting Elections Wrong." *Journal of Democracy*, 23.1: 164–168.

Richards, Alan and John Waterbury (1998). *A Political Economy of the Middle East*. Boulder, CO: Westview Press.

Rokkan, Stein (1969). "Models and Methods in the Comparative Study of Nation Building." *Acta Sociologica*, 12.2: 53–73.

Ross, Michael (2001). "Does Oil Hinder Democracy?" *World Politics*, 53.3: 325–361.

Ross, Michael (2011). "Will Oil Drown the Arab Spring: Democracy and the Resource Curse." *Foreign Affairs*, 90.5: 2–7.

Ross, Michael L. (2013). *The Oil Curse: How Petroleum Wealth Shapes the Development of Nations*. Princeton, NJ: Princeton University Press.

Rueschmeyer, Dietrich, Evelyne Huber Stephens, and John D. Stephens (1992). *Capitalist Development and Democracy*, Cambridge: Cambridge University Press.

Rustow, Dankwart A. (1970). "Transitions to Democracy: Towards a Dynamic Model." *Comparative Politics*, 2.3: 337–363.

Saddy, Rikia (2011). "Social Media Revolutions." *Journal of Professional Communication*, 1.1:31–33.

Sadiki, Larbi (2002). "Political Liberalization in Bin Ali's Tunisia: Façade Democracy." *Democratization*, 9.4: 122–141.

Sattar, Hatita Abdel (2011). "Libya: Searching for a Political Map." *Arab Reform Brief, Arab Reform Initiative 48*, Arab Reform Initiative, April.

Sayigh, Yezid (2013). "Morsi and Egypt's Military," *Al Monitor*, January 8, 2013. <http://www.al-monitor.com/pulse/originals/2013/01/morsi-army-egypt-revolution.html#>, accessed August 14, 2014.

Schedler, Andreas (1996). "Anti-Political-Establishment Parties," *Party Politics*, 2.3: 291–312.

Schedler, Andreas (2002). "The Menu of Manipulation." *Journal of Democracy*, 13.2: 36–50.

Schmitz, Charles (2011). "Yemen's Tribal Showdown," *Foreign Affairs*, June 3, 2011. Available at <http://www.foreignaffairs.com/articles/67877/charles-schmitz/yemens-tribal-showdown>, accessed 16 August, 2014.

Schraeder, Peter J., and Hamadi Redissi (2011). "Ben Ali's Fall." *Journal of Democracy*, 22.3: 5–19.

Schwedler, Jillian (2006). *Faith in Moderation: Islamist Parties in Jordan and Yemen*. Cambridge: Cambridge University Press.

Shokr, Ahmad (2011a). "The 18 Days of Tahrir." *Middle East Report* 258: 14–19.

Shugart, Matthew Soberg and John M. Carey (1992). *Presidents and Assemblies: Constitutional Design and Electoral Dynamics*. Cambridge: Cambridge University Press.

Skocpol, Theda (1979). *States and Social Revolutions*. Cambridge: Cambridge University Press.

Slater, Daniel (2012). "Strong-State Democratization in Malaysia and Singapore." *Journal of Democracy*, 23.2: 19–33.

Slim, Randa (2011). "Hezbollah's Most Serious Challenge," *Foreign Policy*, May 3, 2011. <http://mideast.foreignpolicy.com/posts/2011/05/03/hezbollah_s_most_serious_challenge>, accessed June 11, 2014.

Smith, Benjamin (2004). "Oil Wealth and Regime Survival in the Developing World, 1960–1999'."*American Journal of Political Science*, 48.2: 232–246.

Smith, Benjamin (2007). *Hard Times in the Lands of Plenty: Oil Politics in Iran and Indonesia*. Ithaca, NY: Cornell University Press.

Smith, Benjamin (2013). "Resource Wealth and Political Regimes: How Solid a Link after 40 Years of Research?" *APSA-Comparative Democratization Newsletter*, 11.2: 17–20.

Snyder, Jack (1991). *Myths of Empire: Domestic Politics and International Ambition*. Ithaca, NY: Cornell University Press.

Snyder, Richard (1992). "Explaining Transitions from Neopatrimonial Dictatorships."*Comparative Politics*, 24.2: 379–399.

Snyder, Richard and James Mahoney (1999). "The Missing Variable: Institutions and the Study of Regime Change." *Comparative Politics* 32.1: 103–122.

Springborg, Robert (1991). "State-Society Relations in Egypt: The Debate over Owner-Tenant Relations." *Middle East Journal*, 45.2: 232–249.

Stacher, Joshua (2011). "Reinterpreting Authoritarian Power: Syria's Hereditary Succession."*The Middle East Journal*, 65.2: 197–212.

Stacher, Joshua (2012). *Adaptable Autocrats: Regime Power in Egypt and Syria*. Palo Alto, CA: Stanford University Press.

Stepan, Alfred (2012). "Tunisia's Transition and the Twin Tolerations." *Journal of Democracy*, 23.2: 89–103.

Stepan, Alfred and Juan Linz (2013). "Democratization Theory and the Arab Spring." *Journal of Democracy*. 24:2: 15–30.

Stepan, Alfred with Graeme Robertson (2003). "An 'Arab' More than 'Muslim' Electoral Gap." *Journal of Democracy*, 14.3: 30–44.

Stilt, Kristen (2012). "The End of One Hand: The Egyptian Constitutional Declaration and the Rift between the 'People' and the Supreme Council of the Armed Forces," Northwestern Public Law Research Paper No. 12-10, April 8, 2012. <http://papers.ssrn.com/sol3/papers.cfm?abstract_id=2037563>, accessed August 15, 2014.

Stinchbombe, Arthur (1965). "Social Structure and Organizations." In *Handbook of Organizations*. Ed. James G. March. Chicago: Rand McNally: 142–193.

Stone Sweet, Alec (2000). *Governing with Judges: Constitutional Politics in Europe*. Oxford: Oxford University Press.

Stork, Joe (1973). "Socialist Revolution in Arabia: A Report from the People's Democratic Republic of Yemen," MERIP Reports, No. 15 (March): 1–25.

Telhami, Shibley (2013). *The World Through Arab Eyes: Arab Public Opinion and the Reshaping of the Middle East.* New York: Basic Books.

Thiel, Tobias (2012). "Yemen's Arab Spring: From Youth Revolution to Fragile Political Transition." <http://www.academia.edu/1539006/Yemens_Arab_Spring_From_Youth_Revolution_to_Fragile_Political_Transition>, accessed June 11, 2014.

Thompson, William R. (1980). "Corporate Coup-Maker Grievances and Types of Regime Targets." *Comparative Political Studies*, 12: 485–496.

Tilly, Charles (1985). "War Making and State Making as Organized Crime." In *Bringing the State Back In*. Eds. Peter B. Evans, Dietrich Rueschemeyer, and Theda Skocpol. New York: Cambridge University Press: 169–191.

Tilly, Charles (1992). *Coercion, Capital, and European States AD 990–1992.* Cambridge: Blackwell.

Toensing, Chris (2011). "Tunisian Labor Leaders Reflect Upon Revolt," Middle East Report Online (258). <http://merip.org/mer/mer258/tunisian-labor-leaders-reflect-upon-revolt-0>, accessed June 11, 2014.

Trager, Eric (2012). "The American Media Gets an Egyptian Presidential Candidate All Wrong," *New Republic*, May 3, 2012.

Tufekci, Zeynep and Christopher Wilson (2012). "Social media and the decision to participate in political protest: Observations from Tahrir Square." *Journal of Communication*, 62.2: 363–379.

Vandewalle, Dirk (1998). *Libya Since Independence: Oil and State Building.* London: IB Tauris Publishers.

Vandewalle, Dirk (2012). *A History of Modern Libya*. Cambridge: Cambridge University Press.

Vandewalle, Dirk (2012b). "After Qaddafi: The Surprising Success of the New Libya," Foreign Affairs, November/December.

Waltz, Susan E. (1995). *Human Rights and Reform: Changing the Face of North African Politics*. Berkeley: University of California Press.

Ware, L. B. (1985). "The Role of the Tunisian Military in the Post-Bourgiba Era," *Middle East Journal*, 39.1 (Winter): 27–47.

Weber, Max (1958). "Politics as a Vocation." In *Max Weber: Essays in Sociology*. Eds H. H Gerth and C. Wright Mills. Oxford: Oxford University Press: 78.

Wedeen, Lisa (1999). *Ambiguities of Domination: Politics, Rhetoric, and Symbols in Contemporary Syria* . Chicago: University of Chicago Press.

Wedeen, Lisa (2013). "Ideology and Humor in Dark Times: Notes from Syria." *Critical Inquiry*, 39.4: 841–873.

Wehrey, Frederic (2012). "The Wrath of Libya's Salafis," Sada (Carnegie Endowment for International Peace), September 12, 2012. <http://carnegieendowment.org/2012/09/12/wrath-of-libya-s-salafis/dtdn>, accessed August 17, 2014.

Wells, Madeleine (2012). "Yemen's Houthi Movement and the Revolution," *Foreign Policy*, February 27, 2012. <http://mideastafrica.foreignpolicy.com/posts/2012/02/27/yemen_s_houthi_movement_and_the_revolution>. accessed August 16, 2014.

Werner, Suzanne (1996). "Absolute and Limited War: The Possibility of Foreign-imposed Regime Change." *International Interactions*, 22.1: 67–88.

Weyland, Kurt (2012). "The Arab Spring: Why the Surprising Similarities with the Revolutionary Wave of 1848?" *Perspectives on Politics*, 10.4: 917–934.

Weyland, Kurt (2014). *Making Waves : Democratic Contention in Europe and Latin America Since the Revolutions of 1848*. New York: Cambridge University Press.

Wickham, Carrie Rosefsky (2002). *Mobilizing Islam: Religion, Activism, and Political Change in Egypt*. New York: Columbia University Press.

Wickham, Carrie Rosefsky (2004). "The Path to Moderation: Strategy and Learning in the Formation of Egypt's Wasat Party." *Comparative Politics* 36.2 (January): 205–228.

Wiktorowicz, Quintan (2002). "Islamic Activism and Social Movement Theory: A New Direction for Research." *Mediterrannean Politics*, 7.3: 187–211.

Yashar, Deborah J (1997). *Demanding Democracy: Reform and Reaction in Costa Rica and Guatemala, 1870s–1950s*. Stanford: Stanford University Press.

Yergin, Daniel (2009). *The Prize: The Epic Quest for Oil, Money & Power.* New York: Free Press.

Yom, Sean L. (2011). "Oil, Coalitions, and Regime Durability: The Origins and Persistence of Popular Rentierism in Kuwait." *Studies in Comparative International Development* 46: 217–241.

Yom, Sean L. and F. Gregory Gause III. (2012). "Resilient Royals: How Arab Monarchies Hang On." *Journal of Democracy*, 23.4: 74–88.

Zemni, Sami (2014). "The Extraordinary Politics of the Tunisian Revolution: The Process of Constitution Making," *Mediterranean Politics*: 1–17.

Index

Abbasi, Hussayn 145
Abu Shaqur, Mustafa 160–1
actor-based approaches to transitions 25–8
Afghanistan
  Soviet invasion of 47, 48
Africa 18–19, 28, 30, 40, 42, 49–50, 55, 190
Ahmar, General Ali Mohsen al- 77–8
Ahmida, Ali Abdullatif 158
al-Qaeda 99, 147
Albania 216, 217, 218
Alexander, Christopher 67–8
Algeria 3, 4, 9, 13, 18, 213
  balance of power 27
  first Arab Spring 1, 2
  FIS (Islamic Salvation Front) 2, 49
  institutional profile 29, 30, 33
  internet use 36, 37
  lack of breakdown 22
  lineages of repression 50, 59, 60
  oil resources 53, 54–5
  political continuity 64
Amamou, Slim 127
American Revolution 216
Ammar, Rachid 68–9
Andersen, J¢rgen 53
Anderson, Lisa 153
Annan, Sami 120–1
Arab Spring overview 9–12
Argentina 217
armed forces 15
  and authoritarian breakdown 21–2, 65, 80, 97
  Bahrain 10, 90, 91
  concerted military repression 65
  continuing power of coercion 63
  and crackdowns 80, 97, 221–2
  and dictators 10–11
  Egypt 10, 11, 38, 73, 80, 104, 105, 110, 120–1, 186–7
  Libya 10, 11–12, 38, 154–5
  and lineages of repression 41
  military behaviour 37–8, 186–7
  military expenditure and oil resources 54–5
  military inheritances 190–4
  Syria 38, 63, 91–3, 95
  Tunisia 10, 38, 63, 66, 69, 80, 186, 186–7, 187–8
  Yemen 10, 11–12, 29, 38, 77–8
Assad, Bashar al- 11, 25, 36, 40
  and the Alawis 91–2, 93
  crackdown by 91–5
  and dynastic personalism 56, 57, 58
Assad, Hafez al- 57, 91
Aswany, Alaa al- 223
Attalah, Lina 121
authoritarian breakdown 15, 16, 63
  and the armed forces 21–2, 65, 80, 97
  and authoritarian continuity 41–2
  Bahrain 20, 21, 22, 23, 24
  and completed transitions 169–72
  and democratic transition 211–12
  Egypt 13, 16, 20, 21, 23, 65, 70–5, 97
  future of regimes 227–8
  and leadership change 13, 21–2, 61
  Libya 13, 16, 20, 22, 222
  and lineages of repression 40
  and post-transition process 98, 101
  and structured contingency 39
  and the transition process 16, 98–168, 210
  Tunisia 13, 16, 20, 21, 65, 66–70, 97
  and uprisings 20–5
  Yemen 13, 16, 21, 65, 75–80, 97
authoritarianism
  ability to challenge 39
  in the Arab world 224–6
  continuity of 61
  durability of 14–15, 18, 19, 218–21
  and dynastic personalism 55–9

authoritarianism(*Cont.*)
  and human agency 221
  institutional differences in 28–33
  and oil resources 52–3
  transitions from 25–8, 39
  and unconstrained security states 45–6
  and the Western-dominated international order 35
  see also despotic power
autocratic resilience 19
Ayubi, Nazih N. 44, 155

Badi, Muhammad 110, 116
Bagatu, Hatim 108
Bahrain 13, 211, 212, 213
  armed forces 10, 90, 91
  authoritarian breakdown 20, 21, 22, 23, 24
  Bahraini Shias 87, 88
  balance of power 27
  civil activism 4
  crackdown 13, 65, 80, 80–1, 85–91
  dynastic personalism 59
  foreign intervention 66, 88–9, 90–1
  institutional profile 29, 30, 33
  lack of breakdown 22
  monarchy 86
  oil resources 53, 54–5
  and the United States 47–8
  uprising (2010) 3, 4, 10, 60, 62
  and Yemen 78
Barany, Zoltan 38, 82
Basindwa, Muhammad Salim 148–9
Becker, Jaime 177
Belaid, Chokri 144, 145
Bellin, Eva 38, 173, 188, 195, 206
Ben Ali, Zine El Abidine 2, 10, 11, 21, 32, 38, 220
  overthrow of 40, 66, 67, 68–70, 98, 126, 154, 210
Ben Ammar, Rachid 192
Ben Omar, Jamal 153
Bennett, Andrew 174
Berman, Sheri 215
Bin Ashur, Ayad 129, 130, 133
Bishri, Tariq al- 107, 108
Boduszynski, Mieczystaw 171
Bouazizi, Tarek al-Tayeb 10, 67, 68, 71
Bourguiba, Habib 67, 69, 129, 194, 207
Bratton, Michael 28, 29, 30, 180, 182, 190
Brezhnev, Leonid 6–7
Brown, Nathan 104
Brownlee, Jason 45, 189
Brumberg, Daniel 188
Brynen, Rex 82, 86
Bunce, Valerie 26
Bush, George H.W. 49
Bush, George W.
  "Freedom Agenda" 2–3

capitalist development
  and civil society 184
Carapico, Sheila 179
Carey, John 199, 200–1
Carothers, Thomas 202
Carter, Jimmy 48–9
Chaney, Eric 225
Checkel, Geoffrey 174
China
  and Syria 94
Chobaki, Amr 209–10
Christianity and democracy 223, 225
civil society
  and authoritarianism 226
  and capitalist development 184
  and democratic transition 15, 16–17, 101–2, 214–15
  Egypt 16, 104–5, 203–9, 215
  and infrastructural power 43
  Libya 82, 153–4, 156
  Tunisia 16–17, 67–8, 100, 103, 128–32, 203–9
class
  balance of power and transition 27–8
Clinton, Hillary 73, 90–1, 202
Cold War 1–2, 9, 11, 46
communism
  post-communist democracies 18, 26–7, 47, 216–18
completed transitions *see* transition completion
Cook, Stephen 192, 202
crackdowns 80–95
  and the armed forces 80, 97, 221–1
  Bahrain 13, 65, 80, 80–1, 85–91
  and despotic power 13, 16, 42, 53–4, 61, 65, 80, 96
  and leadership continuity 13, 16, 42, 53–4, 61, 65
  Libya 80, 81–5
  Syria 65, 80, 91–5
Czechoslovakia 5, 6

Dahl, Robert
  Polyarchy 30
democracy/democratic transitions 4–5, 14–15, 16–17, 18–19, 209–10

the "Arab" democracy deficit 224–6
and authoritarian breakdown 20, 23–4
and civil society 15, 16–17, 101–2, 214–15
completion of 101, 154
creation of stable democracies 215–16
and economic development 223–4
and European "springs" 5–6
from authoritarian rule 25–8
institutional differences in 29–31
and lineages of repression 41–2
post-communist democracies 18, 26–7, 47, 216–18
and the second Arab Spring 3
sequencing in 173
and sub-Saharan Africa 18–19
two-turnover test of 100–1
and unconstrained security states 46–7
Yemen 4–5, 14, 16, 17, 80, 152–3
see also elections; transition process
demography
and literature on the Arab Spring 34
despotic power 41, 43–5, 50, 61, 63
and the capacity to govern 176
and crackdowns 13, 16, 42, 53–4, 61, 65, 80, 96
and oil resources 52–3, 54–5
repression in Bahrain 86–7
see also authoritarianism
Diamond, Larry 225
dictators
and the Arab Spring 10–11
and European "springs" 6
overthrow of 40
digital media
and the origins of the uprisings 36–7
Dubcek, Alexander 6
durable authoritarianism 14–15, 18, 19
dynastic personalism 55–9, 65, 96
see also hereditary succession

Eastern Europe 6–7, 18, 27, 40, 41, 174
democratic transition in 216–18
per capita GDPs compared with Arab countries 217, 218
economic development and democracy 223–4
Egypt 13, 17, 215
armed forces 10, 11, 38, 73, 80, 104, 105, 110, 120–1, 186–7
authoritarian breakdown 13, 16, 20, 21, 23, 65, 70–5, 97
balance of power and transition 27–8
"Battle of the Camel" 74, 76
civil society 16, 104–5, 203–9, 215
constitutional declaration 108–9
"Day of Wrath" 71–2
and democratic transition 4, 14, 16, 19, 125, 209–10, 211, 212
despotic power 45
elections 102–3, 110, 113–20, 197
electoral rules 198, 199, 201
ETUF (Trade Union Federation) 206
Fairmont Accord 119–20
first Arab Spring 1, 2
Free Officers coup (1952) 193, 207
future of 226, 227–8
GDP 186
institutional profile 31, 32, 33
interim government 102–3
internet use 36, 37
and Islamic law 208, 209
Islamist-secularist balance 172, 185–6, 188, 190, 194–209
and Israel 48, 49
judiciary and the constitution 121–4
lack of oil resources 53, 54
leadership change 13, 70–5
and Libya 153, 154
lineages of repression 50, 56–8, 59, 60
military inheritances 190, 191–2, 193–4
National Front for Completing the Revolution 119–20
NDP (National Democratic Party) 104, 105
origins of the uprising 34
per capita income 184, 185
and personalism 219, 220
police force 71, 72
political party leaders 188–90
regime change 70–5
SCAF (Supreme Council of the Armed Forces) 74–5, 105, 106, 107–13, 115–16, 170, 186–7, 199
second Arab Spring 3
Simli document 110–13
socio-economic structures 203–9
state effectiveness 176, 177, 178
Supreme Constitutional Court 118–19
and Syria 92
Tamarrod (Rebel) movement 99, 124–5
and transition completion 170, 171, 174, 175, 181–2
and transition maintenance 172–3, 185–209
transition process 98–9, 101, 102–3, 104–25, 165–8
and Tunisia 70–1, 125–6, 185–209

Egypt (*Cont.*)
  uprising (2010) 3–4, 10, 60
  urbanization 204–5, 207
  and Yemen 75, 76–7, 146, 147, 151
  see also Morsi, Mohammad; Mubarak, Hosni; Muslim Brotherhood
El-Ghobashy, Mona 72
ElBaradei, Muhammad 105, 109, 121, 122–3, 180, 194
elections 4–5, 15, 16, 18–19
  and completed transitions 179–85
  and democratic transition 101–2
  Egypt 102–3, 110, 113–17, 113–20, 197
  electoral rules and transition maintenance 198–201
  and institutional differences 29
  Libya 5, 103, 158–60, 161, 162–3, 164–5
  Tunisia 132–9, 146, 197
Eljarh, Mohamed 162
Essebsi, Beji Caid 128–9, 131, 133, 134, 139, 143, 145
Europe
  democratic transition in 215
  European "springs" 5–7
  transitions in Southern Europe 18, 25, 26, 27, 39, 46
European Union 47
Ezz, Ahmed 105

Faisal bin Abdul Aziz, Saudi king 48
Faruq, king of Egypt 104
Fatteh, Khaled 150
Fawzi, Sameh 113
FIRCs (foreign-imposed regime change) 22, 25, 222–3
first Arab Spring 1–2
Fishman, Robert 22
Ford, Robert Stephen 94
foreign-imposed regime change (FIRCs) 22, 25, 222–3
France
  1848 Revolution 5
  and Algeria 2
  and Libya 84
  Second Empire 6
  and Tunisia 70
freedom
  negative degrees of 173
Freedom House scores
  for Arab Spring countries 212, 213
  for Warsaw Pact countries 216
future of the Arab Spring 226–8

Gallagher, Michael 197
Ganzuri, Kamal al- 115, 120
Gates, Robert 88
Gause, F. Gregory 38, 58
Gazzini, Claudia 85
GCC (Gulf Cooperation Council) 11, 24, 64
  and Bahrain 86–7, 89–90
  and Libya 222
  and Yemen 78, 79, 99, 146
Geddes, Barbara 186
Ghannouchi, Mohamed 126, 127–8, 129
Ghannouchi, Rachid 126, 127–8, 129, 133, 141–2, 180
Ghonim, Wael 119
Goemans, Hein 190
Goldstone, Jack 38, 56, 177, 216
governing capacity
  and transition completion 176–9
  see also state effectiveness
Gulf Cooperation Council *see* GCC (Gulf Cooperation Council)

Haas, Mark 35
Haber, Stephen 52–3
Haddad, Bassam 95
Hadi, Abdo Rabbo Mansur 79–80, 99, 146, 147, 148, 150, 151, 152–3
Haiti 220–1
Halliday, Fred 178
Hamdani, Sama'a al- 152
Hamdi, Mohamed Hechimi 137
Hamid, Shadi 135
Hamzawy, Amr 202
Harb, Imad 192
Hatita, Abdel Sattar 157
Herbst, Jeffrey 177
hereditary succession 14, 15–16, 34, 214, 219–20
  in Bahrain 84, 87, 88
  in Egypt 71
  and lineages of repression 40, 42, 55–9, 61
  repression in hereditary regimes 80–95, 97
  Yemen 77
Heydemann, Steven 94
Hiftar, Khalifa 100, 163, 164
Hobbes, Thomas 7, 43
Hobsbawm, Eric 215
Howard, Philip 36, 217
Hudson, Michael 47
human rights
  and transition completion 171
  Tunisia 132, 144
Huntington, Samuel 7, 96, 100–1, 173, 225

Hussain, Muzammil 36
hybrid regimes 30–1

Ibrahim, Admad 127
Ibrahim, Saadeddin 220
India 223
information technology
  and the origins of the uprisings 36–7
infrastructural power 43–5, 176–7
institutional change 3–4, 12
institutional differences 28–33
international intervention 221–6
  FIRCs (foreign-imposed regime change) 22, 25, 222
  in Libya 4, 61, 65, 66, 81, 83–5, 103, 153
Iran 12–13
  Iran–Iraq war 1
  Revolution (1978–1979) 9, 47, 48–9, 62
Iraq 3, 10, 13, 226
  despotic power 45
  internet use 37
  invasion of Kuwait (1990) 1–2
  Iran–Iraq war 1
  IRCs (foreign imposed changes) 22
  US invasion of 2–3, 222
Islam
  and authoritarianism 225
  Bahraini Shias 87, 88
  and post-transition process 98
  Sunni Muslims in Syria 93
Islamic law 208, 209
Islamic State 226
Islamist-secularist balance 172, 185–6, 188–90, 194–209
  and electoral rules 198–201
  and lazy liberalism 202–3
  and socio-economic structures 203–9
Islamists 42, 49, 226, 227
  and democratic transition 215
  FIS (Algeria) 2, 49
  Libya 99, 157, 160, 164
  Tunisia 100, 126, 133, 135, 136, 137, 139–46
  Yemen 148
  see also Muslim Brotherhood
Israel 1, 2, 3, 9, 13, 21
  and lineages of repression 47, 48, 49
  and Syria 48, 91

Jaafar, Mustafa Ben 127, 139
Jalil, Mustafa Abdul 158, 159
Jebali, Hamadi 139, 144
Jibril, Mahmoud 156, 160
Joffe, George 157
Johnsen, Gregory 77, 149
Jomaa, Medhi 146
Jordan 3, 4, 10, 13, 17, 213, 227
  balance of power 27
  dynastic personalism 59
  internet use 37
  lack of breakdown 22
  lack of oil resources 53, 54
  lineages of repression 60, 61
Jribi, Maya 137

Kandil, Hazem 193
Karl, Terry Lynn
  The Arab Spring 15
Karman, Tawakol 152
Kedouri, Elie 225
Kerry, John 227
Khalidi, Rashid 211
Khalifa, Khalifa bin Salman al- 87
Khalifa, Shaikh Hamad ibn Isa al- 86, 88
Khomeini, Ruhollah 48
Kirby, Andrew 179
Kurzman, Charles 62, 226
Kuwait 2, 13, 213
  dynastic personalism 59
  internet use 36, 37
  lack of breakdown 22
  lineages of repression 60
  oil resources 53, 54

Labidi, Meherzia 139
Lacher, Wolfram 159–60
Landis, Joshua 94
Larayedh, Ali 144, 146
Latin America 18, 25, 26, 27, 39, 41, 46, 173, 174
leadership change 3, 12, 13–14, 15–16, 21–2, 61
  Egypt 13, 70–5
  Tunisia 66–70
  Yemen 13, 75–80
leadership continuity 10, 12, 13–14, 15–16
  and crackdowns 13, 16, 42, 53–4, 61
  repression in oil-rich and hereditary regimes 80–95
Lebanon 3, 13
  internet use 37
Lerner, Daniel 223
Lesch, David 35
liberalism
  and the Islamist-secularist balance 202–3
liberalization
  and institutional differences 30
  and lineages of repression 41–2

Index

Libya 9, 13, 212, 213, 214
armed forces 10, 11–12, 38, 154–5
authoritarian breakdown 13, 16, 20, 22, 222
balance of power 27
civil society 82, 153–4, 156
crackdown 65, 80, 81–5
and democratic transition 14, 16, 17, 99–100, 154, 211, 212
despotic power 44, 45
elections 5, 103, 158–60, 161, 162–3, 164–5
foreign intervention 4, 61, 65, 66, 81, 83–5, 103, 153, 184, 222
future of 226, 227
GNC (General National Congress) 158–62, 163, 164, 165
institutional profile 30, 33
interim government 103
internet use 37
IRCs (foreign imposed changes) 22
Islamists 99, 157, 160, 164
leadership change 13
lineages of repression 50, 59, 60, 61
militia politics 163–5
National Forces Alliance 159–62
near-civil war 16
NSFL 156–7
NTC (National Transitional Council) 82, 85, 158, 162–3, 180, 181
oil resources 53, 54, 55, 81
parliamentary and presidential elections 100
per capita income 184, 185
and personalism 219, 220
political isolation law 162, 163
political parties 154, 159–61
regions 155
state effectiveness 176, 177, 179
and Syria 92
and transition completion 170–1, 171, 172, 174, 175, 183, 184
transition process 98, 99–100, 101, 103, 153–65, 167, 168
tribes 155–6
uprising (2010) 3, 4, 10, 60, 62
and Yemen 79
see also Qaddafi, Muammar al-
lineages of repression 15, 20, 39, 40–63, 80, 213–14
cross-regional variations in 41, 42, 45–50
despotic power 41, 43–5, 50
dynastic personalism 55–9
explaining outcomes 59–61
intra-regional variations in 41, 50–1
and oil resources 34, 41, 42, 44, 51–5, 60, 61
uprisings independent of opportunity 62
Linz, Juan J. 14, 31–2, 33, 101, 154, 171, 179
Lippmann, Walter 196
Lipset, Seymour Martin 184, 218
literacy and democracy 223–4
literature on the Arab Spring 34–9
Lust-Okar, Ellen 182
Lynch, Mark 78, 211

McFaul, Michael 26, 27
Mahfouz, Asmaa 71–2
Makki, Mahmud 121
Malek, Abdel 192
Mann, Michael 41, 43, 44
Mansfield, Edward 214
Mansur, Adli 125
Marinov, Nikolay 190
Marzouki, Moncef 127, 135, 136, 137, 139, 142, 144–5
Mauritania 10
Mebazaa, Fouad 126, 129, 130
Menaldo, Victor 52–3
Miqrif, Muhammad al- 156–7, 159, 162
monarchies 31, 33, 59, 214
Arabian Gulf 9
Bahrain 86
and European "springs" 5–6
future of 227
monarchism 19–20
Montesquieu, C. 225
Morocco 3, 4, 10, 13, 17, 18, 213, 227
balance of power 27
dynastic personalism 59
lack of breakdown 22
lack of oil resources 53, 54
lineages of repression 60, 61
political continuity 64
Morsi, Mohammad 99, 117–24, 170, 188, 190
and the Islamist-Secularist Balance 194–5
Moussa, Fadhel 142
Moustafa, Tamir 186
Mubarak, Gamal 57, 71, 72, 105
Mubarak, Hosni 2, 10, 11, 21, 36, 103, 228
and dynastic personalism 56, 57, 58, 71, 72, 77, 220
and Libya 81
overthrow of 23, 70–5, 104, 105, 125, 210, 211
and Yemen 76, 147

Muslim Brotherhood
Egypt 4, 16, 74, 98, 105, 106, 107–8, 109–10, 112–13, 148, 180, 208
and democratic transition 209–10
election victory 113–15, 197
Morsi's presidency 120–4, 188, 194–5
and transition completion 181–2
Libya 157, 160–2, 164

Napoleon III, French emperor 6
Nasser, G. 193, 208
NATO 22
intervention in Libya 61, 83–4, 85, 184, 222
Nicaragua 220
Nicolas I, Tsar of Russia 6
North Yemen 1, 75, 178
Noueihed, Lin 155
Nuwayra, Asma 129

Obama, Barack 70, 75, 84, 90, 94, 211
O'Donnell, Guillermo 25, 190, 196
oil price shock (1973) 47, 48
oil resources 9, 19–20, 34, 96, 214
and authoritarianism 226
and leadership change/continuity 13–14, 65, 66, 76
Libya 53, 54, 55, 81
and lineages of repression 34, 41, 42, 44, 51–5, 60, 61
opposition success in oil-poor regimes 66–80
repression in oil-rich regimes 80–95
Oman 13, 213
dynastic personalism 59
lack of breakdown 22
lineages of repression 60
oil resources 53, 54
Oslo Accords 2
Ottoman Empire 178
Owen, Roger 178

Palestine 1, 2, 3, 21
personalism
in Bahrain 90
and durability 218–21
dynastic 55–9
institutional variations in 31–2
see also hereditary succession
Philippines 46
Pickard, Duncan 181
pluralism
and transitions to democracy 15
political parties
and democratic transition 15, 16
Egypt 104–5, 113–15, 180
Libya 154, 159–61
and transition completion 180
Tunisia 127, 133–9, 140–1, 143, 180
post-transition process
Yemen 98, 99, 103, 146–53
power distribution 19, 25, 27–8
see also despotic power
Prague Spring 5, 6
Przeworski, Adam 201, 217

Qaddafi, Muammar al- 4, 5, 13, 22, 36, 79, 184
and the army 154–5
and civil society 154, 156
overthrow of 81–5, 157, 158, 159
Qandil, Hisham 120
Qatar 13, 213
dynastic personalism 59
internet use 36, 37
lack of breakdown 22, 23
and Libya 83, 84, 85
lineages of repression 60
oil resources 53, 54

Reagan, Ronald 49
Redissi, Hamadi 69, 131
regime change *see* authoritarian breakdown; leadership change
regime continuity *see* leadership continuity
repression
in oil-rich and hereditary regimes 80–95
repressive capacity of regimes 34, 38
theorizing 95–7
see also crackdowns; leadership continuity; lineages of repression
research agenda 7–9
revolutions
and democratic transition 216
Robertson, Graeme 225
Ross, Michael 51–2, 53, 54, 184
Rostow, Dankwart 196, 197
Rueschmeyer, Dietrich 184
Russia 6, 27
and Syria 25, 94

Sadat, Anwar 21
Saddam Hussein 2, 22, 222
Said, Khaled 71

Index

Saleh, Ali Abdullah 10–11, 12, 21, 36, 152
overthrow of 75–80, 99, 146–7
and transition completion 169–70
Salih, Subhi 107–8
Salih, Yahya Muhammad 151, 153
Saudi Arabia 11, 13, 22, 30, 213, 227
and Bahrain 24, 86, 88, 89
dynastic personalism 59
institutional profile 32, 33
lineages of repression 60
oil resources 53, 54–5
and Syria 94
and Yemen 78, 79
Schmitter, P.C. 25, 196
Schraeder, Peter 69
second Arab Spring 2–3
security states 9, 45–50, 52, 97
Shadid, Anthony 109
Shafiq, Ahmed 73, 106, 107, 116, 117–18
Shaqur, Mustafa Abu 160–1
Sharif, Ali Hussein al- 161–2
Shatir, Khayrat al- 116, 117
Simli document 110–13
Sisi, Abd al-Fattah al- 99, 121, 123, 124, 125, 190
Skocpol, Theda 23, 62
Slater, Dan 178
Smith, Benjamin 52
Snyder, Jack 214
social media
and the origins of the uprisings 36–7
and Tunisia 68
socio-economic structures
and democratic transition 210
and Islamist-secularist balance 203–9
South Yemen 1, 75, 178
Soviet Union 42
collapse 1, 46–7, 49
and Eastern Europe 6–7
invasion of Afghanistan 47, 48
Stacher, Joshua 57, 187
state effectiveness
and transition completion 176–9
see also governing capacity
Stepan, Alfred C. 14, 31–2, 33, 101, 154, 169, 171, 179, 187–8, 192, 225
Stephens, Evelyn 184
Stephens, John 184
Stork, Joe 178
strong states
and infrastructural power 43
and transitions to democracy 15
structural theory of regime change 34
structured contingency 28–9
and authoritarian breakdown 39
Sudan 10
Suleiman, Omar 73, 74, 75, 78, 104, 107, 116
Sultan, Faruq 105, 117
sultanistic regimes 31–2, 33, 56–7, 219, 220
Syria 13, 212, 213, 226
armed forces 38, 63, 91–3, 95
authoritarian breakdown 20, 22, 24–5
balance of power 27
civil war 4, 11, 24, 66, 91, 94–5
crackdown 65, 80, 91–5
despotic power 45
foreign intervention 66, 93–4
Hamah rebellion 91
institutional profile 32, 33
and Israel 48, 91
lack of oil resources 53, 54
lineages of repression 40, 50, 56–7, 58–9, 60, 61
and personalism 219–20
uprising (2010) 3, 4, 10, 11, 62
see also Assad, Bashar al-
Syrian National Council 93

Tajikistan 27
Tantawi, Hussein al- 71, 73, 74, 75, 120–1
Tarhouni, Ali al- 163
technology
and literature on the Arab Spring 34
Telhami, Shibley 35
Tibi, Bassam 156
Tilawi, Mirvet al- 110
Tilly, Charles 177
Trabusli, Hadi 199
Trager, Eric 199, 201
transition completion 174, 175–85
and the capacity to govern 176–9
and free and fair elections 179–85
variations in 169–72
transition maintenance 171, 174, 212
divergence in 172–3, 185–209
transition process 16, 98–168
charting transitions 100–3
Egypt 98–9, 101, 102–3, 104–25
five features of the 165–8
Libya 98, 99–100, 101, 103, 153–65
Tunisia 98, 100, 101, 103, 125–46
Traouli, Khaled 134
Tunisia 13, 222
armed forces 10, 38, 63, 66, 69, 80, 186, 186–7, 187–8

authoritarian breakdown 13, 16, 20, 21, 65, 66–70, 97
balance of power and transition 27
civil society 16–17, 67–8, 100, 103, 128–32, 203–9
Constituent Assembly elections 132–9
constitution 100, 140–1, 228
constitutional council 126
and democratic transition 5, 14, 16–17, 19, 100, 209–10, 211, 212, 218
despotic power 44, 45
and Egypt 70–1, 125–6, 185–209
elections 132–9, 146, 197
electoral rules 198–9, 200–1
Ennahdha Movement Party 133, 135, 136, 137, 139–42, 143–4, 145–6, 197
first Arab Spring 1, 2
future of 226, 227–8, 228
GDP 186
HGFRG 129–30, 131–2, 133, 182, 200–1
human rights 132, 144
infrastructure power 44
institutional profile 29, 30, 31, 32, 33
interim government 103, 139–42, 182
internet use 37
and Islamic law 208, 209
Islamist-secularist balance 172, 180, 186, 188, 189–90, 195–209
lack of oil resources 53, 54
and Libya 84, 153, 154
lineages of repression 40, 50, 56, 59, 60
military inheritances 191, 192–3, 194
National Council to Protect the Revolution 128, 129
October 18th Movement 180, 181
origins of the uprising 10, 34
per capita income 184, 185
and personalism 219, 220
police force 69, 96
political parties 127, 133–9, 140–1, 143, 180
political rights 183
politicians 188–90
RCD (Democratic Constitutional Rally) 130–1, 135–6
regime change 66–70
socio-economic structures 203–9
state effectiveness 176, 177, 179
and Syria 92
and transition completion 169, 171, 174, 175, 182, 183, 184
and transition maintenance 172–3, 185–209, 212
transition process 98, 100, 101, 103, 125–46, 166, 168
UGTT (General Union of Tunisian Workers) 67–8, 145–6, 206, 208, 217
uprising (2010) 3–4, 10, 12, 60, 66–70
urbanization 204–5, 207
and Yemen 75, 76–7, 146, 147, 151
Turkey 13

Ukraine 27
unemployment
and the origins of the uprisings 35
in Tunisia 67–8
United Arab Emirates (UAE) 13, 22, 213
dynastic personalism 59
oil resources 53, 54
United Kingdom
withdrawal from Empire 47
United Nations
and military action against Libya 83–4
and Syria 94
and Yemen 79
United States 1, 9
and Bahrain 88, 90–1
and Egypt 73, 75
and Iraq 2–3, 22
and Libya 84–5
and lineages of repression 41–2, 46–50
and Syria 25, 93–4
and Tunisia 70
and Yemen 78
urbanization
and democracy 224
Egypt and Tunisia compared 204–5, 207

van de Walle, Nicolas 28, 29, 30, 182, 190
Vandewalle, Dirk 81, 154–5, 177, 180

Waltz, Susan 207–8
Ward, Michael 179
Warren, Alex 155
Warsaw Pact 6–7
Weber, Max 168
Wedeen, Lisa 57
Wehrey, Frederic 85, 170
Western-dominated international order
and the origins of the uprisings 35–6
World Values Survey
on the internet in Arab countries 36, 37

Index

Yemen 13, 214–15
armed forces 10, 11–12, 29, 38, 77–8
army 10, 11–12, 38, 77–8
authoritarian breakdown 13, 16, 21, 65, 75–80, 97
balance of power 27
Comprehensive Conference for National Dialogue 151–3
"Day of Rage" 76
and democratic transition 4–5, 14, 16, 17, 80, 152–3, 211, 212
despotic power 45
first Arab Spring 1, 2
future of 226, 227
Hadi appointed president 79–80
Houthis 76, 99, 147–8, 151–2
institutional profile 32, 33
interim government 103
internet use 37
JMP (Joint Meeting Parties) 78, 82, 148, 149, 180, 181
lack of oil resources 53, 54
and Libya 153, 154
lineages of repression 50, 59, 60
per capita income 184, 185
and personalism 219, 220
Southern Movement 76, 147–8, 151–2
state effectiveness 176, 177, 178–9
and transition completion 169–70, 171, 174, 181, 182, 183, 184
transition process 98, 99, 103, 146–53, 167, 168
tribes 149–50
unification of 75
uprising (2010) 3–4, 10–11, 12, 60
see also Saleh, Ali Abdullah
Yom, Sean 52, 58
young people
and the origins of the uprisings 34–5
in Tunisia 67–8
youth organizations in Egypt 10–45, 109, 118

Zeiden, Ali 161, 163, 164